Excavations at Gilund:
The Artifacts and Other Studies

Parallel-walled structure on GLD-2.

MUSEUM MONOGRAPH 138

Excavations at Gilund:
The Artifacts and Other Studies

❖

edited by

*Vasant Shinde, Teresa P. Raczek, and
Gregory L. Possehl*

UNIVERSITY OF PENNSYLVANIA MUSEUM OF ARCHAEOLOGY AND ANTHROPOLOGY

PHILADELPHIA

Gilund Archaeological Research Project, jointly in collaboration between Deccan College, Post-Graduate and Research Institute, Deemed University, Pune, India, and the University of Pennsylvania Museum, University of Pennsylvania, Philadelphia, USA.

CIP data available from the Library of Congress

ISBN-13: 978-1-934536-66-7
ISBN-10: 1-934536-66-0

Published for the University of Pennsylvania Museum of Archaeology and Anthropology by the University of Pennsylvania Press.

Printed in the United States of America on acid-free paper.

Contents

Figures

Tables

Contributors

Marta Ameri
College of Arts and Creative Enterprises
Zayed University
Dubai, UAE

Shweta Sinha Deshpande
Deccan College Postgraduate and Research
  Institute
Deemed University
Pune, INDIA

Debasri Dasgupta Ghosh
Deccan College Postgraduate and Research
  Institute
Deemed University
Pune, INDIA

Lorena Giorgio
Department of Archaeology
University of Bologna
Ravenna, ITALY

Praveena Gullapalli
Department of Anthropology
Rhode Island College
Providence, RI
USA

Julie Hanlon
Department of Anthropology
University of Chicago
Chicago, IL
USA

Peter Johansen
Department of Anthropology
University of British Columbia
CANADA

Matthew Landt
Alpine Archaeological Consultants
Montrose, CO
USA

Gregory L. Possehl[†]
Department of Anthropology
University of Pennsylvania

Teresa P. Raczek
Department of Geography and Anthropology
Kennesaw State University
Kennesaw, GA
USA

Vasant Shinde
Deccan College Postgraduate and Research
  Institute
Deemed University
Pune, INDIA

[†]deceased

Foreword

I feel somewhat flattered to have been requested by Professor Gregory L. Possehl to write a Foreword to the report on the excavations at Gilund which he, Professor Vasant Shinde, and their colleagues have carried out at this site from 1999 to 2005. What seems to have impelled Professor Possehl to do so is very likely the fact that a little over a decade ago, prior to the planning of his work at this site, he asked me if I had any objection to his carrying out further excavation there, since it had been excavated by me in 1959–60. I told him that I would be only too glad if he did so, and wished him all the best in his venture.

The Museum of the University of Pennsylvania in Philadelphia, represented by Professor Possehl, and the Deccan College Post-Graduate and Research Institute (a Deemed University), Pune, India, represented by Professor Vasant Shinde, and a host of other field workers and research specialists have done commendable excavations, documentation, and analysis of the excavated material, which is faithfully reflected in this report.

Straightaway, I would like to draw special attention to some new aspects which these excavations have brought to light about this site in particular and in the context of the Ahar-Banas Culture Complex in general. Thus, if we begin with the earliest occupation of the site, the discovery of a separate microlithic basal stratum is indeed very noteworthy, since I had not come across such a deposit in my single season of field work in 1959–60. According to the excavators, this milieu is comparable to the microlithic complex of Bagor to the north. However, it still remains to be determined whether the Ahar-Banas Chalcolithic Culture arose from this Bagor-like complex and, if it did, as may not be unlikely, how exactly the transition took place from a nomadic, microlith-using stage to an agriculture-based, metal-using settled society. I am sure further work at this very site and at other related ones will provide the answer in due course.

In the context of the Ahar-Banas Chalcolithic Complex itself, the renewed excavations at Gilund have brought to light two new elements. The excavation at Balathal, carried out by Professors V.N. Misra and Vasant Shinde, had revealed that the Ahar-Banas settlement over there was provided with a peripheral wall which was duly identified on the eastern side. The work at Gilund has now also thrown up some evidence which seems to suggest that fortifying their settlements may have been a normal practice with the Ahar-Banas people as well, as was doubtless the case with their contemporaries, the Harappans, farther to the north. The Gilund evidence, however, needs to be amplified by conducting further work at the site.

My small-scale excavation in 1959–60 did bring to light the massive "parallel-wall complex" in the northern part of GLD-2. But much welcome further light has been thrown by the work carried out in 1999–2005. What is most significant in this context is the discovery of 214 sealings of clay in a circular bin located in this very area. While these sealings do testify to the fact that some containers had been sealed, what exactly was the purpose of storing such a large number of sealings in a bin close to the "parallel-wall complex" which, for all one can guess, may have been a granary? A record of the contributors? Maybe or maybe not!

Some of the motifs occurring on these sealings have parallels on painted pottery and sealings in Iran (e.g., Tepe Hissar, Tepe Sialk, etc.), which may go as far back as circa 3500 BCE. Again, similar motifs also occur on the sealings/seals in the Bactria-Margiana Archaeological Complex which dates to as late as 1800–1700 BCE. In contrast, the Gilund sealings are dated to circa 2300 BCE. From time to time, various views have been offered to explain these similarities, but each one, I am afraid, has its flaws. The issue is an important one and requires a much more in-depth study before arriving at any conclusion.

The report contains, besides the usual chapters on the architectural remains, ceramics, metal tools, lithics, and floral and faunal remains, some very interesting contributions, such as "Site Catchment Analysis," which provide a meaningful background to the various features of the site. Such studies deserve to be encouraged more and more.

At the end, I would like to congratulate heartily Professors Possehl and Shinde and all their colleagues on presenting such a comprehensive report—well argued and amply illustrated.

B.B. Lal
Los Angeles
July 4, 2009

Acknowledgments

Archaeology is a team effort and our accomplishments at Gilund would not have been possible without the help of many. We owe a deep debt of gratitude to hundreds of people and many institutions who made the five seasons of excavation at Gilund possible. Their names are too many to list in full here, but we would like to acknowledge a few institutions and individuals who provided exceptional assistance.

We are grateful to the Archaeological Survey of India and the Government of India for granting us permission to excavate this centrally protected site. Ultimately, Gilund was successfully excavated because the site has been remarkably well preserved thanks to the extraordinary efforts of the Archaeological Survey of India. The efforts of the central ASI, the Rajasthan Circle, and the site guards that have been posted there since 1960, have prevented illegal digging and other disturbances. The contrast between the preservation of Gilund, a designated "Centrally Protected Monument," and Ahar-Banas sites without protected status is remarkable. Many of these other sites have been lost to farming, soil borrowing, construction, and other activities. This project was only possible because of the work of the ASI at Gilund. We would also like to thank the State Department of Archaeology and Museums, Government of Rajasthan, and the staff at the Government State Museum in Jaipur and Udaipur.

Financial support was provided by the University of Pennsylvania Museum of Archaeology and Anthropology, the National Science Foundation (NSF INT99-08463), the American Institute of Indian Studies, James and Karen Possehl, the Archaeological Survey of India, and Deccan College. The University of Pennsylvania Undergraduate Research fund provided financing for several students to participate in the excavation. Dr. Pradeep Mehendiratta and Purnima Mehta of the American Institute of Indian Studies in Delhi provided valuable counsel and assistance. In addition, Madhav Bhandare visited the site and assisted with visa compliance both in Rajasthan and in Pune.

We would like to thank Deccan College and the University of Pennsylvania Museum of Archaeology and Anthropology. The authorities of Deccan College, particularly Dr. S.N. Pathan, the then acting Director, Dr. K. Paddayya, the then Joint Director, Mr. Kashikar and Mr. Gaware, the then Registrar and Deputy Registrar respectively, provided strong administrative and moral support to this project. At the Penn Museum, Jennifer Bornstein provided administrative assistance. In the Museum's Publications Department, we would like to thank James Mathieu for helping to shepherd this volume through a long editorial process and for being a strong advocate for this volume. We also thank Jennifer Quick in Publications for additional editorial assistance. We appreciate the extensive work of the anonymous reviewers who provided helpful guidance. The authors are grateful to Prof. B.B. Lal not only for writing the Foreword to this volume but providing guidance at various stages while we were excavating and writing this report.

It takes many people to run a camp full of archaeologists. Dighe Bharat Baburao and V. Vishwasrao acted as Camp Managers and oversaw many details. Krishna Malap prepared delicious meals. Shantiba Nai provided many services and acted as a resident grandfather, while Dilip Kumawat ably transported us back and forth to Udaipur and many other locations. Dr. Lalit Pandey and Dr. Jeewan Kharakwal of the Institute of Rajasthan Studies, and Rajasthan Vidhyapeeth deserve special thanks for providing local logistic support during the course of excavation.

Dozens of students offered their time and talents, most notably the dedicated students of Deccan College and the University of Pennsylvania, who performed much of the excavation. Sanjay Desphande, Shweta Sinha Deshpande, and Prabodh Shirvalkar provided extensive leadership throughout. The senior research students like Marta Ameri, Debashree Dasgupta Ghosh, Lorena Giorgio, Praveena Gullapalli, Julie Hanlon, Matthew Landt, Rita Jeney, Peter Johansen, and Shiv Kumar, etc., shouldered various responsibilities ably. The bulk of the work was conducted by dozens of workers from Gilund village who toiled to excavate, screen, and wash artifacts in the coldest part of winter. It is their hard work that allowed us to accomplish so much in five short seasons. Harriet F. (Rae) Beaubien and Claudia Chemello of the Smithsonian Institution helped to preserve the incredibly important and incredibly fragile seal impressions. We also thank the following students from Kennesaw State University who provided assistance in the volume production: Mollie Gilstrap, Allie Ingram, Elise Krause, Jenn Parent, Madyson Price, Samantha Roberts, April Tolley, and Brian LaRaia.

Our warmest gratitude is reserved for the people of Gilund village who opened their hearts and homes each year to multitudes of researchers from across India and around the world. Their patience with our many impositions and cultural confusion has been immense. Many families in the village participated in the excavations in some way. Girish Vyas and his entire family helped to make several complicated arrangements. Omji Bohra and his family graciously hosted the directors, visiting guests, and various researchers throughout the years.

Finally, we would like to say a few words about Gregory L. Possehl, who sadly passed away during the final stages of editing this volume. Dr. Possehl played a critical role in the operations at Gilund, which was his last excavation in India. He was involved in the initial drafts of Chapters 1, 2, 3, and 12 and assisted in the compilation and initial editing of the additional chapters. It was his request to be listed as third author on this volume. Always ready to give an impromptu lecture, Dr. P delighted in working with students at Gilund, and sharing his knowledge of Indian archaeology accumulated over a lifetime. He will be greatly missed.

Vasant Shinde
Teresa P. Raczek

1

Excavations at Gilund 1999–2005: The Artifacts and Other Studies

Vasant Shinde, Teresa P. Raczek, and Gregory L. Possehl

Introduction

As the largest known Chalcolithic settlement in its region, the site of Gilund played an important role in the development of early social, political, and economic forms of the 3rd and 2nd millennia BC in northwest India. The site was home to an ancient community of farmers and artisans who engaged in extensive inter- and intra-regional networks of interaction. The presence of monumental architecture in the form of a large parallel walled mudbrick structure, along with a circumference wall, workshops, and a diverse body of material culture make Gilund an excellent site for studying early social complexity. Moreover, its location on the margins of the Indus Civilization provides a distinctive vantage point for viewing social, political, and economic processes more broadly.

Gilund was first excavated over half of a century ago by B.B. Lal of the Archaeological Survey of India (IAR 1959–60). In order to follow up on his initial finds, new multi-disciplinary excavations were undertaken from 1999–2005 by the University of Pennsylvania and Deccan College, Post-Graduate and Research Institute. These new excavations investigated the role that Gilund played in ongoing regional social processes including increased sedentism, the spread of farming, and the development of trade and exchange networks. In this volume, we present an overview of the artifacts recovered from the new excavations, together with an overview of related studies and significant discoveries. In order to situate these studies, a summary of previous research in the region is presented here.

The Mewar Plain and the Ahar-Banas Complex

The ancient habitation mound of Gilund (25°01′56″ N and 74°15′45″ E, 485 m above sea level, Rajsamand District, Rajasthan) is locally known as Modiya Magari ("bald habitation mound"). Although it was referred to as Bhagwanpura in Lal's first excavation report, it is currently called Gilund after the nearby contemporary village of that name. The site sits in the middle of the Banas Basin in the Mewar Plain, a geological extension of central India's Malwa Plateau. The region is bounded on the west by the Aravalli Mountains, which form the watershed for this part of the subcontinent. The Banas/Berach River and several of its tributaries drain from here to the northeast, eventually emptying into the Chambal River in Madhya Pradesh. The site is located approximately 1.20 km south of the Banas River, which served the occupants of ancient Gilund as a source of water, fish, stone, and potentially reeds and transport. A nulla, or creek, that connects to the Banas passes just south of the site, potentially providing more immediate access to water. Additional water and water-based flora and fauna may also have been obtained from a now dry lake located 2 km to the west.

The region has a semi-arid environment characterized by hot, dry summers (over 45° C); cold, dry winters (under 15° C); and an unpredictable monsoon with an average rainfall of 500 to 800 mm. Until recently, much of the region was covered by thorny scrub forests; some varieties of trees including babul, banyan, tamarind, mango, papal, and neem are still commonly found. Wild animals present

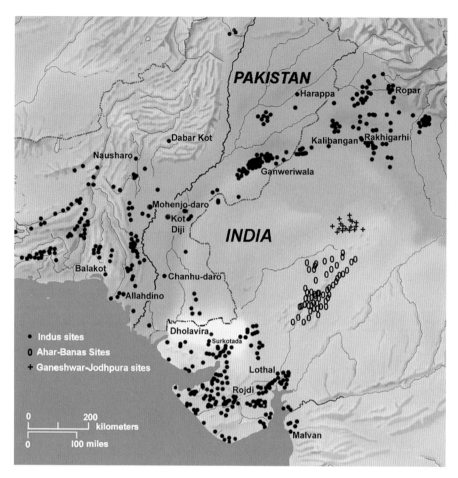

Fig. 1.1. Map of Chalcolithic sites in Ahar-Banas, Ganeshwar-Jodhpura, and Indus regions. (Map by G.L. Possehl)

when Gilund was inhabited include nilgai (a large antelope), tiger, wild boar, and sambar (a large deer).

The land surrounding Gilund is slightly sandy, but arable; crops currently grown in the area include wheat, barley, millet, sorghum, sesame, green gram, black gram, and mustard. Non-agriculturally productive land suitable for pasture is available across the river (between 2 and 4 km away) on several small hillocks covered by coarse red soil. Additional pasturage is available throughout the region. In sum, the local ecological conditions were suitable for both farming and pastoralism.

Although the Mewar Plain was first occupied in the Pleistocene, the population increased in the mid-Holocene (Misra 2002). By the early 3rd millennium BC permanent settlements spread across the region and the occupants began to emphasize agro-pastoralism. Many of these settlements are known collectively as the Ahar-Banas Cultural Complex, named after the first excavated site,

Ahar, and the nearby Banas River. Over 100 sites with Ahar-Banas pottery have been located in southeast Rajasthan near the Banas, Khari, Berach, Kothari, and Gambhiri Rivers and their tributaries (Hooja 1988, Misra 1967) (see Fig. 1.2). Although some of these settlements, like Tarawat, are as small as 0.3 hectares, most are larger, with several in the 5-hectare range. Gilund remains the largest site at approximately 22 hectares.

The past few years have shown a resurgence of interest in the archaeology of the Mewar region as indicated by the large-scale excavations at the sites of Gilund (Raczek and Shinde 2010, Shinde 2010a, 2010b, Shinde and Possehl 2005, Shinde and Raczek 2010, Shinde, Deshpande, and Yasuda 2004, Shinde, Possehl, and Ameri 2005), Balathal in Rajsamand District, and Ojiyana in Bhilwara District, as well as the test excavations at Chatrikhera in Rajsamand District and Purani Marmi in Chitaurgarh District (Fig. 1.3). Together, these studies have clarified regional cultural

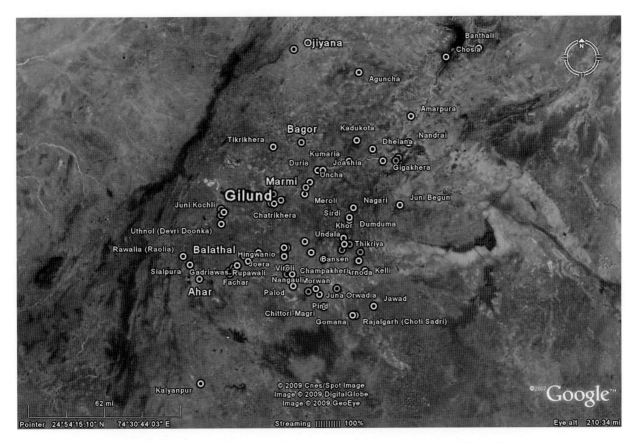

Fig. 1.2. Location of selected Ahar-Banas sites in the Mewar region of Rajasthan.

sequences as well as local variation in material culture. In addition, they have contributed to our understanding of the development of cultural complexity and the expansion of interaction within the Mewar region and beyond. A brief description of excavated sites is presented here in order to provide context to the artifact analyses included in this volume.

Ahar

Ahar (24°35′ N, 73°44′ E), was first excavated in 1952 on a limited scale by A.K. Vyas of the Department of Archaeology, Rajasthan, although this excavation remains unpublished. R.C. Agrawala resumed the excavations in 1954–56 (IAR 1954–55:14–15; IAR 1955–56:11) as did H.D. Sankalia of Deccan College in 1961–62 (Sankalia, Deo, and Ansari 1969). This latter work established a relatively complete cultural sequence for the "Ahar-Banas Complex" of the 3rd and 2nd millennium BC. Located on the Ahar River, a tributary of the Banas, the archaeological site locally known as Dhulkot has a deposit of 12.8 m and is divided into two periods: Period I Ahar-Banas Complex

(2580–1500 BC or later) with three sub-phases, and Period II Iron Age (Sankalia, Deo, and Ansari 1969). While no sterile layer was found separating the two periods, there is a chronological gap. Sankalia and Deo divided the three sub-phases of Period I according to changes in the ceramic assemblage (Deo 1969a, Sankalia 1969b). Phase Ia (2580–2170 BC) is characterized by the presence of Black and Red Ware (especially convex-sided bowls); Buff Ware and imitation Buff-Slipped Ware; Red Ware; some Gray Ware; and the absence of sharply carinated bowls. In Phase Ib (2170–2080 BC) Black and Red Ware continues to be present while Buff and imitation Buff-Slipped Ware are absent. The amount of Gray Ware and Red Ware (including cut and ribbed styles) increases and some new ceramic types appear. Finally, Phase Ic (2080–1500 BC) is characterized by the presence of sharply carinated Black and Red Ware bowls and Lustrous Red Ware similar to that of Rangpur, as well as the absence of sturdy metallic ceramics and dishes-on-stands.

In addition to pottery (Deo 1969a), other artifacts recovered from Ahar include shell bangles, beads made of crystal, terracotta, and lapis lazuli (most of which belong to Phase Ib and Ic), and terracotta figurines of animals like bulls and elephants (Deo 1969b). The archaeologists collected only a few microliths: mainly backed blades, borers, fluted cores, and side scrappers made of chert, chalcedony, and quartz. This led Sankalia to suggest that the people of Ahar depended on copper tools. In fact, he argues that the inhabitants smelted copper using ore procured from local sources in the Aravallis. The Aravallis have extensive metal and mineral deposits, including copper, lead, zinc, silver, and iron. Pointing to finds of copper slag and copper implements like celts, blades, knives, rings, bangles, and kohl sticks he argues that the inhabitants manufactured their own copper tools.

Finally, fauna and flora remains indicate that the peo-

ple of Ahar practiced agriculture and animal husbandry, along with hunting and fishing. Impressions of domestic rice and millet were found in several pot sherds (Vishnu-Mittre 1969). Domesticated animal remains included donkey, cow, buffalo, goat, sheep, and dog, while wild animal remains included fish, turtles, birds, deer, pig, and mongoose (Shah 1969).

Due to the vertical nature of the excavations, no complete house plans were outlined. However, both stone and mud houses were identified along with related storage jars and cooking features, including U-shaped chulhas or hearths (Sankalia 1969c).

Balathal

The site of Balathal (24°43′ N and 73°59′ E) is located 42 km northeast of Udaipur in the Banas River basin. At 2 hectares (150 m N-S and 135 m E-W), it is among the smallest sites of the region. However, it has a deposit of 7 m, indicating long-term occupation. The site is located near a large freshwater lake and is surrounded by agricultural land. Excavations carried out at Balathal between 1993 and 2000 by Deccan College, Post-Graduate and Research Institute, Pune, and the Rajasthan Vidyapeeth, Udaipur, aimed at reconstructing the socio-economic organization of the 3rd and 2nd millennium BC culture of the Mewar region (Misra 1997, Misra et al. 1995, 1997).

The excavators divide the occupation of Balathal into two cultural periods that are separated by a gap of 1600 years—Ahar-Banas (2800–1800 BC) and Early Historic (200–300 BC) (Misra et al. 1995, 1997). The Ahar-Banas period is further divided into three phases based on the pottery. Phase A, Early Ahar-Banas (2800–2500 BC) includes typical Ahar-Banas pottery such as Coarse and Thick Slipped Red Ware, Thin Red Ware, Black and Red Ware, and Thin Red Slipped Ware. In addition, Reserve Slip Ware was found in very early deposits. In this phase, however, the majority of the pottery is hand-made, coarse, thick, and low-fired. Shapes that are common across the region for the Chalcolithic are present in the initial oc-

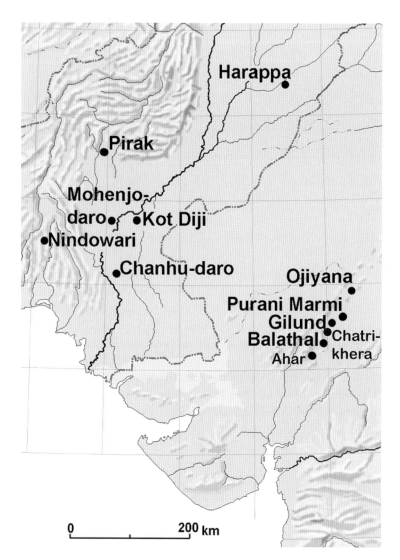

Fig. 1.3. Excavated Ahar-Banas sites in Rajasthan in relation to major sites of the Indus.

cupations (Mishra 2000). These include wide-mouthed deep carinated bowls, small narrow-mouthed jars, and storage jars with beaded rims. In Phase B, the Mature Ahar-Banas (2500–2000 BC), the Balathal pottery has three different traditions: Ahar-Banas (Mewar region), Kayatha (Chambal Valley), and Malwa (Malwa Plateau). Finally, in Phase C, Late Ahar-Banas (2000–1700 BC), the texture of classical Ahar-Banas pottery becomes coarser. The large quantity of the Malwa Ware recovered in Phase C indicates that interaction with the Malwa region continued.

At Balathal, the initial structures of wattle and daub, mud, and stone (Phase A) were built on bedrock. During Phase B, houses were rectangular or square with single or double rooms and storage and cooking facilities. The floors of these structures were made of clay and plastered with cow dung or lime (Boivin 2010). Significantly, a large (30 m E–W by 20 m N–S), roughly rectangular fortified stone enclosure was identified in the middle of the site. Its function is unclear. House complexes were constructed in a rectangular plan around this central structure and all were enclosed by an outer wall.

A wide variety of ethnobotanical remains were recovered from Balathal, including wheat, barley, three varieties of millet, three or four varieties of lentils, and peas (Kajale 1996). Recovered wild plant remains include Job's tears, Indian jujube, and okra (Kajale 1996). In addition, sheep, goat, and cattle were identified (Thomas and Joglekar 1996).

Five burials were recovered from Balathal: three from Early Historic levels and two from Chalcolithic Phase B levels (Robbins et al. 2006, 2007, 2009). One of these, an adult male dated between 2500 and 2000 BC provides the earliest evidence of leprosy in South Asia and the world (Robbins et al. 2009). One skeleton from Early Historic deposits was buried in a seated, upright position.

The excavators suggest that Balathal was a well-planned fortified settlement, where society and economy gradually developed then declined (Misra et al. 1995, 1997, Shinde, Possehl, and Deshpande 2002). They argue that gradual development and technological advancement led to the rise of the Mature Ahar-Banas (Phase B) at Balathal, which included contact with Harappans in Gujarat. Changes during the Late Ahar-Banas Phase (Phase C) included a decline in population at the site, the replacement of large multi-room structures by single- or double-room structures, and a shift from fine to coarse pottery. This later decline is contemporary with the emergence of the Post-urban (or "Late") Harappan.

Purani Marmi

Marmi is also known as Purani Marmi (25°06′ N and 74°26′ E) in order to distinguish it from the contemporary village of the same name. It is located on the banks of the Banas River, and is partly under cultivation at this time. Several major natural alluvial channels run from the middle of the site down to the riverbed. These channels are quite deep and cut through the archaeological deposits as well as the sterile soil underneath. As a result, the site of Marmi is currently disturbed.

Marmi was first identified through survey (IAR 1957–58); more recently two 1 m by 5 m trenches were excavated in 2000 (Joglekar, Thomas, and Mohanty 2003, Mohanty et al. 2000). The excavators used the site's alluvial channels to their advantage and set their trenches so as to create a clean and visible profile. They found that the deposition was 1.5 m to 1.7 m deep and included Ahar-Banas Phase and Early Historic artifacts. Unfortunately, their excavations were not extensive enough to allow them to identify any structures.

Five types of pottery have been identified at Marmi: Black and Red Ware, Thin Red Slipped Ware, Thick Red Slipped Ware, Gray Slipped Ware, and Coarse Red Ware. However, some common Ahar-Banas wares that were identified at Balathal and Ahar were not found at Marmi. These include Tan, Chocolate Slipped, Thin Red, and Reserved Slip (Mohanty et al. 2000:136). These substantial differences between the pottery of Marmi and Balathal may be due to the late occupation of Marmi (approximately 1500–1400 BC) and could represent a fourth phase in the regional Ahar-Banas chronology.

The most distinctive artifacts at Marmi are the terracotta bulls. A team from Deccan College collected 58 terracotta bull figurines during a survey in 1993 (Misra et al. 1993). The analysts divided the bulls into three categories: naturalistic figurines with a hump, naturalistic figurines without a hump, and stylized figurines. Those of the first two categories are formally similar to bulls found at other Ahar-Banas sites such as Ojiyana and Gilund. However, the stylized figurines are unique to Marmi. They do not have any limbs and consist of an upright cylindrical form with two horns on the upper portion. A slight nodule indicates the presence of a face on some figurines, but most bulls are faceless. In addition, the horns are frequently broken and missing. The analysts suggest that these bulls may have been made locally at Marmi for ritual purposes. They present an analogy with several traditions among contemporary Indian communities who also use small bull figurines in their worship. Because Marmi has produced far more bull figurines than other sites, Misra et al. (1993) suggest that Marmi may have been a kind of religious center, although the large size of the mound and the unique depositional circumstance at Marmi may also contribute to the high concentration of figurines (for more on terracotta bulls see Hanlon 2006).

Chatrikhera

Located 3 km southwest of Gilund, Chatrikhera is a small settlement that was occupied during multiple time periods. The main mound at Chatrikhera was first discovered as part of the explorations in southeastern Rajasthan by K.N. Puri (IAR 1957–58:44–45), and was also identified in three other surveys (Misra 1967:149; Hooja 1988:163; Dasgupta 2006a, 2006b). The site was more intensively studied by a joint Indian-American team in 2009 and 2011. Although heavily disturbed, the research team documented evidence that the site was occupied during the Ahar-Banas, Early Historic, Medieval, and Modern periods (Sugandhi et al. 2010, Raczek et al. 2011). Two test trenches were excavated, one in the northern deposit and one in the southern deposit. Mudbrick walls and a hearth were encountered in the layers with Ahar-Banas pottery. Multiple Ahar-Banas wares were recovered including white-painted Black and Red Ware bowls, Thin Red Slipped small pots and jars, Coarse Red Ware pots, Gray Wares, and Burnished Black Ware. A few sherds of Chocolate Wares (possibly Kayatha) were also encountered along with three small terracotta animal figurines.

Ojiyana

Located in the hills of the Aravallis, Ojiyana (25°53′ N and 74°21′ E) is the farthest north of all the excavated Ahar-Banas sites. The site was first identified in 1980 by R.C. Agrawala and first excavated by the Archaeological Survey of India in 2000 (Meena and Tripathi 2000a, 2000b, 2001, 2001–02). The deposit is 7.5 m deep and contains 26 separate layers. The excavators pursued both vertical and horizontal excavation strategies, which allowed them to gather chronological data as well as information about settlement patterns.

Ojiyana has been dated to 3000–1500 BC and the occupation has been divided into three separate phases based on pottery sequences: I, II (a and b), and III. Ahar-Banas white-painted Black and Red Ware was found in all phases. In addition, Black Slipped Ware, Gray Ware, Tan Ware, and Red Slipped Ware were all recovered. Several small terracotta bulls and cows, including some that were painted white, were recovered. Other recovered antiquities are common throughout the Ahar-Banas: spindle whorls, slingballs, toy

cart wheels, "gamesmen" (small baked terracotta objects of various sizes), "hopscotches" (ground pottery sherds), and beads of various materials.

The structures at Ojiyana vary by phase. Phase I structures are made of mud brick with clay floors. Phase II structures consist of multiple rooms and courtyard areas that are made of stone and mud plaster with bamboo and mud roofs. Associated querns and chulhas were found in some rooms. In addition, the excavators argue that one of the structures served as a communal granary. The excavators describe the Phase II settlement as "well-planned," with east-west aligned structures, parallel streets, and a surrounding fortification wall. Phase III structures are smaller than those of Phase II and do not follow any specific orientation. Some are made of stone, others of wattle and daub with clay floors. A number of subterranean lined storage pits were identified and presumably stored grain.

Bagor

The site of Bagor, originally excavated by V.N. Misra (IAR 1967–68b:41–42; 1968–69:26–28; 1969–70:32–34; Misra 1971a, 1973, 1982) and later reopened by Deccan College in 2000 (Deshpande et al. 2004, Shinde 2010a), consists largely of a lithic and pottery scatter that lies on top of a fossilized sand dune. Although it is the only published excavation of a lithic scatter site in southeastern Rajasthan, hundreds of sites like it have been identified throughout the region (Hooja 1988, Misra 1967, and see Ghosh this volume). The site is located at a bend in the Kothari River and has an excellent view of the surrounding area. It was intermittently occupied from 5500 BC until approximately AD 200. Misra divides the site occupations into three phases (1973, 1982). Phase I (5000–2800 BC) is considered to be Mesolithic and is largely aceramic, although some small pieces of eroded pottery were found in these levels. Phase II (2800–600 BC) is characterized by low-fired pottery that resembles both Ahar-Banas and Kayatha pottery sequences. Ahar Black and Red Ware is present, as are other Ahar Red Wares including basins, bowls, and jars that have Ahar designs and motifs. This phase overlaps with the occupations at Gilund and other Ahar-Banas sites. Phase III (600 BC–AD 200) is the historic period occupation. It includes wheel-made pottery, iron artifacts, glass beads, bricks, and tiles. There are fewer lithics in this phase than in previous phases. Shinde, Deshpande, and Yasuda (2004) divide the Bagor sequence into aceramic and ceramic.

The site has no permanent architecture, although some concentrations of schist stone slabs procured from the outcrops across the river were identified in Phase I and

II. These stones may have been used as house floors for superstructures made of portable or perishable materials. Beyond pottery, recovered artifacts in Phase II include stone and carnelian beads, a copper spearhead, a copper awl, and three copper arrowheads described as similar to Harappan arrowheads (Misra 1970, 1973). Hammerstones, groundstones, two perforated stones, and a spindle whorl were also found in Phase II (Misra 1973:105).

Vast quantities of faunal remains were recovered from Bagor; however, most were fragmentary. The initial faunal analysis indicated that Phase I fauna only included wild species; later studies identified domesticated animal remains in Phase I and II including sheep/goat and cattle (Thomas 1975, 1977, 1984). In recent years, the faunal analysis has been challenged since archaeologists have learned more about the comparative osteology of the local wild animals of Rajasthan (Meadow and Patel 2002, Patel 2009). Recent microwear and starch grain analyses conducted on lithics procured during the 2000 excavations indicate that the inhabitants prepared and consumed a variety of fruits, pulses, and grains (Kashyap 2006).

While five burials were recovered, only three are attributed to the time period that is contemporaneous with Gilund: one child and two adults (Kennedy 1982, Kumar 1970–73, Lukacs 1982, Misra 1972). Several pots were buried with the deceased in Phase II along with copper arrowheads and a stone and bone bead necklace (Misra 1982). In addition, one burial with no associated goods was uncovered from Phase I deposits.

Several archaeologists have suggested that the inhabitants of Bagor engaged in exchange with other settlements of the Mewar Plain and beyond (Hooja 1988, 1996, Misra 1971b) (Lukacs 2002, Possehl 2002, Possehl and Kennedy 1979). Recent visual analysis of the lithic raw materials supports the idea that the inhabitants of Bagor may have traveled to areas near the border of the contemporary state of Madhya Pradesh (Raczek 2011), while analysis of the lithic technology confirms a shared technological vocabulary with Gilund (Raczek 2013).

Excavated Ahar-Banas Sites Outside of the Banas-Berach Basin

A number of researchers have observed that Ahar-Banas pottery extends into Madhya Pradesh (Chakrabarti 1999, Dhavalikar 2002, Hanlon 2006; Hooja 1988:43; Possehl and Rissman 1992, Sankalia 1979). For the most part, sites in this area have layers with Ahar-Banas material culture that precede or follow other phases that are not present in the Banas-Berach Basin. Excavated sites include Navdatoli

(Sankalia, Deo and Ansari 1971, Sankalia, Subbarao, and Deo 1958), Kayatha (Ansari and Dhavalikar 1975, IAR 1964–65, 1967–68a, Wakankar 1967), Chichalli (IAR 1998–99, 1999–2000), and Eran (Pandey 1982, Singh 1967a, 1967b).

Common Themes among the Research Projects at Gilund

The studies presented in this volume address four common themes: early sedentism, increasing social complexity, trade and exchange, and the transition between the Ahar-Banas and Early Historic periods. Each study also addresses specific questions that are best suited to the material under analysis. Together, the data generated by these studies enable a synthetic consideration of social processes and practices of the 3rd and 2nd millennia Mewar Plain (see Chapter 12).

Early Sedentism

By the early 3rd millennium BC, many inhabitants of the Mewar region settled into villages and towns like Gilund. Beyond changes in mobility and diet, the new excavations at Gilund investigated shifts in social, economic, and political processes that occurred in concert with increasing sedentism. A deep trench on mound GLD-1 was excavated in order to identify the earliest habitations and document the transformations that occurred during the following occupations. The findings of the deep trench are presented in Chapter 2 while the analysis of artifacts from that trench is presented throughout the remaining chapters. In an effort to study the subsistence regime that developed in concert with sedentism, Matthew Landt presents an analysis of the faunal collection in Chapter 11.

Early Social Complexity

The largest site of the Ahar-Banas, Gilund was also situated at the geographic center of the Mewar Plain. Thus, Gilund's size and location suggest that it played a prominent role in regional economic interactions and political organization. Additionally, the location of the Banas-Berach Basin—on the peripheries of the Indus Civilization—is suitable for examining contemporaneous social and economic processes in a non-urban context. Evidence of specialization and social stratification was identified and studied through the excavation of workshop areas. In addition, re-opening the parallel walls previously discovered by Lal and investigating their surrounding archaeological context allowed the research team to examine questions about monumentality and communality in the form of prominent architecture. These finds are discussed in Chapter 3. The chapters on pottery, small finds, and sealings provide the necessary data to consider questions of complexity, while Raczek's chapter on lithics challenges the idea that stone tools are indices of sites that predate the emergence of complexity.

Trade and Exchange

Previous studies of the Mewar economy identified local and long-distance exchange through such finds as Saurashtra Harappan artifacts from Balathal and pottery and copper artifacts from Bagor (Misra 1973). The new excavations at Gilund provided the opportunity to investigate the intensity and nature of regional interaction as well as interaction between Mewar and regions of the Indus and the Deccan. It had previously been argued that the Harappans may have established contact with the Mewar region in order to obtain raw materials such as copper, zinc, and semi-precious stones including chalcedony, carnelian, and agate. Although Gilund was not located near any deposits of these materials, it was large and centrally located and was thus likely pivotal in both regional and long-distance interactions.

In order to situate the finds at Gilund, a systematic site catchment and locational analysis was undertaken by Debashri Dasgupta Ghosh who identifies locally available raw materials and describes other nearby sites that may have engaged in trade and exchange with Gilund (Chapter 5). Questions regarding the procurement of raw materials and the production and circulation of goods were approached through systematic and scientific study of various artifact classes. For example, Lorena Giorgio's and Shweta Sinha Deshpande's pottery analyses identified sherds that came to Gilund from far-away places (Chapters 6 and 7). Julie Hanlon's discussion of antiquities presents additional evidence of long-distance interaction (Chapter 8), as does Marta Ameri's discussion on the seal impressions (Chapter 9), and Teresa Raczek's lithic analysis, which includes a description of non-local raw materials (Chapter 10).

Transitions

Finally, little is known archaeologically about the transition between the Ahar-Banas and Early Historic periods. The problem of the so-called gap or "Dark Age" between these time periods in western and central India is reinforced by the paucity of research at occupations that span 1200 BC to 600 BC. Earlier explorations carried out on the eastern mound at Gilund identified the presence of fine Gray Ware, which often dates to 7th or 8th century BC. As a result, Gilund was seen as a fit candidate to study this transition and a trench was opened on GLD-I. Praveena Gullapalli and Peter Johansen present their finds of the Early Historic occupations in Chapter 4. Hanlon's presentation of the small finds also includes an Early Historic section and both pottery chapters document shifts in pottery production at the transition.

Plan of the Work

The chapters that follow present the finds and analyses undertaken in conjunction with the new excavations at Gilund. Chapters 2 and 3 provide the necessary context by summarizing methods, areas of excavation, and work conducted and presenting the site stratigraphy, architecture, and prominent features. Chapter 4 by Gullapalli and Johansen focuses on the Early Historic excavations and presents the stratigraphy, architecture, and features encountered in that part of the site. Chapter 5 by Ghosh presents the results of a detailed systematic survey of the area surrounding Gilund. In this chapter, nearby sites are described and natural resources available to the inhabitants of Gilund are identified. The chapter situates Gilund in a broader context among its geographic surroundings and nearest neighbors.

The analyses of artifacts from Gilund are presented in Chapters 6 through 11. Two separate pottery studies are presented (Chapter 6 by Deshpande and Chapter 7 by Giorgio) in order to provide both a chronological analysis and overall description of the pottery finds. These chapters highlight the most common Ahar-Banas pottery types, as well as select sherds that were brought to the site from other regions. In addition, a consideration of chronological changes in the pottery assemblage is presented.

Chapter 8 by Hanlon presents the antiquities collected at Gilund over the five seasons of excavation. Hanlon separates the antiquities by material class, and presents individual photos as well as summary tables of her finds. Her analysis also includes a discussion of how these small finds link Gilund to other sites both near and far (see also Hanlon 2010). Ameri's Chapter 9 on the seals and seal impressions found at Gilund provides additional analysis into Gilund's interactions with the wider world. Photos of the seals and impressions are presented along with a discussion of other sites where similar items can be found (see also Ameri 2010).

Chapter 10 by Raczek offers an in-depth analysis of technology used at Gilund by presenting the stone tool and debitage collection recovered during excavations. The study includes a typology, attribute analysis, and raw material analysis, and compares the Gilund collection to those from other sites in the region. Chapter 11 by Landt presents the faunal collection and offers some thoughts on the pastoral and hunting economies and activities of the residents at Gilund. His analysis contributes to our understanding of diet and subsistence during the Ahar-Banas period in the Mewar Plain. Finally, Chapter 12 summarizes the major finds of the research project and synthesizes the data to comment on the four themes discussed above. It concludes by offering suggestions for next steps in further research in the Mewar Plain.

2

Excavation Methods and Stratigraphy

Vasant Shinde and Gregory L. Possehl

The Site and Its Location

The site of Gilund measures roughly 500 m (E–W) by 450 m (N–S) and is comprised of two prominent mounds. The top of the eastern mound, GLD-1, rises 15 m higher than the surrounding area while the top of the western mound, GLD-2, rises 8 m higher than the surrounding area. However, as both mounds were built on top of an existing stabilized sand dune, the depth of the habitation deposit of GLD-1 is 9.40 m and that of GLD-2 is 5.40 m. The two mounds are somewhat elliptically shaped, oriented roughly north-south, and separated by a gap which currently resembles a rain gully (Fig. 2.1). A Historic period deposit and modern temple are located at the top of the southern part of GLD-1. As will be discussed in Chapter 3, there is some evidence that a thick enclosure wall may have once surrounded this mound, and a 35-m-wide gap located near the modern temple may have been an entrance or opening in that wall. GLD-2 has three circular ridges, a prominent one on the northern part (diameter = 70 m, 2 m above the rest of the mound), a second in the middle (diameter = 35 m, 15 cm above the rest of the mound), and a third along the southern portion of the mound (diameter = 25 m, 20 cm above the rest of the mound). The uneven surface of GLD-2 results from well-preserved architectural remains, including the large parallel mud-brick wall complex, that lie just underneath the surface. While much of the mound has been subject to deflation, areas with structural remains were somewhat protected.

Excavation Areas

Five areas on the site were selected for excavation. The excavation plan combined vertical and horizontal strategies in order to investigate diachronic and synchronic processes.

See Figure 2.2 for the location of each excavation area.

Excavation on GLD-1 (Eastern Mound)

A deep, vertically oriented Index Trench was placed on mound GLD-1 in order to determine the sequence of the site.

Index Trench (Trenches: 4A, B, C, D, E, F, G, H, I, J, K)

The Index Trench (Trench 4) was placed on the western slope of GLD-1, extending in a rough northwest-southeast line as a step-trench. An uneven exposure was created as a response to the acute slope of the mound. Each 5 m by 5 m unit of the Index Trench was assigned a letter, starting with A at the highest point and continuing through K, the lowest point. The northwest quadrant of Trench 4F was sunk down to unoccupied soil in order to provide the complete stratigraphic sequence of the mound (see Fig. 2.7). A total of 32 layers were encountered in the Index Trench (see Table 2.1 for a full description of these layers).

Excavation on GLD-2 (Western Mound)

Excavation on GLD-2 was divided into four distinct locales in order to sample a range of activity and occupation areas. See Figure 2.6 for the layout of trenches in each area.

Area I

Area I was located on the northern part of GLD-2. Horizontal excavation was undertaken on the eastern face of this area in order to investigate the function and context of the parallel wall complex that had been found during the original excavations (IAR 1959–60). A series of trenches was laid at the top of the slope, starting with an initial line of Trenches 5 through 11. New trenches were opened in sequence in

Fig. 2.1. Satellite photo of Gilund.

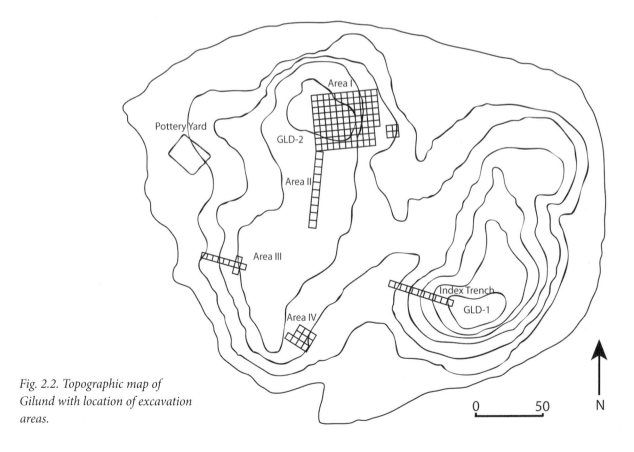

Fig. 2.2. Topographic map of Gilund with location of excavation areas.

order to follow walls, features, and other depositions.

Area II

Area II was excavated in order to understand the connection between the northern and middle rises of mound GLD-2. Five trenches were laid in a rough north-south line, starting with number 101 on the northern end. This area was informally termed the "Swale Operation" during excavation.

Area III

Excavation in Area III was undertaken in order to assess the architecture visible from the surface, identify the activities that occurred there, and to determine the presence of an enclosure wall. A series of east-west trenches were laid on the western slope of GLD-1 starting with Trench 201 at the top of the rise and continuing to Trench 208 at the western end. In order to excavate the extension of the burned structure discovered in Trench 201, three more trenches were laid (Trenches 209, 210, 211).

Area IV

Surface study of the southern end of GLD-2 indicated industrial activity on the eastern slope in the form of visible burning and burned-brick structures. To study this activity, ten trenches were laid starting with 301 near the top of the slope. Trenches were opened in order to follow walls, features, and burned areas. Thus, the trenches lie in a rough block formation, with Trench 310 located just to the west of 301.

Methods

The Archaeological Survey of India had previously set a datum at the highest point of GLD-1 near the northwest corner of the temple. This datum was reused for the new excavations and additional datums were fixed throughout GLD-1 and GLD-2 as a guide for laying trenches and for use in depth measurement. A grid system that emphasized the contours of the site was implemented. Trenches were laid in locations that best addressed the archaeological context and research questions, instead of in a rigid north-south direction, as in an arbitrary Cartesian system. Each trench measured 5 m by 5 m and all trenches were given Arabic numerals, starting with 4 as trench numbers 1–3 had been used by Lal in the 1959–60 season. The remaining trench numbers were assigned as the trenches were excavated.

Excavators dug by stratigraphic levels except when stratigraphic levels exceeded 5 cm. In those cases, archae-

Fig. 2.3. GLD-1, Trench 4, Step Trench.

TABLE 2.1. Stratigraphy of index trench, GLD-1

Layer	Time Period	Depth	Description
1	Early Historic	Generally uneven; a 10 cm thick deposit remains along the eastern edge of trench	Humus
2	Early Historic	Generally uneven; average thickness = 15 cm	Loose, dark gray, and homogeneous
3	Early Historic	Average thickness = 22 cm in the southeast. Thinner in north, where it merges with Layer 2	Deposit mainly exists in the eastern part of Trench 4C; a 1.50 m-long deposit is also present in west; hard, light gray, and homogeneous
4	Early Historic	Thickness = 45 cm	Darker gray than Layer 3 and loose in composition. Layer is disturbed in places, particularly in the north due to a number of later pits. Disturbed in the north by later pit
5	Early Historic	Average thickness = 25 to 30 cm	Similar dark gray to Layer 4, but made of mud and mud-brick material and therefore more compact. Homogeneous with the exception of yellow patches. Disturbed in the north by later pit
6	Early Historic	Average thickness = 22 cm	Roughly horizontal on top, dark gray, and disturbed in the northeast corner by a later pit. The top 15 cm is similar to Layer 5 but harder and more homogeneous; composed of typical wall material. The bottom 7 cm is coarse light gray clay and contains pebbly floor material. A cylindrical storage bin lies in the northeast corner of the base of Trench 4D and extends into the southwest section of Trench 4C. It is 1.75 m in diameter, 65 cm deep, and has vertical sides and flat base, both plastered with lime and clay. It starts from the base of Layer 6 and was filled with ash, pottery, brick fragments, and stones.
7	Chalcolithic	Considerably thick	Nearly horizontal on top and disturbed in northeast and southeast corners of Trench 4D by later pits. The base is exposed in the east half of Trench 4D in a small area that measures 5 m by 2.5 m. Light brown, composed of homogeneous clay material which appears to have come from nearby walls; contains potsherds and burnt clods of clay. Shallow circular pit, (diameter = 2.50 m; depth = 10 cm) belongs to the upper levels of the Historic Period. Cut in the west half of the trench, the pit has a gradual slope but is flat in the center. Could be associated with structure. Pit and surrounding area have smooth surfaces, indicating that it was part of a floor found at the base of Layer 6 belonging to structural phase 1.
8	Chalcolithic	Perfectly horizontal on top and bottom. Average thickness = 30 cm; thins towards north	Observed in Trench 4D; typical habitation layer, composed of loose white material with potsherds and stones. Cut in the upper part by a shallow pit.
9	Chalcolithic	Average thickness = 35 cm	A 1.55 m-long area is exposed in the west half of Trench 4D; light gray, medium compactness. Well-preserved southeast corner of mud structure (2nd structural phase of Chalcolithic) lies at base of layer in the west half of trench. The remains of the east wall are 1.30 m long and run north-south. The remains of the south wall are 2 m long and run east-west. The remains of both walls are 10 cm high and 75 cm wide.
10	Chalcolithic	Top of layer is uneven, but base is even. Average thickness = 15–20 cm	Exposed in west part of Trench 4D; loose and white, composed of compressed ash and small horizontal strips of black burnt material. Few artifacts.

TABLE 2.1 cont'd.

Layer	Time Period	Depth	Description
11	Chalcolithic	Average thickness = 30 cm in the west part of Trench 4D	Composed of mixed loose, dark gray material with thin lenses of ash, brown clay, black burnt material, and a few bone fragments. Disturbed in north half and southwest corner of Trench 4D by later pits and fox-holes
12	Chalcolithic	Average thickness = 10 cm in the west part of Trench 4D	Compact homogeneous white ash
13	Chalcolithic	Average thickness = 25 cm in the west part of Trench 4D	Brown and homogenous; appears to have formed from wall material; contains some pebbles at base. Disturbed in the north by later pits
14	Chalcolithic	Uneven thickness. Layer only exists in small part of north-west corner of the trench.	Loose, brown and contains burnt clods and ash
15	Chalcolithic	Uneven thickness. Layer only exists in small part of north-west corner of the trench.	Similar to Layer 14: loose, brown, and contains burnt clods and ash which are concentrated in lower parts of the layer.
16	Chalcolithic	Uniformly horizontal with a thickness of 25 cm in center of trench; thins to 15 cm to-wards the north	Compact, light brown, homogeneous; contains few artifacts. Disturbed in south half by presence of horizontal tandoor
17	Chalcolithic	Uniformly horizontal; average thickness = 15 cm	Present only in the northeast corner of Trench 4F due to the presence of the tandoor in this layer. Dark gray, compact, and homogeneous
17A	Chalcolithic	20 cm thick in southeast cor-ner; slopes and thins to west, and almost disappears in the southwest corner	Dark gray, loose, and heterogeneous. Contains small pebbles, pottery, and erosion deposits from the surface. Differentiated from Layer 17 as it was formed from erosion debris
18	Chalcolithic	Thickness = 40 cm	Heterogeneous; upper 12 cm is brown; below this, 12–20 cm is blackish gray, 20–25 cm is brown, 25–30 cm is light gray, and 30–40 cm is light brown. The brown sub-layers are slightly harder and more compact than the others which are loose in composition.
19	Chalcolithic	Average thickness = 25 cm	Brown, very hard, homogenous, and composed of very hard mud-brick fragments; possibly wall material
20	Chalcolithic	Average thickness = 17 cm; slopes towards the east	Light gray and loose. Composed of mixed wall material and ash; con-tains very few artifacts
21	Chalcolithic	Average thickness = 30 cm; slopes towards the east	Dark gray and contains thin lenses (average thickness = 3 cm) of ash and charcoal. Loose in composition, and contains high density of pot-tery and charcoal
22	Chalcolithic	Even thickness = 14 cm; slopes gradually towards the east	Similar to Layer 21 but with more ashy material in the lower portion, which is loose and disturbed. A sub-layer of pottery sherds lies at base of layer.
23	Chalcolithic	Even thickness = 18 cm; slopes slightly towards east	Composed of wall material that is brown, hard, and uniformly homoge-nous; few artifacts
24	Chalcolithic	Thickness = 6 cm; gradually broadens towards west; base is horizontal	Loose, ashy material with charcoal and pottery fragments
25	Chalcolithic	Even thickness = 20 cm	Composed of mixed wall, floor, and habitation material. Light brown, medium hard, and contains charcoal, pottery fragments, and pebbles

cont'd.

TABLE 2.1 cont'd.

Layer	Time Period	Depth	Description
26	Chalcolithic	Maximum thickness = 1.25 m	Base (foundation) of circumference wall. Made of fine clay, silt, clay loaves, and brick bats. Brown, very compact, and homogenous
27	Chalcolithic	It is uniformly horizontal and has a thickness of 32 cm	Light brown, medium hard, homogenous, and contains charcoal and pebbles. Composed of mixed wall and habitation material
28	Chalcolithic	Thickness in west = 15 cm; tapers to east and gradually disappears to northeast	Made of series of thin and loose to semi-compact sub-layers representing multiple deposits. Sub-layers include: 3 cm pink, 1 cm green road, 1 cm pink, 1 cm greenish-white, 2 cm pink, 3 cm green, 1 cm pink, 1 cm white. Reserved Slip Ware sherd found in this layer.
29	Chalcolithic	36 cm thick in south and west; thins down to 10 cm in east. Slopes to northeast corner of trench	Charcoal flecks on the surface along east. Uniformly light black, very compact, and with brick wall fragments
30	Chalcolithic	Average thickness = 12 cm in southeast; absent in north and west	Gray, loose, and contains charcoal flecks and small pebbles
31	Chalcolithic	Average thickness = 22 cm, but 40 cm thick in northwest corner	Resembles Layer 29; homogeneous layer of black wall material, with some yellow mud-mortar deposits; no artifacts. Brick wall in northwest corner
32	Chalcolithic	Average thickness = 20 cm	Mixed gray coarse and fine sand. Some large lumps of brick present. Base of wall that forms the above layer is present.
32A	Uncertain	Uncertain	Uniform loose, fine sand with few artifacts or evidence of occupation; potentially original ground surface

ologists dug by 5 cm arbitrary levels or until a new archaeological context was encountered. Depths were taken at the bottom of each digging episode, notes were made, and photos were taken when appropriate. The excavation implemented a lot-based recording system in order to maintain the proper provenience of objects and other features. Each episode of digging in a trench was treated as a separate lot and assigned a sequential number. All artifacts encountered in that digging episode were assigned the same lot number which was written on all forms and artifact bags. Depending on the archaeological context, excavators either included the entire 5 m by 5 m trench in their lot or they subdivided their trench into 2.5 m by 2.5 m quadrants or 5 m by 2.5 m halves. In addition, separate lot numbers were assigned to each excavated feature. Lots were numbered sequentially, starting with 1001 for each trench.

Excavators were required to fully record their work in notebooks and on lot forms. The lot forms requested basic information such as excavator initials, trench number, lot number, start and end depths, stratum number, artifacts encountered, features encountered, and soil type (see Appendix 1). The lot form also asked questions about methods used and observed depositional processes. The majority of the lot form consisted of boxes to check, which allowed for a speedy collection of data at the side of the trench. However, the forms also included a small box for drawing features encountered in the trench, as well as a space for comments. Excavators also discussed their work in their trench notebooks, which served as a redundant source of information, as well as an elaboration on daily discoveries. Work at the site was also documented by the Project Directors in a summary notebook that described the work at each trench and interpreted the finds. Trench photographs were taken when a new stratum or features were encountered. All features were drawn and one or two profiles were drawn for each trench at the end of each season. A selection of available photographs and drawings are included in this report.

Fig. 2.4. GLD-2, Area III.

Excavation crews consisted of the Area or Trench supervisor, 1–3 graduate student assistants, 1–3 undergraduate student assistants, and 3–5 local workers. The project was international in scope as students from Deccan College and the University of Pennsylvania were joined by students representing over twenty universities from nine different countries (see Appendix 2). A diverse set of Indian students joined in the excavation from the Maharashtra Vidyapeeth (Pune), St. Xavier College (Mumbai), Bombay University, Rajasthan University, M.S. University of Baroda, Pune University, and the Indian Archaeological Society. In addition, researchers from the International Research Center for Japanese Studies in Kyoto, Japan, and Tokyo Metropolitan University participated in the initial stages of the project. Over 100 villagers from Gilund participated in the original excavations by Professor Lal and an additional 100 participated in the new excavations reported here. Two village residents, Lehruba, and Shantiba Nai participated in both excavations and provided the new project team with valuable insight regarding the original excavations.

Excavations were conducted with small hand picks, powdahs (small straight-edged shovels), and trowels. During excavations, 100% of the soil from each lot was screened through very fine screens (less than 0.3 cm), with the exception of soil that came from very disturbed contexts (such as erosion deposition). Screeners were trained to collect all artifacts encountered and to group them by lot. For each lot, pottery was collected and sent to the pottery yard where it was washed, dried, and sorted. Select pieces were drawn. In addition, fauna was collected in paper envelopes, as were lithics. All other artifacts were treated as antiquities and were given special care. They were collected by the designated antiquities keeper at the end of each day and most were then individually packed in plastic

Fig. 2.5. GLD-2, Area IV, pyrotechnic feature and related structure.

boxes with protective cotton. Where appropriate, alternative storage methods were used. A separate antiquities log documented each of these artifacts.

Stratigraphy

The stratigraphy for GLD-1 and GLD-2 varies somewhat. Table 2.1 and Figure 2.7 present the stratigraphy for GLD-1, based on the index trench. Table 2.2 presents stratigraphy for GLD-2, based on excavations across the mound, and Figures 2.8 and 2.9 show the stratigraphy as seen in Trench 9. Both tables provide a description of each layer, presented from the mound surface downward.

Index Trench on GLD-1

The occupation of GLD-1 potentially spans from pre- or very early Chalcolithic levels through historic periods.

Chalcolithic Phase

The Chalcolithic phase on GLD-1 was first encountered in Trench 4D and is comprised of Layers 7–32 and runs from a depth of 1.50 m to 10.80 m. Layer 32A, the bottommost, is an unoccupied layer of uniform and loose

fine sand. As the Chalcolithic habitation was established on top of this layer, it appears that the initial occupation at Gilund was built on the surface of a natural dune formation. The earliest occupations appear to predate architecture and include microlithic tools. The deposits in Layers 31 and 32 resemble deposits at the site of Bagor, a contemporaneous temporary occupation also located on top of a sand dune (see Misra 1973). It is possible that Gilund also served as a temporary occupation site prior to full settlement.

An Early Chalcolithic phase has been identified in the Index Trench based on pottery and mud-brick construction collected from Layers 28–31. Similar evidence was found at the site of Balathal, where handmade ceramics and circular huts appeared towards the middle of the 4th millennium BC. However, the pottery from the lower layers at Gilund is finer than that from Balathal. In addition, three dates run on charcoal samples from the earliest levels are somewhat later than Balathal (see Appendix 1). The calibrated sample from Layer 29 dates to 2460–2200 BC, the calibrated sample from Layer 30 dates to 2330–2130 BC and 2080–2060 BC, and the calibrated sample from Layer 32 dates to 2450–2190 BC and 2170–2150 BC. The presence of later dates in the context of Early Chalcolithic pottery might be attributed to mixing. As the earliest deposits lie on top of a stabilized sand dune, some mixing is to be expected in the context of the sand.

Historic Period

At the top of GLD-1 a Historic period occupation was identified in Layers 1–6 with a total depth of 1.20 m. Based on the artifact assemblage, the occupation is subdivided into two periods: 3rd century BC, represented by Layers 4–6 (the lower 70 cm of the deposit), and Kushan period, 2nd century BC to 3rd century AD, represented by Layers 1–3 (the upper 50 cm of the deposit). As three separate structures were identified in Layers 4, 5, and 6, the 3rd century BC deposit appears to represent three separate architectural phases. Each of these layers contains either wall or floor material. Within the Kushan period deposits, two

distinct structural phases were identified. The first appears in Layer 3 and consists of wall material. The latest structural phase consists of a rectangular structure complex composed of mud, stones, and brickbats (Structure No. 1, located in Trench 4A and B).

Stratigraphy of GLD-2

A total of 26 layers, from the mound surface to unoccupied soil, were identified on GLD-2 (see Table 2.2). As there is no indication of Early Historic deposits on GLD-2, all layers are considered to be Chalcolithic. Layer 1 is the surface layer and is found across the site. Layers 2–6

GLD-1, Index Trench

4K	4J	4I	4H	4G	4F	4E	4D	4C	4B	4A

GLD-2, Area I

119	110	50	51	52	53	54	55	56	36	37
120	111	57	58	59	60	61	62	63	35	34
121	112	64	65	66	67	16	15	14	13	12
122	113	68	69	5	6	7	8	9	10	11
123	114	70	71	72	73	31	30	17	18	19
124	115	74	75	76	77	32	25	20	21	22
125	116	78	79	80	81	33	29	23	24	
126	117	82	83	84	85	86	87	26	27	
127	118	88	89	90	91	92	93	94	28	

38	40
39	41

GLD-2, Area II

105	104	103	102	101	99	98	97	96	95

GLD-2, Area III

						210	
208	207	206	205	204	203	201	209
						211	

GLD-2, Area IV

	307	308	309
	304	305	206
310	301	302	303

Fig. 2.6. Plan of trenches excavated at Gilund, 1999–2005.

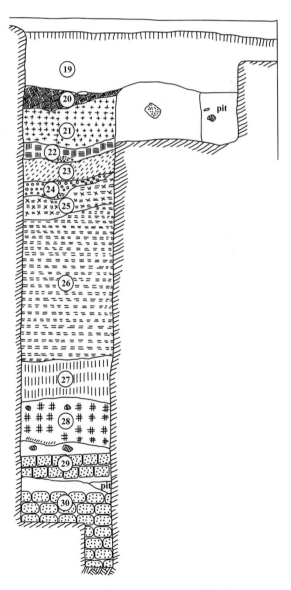

Fig. 2.7. Index trench, Trench 4F profile.

Excavations at Gilund

TABLE 2.2. Stratigraphy of GLD-2

Layer	Depth	Description
1	Thickness = 5 cm to 15 cm; follows the contour of the mound and thus thins down towards the eastern slope of the mound	Present throughout the mound; post-occupation layer formed of erosion material. Gray with many small pebbles and artifacts. Loose to semi-compact
2	Average thickness = 15 cm to 20 cm; dips slightly towards the east but damaged in some sections due to erosion	Gray semi-compact; high density of artifacts; some small pebbles
3	Thickness = 15 cm to 20 cm	Yellow-brown and loose; contains pebbles, indicating presence of floor levels, though no structural elements were observed
4	Thickness = 15 cm to 40 cm	Yellow-brown, uniform loose composition; includes eroded material from walls or mud bricks. Contains habitation floors and structures with clay walls
5	Thickness = 10 cm to 15 cm	Light brown to whitish-brown; semi-compact to compact, with bricks, brick fragments, prepared floors, and mud-brick structures
6	Thickness = 30 cm to 40 cm	Light sandy brown; loose to semi-compact, with artifacts, charcoal, and stones
7	Thickness = 10 cm to12 cm	Light brown, sandy layer made of multiple 1–2 mm thick fine sand layers
8	Thickness = 10 cm to 15 cm; made of 6 sub-layers	Sub-layers are composed of alternating semi-compact brown sand and thin loose rain-deposited brown sand.
9		Similar to Layer 8; made up of alternating semi-compact prepared sandy floors and loose sandy deposits. Loose deposits are almost as thick as the floors under them.
10	Thickness = 30 cm	Made of 15–20 sub-layers of loose material. Heterogeneous with ashy, brown, greenish-gray, or a mix of colors.
11	Thickness = 35 cm; slopes towards west from wall NS5	Made of ashy or brown loose soil patches. Waterlogged sands and burnt patches of soil that represent dumping episodes
12	Thickness = 37 cm	Series of thin ashy layers and thicker brown sand layers
13	Thickness = 17 cm	Comparatively loose layer with fragments of pottery, bones, and charcoal; 5 distinct sublayers: (from top to bottom) brown sand, gray ash, white ash, brown sand, and gray ash.
14	Thickness = 34 cm	Similar to Layer 13 but with 10 sub-layers. Contains fragments of pottery, bones, and charcoal. Originally excavated by B.B. Lal
15	Thickness = 8 cm	Semi-compact and uniform yellowish-brown sand; contains pottery, bones and charcoal
16	Two distinct sub-layers: 16A thickness = 9 cm; 16B thickness = 11 cm	16A has five thin, fine and loose pathway deposits, the lowermost of which is a white lime floor. 16B is made of two semi-compact yellowish-brown sandy sub-layers. These may represent either floors or prepared bases for floors like the white lime floor at the base of 16A.
17	Two distinct sub-layers: 17A thickness = 7 cm; 17B thickness = 10 cm	Sub-layer 17A: gray mud brick and floors made of brick fragments. Sub-layer 17B: rammed compact clay mixture. Both are prepared bases for floors made of mud-brick and brick fragments.

TABLE 2.2 cont'd.

Layer	Depth	Description
18	Two distinct sub-layers: 18A thickness = 6 cm; 18B thickness = 3 cm	Both sub-layers made of rammed compact clay mixture with gray mud-brick and brick fragments. Both are prepared bases for floors made of mud bricks and brick fragments.
19	Thickness = 1-3 cm; protrudes 50 cm from the wall and lies on wall's footer courses	Thin, indistinct layer of red burnt material that appear to have been dumped along Wall NS5.
20	Two distinct sub-layers: 20A thickness = 13 cm; 20B thickness =10 cm	Both sub-layers are similar in appearance, made of semi-compact to compact brown sand, and separated by a very thin ashy layer. Both may represent prepared floors
21	Thickness = 15 cm	Compact brown sand similar to Layer 20, but more compact and with some brick fragments
22	Thickness = 6 cm; begins at a depth of -9.61 m	Semi-compact to compact hard layer of mixed brown sand and straw used as binding material. The layer has developed vertical and horizontal cracks, giving the impression that it is made of mud bricks. Wall NS5 of the parallel-wall complex sits on this layer; may represent a prepared base for the wall.
23	Thickness = 9 cm	White tinged brown sand and semi-compact; resembles Layer 22 above and may represent a prepared base or floor
24	Thickness = 29 cm	Very hard, compact clay and sand mixture formed from wall material
25	The base of this layer is at -10.28 m.	Semi-compact to compact clay and sand mixture with white tinge; lowermost habitation layer; bottom 1 cm appears to be a burnt white lime floor.
26	Thickness = 1.25 m; when the excavation halted a depth of -11.50 m had been reached.	Loose, well-sorted medium-grained yellow sand with some cultural remains including pottery, bone fragments, a terracotta slingball, and numerous quartz blades and flakes. Excavation in limited area because of the great depth of the trench.

were found in Areas I, II, and III. Layers 7–13 are visible in Area I in Trenches 9, 17, 18, 20, and 21. Layers 14–21 are identified through excavation of the deep trench located in the southwest quad of Trench 18. In Trench 18, Layers 7–21 all represent pathway deposits that have accumulated in-between the mud-brick complex represented here by wall NS5 and the unexcavated structures that lie to its west. In the excavation area immediately next to wall NS5, the layers sloped up against the wall, displaying a feature characteristic of pathway deposits.

Cultural Sequence of Gilund

The following cultural sequence at Gilund derives from analysis of the excavated layers, structures, features, and artifacts:

Period I: Initial occupation
Period II: Chalcolithic (Early, Middle, and Late Phases)
Period III: Historic (3rd century BC to 3rd century AD, including Kushan period)

Initial Occupation

The initial inhabitants at Gilund established their occupation on top of one or more stabilized sand dunes and may have been largely mobile. Unfortunately, due to the limited excavation of the deepest layers of the site, a full investigation into the earliest occupation was not possible. A burned patch was identified on the top of the sand dune deposit on GLD-1, but due to the small area under excavation, nothing conclusive can be stated about its nature.

Fig. 2.8. GLD-2, Area I, Trench 9 profiles looking NW.

A small trench on GLD-2, excavated between walls NS4 and NS5 down to the sand dune, revealed similar evidence of burning including ash, charcoal, and red soil. Such evidence was also reported from the base of the Chalcolithic level at Balathal (Shinde 2000) and may indicate natural burning episodes.

Deposits of lithic remains (microliths and debitage)

were identified in the upper levels of the sand dune, just above sterile soil in five separate areas of the site (see Raczek, this volume). These areas include: a small trench (1 m by 1 m) on the western side of wall NS5 of the parallel-wall structure, a small trench in-between two parallel walls of the same structure, two 2.5 m by 5 m trenches south of the parallel walls, four 2.5 m by 5 m trenches to the southeast of the

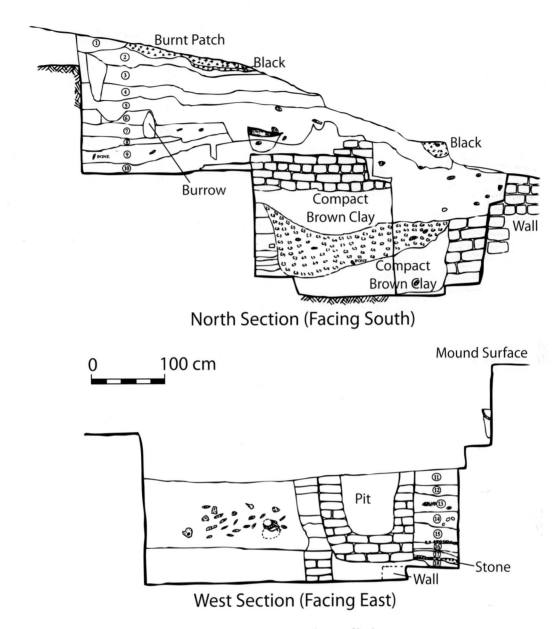

Fig. 2.9. GLD-2, Area I, Trench 9 profile drawings.

parallel walls, and the bottom of the Index Trench on GLD-1. Some of these areas included degraded pottery as well. Gilund appears to be unique in the region for the construction of a permanent settlement on a sand dune. In addition, Gilund may also uniquely represent the transformation of a temporary occupation to a permanent settlement.

Chalcolithic

The Chalcolithic period is divided into Early, Middle, and Late based on changes in architecture, ceramics, and

other artifacts. This convention follows that used at other Ahar-Banas sites in the region.

Early Chalcolithic (3200–2600 BC): The Early Chalcolithic Phase represents the earliest Chalcolithic occupation at the site. Stratigraphically, Layers 22–25 on GLD-2 and 28–31 on GLD-1 are attributed to this level. This phase appears to be comparable to Phase A at Balathal; however, further excavation is required before more conclusive statements about the relationship between the early phases at Gilund and other sites can be made.

Middle Chalcolithic (2500–2000 BC): The Middle Chalcolithic Phase shows an increase in the density of structures (five domestic structures have been excavated) and the introduction of large architecture in the form of a mud-brick parallel-wall complex. Most structures are made of mud brick. Most of the regional Chalcolithic ceramic wares and forms as well as other common regional artifacts are found in these levels. Stratigraphically, Layers 5 to 21 on GLD-2 represent this Phase.

Late Chalcolithic (1900–1700 BC): The evidence from the Late Chalcolithic Phase indicates a major shift in the material culture. Spacious mud-brick rectangular structure complexes are largely replaced by structures made of wattle and daub or mud and wood. The ceramic assemblage also changes. Chronologically, this phase is contemporary with the first part of the Late Harappan culture (1900–1300 BC). Stratigraphically, Layers 1 to 4 represent this Phase on the northern end of GLD-2.

Historic

The Historic period at the site is only present in the index trench on GLD-1. The 1959–60 excavation report noted the presence of Medieval period glazed pottery. However, no such evidence was identified by the current excavators. The Historic period pottery and artifacts appear to suggest that they date from the 3rd century BC to the Kushan period. This final occupation at the site was much smaller than the Chalcolithic period occupation. No evidence was uncovered to indicate why the site was ultimately abandoned. However, the temple on top of GLD-1 continues to be in use today.

3

Chalcolithic Structures and Features

Vasant Shinde and Gregory L. Possehl

A total of 17 structures were identified during the excavations at Gilund.[1] Five Middle Chalcolithic structures were partially exposed in the Index Trench on GLD-1. Six Middle Chalcolithic structures were unearthed on GLD-2, including three domestic structures (in Area I and Area III), two workshops (in Area IV), and a large mud-brick parallel-walled complex (in Area I). Six additional structures were found in Late Chalcolithic contexts on GLD-2, all from Area I: four domestic, one storage, and one of uncertain function. In addition to these structures, a circumference wall was identified on both GLD-1 and GLD-2. No structures were found in Early Chalcolithic deposits.

GLD-1, Trench 4 (Index Trench)

The five Middle Chalcolithic structures on GLD-1 were only partially exposed due to the vertical orientation of the Index Trench. As a result, their function remains unclear. The architectural remains are presented here in the order in which they were discovered. Thus, the descriptions begin with the Middle Chalcolithic and proceed from the top of the archaeological deposits to the bottom, that is, from the most recent to the oldest architectural remains.

Structure 1. A prepared floor was exposed in Layer 7 in the east half of Trench 4D in a 5 m by 2.5 m area. No associated walls were identified.

Structure 2. At the base of Layer 9 in the northwest quadrant of Trench 4D, the southeast corner of a well-preserved mud-wall structure was identified. A 1.30 m long portion of the north-south running east wall was exposed, as well as a 2 m long portion of the east-west running south wall. The remains of both walls are 75 cm wide and 10 cm high. The structure may have been rectangular or square.

Structure 3. A partially excavated rectangular structure in Layer 12 of Trench 4E has at least two rooms. A 4.60 m long segment of the north wall appears in the northwest part of the trench. Part of the base of the south wall sits in the southeast corner of the trench (length = 4.40 m). Both the north and south walls are approximately 50 cm wide and run in a rough northeast-southeast direction. Their west sides have eroded due to the mound's slope to the west. A partition wall is located 2.80 m west of the east end of the north wall and runs 1.50 m to the north of the north wall. However, as it continues into the unexcavated area north of trench 4E, its total length is greater than 1.50 m.

The structure has multiple floors, three of which have been exposed. The composition of each floor includes alternate layers of silt and clay that have been rammed hard and plastered. A few flat stones near the western ends of both the north and south walls are present. A fire pit abuts the middle of the inner face of the south wall. In addition, a fragmentary Coarse Red Ware pot with an everted rim, vertical short neck, and a globular body is located 1.10 m north of the fireplace. A second fragmented vessel—a large Coarse Black and Red Ware wide-mouthed jar—is located 60 cm north of the Coarse Red Ware pot.

Structure 4. One wall of Structure 4 lies in the north part of Trench 4F in Layer 14. The west end of the wall is completely eroded away. The remaining portion is 4.40 m long, starts in the northeast corner of the trench, and runs east-west. It has an uneven width; towards the west end it is 70 cm wide whereas at the east end it is 45 cm wide. The mud and clay loaf wall is potentially the north wall of the structure and its remains are 40 cm high. It is associated with a horizontal tandoor (enclosed fireplace).

Tandoor. The tandoor is located in the southeast quadrant of Trench 4F, although its south end partially extends into the southwest quadrant of Trench 4E. The sides, bottom, and area around the *tandoor* are burned red. The north end, located 2.40 m south of the north trench line, is partially cut by a later circular pit (1.10 m diameter). The *tandoor* is horizontal, roughly circular, with a conical base. It is 2.55 m long (north-south) but its width varies between 90 cm (north end) to 1.25 cm (in the middle) to 80 cm (south end). The inner surface has been smoothed. The maximum thickness of the fine clay walls is 20 cm along its west edge. The width of the top of the *tandoor* is 1.20 m but it tapers towards the base, which is 10 cm wide. The upper dome structure has collapsed and fallen inside. The bottom half (40 cm) was built in a pit, while the rest (30 cm) lies above ground. The *tandoor* has two openings: the north one is horizontal (diameter=50 cm) while the middle one is vertical (diameter=15 cm). Clay pillars, one of which remains intact in the middle of the *tandoor*, once supported the dome. Stones found in the *tandoor* may have served as additional dome support. Near the south end (40 cm to the north of the southern tip), along the western margin, is a flat area (30 cm by 35 cm) on top of which lies a long, charred cattle bone which may indicate roasting activity. Two roughly oval, convex, smoothed terracotta objects were found inside the *tandoor*. They resemble modern wooden objects used for placing *roti* (flat bread) inside the *tandoor*. In current practice, *rotis* are usually stuck to the sides of the *tandoor* for baking and then removed with the help of a long metal rod.

Gilund is one of the few Chalcolithic sites in India where the physical remains of a *tandoor* have been found. Although *tandoors* were found at Oriyo Timbo (Rissman and Chitalwala 1990) and at Kalibangan, a Harappan site in the Ghaggar basin (Joshi 2003:73), the one from Gilund appears to be distinct in that it is horizontal instead of vertical and cylindrical like most *tandoors*.

Structure 5. A very well preserved thick mud-brick wall was identified in Layer 19 in a 1 m by 1 m area just north of the Index Trench (4F, deep trench). The wall is 80 cm wide and plastered on both sides with 4-cm-thick plaster. Five courses of the wall remain (height=80 cm). **Circumference wall** (in Trenches 4F, 4G and 4H). The outer circumference wall runs in a rough north-south direction and is made of rammed black clay and brown silt as well as clay loaves and brick fragments. The wall and its support ramps were built on a solid platform made of mud and mud-bricks. The thickness of the wall at the top is 7.3 m. A span of 5 m was exposed. The wall has eroded down towards the west due to the presence of a slope. As a result, the wall is currently 1.80 m high on the east side and 40 cm high on

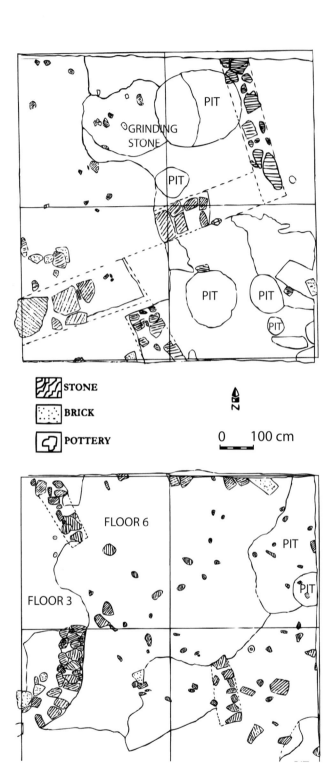

Fig. 3.1. GLD-1, Trench 4B.

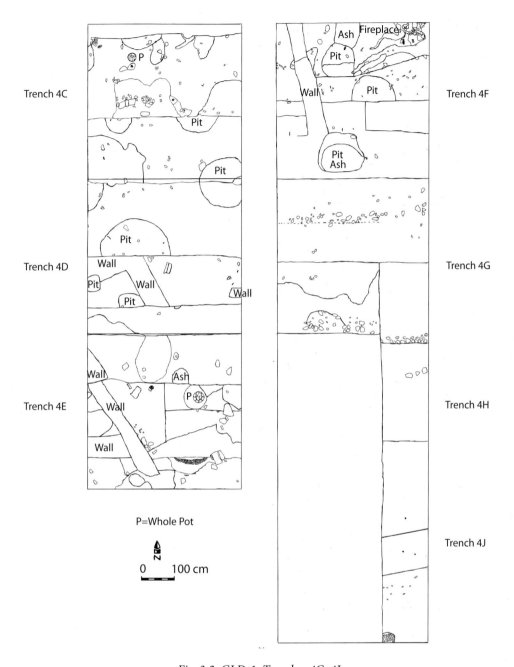

Trench 4C

Trench 4D

Trench 4E

Trench 4F

Trench 4G

Trench 4H

Trench 4J

P=Whole Pot

0   100 cm

Fig. 3.2. GLD-1, Trenches 4C–4J.

the west side. The vertical wall is supported from the outside by a 4.20-m-thick compact mud ramp, which is thicker along the wall and slopes down considerably towards the west end. The clay used for construction of the ramp contains calcium carbonate and gravel.

Road. Immediately to the west of the ramp lies a possible road that runs in a rough north-south direction between the circumference walls of GLD-1 and GLD-2. The feature consists of a very compact surface with alternate layers of clay, silt, and gravel. Wheel marks and cattle hoof traces were identified on its surface. The surface starts from the western edge of the ramp in the eastern margin of Trench 4I and continues through Trenches J and K towards the west. The total width of the exposed surface is 7.20 m and it is concave in the middle potentially due to constant use. As the edges of the surface join the outer circumference walls of GLD-1 and GLD-2, it appears that all three features are contemporaneous. The average width of the wheel marks is 2.5 cm. A bullock cart track was also identified at the site of Harappa, now located in the Punjab province of Pakistan.

GLD-2

A number of Middle and Late Chalcolithic structures were partially or fully excavated on GLD-2. As above, the architectural remains are presented here in the order in which they were discovered. Thus, the descriptions begin with the Late Chalcolithic and continue to the Middle Chalcolithic, proceeding from the most recent to the oldest architectural remains.

Late Chalcolithic

The top layers of GLD-2 date to the Late Chalcolithic. Multiple domestic structures were identified based on the presence of hearths, querns, cooking vessels, and storage bins or pits. The houses were rectangular or square, made of mud-brick or wattle and daub, and with one or more plastered floors. In addition, a unique rectangular storage facility was identified based on the presence of thick wall plaster and a surrounding "moat" filled with ash, presumably constructed to prevent pests from entering the facility. Most structures were not completely intact and had suffered from intrusive pits or erosion due to their location on a slope.

Area I
Structure 2 (Trench 9). A small rectangular structure was uncovered 76 cm below the surface in Trench 9 (sealed by Layer 4) on the eastern slope of mound GLD-2. As a result of the slope, the entire east half of the structure was eroded. In addition, a very large later pit (sealed by Layer 1) destroyed large parts of the structure's south half. The remaining portions of the structure are made of mud brick with rammed brick fragments and a mud-plastered floor. Its dimensions are 2.80 m (east-west) by 4.40 m (north-south) and it is located 1.90 m west of the east line of the trench.

A circular grass-lined pit (diameter = 1 m, depth = 90 cm) lies 3.40 m west of the east trench line and 1.30 m north of the south trench line. A large, intensively used concave saddle quern (60 cm by 50 cm; depth = 12 cm) sits 10 cm to the north of this pit. A large circular depression that is presumably a posthole (diameter = 25 cm) lies 27 cm to the west of the quern. Part of the north-south wall was exposed (length = 1.50 m, width = 35 cm). The wall is made of two lines of mud bricks set in mud mortar, only two

courses of which remain. Two flat stones lie to its west: the first is 64 cm west of the wall (dimensions = 34 cm by 14 cm east-west) and the second is 8 cm further west (dimensions = 43 cm by 15 cm east-west). A grinding stone is located 20 cm north of the quern and a muller (grinder) was located an additional 15 cm away. A second grinding stone was found immediately to the west of the second flat stone. A nearly complete Coarse Red Ware pot was found 35 cm east of the wall and 1.05 m south of the north trench line. Three grinding stones were found near the pot. These associated artifacts suggest that this was a domestic structure.

Structure 3 (Trench 5). At the base of Layer 4, Trench 5, a domestic structure composed of mud and wattle and daub was identified. Only its south wall is present in the trench. It runs in a rough northeast-southwest direction and its remaining section is 3.30 m long (average thickness = 35 cm). The wall is made of clay and has within it eight postholes that are approximately 15 cm apart. Thus, the clay wall was formed around a superstructure of perishable materials. The average depth of these postholes is 30 cm and they have a diameter of 15 cm. The structure has a prepared floor that has been destroyed in places by later pits. It contains two large globular Gray Ware pots (one of which is intact), a domestic hearth, and a small pit containing the upside-down rim of a pot. The intact Gray Ware pot (height = 50 cm, mouth diameter = 20 cm) is located 2.50 m north of the south wall and 1.35 m west of the east trench line. It has four low ridges on its shoulder and the upper 15 cm is treated with a gray slip, while the remainder is coarse and untreated. The other pot, which is crushed, lies 2 m to the south, close to the east end of the south wall. This pot appears to be as large as the intact pot. The circular pit containing the upper half of a jar was probably used as the basal support of another storage jar. This pit is located 1.20 m north of the south wall and 2.05 m west of the east trench line. It is roughly square (45 cm by 42 cm) and has rounded corners. The pit is shallow, with a depth of about 5 cm. The rim portion of the pot (mouth diameter =15 cm) lies near its western margin. The floor of this structure in the northeast corner of the trench appears to be disturbed by burning activity and may possibly have been a fireplace.

A U-shaped, or two-armed domestic hearth that faces west is located approximately 90 cm to the north of this pit. The sides and base of the hearth are clay lined and burned red (average thickness = 8 cm). It is roughly square with sides that are approximately 40 cm long. Its mouth has an opening of 20 cm and its height is 15 cm. A radiocarbon sample from the hearth dates to 1742 BC, calibrated (see

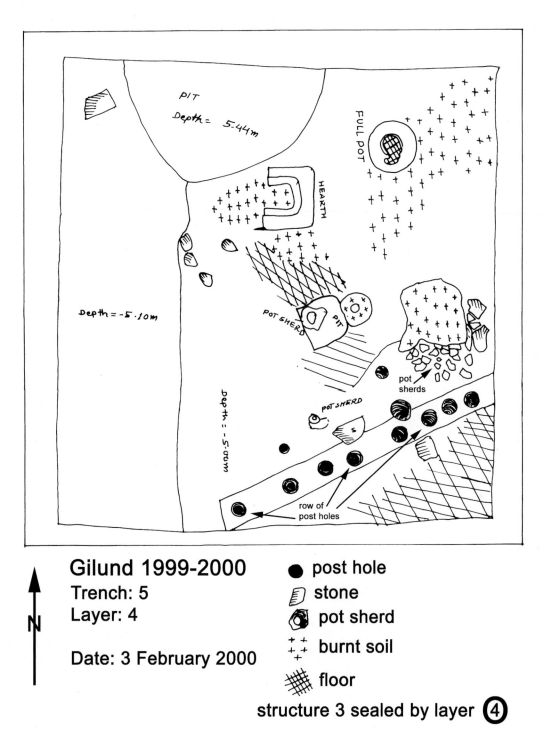

Gilund 1999-2000
Trench: 5
Layer: 4

Date: 3 February 2000

● post hole
🗐 stone
🗐 pot sherd
+ + burnt soil
+ +
▦ floor

structure 3 sealed by layer ④

Fig. 3.3. GLD-2, Area I, Trench 5, Layer 4, Structure 3.

Appendix 1). Next to the hearth is a burned circular mark on the floor, suggesting hot vessels were once placed there. This structure also has within it a large pit (diameter = 2 m), located 2.2 m north of the east trench line. The pit is 55 cm deep and contains ash, burned earth, pottery, and bone fragments.

Structure 4 (Trench 6). A rectangular structure was uncovered at the base of Layer 4, in the east half of Trench 6. The west half of the structure remains and measures 1.62 m north-south by 1.60 m east-west. The complete west wall is

1.62 m long and 40 cm wide. The south wall is also 40 cm wide, but only a portion remains (length = 1.35 m). It runs in a rough east-west direction while a 2.05-m-long portion of the north wall that has survived runs slightly NE-SW. This wall's width cannot be measured as an animal burrow has destroyed its north face. The remains of the walls are only 5 cm high, due to the poor preservation of the structure. The structure's floor is comprised of clay and brick fragments that were rammed into a hard surface and then plastered. A few fragments of Coarse Gray Ware pottery were recovered from the south part of the structure.

Two associated pits are located outside the structure. The first is a large oval pit in the northwest quadrant of Trench 6 (2.60 m west of the east trench line and 2.55 m north of the south trench line). It measures 2.20 m (east-west) by 1.40 m (north-south). It gradually slopes and deepens toward the center, where the maximum depth is 45 cm. The surface of the pit is prepared, and it is quite possible that it was used for storage. It was later filled with garbage including fragments of pottery and bones.

The other pit is located in the center of the south trench line, 2.25 m west of the east trench line. Only half of its circumference is visible in Trench 6. The pit is circular

(diameter = 1.50 m, depth = 30 cm). It was later filled with mud and stones. This structure appears to represent a small domestic unit.

Structure 5 (Trench 7). An east-west running mud-brick wall was identified 2.80 m north of Trench 7's south trench line at the base of Layer 4. Only the base course of the wall remains (height = 15 cm, length = 3.40 m, width = 50 cm). The bricks are placed vertically in an east-west direction. The average brick size, visible on the surface, measures 32 cm by 10 cm. The west end of the wall is cut by a later circular pit (diameter = 1.20 m) that is 60 cm deep with a flat and smooth bottom. Two successive floor levels related to the wall are located on the south side of the wall, both made of alternate layers of brown silt and fine sand rammed hard and then plastered with cow dung. The later 5-cm-thick floor was exposed on the west side of the trench in an area that measures 2.60 m (north-south) by 2.90 m (east-west). The earlier floor level is relatively better preserved along the south side of the wall in an area that measures 5 m (east-west) by 2.60 m (north-south). A shallow rectangular pit (1.20 m east-west by 1 m north-south, depth = 20 cm) with rounded corners is located along the east trench line, 75 cm to the south of the mud-brick wall. The south face of the

Fig. 3.4. GLD-2, Area I, Trench 5, chulha and pot.

wall seems to be the inner side of the structure, as the north face is not associated with a prepared floor. The west end of the wall was destroyed by a later lime-plastered circular storage pit (diameter = 1.20 m, depth = 60 cm).

Structure 6 (Trench 8). Several mud bricks were scattered at the base of Layer 4, in Trench 8. On closer examination, two distinct features were revealed: (1) a mud-brick platform in the southeast quadrant and (2) a rectangular mud-brick structure to its north. The platform appears to be slightly later than the structure and it has destroyed the south wall and floor of the structure. The platform was exposed over an area of 2.60 m (north-south) and 1.60 m (east-west) and has a height of 6 cm. The surface of the platform has been disturbed by later postholes and insect and animal burrows. From the surface, however, it is clear that the platform was once made of mud bricks (36 cm by 10 cm) that were arranged vertically and held in place with yellow mud mortar. This unusual brick placement has resulted in the platform appearing to be both compact and sturdy. Mud bricks made of black clay and yellow silt were also used. A few mud bricks at the platform's northern margin are burned due to the presence of a later fire pit. The function of the platform is not clear as its southern portion lies outside the trench and has not yet been excavated.

The earlier structure that was partially cut by the platform is made of mud bricks, brick fragments, and mud. Parts of the west and north walls of the structure are present. A 2.35-m-long section of the west wall has survived, 1.35 m to the east of the west trench line. It runs north-south as do its mud bricks. It was plastered on the inner surface with a 3 cm thick plaster. The average thickness of the wall is 45 cm and the remains are 15 cm high. The northwest corner of this structure was disturbed by a later pit. A later nearby saddle quern is oriented north-south (length = 50 cm, width = 30 cm). Its concave surface is 12 cm deep. The quern was used until a hole developed in the center at which time it was likely discarded. The remains of the north wall, which is disturbed near its east end by a later circular pit (depth = 70 cm), are 16 cm high, 2.50 m long, and 45 cm wide on average. The mud brick size is 32 cm by 16 cm by 10 cm. The floor within the structure is prepared and appears to have been rammed. It is exposed in an area that measures 2.70 m (east-west) by 1.85 m (north-south).

A well-made circular pit with a diameter of 60 cm was found associated with the floor of this structure. It is located 1.95 m east of the west wall and 80 cm south of the north wall. The pit has a 5 cm thick mud lining and is 25 cm deep. Two flat stones were found lying nearby on the floor. The first, 20 cm by 20 cm, lies 8 cm east of the west wall and

1.60 m south of the north wall, and the second lies 1.50 m east of the first. As the majority of the structure has been destroyed, its exact dimensions cannot be determined. The structure appears to be domestic.

Structure 8 and its associated features. A nearly complete mud-house covers the area of four trenches (25, 30, 31, and 32) at the base of Layer 2. It may extend further into the trenches on all sides. It is contemporaneous with Structure 3 (in Trench 5) and dated to 1800 BC based on ceramic analysis. The structure is also associated with a storage bin (in Trenches 25 and 30), and two surviving platforms that were probably used for supporting storage bins (Storage Platform 1 in Trench 30, Storage Platform 2 in Trench 25).

The structure is rectangular with the longer axis running in a roughly northwest-southeast direction. Although the southeast corner is slightly damaged, the remaining portions were better preserved. A well-defined wall on the south side divides the floor and creates two distinct rooms. The south room is badly eroded. However, the north room was completely excavated and measures 8.75 m long by 5.70 m wide. A 10-m-long portion of the western wall was exposed; 8.75 m borders the north room while the remaining 1.25 m borders the south room. It is a mud wall with an average width of 22 cm and a number of postholes in its outer periphery. The south wall is similar to the west wall and its remains are 2.45 m long. The northern periphery of the structure is represented by a series of five post-holes running in an east-west direction, with the remains of wattle and daub along the periphery. These postholes are situated almost equidistant from each other with an average diameter of 25 cm. The east wall is similar to the north wall, which is also represented by a series of four postholes.

The floor is prepared of alternate layers of silt and clay, and plastered with cow dung. It shows distinct signs of periodic repairs. Three different floor levels have been identified, indicating that the structure was in use for a considerably long duration. There are a number of intrusive postholes on the floor, which belong to structures of later levels. A storage bin and two Gray Ware storage jars sit in the interior of the structure, along the north wall.

Cooking activities were carried out in the western part of the structure which may have been a room or an open veranda. A relatively large fire pit that may have been a domestic hearth was identified 30 cm west of the western wall and 3.60 cm south of the northwest corner of the structure. The fire pit is 10 cm deep, and its sides and base are lined with a thin layer of clay (thickness = 5 cm). It lies in a northeast-southwest direction and is roughly rectangular

Fig. 3.5. GLD-2, Area I, Trenches 31–32, rectangular storage structure.

(90 cm by 65 cm). Within the pit lie burned clods of earth, ash, and charcoal pieces, as well as a fragment of a saddle quern in the southeast corner. A north-south row of three shallow circular depressions are located 80 cm south of the pit. Their various sizes may have supported different sizes of round-based pots.

Storage bin in Trenches 25 and 30. A large, circular underground storage bin associated with Structure 8 sits at the junction of Trenches 25 and 30. One quadrant of the bin lies in the southwest quadrant of Trench 30 and the rest lies in the northwest part of Trench 25. The west half of the bin was destroyed by a later structure. The bin is circular with inner and outer diameters of 3 m and 3.40 m, respectively. It has a depth of 1.60 m and was built in a pit. Its periphery was lined with a framework of flat gneiss stones (25 cm by 12 cm), over which a thick (4 cm) coating of lime and clay mixed with chopped grass was applied. The surface was further smoothed by applying a thin layer of fine cow dung and lime paste. The upper 75–80 cm of the bin is made of burned and semi-burned bricks and brick fragments. The average thickness of the bin wall is 20 cm. The bottom of the pit is prepared, flat, and plastered with lime

and clay. It appears from the stratigraphic sequence that it was filled in two stages, first with a thick (45 cm) deposit of ash, then with a uniform layer of clay.

Storage Platform 1 in Trench 30 sealed by Layer 2. Seventy cm to the northeast of the storage bin described above lies circular storage Platform 1. The platform has a diameter of 3 m and its remains are 80 cm high. The exterior of this feature is made of vertical bricks and the interior is comprised of rammed clay. It is isolated by a narrow trough (15 cm) that was dug around it and filled with ash. This unique aspect indicates that it may have been used for supporting storage bins or baskets that contained grains. This is because the ash trough prevents moisture and discourages rodents and insects from accessing the platform.

Storage Platform 2 in Trench 25 sealed by Layer 2. A second circular storage platform (diameter = 2.50 m, depth = 1 m) is located 60 cm to the southeast of the storage bin and is associated with Structure 8. The platform has vertical sides and a clay base. The sides and bottom are plastered with clay and lime.

The east side of the residential structure (Structure 8) where these features are located was probably a storage area.

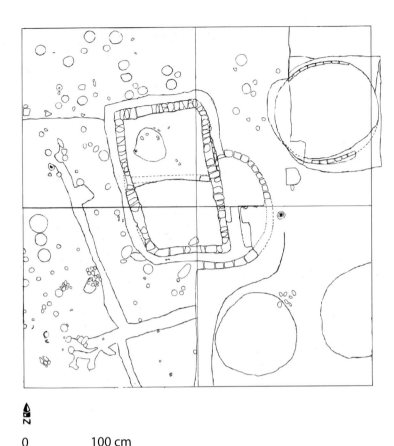

0   100 cm

Fig. 3.6. GLD-2, Area I, Trenches 31–32, plan of rectangular storage structure.

thick coating of lime and clay and the floor has a flat, 20-cm-thick prepared clay surface topped with a 2-cm-thick coating of lime.

A deep and narrow (30 cm) ash-filled trench surrounds the structure. This feature is unique to Gilund. On the periphery of the structure just outside of the ash area, a number of postholes suggest the presence of a superstructure. Additional postholes are located within the stone walls, three each on the east and west walls, placed opposite each other, and one each on the north and south sides. This indicates that the structure was probably protected by a roof.

Middle Chalcolithic Structures

Area I
Structure 7. Part of a large rectangular mud-brick structure was uncovered in Trenches 17, 20, 25, and 29, south of Trench 9. Due to erosion on the slope of the mound, most of the structure is badly destroyed. However, several components of the structure were found somewhat intact. The structure contains three different floor levels: the last occupational level is at the base of Layer 5, the middle at the base of Layer 6, and the earliest at the base of Layer 8.

The east half of this structure, including the east wall that runs nearly north-south, is 9.70 m long with an average thickness of 50 cm. Near the southeast corner the remains are 60 cm high. The north section of this wall is badly disturbed. It is constructed of black clay plastered inside and out with yellow mud. Using a common wall construction technique for the time, the builders laid the bricks on the west side of the wall vertically in an east-west orientation,

However, this area is badly destroyed due to erosion and it is therefore not possible to determine whether these features were located inside or outside the structure. It appears that at one time the structure extended farther to the east. The east wall of Structure 8, represented by postholes, may actually have been a partition wall since it differs from the western periphery wall of the structure.

Storage building. A rectangular stone building, which cut the west half of the storage bin sealed by Layer 2, is later than Structure 8 and lies at the base of Layer 1 in the southeast of Trench 31 and the northeast of Trench 32 and 25. This feature is 2.60 m wide on the north side and in the middle, and 2.30 m on the south. The length of the feature also varies; to the west it is 4.15 m long while to the east it is 4.30 m long. The intact original surface of the structure visible in the southwest corner indicates that the original height of the wall was 1.5 m. The structure is made of eleven regular courses of flat to sub-round stones set in mud mortar. This is capped with a single course of burned bricks of two sizes: 30 cm by 15 cm by 10 cm and 30 cm by 20 cm by 10 cm. The inside of the structure's walls are plastered with a and those on the east side in a north-south orientation.

The south wall of the structure slopes toward the east (average width = 60 cm, maximum height = 60 cm). It is composed of red mud bricks that were made by mixing yellow silt and fine sand with clay. The wall was also plastered on both surfaces. An intrusive saddle quern, most likely later in age, was found sitting on the outer edge of this wall, located 2.60 m west of the southeast corner of the structure. The quern is 60 cm long, 35 cm wide and 15 cm thick. The worked surface of the quern is 30 cm by 24 cm and its concave surface is 6 cm deep.

The north wall of the structure, running east-west, is the thickest wall of the structure (80 cm). A 3.95-m-long section of it was exposed. The wall is 1 m high in the northwest corner of Trench 17. Near this corner, only the base course of the wall has survived and animal burrowing has disturbed the outer face of the wall. Like the south wall, it is made of red bricks set in yellow mud mortar and plastered with yellow mud on both surfaces.

The presence of three different floors suggests a long period of activity. A 2.65 m (north-south) by 1 m (east-west) area of the youngest floor was exposed. It is located up slope and 2.35 m west of the east wall. This floor was prepared with a pebble and gravel base, covered with fine silt, rammed hard, and plastered. A domestic hearth and a north-south running mud-brick wall were found associated with this floor. Only the base course remains of this wall (length = 2.60 m, width = 30 cm) which is made of black mud bricks. A domestic hearth is attached to its western surface. A 5-cm-thick yellow plaster covers the hearth side of the wall as well as the surface of the hearth. The wall was possibly built to protect the flames of the hearth, as well as to create a small room that might act as a kitchen for this structure.

The domestic hearth located west and north of the small wall is roughly rectangular with rounded corners. A burned red square support made of clay-plastered brick fragments lies at the south end of the fireplace. The remains taper towards the top (height = 20 cm). The north side of the fireplace has three intact, plastered flat-topped conical clay supports that are arranged in a rough triangle pattern. They were possibly used to support cooking vessels. All three are 24 cm high, but they vary in diameter from 15 cm to 20 cm.

A rectangular gap (25 cm by 30 cm) that may have served as an opening for the hearth lies between the square support and the hearth. Two additional openings are associated with the hearth itself; one faces west and the other north. All three openings could have served as points for firewood insertion. The hearth has visible signs of burning and resembles kitchen hearths used in the region today (see for example Boivin 2010).

A shallow, circular convex silo is located 80 cm to the north of the hearth (diameter = 1.35 m, depth = 25 cm) and may be associated with this floor level. However, because of erosion between the silo and the floor, no direct contact can be established. The sides and base are lime-plastered and possibly lined with grass. Considering its smooth surface and shape, it is identified as a storage pit.

A second storage pit was found 1.50 m to the north of the grass-lined silo. It is 70 cm by 75 cm, roughly square, with rounded corners. It has a prepared, smooth surface with straight sides and a flat bottom and it is lined with mud bricks and clay. The combination of these storage pits with the domestic cooking hearth indicates domestic activities during this occupation.

A 2.20-m-wide portion of the second or middle floor was found along the east wall and appeared similar in nature to that of the later floor. There is strong evidence that this floor functioned as a storage facility. In all, seven storage pits were uncovered inside the east and south walls. Of these, three pits lie along the south wall and four along the east wall. All are lined with yellowish clay plaster, a material that was also used as mud-brick mortar throughout this area. Seven additional prepared underground pits are identified here as clay storage bins (see Table 3.1). They differ from grain silos which are usually larger in plan, circular, plastered with lime, and lined with grass.

Since only a small portion of the structure is exposed, it is difficult to identify its function. However, it can potentially be associated with some kind of industrial or mercantile activity. Pit 10 contained a large amount of fine clay that may have been used as a raw material required for pottery production, for preparing new storage bins, or for sealing. Alternatively, the pits of different dimensions located along the walls in a straight line may have been used to separate different items similar to the way shopkeepers organize their goods today. After the pits were abandoned, they were used for dumping garbage including ash, broken pots, and bones.

A north-south running partition wall that is parallel to the east wall is associated with the second phase floor. It originates at the north wall, at a distance of 2.25 m from the northeast corner of the structure. It is made of black mud bricks that have plaster on both faces. It is 5.40 m long, 45 cm wide, and appears to turn west at its south end. However, the south end is partly destroyed by a later silo.

Parallel-Wall Mud-brick Structure Complex (Trenches 10, 11, 12, 13, 18, 19, 21, and 22). The first excavation

TABLE 3.1. Pits associated with Structure 7

Pit	Location	Shape	Measurements	Depth	Lining	Notes
5	8 cm N of S wall, 1.70 m from SE corner of structure	Circular, with slight elongation in N-S direction	50 cm by 45 cm	54 cm	5 cm thick clay lining	The sides are vertical and it has a flat base.
6	10 m E of Pit 5	Circular	Diameter = 60 cm	70 cm	5 cm thick clay lining	
7	5 cm E of Pit 6	Irregular	50 cm (N-S) by 35 cm (E-W)	35 cm	Clay lining; thickness varies from 5–8 cm; may have been made with coil method	
8	5 cm N of Pit 7 along E wall	Oval	85 cm (N-S) by 70 cm (E-W)	45 cm	6 cm thick	Contemporaneous with Pit 7; E portion is damaged by erosion; base dips to W
9	10 cm N of Pit 8, 15 cm from E wall	Apsidal	1.35 m (N-S) by 77 cm (E-W)	40 cm in S and 55 cm in N	7 cm clay lining	Erosion has destroyed eastern part
10	25 cm N of Pit 9, close to E wall	Oval	75 cm (N-S) by 68 cm (E-W)	70 cm	4 cm thick clay lining	Base slopes to W
11	20 cm N of Pit 10	Oval	90 cm (E-W) by 80 cm (N-S)	55 cm on W and 20 cm on E	5 cm thick clay lining	Base steeply slopes to W; N part is destroyed by erosion
12	In NE corner, partly under N wall	Circular	Diameter 40 cm		3 cm thick clay lining	Base slopes to W; associated with earliest floor; only partially exposed
13	15 cm W of Pit 12	Circular	Diameter 40 cm	40 cm	3 cm thick clay lining, with flat bottom and straight sides	

carried out by B.B. Lal and the ASI (IAR 1959–60) reported the evidence of a unique structure, made up of parallel running mud-brick walls with narrow spaces in-between. However, as Lal was unable to excavate the structure completely, the new excavations aimed to restudy the structure. While cleaning debris in Trenches 21 and 22, part of the structure was rediscovered along with modern metal tags used by the ASI to mark layers. During cleaning, it soon became clear that parts of the structure had not yet been excavated.

The longer north-south axis of the structure was measured at 19.70 m. However, the north portion of the com-

plex appears to continue beyond the trench and remains unexcavated. Similarly, the structure's 10 m long east-west measurement is only partial; the structure appears to continue east onto private property where excavation could not be conducted. The south and west sides of the structure have been satisfactorily identified. The structure is identified here as a "complex" since it is comprised of multiple parallel north-south walls (eight located) attached to parallel east-west walls (two located). The walls have been given Arabic numerals.

East-West Wall No. 2 (EW2). Wall EW2 represents the earliest phase of this complex. It has an orientation of

Fig. 3.7. GLD-2, Area I, Trench 9, brick-lined pit.

Fig. 3.8. GLD-2, Area I, parallel-walled structure.

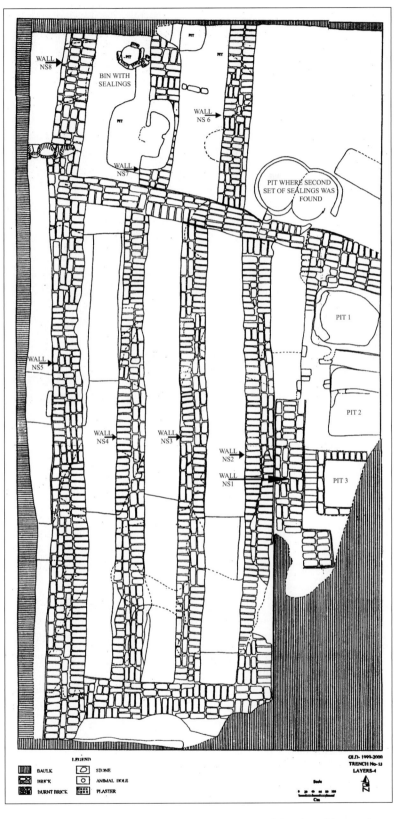

Fig. 3.9. GLD-2, Area I, parallel-walled structure with brick and bin outlines.

290° and a measured length of 10 m, although its east end has not been uncovered. It is made of black mud-bricks in the middle of the wall and red mud-bricks on the peripheries. The wall is plastered on both sides with thick yellow clay (average thickness 2.5 cm). Subsequent to its construction, a number of north-south walls were attached to it. The construction sequence was determined when yellow plaster was identified between EW2 and the attached north-south walls: NS5 which runs to the south and NS8 which runs to the north. The average width of EW2 is 70 cm; however, at both ends it is 65 cm wide. On its north side where it meets NS6, a small portion has been damaged by the construction of a later pit. As a result of the eastern orientation of the slope and related erosion, the wall is 1 m thick towards the west side and 20 cm thick towards the east end.

East-West Wall No. 1 (EW1). In the second construction stage of this complex, EW1, NS2, and NS5 walls were added to EW2. The construction sequence was determined by examining the bonding between each of these walls. A 6-m-long portion of wall EW1 was exposed and like EW2, its east end is unknown. The height of the wall is 45 cm and its average width is 1.10 m. Four courses of mud bricks are visible and the wall is plastered on both sides. Subsequent to its original construction, the outside of the wall was broadened by the placement of additional mud bricks, most probably to strengthen it. The entire exposed wall is made of reddish mud bricks with yellow mortar. The mud bricks were laid using a header and stretcher method, with the exception of the corner at the west end where the mud bricks were laid in a haphazard manner.

North-South Wall No. 1 (NS1). Located along the eastern margin of the complex, this north-south running wall is currently 9.60 m long and its width varies from 70 cm to 80 cm. Since the wall is located on the periphery, it is badly eroded on the surface and only three brick courses have survived (height = 45 cm). The wall was added subsequent to the construction of EW2 as mentioned above. Since the south end of the wall extends into private property and could not be traced, it is not possible to observe the relationship between EW1 and NS1. The wall is plastered on both sides. Two possible phases of construction are visible; the earlier phase of the wall consists of the bottom courses and projects 25 cm beyond the later or upper courses.

Area to the east of North-South Wall 1 (Trench 11). Three rectangular storage pits with rounded corners are located on the east side of the wall NS1 and postdate the structure. The pits lie in a row and were separated by thin mud-brick walls running in an east-west direction. As they were close to the surface, they have deteriorated considerably and only the bases have survived. Pit 1, close to EW2, was built by carving out a portion (50 cm) of wall NS1 near its north end. The remaining 25 cm portion of the wall served as the western periphery of the pit. On the north side of the pit, a 65 cm wide and 2 m long mud-brick wall was added to the south face of EW2. The pit measures 1.80 m (east-west) by 1.70 m (north-south) and appears to have been lined with grass and plastered with lime.

Pit 2, located south of Pit 1, lies in both Trench 11 and Trench 19. It is separated from Pit 2 by a thin east-west mud-brick wall (1.70 m long by 45 cm wide) that is plastered on both sides. The eastern face of NS1 served as the western boundary of Pit 2, which is deeper than Pit 1 by 50 cm. The pit is roughly square in plan, measuring 1.75 m (north-south) by 1.80 m (east-west), and is plastered with lime and lined with grass.

Pit 3, located south of Pit 2, is exactly in alignment with Pits 1 and 2, but is smaller and separated from Pit 2 by a 35-cm-thick east-west wall (currently 1.60 m long). The eastern face of NS1 served as the western periphery of the pit. To the south lies an east-west running wall, which is 50 cm wide and 1.10 m long. The pit is roughly square, measuring 1.20 m by 1.30 m and 25 cm deep.

These pits seem to have been used for storage as they were lined with grass and plastered with lime. Even though they were added later to the complex of parallel mud-brick walls, they seem to have been used in the second phase of the structure complex.

North-South Wall No. 2 (NS2). NS2 is located 95 cm to the west of NS1. The inner sides of both walls were plastered with yellow mortar and the gap between them is 1 m near the north end and 70 cm near the south end. A por-

tion of that gap was subsequently closed by laying an additional brick wall that measures 78 cm wide and 3.50 m long. The result is a mud-brick platform, 2.35 m wide and 3.50 m long, that reuses materials of walls NS1 and NS2.

NS2 is parallel to wall NS1, 12.35 m long, and 80 cm wide on average. It was built at the same time as EW1. Its north side is 40 cm high with four visible plastered brick courses. A 2-m-long portion of the south side has been destroyed by erosion. The space between NS2 and NS3 is 1 m. At least two different floor levels can be identified, with one sitting directly above the other. Both floor levels are made of brick, brick fragments, and rammed hard clay. The second or younger floor is 25 cm thick.

North-South Wall No. 3 (NS3). Located west of and parallel to NS1 and NS2, NS3 is 12.54 m long and comparatively better preserved, particularly a 7.30-m-long portion of its north side. However, a 1-m-long section has been cut out near the south end, possibly due to erosion. Only one phase of the wall is currently visible. Both wall faces are perfectly vertical and the original plaster has been largely peeled away. Its average width is 65 cm and maximum height is currently 85 cm, with seven courses of bricks visible near the north end. This wall was constructed later than EW1 and EW2.

A long rectangular chamber-like space lies between walls NS3 and NS4 and runs parallel to both of them (average width = 95 cm). Two separate floors, similar to that noticed between walls 2 and 3, were found.

North-South Wall No. 4 (NS4). This wall is located on the west side of NS3 and its south end is badly destroyed by erosion. Otherwise, it is a comparatively better-preserved wall, with a surviving height of 1.20 m (11 courses of bricks). It is 12.75 m long and ranges from 70 cm to 75 cm wide. It is evident that this wall was added after EW1 and EW2 were constructed.

Between NS4 and NS5 is a 90-cm-wide space. Three floors are clearly visible, each built of bricks and brick fragments that were rammed hard. The second (middle) and the third (youngest) are each 30 cm thick.

North-South Wall No. 5 (NS5). NS5 is 13 m long with 15 courses of bricks. This is the westernmost limit of the complex, and is comparatively well preserved with the exception of the south end which is slightly eroded. The wall was built in two phases; the lower phase of construction is parallel to wall NS4 and is 65 cm high and 1.10 m wide. On the north side the second phase (height = 75 cm, width = 85 cm) is preserved on top of the earlier phase and inclines to the west. This wall was plastered on the outside with a thick coating (10 cm) of fine yellow silt, which has survived

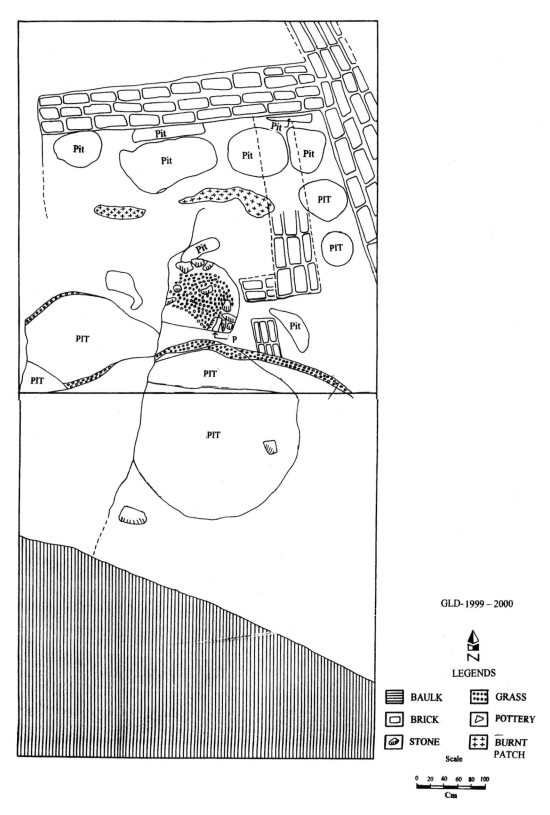

Fig. 3.10. GLD-2, Area I, pits in Trench 11 and 12.

near the south end. It is this wall on the western periphery that was constructed simultaneously with EW1 and EW2 and even extended towards the north on the other side of EW1. The extended portion of the wall on the north side is identified as wall NS8. It is also parallel to NS4. This wall is thicker and well plastered, with five plaster coats, possibly because it is on the periphery. The first two coats were made of mud while the last three coats were made of lime plaster. Through the excavation of a deep trench in this area, the base of the wall was identified at 9.61 m below the datum. It was built on a compact clay layer that serves as a foundation support (Layer 22).

North-South Wall No. 8 (NS8). This wall runs north-south starting at the west end of EW1. It is the north extension of wall NS5. Like NS7, NS8 is not perfectly aligned with NS3 and NS4. It appears to have been built in the second phase of construction, and is contemporary with the second phase of NS5. A 4-m-long section was exposed. The average width is 85 cm and its current height is 50 cm, with three courses of bricks clearly visible.

North-South Wall No. 7 (NS7). It was determined that this wall postdates other walls of the complex because it includes innovations in brick composition and construction methods. Seven courses of black bricks were identified, but they are not laid in the header and stretcher method. A 4.55-m-long portion of the wall was exposed (average width = 80 cm), both surfaces of which are badly eroded. The middle of this wall is badly disturbed due to an intrusive large circular pit that postdates the wall. This disturbance is located 35 cm north of the south end and continues for 1.90 m. Near the north end of the wall, another large circular pit cuts the wall. A third circular pit is located in the northeast corner of a 1.60-m-long space between walls NS7 and NS8. This pit (diameter = 45 cm, depth = 40 cm) has a 16-cm-thick brick lining and contains large sherds of Gray and Red Ware and fragments of clay seal impressions (for details on sealings see chapter by Ameri in this volume). It appears to be contemporary with NS7.

North-South Wall No. 6 (NS6). Located to the east of NS7 and almost parallel to it, NS6 has an average thickness of 70 cm and a height of 60 cm. A 5-m-long section was exposed. The surface of the wall is badly eroded because of its proximity to a pit to the north. The wall is made of red bricks and was built later than walls EW1 and EW2. The space between NS6 and NS7 is narrow (1.30 m) compared to the space between NS7 and NS8.

The composition of the floor is similar to the floor between NS3 and NS4. A large circular storage pit (diameter = 1.40 m) is located approximately 30 cm to the east

Fig. 3.11. GLD-2, Area I, Trench 18 deep trench.

of NS6 and 30 cm to the north of EW2. It is lined with a 6-cm-thick clay ring. This pit was cut by another circular pit (diameter = 1.20 m) on the east side. Both pits postdate the walls.

Summary. The huge complex of parallel walls is composed of mud and mud-brick walls that were plastered on both sides. In order to establish its chronological position and construction phases, three separate areas were excavated: between NS4 and NS5, between NS7 and NS8, and immediately west of NS5 (Trench 9). The first area was excavated to unoccupied soil and revealed two clear phases of construction as well as a prepared floor with plastered bricks and brick fragments. The second excavated area revealed a bin. The third area was excavated to the base of the wall, revealing that the entire structure was made on a thick platform built of rammed mud and brick fragments. Together, these finds indicate that the long, narrow rooms may have been used for storage, as in a "magazine"-style facility, with goods lined up, leaning against the supporting walls (Posse-

hl 2007, Possehl, Shinde, and Ameri 2004, Shinde, Possehl, and Ameri 2005). The evidence such as plastered walls, prepared floors between walls, and a strong waterproof base further support this hypothesis. In addition, the identification of a series of seal impressions in and around a clay bin located within the structure suggests that goods and containers were sealed in and around the complex (Ameri 2010 and see Chapter 9). Excavations in Trench 9 (immediately west of NS5) indicated that the structure was built in the beginning of the Middle Chalcolithic, around 2500 BC.

Area III

Structure 9. The remains of a burned wattle-and-daub structure were found in Trenches 201, 209, 210, and 211. Located at the base of Layer 2 (depth = 30 cm), the structure possibly dates to the last phase of the Middle Chalcolithic (around 2000 BC). Thick, flat burned clay lumps, which may have been part of the roof and walls, cover the interior of the structure. A 5.60-m-long portion of the north wall (average thickness = 50 cm) consists of a mud base with the burned remains of a wattle-and-daub superstructure located just inside. The wall is visible near the northern margin of Trenches 201 and 211 and it runs in a roughly northeast-southwest direction. The west wall (length = 7.60 m) is similar in composition and was fully excavated in the north half of Trench 211. Although the east and south walls were not excavated, the structure appears to be rectangular.

The structure contains a number of whole pots, most of which are crushed or cracked by fallen debris. Twelve pots of various sizes were found in Trench 201. Three pots of Coarse Red Ware were identified near the west wall. One of these, a large wide-mouth bowl, is located 1.40 m east of the west trench line and 1.30 m north of the south trench line. A large globular pot almost touches a bowl to the southwest. A medium globu-

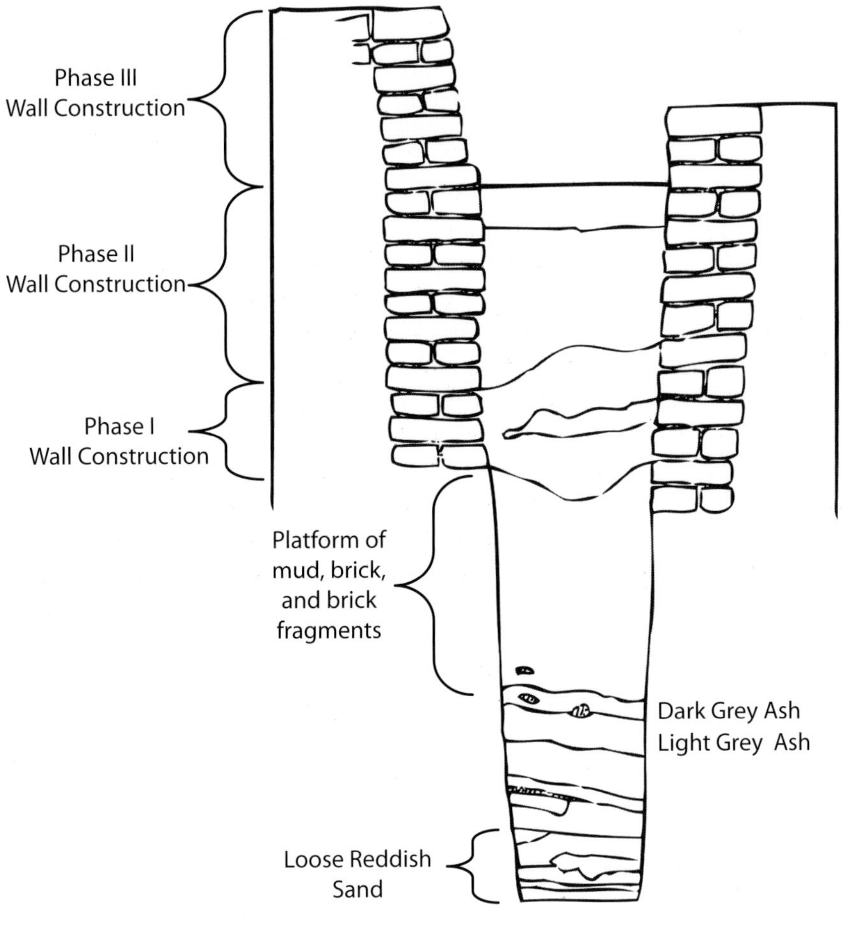

Fig. 3.12. GLD-2, Area I, Trench 18 deep trench profile.

lar pot is located 30 cm west of the clay bins described below. A larger globular storage jar is located 50 cm southeast of the bowl. Two more small globular pots are located very close to the storage jar in this line. In the southeast corner of the trench lies a large storage jar (circumference = 50 cm); it is 40 cm to the west of the east trench line and 50 cm to the north of the south trench line. The upper half of the storage jar has broken and fallen inside. An upside-down small globular pot of Coarse Gray Ware lies 30 cm to the north of the jar. A fragmented Gray Ware pot is located 50 cm to its east.

A number of pots of different sizes can also be found inside the structure in the northeast quadrant of the trench. A cluster of three pots, all of Coarse Red Ware, is located 70 cm to the west of the east trench line and 1.60 cm to the south of the north trench line. These three pots lie close to each other in a rough triangle. One pot is larger than the two globular Red Ware pots; it is located 70 cm east of the first. All were badly damaged by fallen architectural debris. Three additional pots can be found near the east end of the north wall, along its inner edge. Two of these are medium and globular and lie 20 cm apart. The third pot is a wide, shallow round Coarse Red Ware pot. It is located 60 cm south of the north trench line and 90 cm to the west of the east trench line. Two additional large pots lie in Trench 211, just south of Trench 201.

In addition to the pots, three main features were found inside the structure. These include a circular fireplace (diameter = 60 cm) with a large number of burned jujube seeds located 50 cm south of the north wall and 2.70 m east of the west wall. A second circular fire pit was identified to the east and a tubular shell bead was found in-between these two fire features. In addition, traces of burned red clay bins were identified in the northeast and southeast corners of Trench 201. This structure is classified as domestic due to the large number of coarse pots, domestic hearths, and storage facilities found within it.

Structure 10 (Trenches 205 and part of 206). The team excavated three walls of this structure which was sealed by Layer 3. Although the west half of the structure was damaged by erosion, the east wall is complete with the exception of its corner. The remains of the east wall run in a slight northwest-southeast direction. The walls are 5 cm high, 4.50 m long, and 70 cm wide. There are two postholes in the wall: one at the junction of the east and south walls and the other 90 cm north of the north end of the wall. The first has a diameter of 25 cm and a depth of 20 cm. The second has roughly the same diameter, but is 25 cm deep. The north and south walls of the structure run in a slight northwest-southeast direction. The east ends of the walls

lie in the eastern part of Trench 206 and have been cut by erosion. The partial remains of these walls are 3 m long and their average thickness is 50 cm.

A large shallow circular pit (diameter = 1.65 m, depth = 25 cm) lies near the northeast corner of the structure; the edge of the pit merges with the floor of the structure. Inside the pit lies a large Coarse Red Ware storage jar with elongated neck that has a pointed base, narrow vertical neck, flat projecting rim, and sloping shoulders (circumference = 60 cm). The neck of the jar is decorated with two incised panels separated by an undecorated slipped area. The first panel consists of rows of short vertical incised lines separated by horizontal lines. The second panel consists of a row of incised hatched diamonds interspersed with groups of four slanting lines and set between two horizontal incised lines. Four appliqué knobs with fingertip impressions are found at regular intervals around the lower horizontal line. Based on the size of the structure and the storage facilities within it, it is characterized as domestic.

Circumference wall on the east side of GLD-2. Traces of a circumference wall were encountered on the eastern margin of GLD-2 and excavated in Trench 4K, the last in the series of trenches that line the western slope of GLD-1. The section of wall exposed here potentially belongs to a separate circumference wall from the one excavated in Trenches 206, 207, and 208. As the wall was only partially excavated, the thickness, shape, and height of the wall could not be traced. However, the surface of the wall had a width of 7.50 m. The wall was built of the same material used in the wall uncovered in Trenches 206, 207, and 208.

Circumference wall in Trenches 206, 207, and 208. These three trenches were excavated to an average depth of 25–30 cm in order to trace the circumference wall. Traces of the top of the wall were identified at the base of Layer 1 and a 5.5 m length of the northwest-southeast running wall was exposed (width = 7.50 m). The wall is made of rammed clay, clay loafs, and mud-brick fragments. One portion of the wall is very compact, homogeneous, and made of silt material. The wall surface is disturbed at places due to later pits and rodent holes. Disintegration of the building material made the task of identifying the wall's edges difficult. However, an unseasonal rainfall helped to highlight the outline of the wall and a supporting feature in Trench 208. The supporting feature runs southwest-northeast, is comprised of the same material as the rest of the wall, and is attached to the outer face of the wall (exposed length of support = 4.30 m, width = 4.10 m). Only the upper 15–20 cm portion of the wall has been excavated in these trenches.

The outer circumference wall excavated on GLD-1 and GLD-2 and the road between them are contemporaneous and belong to the Middle Chalcolithic phase of the site.

Area IV, Industrial Area

A number of complete and partial structures were excavated on the south end of GLD-2. Most yielded furnaces, slag deposits, and burning activities and as a result, these structures are identified together as an "Industrial Area."

Structure 11 (Trenches 301, 304, and 310) Sealing Layer 2, Middle Chalcolithic. Structure 11 is comprised of three mud-brick walls laid at right angles. As no trace of a north wall was identified, it is considered to be an open structure. The south wall runs in a northeast-southwest direction. It is thin (14 cm) near the west and broadens towards the east (33 cm). The remains are 27 cm high. The western part of the wall runs due east for 220 m, then makes a 160° turn, and runs in a northeast-southwest direction for 2.70 m. The remains of the east wall are 1.15 m long and 45 cm wide. A 2.80-m-long section of the west wall is visible in the baulk of Trenches 301 and 310, but it is cut in the north by a later pit. The remains are 45 cm wide, 15 cm high, and run northwest-southeast.

The structure shows evidence of burning in the form of vitrified clay, on top of which lies one surviving course of a later burned brick wall. The bricks are laid horizontally on the east side and vertical on the west side. The remains of the wall run north-south and are 1.30 m long and 45 cm wide. The structure has a prepared floor on top of which lies a thin layer of ash followed by vitrified clay and cow dung. The burned clay and cow dung appear to postdate the floor due to the uneven nature of the burning. On the west side of the west wall is a large kiln-like feature that also appears to postdate the structure. The burned material may be dumped kiln waste. In the absence of a domestic hearth and storage facility, the structure is classified here as non-residential. It belongs to the second structural phase on this side of the mound and it sits in the level overlying Structure 12.

Structure 12 (Trenches 301, 302, 304, and 305) sealed by Layer 2 on the slope. This rectangular structure is located on the eastern slope of the south end of GLD-2. The top course of the east wall was visible on the mound's surface and it belongs to the first structural phase on this side of mound. The east half of the structure was burned. The east wall lies in both Trench 302 and Trench 305 and is oriented north-south with a slight curve in the center due to a slope towards the outside (east). It is made of burned bricks and plastered on the inside. The wall is 6 m long, 50 cm wide, and 35 cm high. Four courses of bricks remain and are ar-

ranged in a header-stretcher method. A 1.30-m-long and 40-cm-wide opening lies in the east wall near the north end. As the face of the wall is finished at this point, it appears to be a constructed entrance. The threshold is 25 cm high and is made of two courses of bricks that were plastered on all sides. A 1.40-m-long area of clay plaster was identified south of the entrance on the inner surface of the wall. The plaster is 2 cm thick and is made of clay, cow dung, and chopped hay or grass. Its surface is smooth and bears impressions of grass and fingers. The entire wall, including the plaster and mortar, appears to have been burned.

A 2-m-long portion of an east-west running north wall was excavated near the northeast corner of the structure. Its average thickness is 50 cm and remaining height is 40 cm. Three courses of burned brick are visible. One of the intact bricks measures 36 cm by 11 cm by 13 cm. The west side of the north wall has yet to be excavated.

A large brick-lined depression (1.40 m by 1.40 m) was identified below the north wall. It is 45 cm deep in the center and rises gradually towards the edge, where it is 35 cm deep. The burned surface and edges suggest that it was subjected to firing activity. The gap between the wall and this feature indicates that they belong to two different phases.

The south wall, visible in Trench 301 and Trench 302, has a stone foundation. It runs in an east-west direction and a 4.50-m-long section was excavated near the southeast corner where a 1.20-m-long segment of the wall is intact. Three courses of bricks have survived (wall height = 60 cm). Three large stones lie nearby to the west. A later circular pit (diameter = 1.50 m) cuts part of the end of the wall. In addition, two circular clay bins were identified beneath the southeast corner and parts of the south wall. The rest of the south wall underlies the later stone and mud wall described below.

A 5-m-long portion of a later east-west running stone wall in Trenches 302 and 301 has survived and was built on top of an earlier pit. An entrance (length = 1.20 m) lies 2.50 m from the east end of the wall. A pair of north-south running mud-brick walls is attached to the south of the wall and contains the remains of pits. The first (exposed length = 1.55 m) is located 1.50 m to the west of the east trench line of Trench 301. It is 45 cm wide and 20 cm high. The second is located 1.35 m to the west of the first wall. A 1.05-m-portion of this wall has been excavated. The remains are 80 cm wide and 30 cm high. Other parts of the structure are completely damaged.

Two-armed domestic hearth (Trench 304, sealed by Layer 1, contemporaneous with the stone wall in Trench 301). A well-preserved two-armed domestic hearth lies at the base of Layer 1 at the north trench line of Trench 304. Part of one of the arms extends into the non-excavated north half of the trench. The hearth is located 1.20 m west of the northeast corner of the trench. The unexposed hearth arm is 65 cm long (east-west) and 27 cm wide. The other arm is 60 cm long and 20 cm wide. Both arms are 5 cm high. The hearth has a well-made base. The sides and base are smooth and plastered and have been burned red. As with the hearth above, the hearth resembles two-armed domestic hearths (*chulhas*) that are in use today in the vicinity of Gilund.

Kiln in Trench 310. A kiln-like feature was discovered 1.20 m below the surface of the mound, at the base of Layer 4. A 4.20-m-long and 80-cm-wide portion was exposed. The feature is oriented north-south and parts of the north side extend into the north section of the trench. It was built in a shallow depression (center depth = 20 cm) and lined with a thin mud wall (15 cm thick). Parts of the east wall of the kiln survived (height = 20 cm) and are completely burned along with a prepared floor. Interior clay projections occur at regular intervals including two circular projections that lie 20 cm apart, 90 cm south of the north trench line. Another projection comes from the inner face of the east edge of the feature (average diameter = 25 cm). Twenty cm to the east of this projection lies an outer projection, (diameter = 25 cm). Two additional projections occur at regular intervals of 40 cm from the first projection. Like the others, they are circular with an average diameter of 25 cm. The gap between the middle and southern projections is 15 cm. Near the north section, at a distance of 1 m from the eastern margin of the kiln, is a circular pit (diameter 25 cm) that was not excavated. As only a portion of the kiln was excavated, it was not possible to determine how it was used. However, a thick layer of ash and vitrified clay lie on top of the floor inside the kiln, indicating high-temperature firing. As mentioned above, the vitrified clay and ash layer resembles that found dumped inside Structure 11, located 80 cm to the east of the kiln, indicating a relationship between this feature and that structure.

Burned brick wall (Trenches 302 and 305 sealed by Layer 1). A single wall of burned bricks (length = 4.20 m, width = 36 cm) with a burned and plastered western face lies 1.20 m to the east of Structure 12. The wall slightly inclines towards the east. Related walls are located to the west and were not excavated. This wall appears to be earlier than Structure 12 and may be contemporaneous with the saddle querns and kiln-like structure beneath the north wall of Structure 12. The portion of the wall near the southeast corner is broken and only a single course of stone, probably the foundation portion, has survived (length = 80 cm). The east wall runs in a north-south direction and the southern in an east-west direction.

Just outside of the southeast corner of the structure described above is a large rectangular saddle quern (length = 80 cm, width = 45 cm). It has a gentle concave (depth = 13 cm) surface. Immediately to the south of the saddle quern is a prepared floor made of mud bricks (155 m east-west by 1.05 m north-south). It is not clear whether the floor belongs to the structure or not. To the west of this floor lies a large circular saddle quern (diameter = 45 cm) with a concave surface (depth = 10 cm). Traces of a mud-brick wall were identified along the south trench line of Trench 302 and continuing into the unexcavated area. A third, broken saddle quern is located 20 cm to the north of these walls and 30 cm to the west of the circular saddle quern. All three saddle querns found in the southeast quadrant of Trench 302 are made of locally available gneissic rock.

In sum, a number of structures and features from different phases were found in a 15 m by 10 m area. Given the presence of a number of kilns and furnaces, this area is identified as an industrial or craft manufacturing area.

NOTE

3.1. The emphasis on horizontal excavation resulted in a greater exposure of Late and Middle Chalcolithic contexts compared to Early Chalcolithic. The soil volume excavated for each phase must be considered when comparing the numbers of structures or other artifacts recovered from each phase.

4

Excavation of Early Historic Deposits, Gilund 1999–2001

Praveena Gullapalli and Peter Johansen

Early Historic archaeological remains at Gilund are located on the eastern mound (GLD-1) and are confined to approximately the top 1.5 m of excavated deposits. Early Historic period deposits have been disturbed by an abundance of postdepositional activities including those associated with the construction of a small temple on top of the mound and the erosion of the mound surface. Excavations in the upper three squares of the GLD-1 step trench (Trenches 4A, 4B, and 4C) and an adjacent side square (Trench 5B) exposed deposits of Early Historic period artifacts (e.g., ceramics, metal artifacts, "slags") and features (stone walls and prepared surfaces) that appear to date to the early 1st millennium AD. Trenches 4A and 4B were excavated in full; however, Historic period deposits were only exposed in the western third of Trench 4C due to the erosion of the west side of the mound. Excavations in Trench 5B were restricted to the southern half (2.5 m).

Trenches 4A and 4B were excavated during the 1999–2000 and 2000–01 field seasons. Trench 4C was excavated only during 1999–2000, while excavation in Trench 5B was confined to the 2000–01 field season. Excavations further down the western slope of GLD-1 continued in subsequent years, with the goal of exposing Chalcolithic deposits. Although post-Chalcolithic material was exposed during these later excavations (see Chapters 2 and 3), our focus here will be on the results of the 1999–2001 seasons.

Excavation was most substantial in Trenches 4A and 4B, where a series of floors, walls, and pits were revealed that defined three structural phases. The succession of exposed walls and floors appears to maintain a consistency in orientation and in the distinction between internal and external spaces. Excavation in Trenches 4C and 5B exposed similar deposits but excavation in these trenches was more limited in scope. Ceramics were by far the most frequently recovered class of artifacts, but these trenches also exposed significant quantities of groundstone tools, iron artifacts, concentrations of shell (see Landt, this volume) and carbonized botanical remains. Extensive pitting and the modification of architectural elements particularly during the later occupation of the mound have made it difficult to establish a coherent picture of past activity in the area exposed by excavations. Yet well-constructed walls and variation in prepared surfaces suggest that this area was for some time the location of clearly demarcated architectural and extramural spaces which may have been associated with domestic or other Early Historic Period settlement activities.

The following discussion will outline the deposits excavated in each of the four upper squares of the GLD-1 step trench. Trenches 4A and 4B are discussed together as their deposits were overlapping and largely continuous through each of the three occupational phases; 4C and 5B are discussed separately. Excavations in Trenches 4C and 5B were limited in areal exposure and in the case of 4C exposed poorly preserved floors and walls. Due to the fragmentary nature of the exposed material we have not discussed them in their proper structural sequence. Rather, we have briefly discussed each trench in turn after our discussion of the structural phases.

Trenches 4A and 4B

Archaeological deposits in Trenches 4A and 4B are divided into three occupational phases based on the stratigraphic relationship of architectural features, surfaces, and individual layers of artifact-rich sediments. Of these three phases, Phase 3 is the latest and most heavily disturbed, preceded by Phase 2 and Phase 1. Each are described and discussed individually below.

Phase 1

Phase 1 is the earliest phase and is dominated by a number of floors. One of these, Floor 4, is quite extensive, however the majority of others were broken up and largely discontinuous. Floors 3 and 4 appear to be associated with an east-west oriented wall (Wall 4). The Phase 1 surfaces and surface deposits on either side of Wall 4 appear similar, especially early in the phase, which may indicate less variation in the activities structuring deposits on either side of the barrier than what emerges later in Phase 2 (see below). Wall 4 consists of an alignment of large undressed field stones to the west, as well as a trench of semi-compact fill

TABLE 4.1. Early Historic Wall and Floor Designations, Trenches 4A, 4B

As Excavated	In Text	Phase
4A Wall 1	Wall 1	Phase 2
4A Wall 2	Wall 2	Phase 2
4A Floor 1	Floor 1	Phase 2
4A Floor 2	Floor 2	Phase 2
4A Floor 3	Floor 3	Phase 1
4A/B Wall 4	Wall 4	Phase 1
4B Floor 1	Floor 3*	Phase 1
4B Wall 2	Wall 3	Phase 1
4A/B Lowest floor	Floor 4	Phase 1

*Floor 1 in 4B is a continuation of Floor 3 from 4A, so both are designated as Floor 3.

along the stone wall elements that extend to the east.

The most extensive of the Phase 1 surfaces was Floor 4, a hard and compact well-prepared surface. Floor 4 was exposed both north and south of Wall 4 although it disappears towards the eastern end of Trench 4A and breaks up 2–3 meters north of the southern baulk in both Trenches 4A and 4B. It is best preserved north of Wall 4.

To the north of Wall 4 ashy deposits covered Floor 4. Excavation of these ashy deposits exposed the articulation of Floor 4 with Wall 4 through Trenches 4A and 4B

and with a western north-south oriented wall (Wall 3) in Trench 4B (Fig. 4.1). Wall 3's foundation trench consisted of a semi-compact matrix with large cobbles and broken groundstone quern fragments as fill. Both Wall 3 and Floor 4 appear to continue beyond the north baulk of Trench 4B.

Floor 4 also continues to the east, into the northwestern quadrant of Trench 4A where it was cut by several small postholes. Further east Floor 4 abutted a heterogeneous matrix of mixed compaction that was of considerably higher elevation than the floor surface. These deposits consisted primarily of small discontinuous surfaces and lenses of variable horizontal extent that interdigitated with one another and with isolated patches of softer fill.

At the base of these discontinuous surfaces three superimposed surfaces with much greater areal dimensions were exposed. The highest of these terminated to the east at a narrow, shallow north-south oriented trench (possibly associated with construction of the later Wall 2, of Phase 2). Another well-prepared surface, possibly at one time continuous with the floor west of this trench, extended to the east where it disintegrated approximately 0.5 m west of the east baulk of Trench 4A. The trench terminated to the south at the eastern end of an east-west alignment of approximately seven large stones embedded in, and projecting from, a very narrow trench at the base of the lowest of the above-mentioned surfaces. This entrenched east-west oriented stone alignment appears to be an eastern extension of Wall 4 construction, and may have been an early attempt at the structural demarcation of northern and southern spaces that is evident in later phases.

Floor 4 continues south in Trench 4A beneath Floor 3, dipping in elevation towards the southwestern quadrant of the trench. In this area, the floor is associated with the fragmentary remains of a masonry feature with a curved wall. This feature has between one and three courses of masonry. The remains of at least one highly eroded mud brick or a consolidation of daub sits on the upper course of the fieldstone masonry. The upper masonry course extends north where at least four of its structural elements are associated with the floor. No other floors or surfaces could be associated with the south side of the curved-wall feature.

This feature was oriented north-south but curved to the west in a south-rounding corner. Most of the interior of this feature, and indeed all of its western dimensions have been destroyed by subsequent construction activities, most notably a large pit in the southeastern quadrant of Trench 4B (Fig. 4.2). Despite the very fragmentary nature of the feature part of its interior appeared intact, consisting of several layers of black ash, broken ceramics, and a large

Fig. 4.1. Trench 4A, looking north, with Wall 3 (at left, in northeastern corner of Trench 4B) and Wall 4 visible in center.

amount of carbonized macrobotanical remains.

Although Floor 4 has been traced through significant portions of Trenches 4A and 4B, it should be noted that it has also been extensively cut by pits. The pits range from 25 cm to 2 m in diameter and are characterized by ashy fill. They are spread throughout the excavated exposure, but not in the Phase 3 foundation trench (see below) in the western part of Trench 4B. Among the pits were two possible postholes that are rectangular in shape, to the south of Wall 4 in Trench 4B. In total 11 small postholes were exposed in Floor 4, although no definitive alignments were discerned.

South of Wall 4 and covered by a series of heavily pitted deposits is also Floor 3, a later compact well-prepared surface. Floor 3 was exposed throughout the southern portion of Trench 4B and the southwestern portion of Trench 4A. Floor 3 does not continue north past its articulation with Wall 4. A large Phase 3 trench (described below) cuts the western extent of Floor 3 in Trench 4B.

Small finds in Phase 1 include a large iron hoe and axe recovered from Floor 4 north of Wall 4 in Trench 4B. Other iron artifacts including bells, a bowl, chisel fragments, and numerous unidentifiable fragments were also recovered from deposits in this phase. Further small finds include a terracotta bull, four carnelian beads, and a miniature pot.

Phase 2

The subsequent structural/occupational phase is dominated by an east-west oriented core and veneer fieldstone masonry wall (Wall 1) that spans much of the breadth of Trenches 4A and 4B. This wall is a more substantial successor to Wall 4 discussed above; Wall 1 follows the same alignment as Wall 4, but was built slightly to the south of the earlier Phase 1 wall. Wall 1 is constructed of two plumb exterior veneers of undressed fieldstones with an artifact rich trash-filled sediment core. Wall 1 is approximately 6.5 m long and is associated with two cross walls that enclose the area north of Wall 1. One of these cross walls (Wall 2) is characterized by a 2 m segment of articulated stone masonry extending north from the eastern end of Wall 1 and by more fragmentary remains extending to the south as well. The masonry foundations of each of these walls consist of one to three courses of faced field stones and discarded whole and fragmentary groundstone tools (mostly querns). The cores of these walls were arti-fact rich and included slaggy debris that may be associat-ed with metallurgy elsewhere on the mound. The western end of Wall 1 is cut by later constructions associated with Phase 3.

To the south of Wall 1 is Floor 1, a well-made white-gray surface of hard-packed earth and clay. Floor 1 dips down sharply to the south, with cracks from subsidence visible in arcs along its surface. At its southern extreme, Floor 1 was covered by a hard gray sediment yielding high densities of ceramic sherds and bone. This gray matrix has a fine texture that suggests it was waterlaid. Above this de-

Fig. 4.2. GLD 1900, feature with curved wall in Trench 4B.

posit the remains of a gray surface extend north approxi-mately 1 m from the south baulk, sloping down towards but not articulating with Floor 1. This surface is visible in section in the east baulk through which it can be connect-ed with another surface east of Wall 2. At or slightly above the level of this upper surface are the remains of an east-west oriented mudbrick wall to the south of Wall 1. This mudbrick wall may be contemporary with Wall 2. Above the upper gray surface is a deposit of dark brown compact sediment together with a more crumbly, less consolidated deposit and a consolidated trash deposit in the southeast corner of the exposure.

In the southwest corner of Trench 4A, Floor 1 is cut by a pit. Along the northern inside edge of the pit there is a mudbrick construction that in section appears to be aligned with the remains of the mudbrick wall mentioned above. If this is indeed a preserved western section of the wall to the east then these two dilapidated mud-brick features may have at some point con-stituted an east-west oriented barrier wall parallel with and south of Wall 1. Trash deposits line the southern side of this mudbrick alignment.

The southern portion of Phase 2 de-posits in Trench 4A is extensively pitted, especially along the southern baulk and in the southeastern corner, with six of the seven pits from this phase (and possibly from Phase 3) located in this area. The pits range in size from approximately 25 cm to 2 m in diameter. They all appear to be unlined trash pits. The area to the south of Wall 1, then, seems to be a heavily pitted extramural area whose southern bound-ary may have been defined by relatively ephemeral perimeter walls of mud brick at some point during the latter part of Phase 2. The trash dumping along the southern side of the mudbrick wall suggests that this use of space continued through later Phase 2 structural renovations.

North of Wall 1 is Floor 2, a con-structed pebble surface. Along the north side of Wall 1, dug into Floor 2, is a small burnt patch of ash approximately 20 cm long without structural remains or clearly defined edges. This burned feature may be a hearth. To the west of this burned ashy deposit four flat stones are aligned tightly against Wall 1. This alignment may have functioned as part of a step or bench.

Floor 2 abruptly disappears approximately 1 m west of Wall 2 in the eastern part of Trench 4. Floor 2 may not have originally extended this far to the east. However, its absence here may be due to a large later pit whose edges have yet to be defined. A structural explanation for this eastern breach in Floor 2 may point to Wall 2 as a later articulated addition to Wall 1.

Floor 2 is disturbed along the junction of Trenches 4A and 4B by the roots of two small trees. The level of the floor terminates in patches along a north-south oriented alignment of stones that may be the remnants of a cross wall in Trench 4B. This area to the north of Wall 1, with its better-made surface relative to the south could indicate either an indoor space or a transitional space between interior and exterior spaces. This is a distinction, between the northern and southern sides of Wall 1, which arises in Phase 2 and does not seem to have existed in Phase 1 (i.e., to the north and south of Wall 4).

The floor deposits of this phase contain very little artifactual material and the objects that were recovered were highly fragmented. This suggests well-maintained surfaces prior to the abandonment of the Phase 2 occupation. Small finds in Phase 2 are dominated by shell bangle fragments that occur in a variety of contexts. Other small finds include terracotta beads, iron fragments, and projectile points. Cowries and shell fragments were also recovered from a variety of contexts. Samples of what may be animal dung were found in the northeast quadrant of Trench 4A and the northwest quadrant of Trench 4B. The northeast quadrant of Trench 4B has yielded a large number of bivalve shells. Several contexts in Trench 4B, especially Pit 2, yielded large amounts of slaggy material. The small blue-green highly vitrified pieces have been associated with copper smelting (at Ahar), but are more likely to be vitrified fuel ash or broken-up refractory material.

Fig. 4.3. GLD 1899, Trench 4A, looking west, with Wall 1 at left and associated Wall 2 in foreground.

Phase 3

Phase 3 is the latest phase of occupation and is preserved in very fragmentary form. Phase 3 consists of a long foundation trench within which are the remains of a paved surface and two very large walls whose stone footings form a corner in the southwest quadrant of 4B. The fill of the trench is characterized by dark brown sediments (contrasted with the ashy material through which it is cut). The trench traverses the western third of Trench 4B and continues into Trench 5B. It is oriented roughly in a north-south diagonal axis across the excavated exposure. Unfortunately, the erosion of the mound has destroyed the western extent of the trench, thus leaving this surface and structure only minimally preserved.

Trench 4C

Work in Trench 4C was very limited, focusing on a 1-m-wide swath along the western border of Trench 4B. These deposits are associated with a foundation trench from Phase 3. The section of a large pit in the southeastern corner of this trench has revealed at least two more superimposed floors and another wall beneath the Phase 3 structural remains. A small find of note from the pit in this trench is an unfired terracotta lamp.

Trench 5B

The southwest and southeast quadrants of Trench 5B were excavated in an effort to better understand the nature and extent of the structural remains excavated in Trenches 4A and 4B. Excavations were very brief and terminated approximately 10 cm below surface grade on a very patchy plastered floor surface exposed in both quadrants. An east-west oriented masonry wall was also exposed which was of a very similar construction, orientation, and dimensions of both Walls 1 and 4 in Trench 4B. The articulation of this wall with the plastered floor is at present uncertain and must await further excavation. In addition, the northern continuation of the large Phase 3 trench cut exposed in Trench 4B was exposed in the southwest quadrant of Trench 5B.

The surface and wall feature exposed in Trench 5B appear to represent either an earlier component of Structural Phase 3 prior to the excavation of the large foundation trench associated with this phase or an earlier independent structural phase that was eroded or destroyed in the trenches to the south.

Summary

The excavations in Trenches 4A, 4B, 4C, and 5B reveal three distinct occupational phases. These phases document the construction of a series of walls, floors, exterior surfaces, and other features that were rebuilt, renovated, and refurbished over the course of an undetermined period. There appears to be some continuity in terms of the design and orientation of these features across each of the three occupational phases. Common orientations of wall alignments and construction techniques (wall construction and floor preparation) were observed in the exposed occupation layers in the four units excavated over the two seasons.

Over time it appears that a relatively undifferentiated extramural space (Phase 1) was partitioned into two areas whose activities left markedly different traces on the northern and southern sides of the exposure's main superimposed east-west walls (Phase 2). Although the Phase 2 surfaces on either side of Wall 1 have been suggested as interior (northern) and exterior (southern) spaces, this assessment remains tentative, awaiting corroboration from further excavation. These surfaced spaces underwent further modification as indicated by remnants of mudbrick walls (Phase 2) and the extensive trash pitting (Phases 2 and 3), especially along the southern and western perimeters of the excavated area. This latter activity may have been associated with construction following the cutting of the foundation trench from Phase 3. Unfortunately, the limited area of excavation combined with the erosion of the mound surface to the west limit the evidence available for evaluating such an interpretation.

The assessment of the chronological parameters of the post-Chalcolithic deposits is based first on the ceramic assemblage that has been characterized as Early Historic (Sunga-Kushan, 2nd century BC to 3rd century AD) (Deshpande, this volume). This assemblage includes globular pots of Red Slipped Ware and Red Micaceous Ware and a variety of Unslipped Red Ware forms including carinated pots, lids, and cups with flaring sides. Iron tools and objects also date these deposits as post-Chalcolithic and resemble Early Historic materials from Ahar and Balathal (Sankalia, Deo, and Ansari 1969, Misra et al. 1995). Phases 1–3 discussed above belong to the latter part of the time frame.

These excavations have provided needed additional (albeit limited) data regarding the settlements of the late 1st millennium BC and early 1st millennium AD in southeastern Rajasthan. Other Early Historic/post-Chalcolithic sites of southeastern Rajasthan and northern Gujarat provide a glimpse into a variety of architectural styles—wattle and daub, stone, brick—perhaps pointing to domestic, craft, or ritual spaces. Unfortunately, the limited excavation of contemporary levels at sites in the region—such as Ahar (Sankalia, Deo, and Ansari 1969), Balathal (Misra et al. 1995), and Nagari (Bhandarkar 1920) in Rajasthan, and Shamalaji (Mehta and Patel 1967) and Nagara (Mehta and Shah 1968) in northern Gujarat—make it difficult to assess the nature of the Early Historic period deposits at Gilund. Although these sites have been described as villages and towns (rather than cities), the relative lack of consistent horizontal excavation limits our understanding of how space was organized, partitioned, and produced within and between settlements. Like the later occupations at Ahar and Balathal, the Early Historic settlement at Gilund seems to be significantly smaller and less substantial than that of the Chalcolithic period; however, the architecture at Gilund seems to be more akin to that at Nagari in its use of stone and rubble for walls and foundations. The fact that Balathal and Shamalaji have yielded evidence for various pyrotechnological activities may lend support to the interpretation that such activities may have been taking place at Gilund as well. The presence of slaggy materials, albeit in secondary contexts, suggests that iron or copper metallurgy may have been practiced nearby during the Early Historic period. Any further discussion of Early Historic settlement at Gilund, however, must remain tentative until further excavation and research provide more systematic data.

5

Site Catchment Analysis

Debasri Dasgupta Ghosh

Introduction

The reconstruction of human culture in archaeology requires the employment of multiple approaches. Site catchment analysis provides archaeologists with important insights about the relationship between technology and the natural resources that lie in the catchment area: land within a reasonable walking distance from the site that can be exploited for its natural resources (Vita-Finzi and Higgs 1970). Using the data provided by site catchment analysis, archaeologists can reconstruct the relationship between humans and their environment. In India very few studies on site catchment analysis have been conducted, with the exceptions of the work of R.S. Pappu at Inamgaon (1988), Shinde and Pappu at Daimabad (1990), Pappu and Shinde in the central Tapi basin (1990), and Dibyopama at Balathal (2010). The site catchment analysis at Gilund was carried out in order to identify resources available for various subsistence strategies, to locate raw material resources exploited by the inhabitants, and to analyze the relationship between Gilund and nearby sites.

Vita-Finzi and Higgs (1970) introduced the concept of site catchment in their study of prehistoric Mount Carmel when they estimated the probable size of the catchment area associated with that community. They felt that areas located far from the site were less likely to be exploited due to the fact that the energy consumed traveling to and from those areas would cancel out the energy derived from the resources obtained. Their research was based on Lee's (1969) study of !Kung hunter-gatherers in southern Africa which concluded that hunter-gatherers are unlikely to exploit areas beyond two hours walking distance, or 10 km, of their camp. The Vita-Finzi and Higgs study was also informed by Chisholm's study of rural European communities (1979), which found that agriculturalists rarely travel beyond one

hour walking distance, or 5 km, without moving their camp (Higgs 1975). Based on these ethnographic examples, Vita-Finzi and Higgs developed a method for archaeologists to evaluate the resources that are readily accessible to the past inhabitants of an archaeological site. The method emphasizes subsistence practices and takes into consideration site function and location as well as variation in the biophysical environment.

A number of scholars, particularly Americans and Europeans, have identified several problems with the method. Flannery (1976) challenged the practice of labeling sites as non-agricultural when only a small percentage of the surrounding land is arable. Instead, he argued that population estimates must be taken into account. For example, although only a small percentage of the catchment area may consist of arable land, the available acreage may be adequate to support a small prehistoric population (Flannery 1976).

A second objection concerns the use of modern environmental conditions and land use as a basis for reconstructing prehistoric land use (Hodder and Orton 1976). However, Jarman et al. (1982) argue that modern conditions should be taken as a critical source of information, particularly with regard to land use potential, as long as an attempt is made to determine the extent and nature of environmental changes during and since the site's occupation. The present study draws on Jarman et al.'s perspective and considers the environmental changes that took place over the period of the thousand years since Gilund was occupied. The study area presently has a semi-arid climate, similar to the climate during the Chalcolithic (Singh 1971). While the natural vegetation has been significantly reduced due to deforestation and extensive cultivation, it is presumed here that the distribution of ancient and modern resource spaces correspond with each other. That is, deposits of raw materials remain in place and although the land is currently

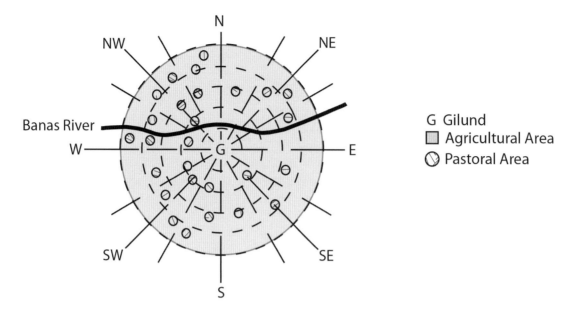

Fig. 5.1. Agricultural and pastoral land near Gilund, 0–10 km.

more densely occupied and cultivated, it had the potential to serve similar purposes in the past. For example, stony land that is currently used for pasture is unlikely to have been used for agriculture in the past. Similarly, soil that is currently fertile had the potential to be cultivated in the past as well.

Even with criticisms, site catchment analysis has proven to be an important device for archaeologists. It has been used for reconstruction of culture histories (e.g., Barker 1972, 1973, 1975a, 1975b), determining the feasibility of economic strategies (e.g., Higgs et al. 1967, Vita-Finzi and Higgs 1970), modeling settlement patterns (Peebles 1978), and studying demographic processes (Browman 1976, Brumfiel 1976). This study uses site catchment analysis to examine the economy at Gilund in two ways. First, the study identifies local land use practices and resources. Second, it identifies Gilund's nearest neighbors and presents hypotheses about the subsistence strategies that they pursued, given the nature of the environment.

Multiple methods are available for conducting a site catchment analysis. Some scholars have used time contours for delimiting the territory of site catchment analysis (Webley 1972, Barker 1972, 1973, 1975b, Jarman and Webley 1975, Jarman 1976). Others have used circles of fixed radii to delimit an area for examining site catchment (Barker 1975a, Fagan 1976, Moore, Hillman, and Legge 1975, Noy, Legge, and Higgs 1973, Clarke 1972, Dennel and Webley 1975, Higgs and Webley 1971, Ellison and Harris 1972, Rossman 1976, Roper 1974, 1979, and Peebles 1978).

In this analysis, a systematic survey was conducted within a 10 km radius of Gilund. The area was divided into concentric 1 km radii, and twelve directional sectors. Topographic maps were used to demarcate the area of survey. The study documented the location and nature of natural resources including cultivable fields, barren lands, pasture lands, types of soil, types of flora and fauna, sources of bricks and other building materials, clay for pottery and terracotta objects, semi-precious stones, and sources of water. Nearby settlements have also been described.

Site Catchment Analysis of Gilund

The site of Gilund has dense deposits of storage pits, querns, mullers, and hammerstones. In addition, the faunal remains include sheep, goat, and cattle. This study's examination of the 1 km radius catchment area identified suitable arable land around the site as well as good pasture (see Fig. 5.1). Together, the evidence indicates that the main occupation of the people at Gilund was agriculture and that they also practiced some form of pastoralism.

The Gilund excavators have uncovered mudbrick and burnt-brick structures (see Chapter 3), a rich pottery assemblage (see chapters by Giorgio and Deshpande, this volume), and a microlithic blade industry (see Raczek, this volume). The antiquities include items made of steatite, shell, bone, terracotta, carnelian, agate, turquoise, and copper (see chapter by Hanlon, this volume). In addition, querns, pounders, and slingballs are made of quartzite,

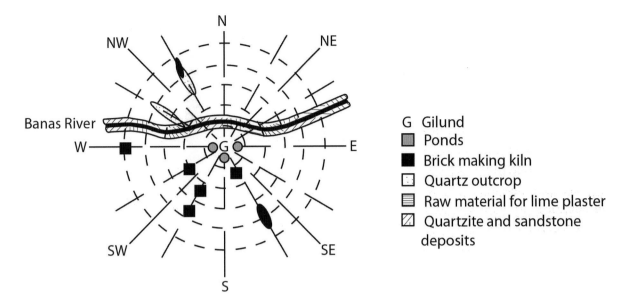

Fig. 5.2. Resources near Gilund, 0–5 km.

sandstone, and schist, while microliths are mostly made of quartz, chert, and chalcedony (see chapters by Hanlon and Raczek, this volume). Limestone, the main ingredient in lime plaster, was used at Gilund in floor and wall construction. This study sought to find potential local sources that were exploited for these materials (see Figs. 5.2 and 5.3).

A quartz outcrop was found approximately 2 km to the northwest. At 5 km to the northwest another quartz outcrop was found along with a limestone outcrop. Addi-

tional limestone outcrops are present 3 km northeast and 3.5 km southeast of Gilund. The latter continues for a distance of 2 km southeast of Gilund. Chert is present in the form of small lumps in negligible quantity in some of the stone outcrops. Sandstone and quartzite occur in abundance in the bed of the Banas River and in a 2 km radius north of Gilund. Schist is present in all directions.

The soil around the site is currently used for making mud brick and baked brick. In addition, two contemporary

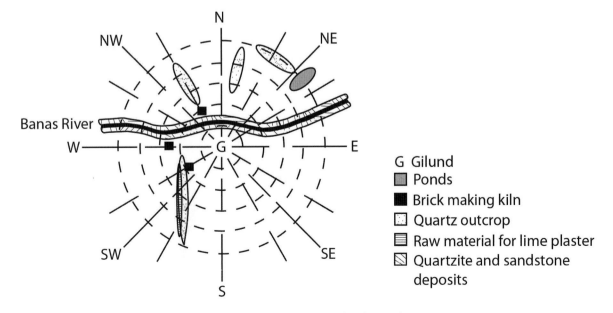

Fig. 5.3. Resources near Gilund, 5–10 km.

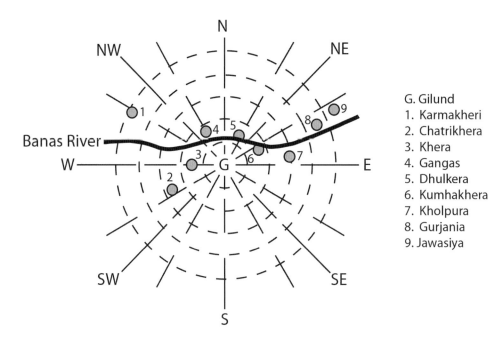

Fig. 5.4. Sites near Gilund, 0–5 km.

brick kilns are located roughly 2 km away. An area near modern Gilund village is also sometimes used by villagers for collecting soil that is used to build houses and enrich fields. The soil is also suitable for pottery production. While it was not possible to identify clay beds used in the past, it is clear that the raw materials for building construction were locally available and plentiful.

Sites Located in the Radius of 5 km around Gilund

A number of sites were also discovered in the course of survey (see Figs. 5.4 and 5.5). They are described below.

Chatrikhera is a Chalcolithic and Historic site located 3 km to the southwest of Gilund inside the contemporary village of Chatrikhera. The height of the Chalcolithic deposit is approximately 3 m, and it lies underneath Early Historic and Medieval period deposits. Agricultural and pasture lands surround Chatrikhera, and may have been utilized in the past. There is also a potentially related microlithic site located on a quartz outcrop to the south of the main mound.

Dhulkhera is a Chalcolithic site that yielded both Historic and Chalcolithic potsherds. It is situated 1.5 km northwest of Gilund, on the left bank of the Banas, next to a quartz deposit. The site has a small (54 m EW by 38 m NS) deposit. The east side of the deposit has been cut away. The northwest part of the site borders cultivated land; another

field is located to the south. As abundant pastureland is located nearby, the site was potentially used for pastoralism and collecting lithic raw material.

Gangas has both Chalcolithic and Historic deposits and is located 0.50 km to the west of the contemporary village of Gangas, 0.50 km north of the Banas River, and 4 km northwest of Gilund. It measures 107 m NS by 56 m EW, with a height of 1.5 m. To the west of the mound is a field that contains potsherds. The mound is currently cultivated, and quartz and granite stones are present. It has been cut away on all sides due to agricultural purposes, although it is surrounded on all sides by pasturelands where the soil is stony. The site may have been used for agriculture and pastoralism.

Gurjaniya is a large Chalcolithic mound located 4 km northeast of Gilund between the villages of Jawasiya and Gurjaniya. This site is situated on the left bank of the Banas and is spread across an area of 2 acres by 2 acres. This mound is very disturbed as the villagers have been taking soil for cultivation purposes. As the mound is nearly destroyed, the height cannot be measured. Potsherds of mainly Black and Red Ware and also Red and Gray Ware are visible throughout the remaining section along with bone. Fertile agricultural lands surround this site as the water level is very high. Given these conditions, Gurjaniya was most likely an agricultural site.

Jawasiya is a microlithic sand dune site located 5 km northeast of Gilund and 1 km north of the Banas River. There is a large pond (approximately 2 km by 2 km) approximately

0.50 km to the north. Immediately next to the dune is a field about 0.50 km in size which cannot be cultivated because the soil is too sandy. The area beyond as well as areas to the east and west are arable. Worked lithics, potsherds, and few pieces of broken hammerstones are concentrated on the upper half of the dune in an area 125 m NS by 67 m EW; no artifacts are found on the bottom half. A second sand dune is located southeast of the first. The two have been separated as villagers cut into the dune to collect soil. A few lithics, potsherds, and bones were found on the second dune, which is very disturbed.

Karmakheri is a Chalcolithic site located 5 km northeast of Gilund. The deposit measures 81 m EW by 49 m NS and the height is 1.30 m above the surrounding ground level. It is a small mound cut away on the north, east, and west sides by the villagers; houses are located to the south. The top is covered with thorny bushes and as a result the visibility is poor. Ceramics are scattered across the mound.

Khera is a Chalcolithic site located 1.5 km west of Gilund, on the right bank of the Banas. This site measures 45 m EW by 75 m NS and is located at the end of a small field. Lithics were found in the center of the site and potsherds were found on the east and west sides of the site; the latter pottery scatter lessens towards both the south and north. Two modern pits (approximately 1.5 m by 1.5 m) have been excavated, one in the southwest and one in the center of the site. Lithics and pottery remains are visible in and around both pits and are scattered across two nearby fields. The site's location near both pasture and arable land would have made it suitable for both agriculture and pastoralism.

Kolpura is a Chalcolithic site located 3 km east of Gilund. It measures 70 m NS by 60 m EW, and is approximately 3 m high. Until recently, the contemporary village was situated on top of the mound. Although it has now been abandoned, stone structures are still visible on top of the mound which has been cut on all sides. Chalcolithic wares found at this site include Thick Coarse Red Ware, Thin Coarse Red Ware, Coarse Cream Slipped Ware, and Fine Gray Ware. The site is situated in the midst of fertile lands and was possibly established by the Chalcolithic people of Gilund as a farmstead.

Kumhakhera is a Chalcolithic and Historic period site located 1.5 km northeast of Gilund, and 20 m south of the river Nalli. The river bed is full of various stones that may have served as raw material for a variety of purposes. The site measures 100 m EW by 75 m NS with a habitation deposit of 2 m. Potsherds, hammerstones, and saddle querns were visible on the surface along with architectural remains. The surrounding fields are suitable for agriculture and the water level in them is quite high. This site may have been a farmstead due to its location and minimal deposit.

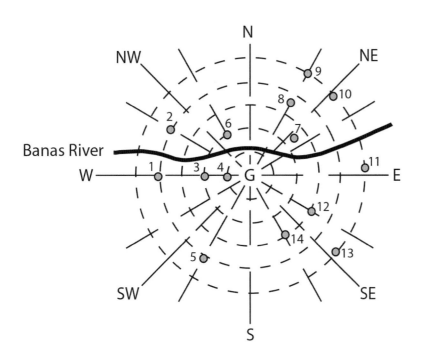

G. Gilund
1. Champakheri
2. Bethumbi
3. Pachamta
4. Pachamta Powerhouse
5. Jashma
6. Surawas
7. Arni
8. Gopalpura
9. Aloli
10. Kiron ka Khera
11. Gandrop
12. Ganeshpura
13. Nangpura
14. Damana Dam

Fig. 5.5. Sites near Gilund, 5–10 km.

Sites Located in a Radius of 5 to 10 km around Gilund

Aloli is a Chalcolithic site with a small deposit that is about 22 m EW by 20 m NS and elevated to a level of about 2 m. Potsherds and quartz are scattered on the surface and some are embedded in the deposit. As pastureland lies all around the site, this could have been a campsite set up by the Chalcolithic people to exploit the pasture area.

Arni is a Chalcolithic site located 7.5 km northeast of Gilund, near contemporary Arni village. The site measures 49 m NS by 27 m EW and has a habitation deposit of 1.5 m; the rest has been cut away by encroaching fields. The surrounding soil is very fertile. Two mudbrick walls and four stone walls were observed along with burned potsherds and charcoal. Potsherds were also found in the nearby fields in a 15-m-long area (NS). This seems to have been a temporary agricultural settlement.

Bethumbi is situated 10 km northwest of Gilund and 1 km from Bethumbi village. The large site has five mounds and mainly Historic period deposits, with some evidence of Chalcolithic occupation. Green fields surround the area. Mounds I and II are separated by a deep ditch and both slope down to Mound III, which is 4 m high and occupies an area that is roughly 120 m² NE/SW. Mound III has three or four visible levels at the top, and the surface is uneven. Several stone structures are also visible as well as a wall. Mound IV extends approximately 13 ha from southeast to northwest. Mound V, located to the north of Mound IV, is 5 ha long and has a temple at the top. Both Mound IV and Mound V are approximately 50 m high. Ceramics found across the mounds include Early Historic, Medieval, and some Chalcolithic. The site also has dense deposits of potsherds, large pebbles, and iron slag. A deep pit in Mounds III and IV was dug by local villagers for the removal of zinc, iron, lead, copper, and glass. Silver coins were also found during digging. The paucity of artifacts for the Chalcolithic period indicates that this site may have been a temporary settlement at the time, perhaps used for exploiting the surrounding land.

Champakheri is a Chalcolithic site located 9 km west of Gilund and 0.50 km southwest of Champakheri village. Potsherds were found across the site. The site may be a camp settlement due to the lack of a habitation deposit.

Dhamana Dam is situated next to the dam of the same name and surrounded by pastureland. It measures 24 m EW by 30 m NS, and is 1.40 m high. A few Mesolithic sherds were found along with Chalcolithic sherds and quartz pieces. This seems to have been a small herding unit of the Chalcolithic people.

Gandrop is located 10 km northeast of Gilund, 0.75 km south of the Banas River, 2 km south of Talav of Rashmi, and at the entrance to Gandrop village. The site includes Gandrop I and Gandrop II. At Gandrop I, both Chalcolithic and Historic period deposits are found in a 0.75 ha mound situated on top of a rocky outcrop. The site is presently covered with trees and some contemporary pits have been excavated. Potsherds were found throughout the site, particularly to the east and in the excavated pits. Quartz and chert lithics were visible along with burnt bricks, bones, mica, and other stones. Two stone walls and one mudbrick wall were visible in the pits along with ash. Gandrop II refers to a 40 m by 41 m area that has only Chalcolithic deposits. The entire site is surrounded with soil that is considered to be very fertile. This site seems to have been another agricultural settlement, which also carried on pastoral activities.

Ganeshpura is situated 7 km southeast of Gilund in the fields of contemporary Ganeshpura. It has both Chalcolithic and Historic deposits. The site is approximately 2 ha with a 4-m-high habitation deposit. The majority of the deposit consists of Historic sherds, but Chalcolithic sherds are visible a few meters below the historical deposit. Contemporary pits have exposed stone walls. The site is surrounded by fertile agricultural soil and there is little pastureland. As a result, it is most likely that the site emphasized agriculture.

Gopalpura site is situated in the jungle of Gopalpura and is surrounded by pasturelands full of small shrubs. Chalcolithic as well as Historic potsherds are found spread across two separate deposits. This seems to have been a small camp or herding unit of the Chalcolithic people.

Jashma I is a microlithic site located about 8 km southwest of Gilund. The deposits are spread across an area that measures 22 m NS by 12 m EW. The height of the mound is 1.60 m. The land around the site is best suited for pasture, indicating that the site may have been inhabited by pastoralists.

Jashma II is situated 9 km southwest of Gilund and 1 km to the north of Jashma I. It has both Chalcolithic and Historic deposits. The site is spread over an area of approximately 4 ha and has a habitation deposit of 5 m. The mound has been cut into, possibly for field fertilizer, as potsherds were found scattered across the fields. As the nearby soil is considered to be fertile, the site may have been another agricultural settlement.

Kiron Ka Khera is a Chalcolithic site situated 10 km northeast of Gilund. A few Chalcolithic potsherds were found around the well of Kiron Ka Khera in an area measuring, 21 m EW by 12 m NS. The height of the deposit is

0.70 m. A second deposit next to the well measures 7 m NS by 4 m EW, with a height of 0.40 m. The surrounding area has soil that is considered to be very fertile. As no full settlement was identified, this site is identified as a temporary camp of the Chalcolithic people.

Nangpura is 10 km to the southeast of Gilund, located in the fields of contemporary Nangpura. The site has both Chalcolithic and Historic deposits in an area of 100 m EW by 120 m NS, with a habitation deposit of 3 m. The sides of the mound have been cut away from plowing and the mound itself has also been plowed. A deposit of ceramics was found across the mound. The area around the site is considered to be very fertile and, therefore, the site seems to have been an agricultural settlement of the Chalcolithic people.

Pachamta is situated 7 km west of Gilund and has both Chalcolithic and Historic deposits. The site is comprised of five mounds, which range in height from 3 m to 3.5 m. The entire modern village of Pachamta sits on the remains of the mound. PCT-I, PCT-III, PCT-IV, and PCT-V have Chalcolithic sections, while PCT-II has an Early Historic section. Potteries found at the site include Black and Red Ware, Gray Ware, and Thin Red Ware. Historic sherds were also observed. This site seems to have been an agricultural and pastoral settlement of the Chalcolithic people as there are both arable and pasture lands located near the site.

Pachamta Powerhouse is a Chalcolithic site located 7 km west of Gilund. The deposit runs 25 m EW by 30 m NS with a height of 0.50 m. A few potsherds are found scattered on the deposit, but no structures are visible. The deposit is disturbed as it has been slowly cut away into nearby fields and a powerhouse is situated at the top of the mound. The villagers consider the soil to be less fertile. Thus, the area immediately around the mound is used for pasture. The scant deposits and poor agricultural land suggest that the site may have been a campsite. A little less than 0.50 km to the north of the site lie cultivable fields. A brick kiln is located 0.50 km away from the site.

Surawas I is located 7 km northeast of Gilund, next to a brick kiln in the fields of Surawas. It has both Chalcolithic and Historic deposits. The intact mound measures 115 m NE/SW and the height is approximately 3 m. It has been cut away on all sides into plowed fields. Cut sections on the east reveal stones, ceramics, and iron. Potsherds are found on both the mound and the plowed fields. The high density

of stones in the mound suggests previous building activity, although structures are not currently visible. The stones are mostly granite and quartzite with some quartz. The area around the site is considered to be fertile. Pasture is also located 0.50 km north of this area. The site may have been used for both agriculture and pasture.

Conclusion

In the course of survey, a number of sites were located in the vicinity of Gilund. Sources of water were also identified and the potential of land for agriculture and grazing was assessed. In addition to agricultural and pastoral products, the raw materials for basic necessities were available within the 10 km catchment of Gilund. The Chalcolithic people of Gilund acquired quartz for manufacturing lithics and slingballs. Quartzite and sandstone were obtained for use as querns, hammerstones, pounders, and mullers. The stones used in construction seem to have been acquired locally. Lime plaster has been abundantly used in the structures excavated at the site of Gilund and appears to have been made from locally acquired raw material. The soil in the 10 km catchment area is suitable for construction of mud houses, making mud brick and burnt brick, and in the production of pottery at the site. The soil around Gilund also seems to have been used for making terracotta objects like beads and animal figurines that were found in large quantities. All other products were acquired from areas outside of the 10 km catchment of Gilund and may have been obtained through trade.

Several sites were found near land that had potential for good crops as well as near areas with good pasture. Most of these sites do not have deep habitation deposits and therefore may have been temporary. Such temporary sites have been documented ethnographically as pastoral camps and seasonal farmsteads. In the ethnographic record, the occupants of such sites are connected to permanent villages such as Gilund. It is possible that the occupants of the temporary archaeological sites described here may have been part-time residents of the site of Gilund. These finds enhance the idea that Gilund subsisted mainly on agricultural products, which were also procured through setting up small camps and in some cases semi-permanent settlements in distant areas.

6

Ceramic Assemblages at Gilund

Shweta Sinha Deshpande

Introduction

The most common artifacts found among the sedentary agriculturist and pastoralist communities of Chalcolithic South Asia are ceramics. Previously, most ceramic studies in South Asia emphasized typological categorization in reports and articles. In recent years, however, archaeologists have begun to use ceramics to answer questions of a social nature with a goal of better understanding cultures and their interactions. Such studies also reveal the life of ancient people who have left us nothing but their broken pottery, structures, tools, and small objects in the form of a three-dimensional puzzle.

General Description

The Chalcolithic pottery at Gilund is very similar to the assemblage at Ahar, with a predominance of white-painted Black and Red Ware, Red Ware, and Gray Ware. However, the fabric seen at Gilund is coarser than that found at the other Ahar sites, even in the Middle Chalcolithic phase. The majority of the pottery at Gilund has been low or unevenly fired, has a gray core, and generally does not have the metallic ring that is a feature of the pottery of the neighboring Harappan Civilization. Rims are often luted to the body and the lower body portions of larger vessels are rusticated, or texturized. Handmade pottery is largely absent; the majority is wheelmade or occasionally molded, although a few handmade sherds are present in the lower levels.

Slips and decorations including painting are usually present on the rim, neck, and shoulder portions of the vessels. The painting, slip, and burnishing are always applied pre-firing, which is a characteristic feature of the Ahar-Banas Complex. Although most paint is white, the inhabitants occasionally used red or black paint. Decoration includes appliqué, incising, ridges, and rope impressions. Shapes and sizes are diverse, ranging from miniature pots to large pots and basins. Both deluxe and utilitarian wares are present throughout the assemblage. Study of the complete pots recovered at Gilund demonstrates that the Rusticated Ware from Ahar (Sankalia, Ansari, and Deo 1969) does not appear to exist here; instead, rustication is restricted to the lower portions of globular pots that served utilitarian purposes.

Ceramic analysts frequently divide vessels into fine and coarse wares based on the degree of purity of clay, surface treatment, nature of firing, vessel forms, and decoration. Fine pottery is made of refined, well-levigated clay, has a thin and highly burnished slip, and is baked at a very high temperature (above 700°). Because of these features, it is sturdy, has a reddish core, produces a metallic sound, looks attractive, and therefore constitutes deluxe pottery. The common vessel types include dishes, globular pots, and bowls (with or without a stand) in various sizes. The presence of such high-quality pottery at Gilund suggests the existence of an elite section within the society. The coarse variety is made of unrefined clay, is low fired, has a gray or black core, and is mainly decorated with incised and appliqué designs. The vessel forms in this variety are mainly comprised of large globular pots that were probably used for storage and cooking as well as for other purposes by the masses.

The Ahar-Banas Complex is characterized by three basic pottery types: Red Ware, Black and Red Ware, and Gray Ware. These can be further subdivided into those with fine fabric, like Thin Red Ware, Black and Red Ware painted in white, Tan Ware, and Reserve Slipped Ware; and coarse fabric types such as the Thick Bright Slipped Red Ware and Gray Ware, which are also common at Gilund and seem to have been manufactured on-site. The various types of wares found at the site of Gilund are discussed below.

Black and Red Ware (B&RW)

B&RW is appropriately named as the interior and the shoulder portion of the outer surface of the vessel is black while the rest of the exterior surface is red or plum red, although occasionally it tends to be brownish red, tan, or chocolate. This effect is believed to have been achieved by the application of an inverted firing technique. Both surfaces are treated with a slip and burnished. The decorations are painted in white pigment on the interior or exterior of the pot, possibly pre-firing, and in some cases the paint tends to peel off, leaving only a faded image of the design. The motifs include groups of straight or wavy lines, spirals, dots, hatched diamonds, concentric circles, and chevrons filled with dots and circles (Deo 1969a:88–98). The shapes in this ware are mostly wide-mouthed, convex-sided bowls of varying sizes.

Excavations at the site of Gilund have revealed some new features of the B&RW as the site has produced not only small tablewares, such as bowls and dishes, but also many large and medium size pots of coarse and medium fabric that appear to be both a deluxe and a utilitarian ware (unlike at the sites of Balathal or Ahar). The fabric is coarse due to the use of tempering material like tiny grains of stone and sand which makes the pottery gritty and brittle. B&RW at the site of Gilund is representative of typical Ahar-Banas Complex B&RW and can be divided into four different varieties: coarse and thick, coarse and thin, fine and thick, and fine and thin. The thicker varieties typically belong to large vessels, like globular pots with wide or narrow mouth, jar/pots, and even basins with grooved rims and thin sections, while the thinner varieties are generally medium to small vessels, like bowls such as convex-sided deep, shallow bowls, everted rim carinated bowls, featureless convex bowls, globular bowls (seen in the Middle phase), basins, and small globular pots. As at Ahar, where B&RW is in the washed category, two sherds at Gilund have a wash-like treatment instead of the thick slip that helped hide the coarseness of the fabric. The decorative treatment of large vessels used for storage is similar to the Coarse Red Ware pottery where the slip and burnishing is restricted to the shoulder and even incised decorations are used. Very few large and coarse pots seem to be painted in white, which is a feature restricted to smaller vessels.

The earliest levels at the site have not yet been excavated sufficiently to reveal the ceramic assemblage for those phases, but the middle levels at the site indicate that B&RW is both fine and coarse. Large and small vessels in B&RW are outnumbered by the Gray or Red Wares. In the middle levels the pottery is less coarse, especially when compared to the site's upper levels where it becomes coarse with a large amount of tempering, including large chunks and dust of mica. Interestingly, in the last phase of the Chalcolithic, the fine variety has only been found in and around the large storage structure on GLD-2. It is presumed that this area played an important role in the late phase.

Burnished Black Ware

This ware was encountered in the lower levels of the Middle Chalcolithic at Gilund and is uncommon, although some sherds were found at Ahar (Sankalia, Deo, and Ansari 1969). This pottery is wheelmade, has fine and coarse varieties with little or no tempering, and a deep black colored core and surface. The surface is black slipped and highly burnished on its entire exterior surface and rim. Some of the sherds have white painted decorations done prior to firing on the shoulder. Designs include patterns made of multiple dots, hatched diamonds, and chevrons in white paint that has been preserved and has not peeled away. As very few sherds have been located, the shapes present at Gilund are still to be determined. However, some interesting shapes include an everted rim, straight elongated neck globular small pot (a similar shape has been found in very fine Thin Red Ware), vessels on stands like the bowl on a corrugated, elongated stand, and other shapes on broad bases. The context of use is not yet identifiable, but it can be presumed to be either a deluxe ware or a ware meant for special occasions. A single sherd of this ware has been found in the late phase from the area around the storage structure, which also suggests its significance.

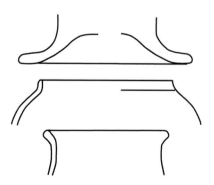

Fig. 6.1 Burnished Black Ware.

Red Wares

Red Wares are the most common wares at Gilund and throughout the Chalcolithic Ahar-Banas Complex. They are categorized into sub-varieties based on the fabric and the surface treatment including Coarse Red, Thin Red, Tan, Chocolate Slipped, and Polychrome wares. The Coarse Red Ware resembles Coarse Gray Ware in fabric, surface treatment, and shapes and is used for utilitarian purposes like storage and cooking. Coarse Red Ware is the most common of the Red Wares and Thin Red, while not plentiful, is found throughout. The other three varieties are rare and in some cases may have been imported from other sites.

1. Coarse Red Ware. Coarse Red Ware in the Chalcolithic is typically represented by Thick Bright Slipped Red Ware that is locally produced, primarily used for storage and cooking, and demonstrates uniformity throughout the Ahar-Banas with the exception of a few shapes. The wares, as described above, are made of poorly fired coarse clay and mainly decorated with incised and appliqué designs. The Coarse Red Ware is dominated by large, narrow-mouthed and wide-mouthed globular jars, small handis (cooking pots), storage jars, basins, other utilitarian shapes, and dishes on stands. These are treated with a highly burnished, bright red slip on the upper part or the rim and shoulder of the exterior surface. The body or middle part of the external surface is decorated with two or more parallel, raised bands/ridges and a variety of incised designs like multiple wavy lines, chevrons, herringbone patterns, criss-crosses, loops, triangular incisions, and punctured and appliqué patterns. At Ahar-Banas sites, Coarse Red Ware decoration is located on the shoulder or upper part of the vessel while the rim, neck, and base are left plain.

At Gilund, as at the other Ahar-Banas sites, Coarse Red Ware is very common, utilitarian in nature, and used for storage and cooking purposes. It is present across the site and represented by a wide range of pottery sizes from small to large. This pottery is sometimes wheelmade and at other times molded. The fabric is gritty with coarse to medium grained temper such as granular sand, chopped grass, and mica flakes. In the Late Phase of the Early Chalcolithic at Gilund, the fabric is coarse and the pottery is wheelmade, which suggests that it is later than the earliest phase at Balathal (Phase A). Here the core tends to be blackish as the pottery is often low fired. The slip varies from orange to dark red and is thickly applied, mostly on a burnished exterior surface. The interior is either red with no slip or gray depending on the firing conditions.

The Middle Phase at Gilund sees a well-fired Coarse Red Ware assemblage with a finer fabric that is not seen at any other level and described as "medium Coarse Red Ware." By the Late Phase, the ware has again become much coarser and tempering includes chunks of mica, stone, and chopped grass in large quantities. As with Coarse Gray Ware, the shoulder and area above it are slipped and may also be decorated and burnished; the lower portions are plain or rusticated. Decorations are made in appliqué, incised, ridged, or rope-impressed styles. Appliqué designs included spirals and circles similar to those found at the site of Ojiyana (Meena and Tripathi 2001–2002). Incised designs include, among others, chequered, combed,

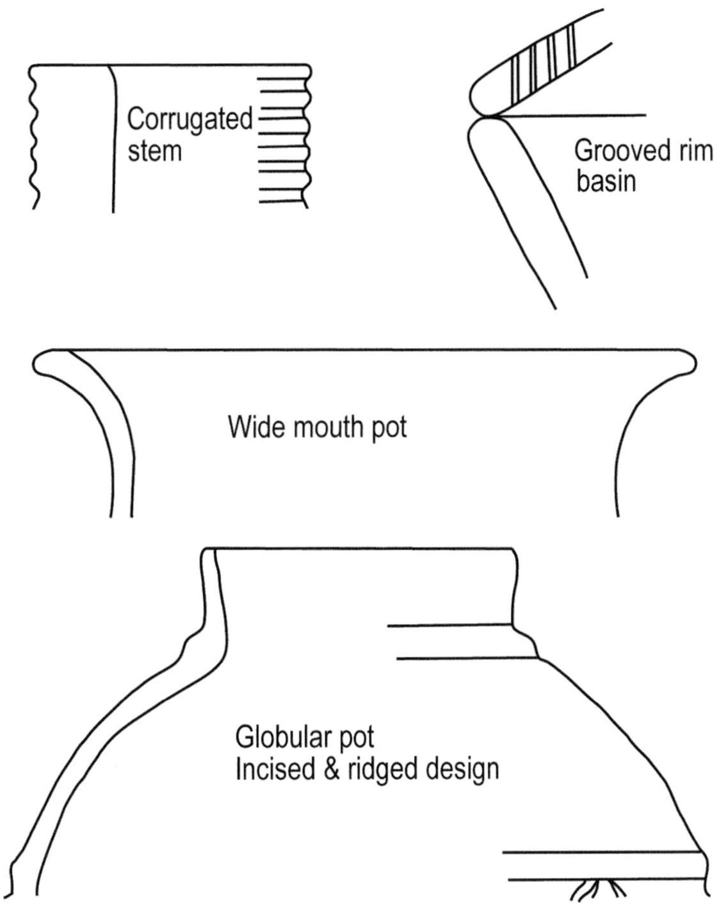

Fig. 6.2. Coarse Red Ware.

hatched diamonds, and diagonal or linear lines. Ridged designs are invariably parallel linear lines on the neck and shoulder portions, while rope-impressed designs are both true impressions or made to look like them by incising ridges. The decorations are finer and deeper with a careful, meticulous deliberation in the middle or Middle Phase, while in the Late Phase there appears to be a careless frenzy in their execution. Paintings are rare in this variety, and the painted versions of Coarse Red have been identified as either an imitation of or a local variation on Malwa Ware, which is present in the Late Chalcolithic Phase at the site. The majority of pottery shapes in this ware are globular pots with narrow or wide mouths, basins, dishes, lids, pots with handles, and very large storage jars.

2. Polychrome Ware. Polychrome Ware at Gilund is a Coarse Red Ware of medium coarse fabric, classified separately because of its distinctive surface treatment. This surface treatment consists of a combination of white, black, and red painted decorations mostly of single or interlaced diamonds. The shapes are difficult to identify as only a few body sherds have been found from the middle and lower levels at the site. A similar ware was found at the site of Ahar (Deo 1969a, Sankalia 1969b), but there too the sherds were limited and shapes unidentifiable.

3. Thin Red Ware. This ware has a thin, highly bur-

nished plum red or occasionally brownish red, tan, or chocolate slip on the external surface, while the inner surface is without any slip or washes and is generally gray or tan. The shapes include convex-sided deep bowls of various sizes and occasionally small globular vessels with everted rim, narrow mouth, and high neck. They are decorated with a single row of punctured or incised triangles and occasionally by single or double ridges in low relief on the shoulder. The rim in some cases is made separately and luted to the body. At the site of Gilund, Thin Red Ware has both fine and coarse varieties (see Table 6.1). The finer variety is uncommon and is present mostly in the Middle Chalcolithic. It is present in fewer numbers by the end of this phase and is completely absent in the Late Chalcolithic Phase.

An interesting feature observed in the Middle Chalcolithic at Gilund is the presence of a few sherds of the Thin Red Ware showing a combination of black and red color on the outer slipped surface. The rim along with some portion of the neck is black while the rest of the pot is red. It resembles the Black and Red Ware except that the fabric and the technique of producing the twin color effect seem different as the interior of the pot is red and unslipped unlike the Black and Red Ware. The pottery is a fine ware, typically thin to medium in section, high fired with a thick slip, highly burnished, and without painted decoration, al-

Table 6.1. Varieties of Thin Red Ware at Gilund

	Fine	Coarse
Fabric	Fine	Similar to the thin coarse variety of Black and Red Ware
Temper	Fine sand	Granular quartz
Firing	High	Low and uneven reduction
Body	Thin	Thin to medium thick
Core	Gray or tan	Gray
Interior surface	Red unburnished, unslipped	Gray with no surface treatment
Exterior	Bright red slip, highly burnished	Bright red slip, gray blotches due to uneven firing technique
Exterior Decorations	Single or double parallel ridges on the shoulder, checkered incised decorations, or a line of punctured wedge shapes	White paintings similar to Black and Red Ware in a number of cases
Shapes	Convex-sided deep bowls, wide-mouth globular bowls, flasks, small pots, bowls on flared hollow stands, flared rim jars, and everted rim, elongated straight neck globular pots	Narrow- or wide-mouth pots and small to large sized globular pots
Rims	Nail-headed rims (a few fragments located). Rims are made separately on a fast wheel and then luted to the body.	Everted rims
Purpose	Deluxe ware	Utilitarian ware used for cooking and serving

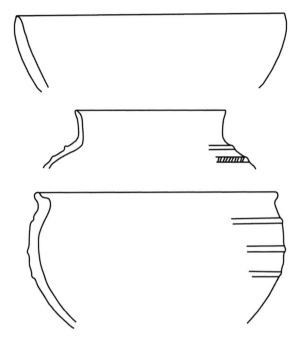

Fig. 6.3. Thin Red Ware.

the latter, however, it lacks painted decorations.

In contrast to Ahar and Balathal where this ware is found in large quantities, at Gilund Tan Ware is rare and Chocolate Ware has not yet been found. Here the Tan Ware is well fired, has a fine to medium coarse fabric with a medium-thick body section, and is undecorated. Initially, only a few body fragments were identified; however, in the last season two complete shapes—a beaded rim globular pot and a featureless concave, carinated shallow bowl—were found.

Gray Ware

This ware has two varieties, a burnished and a plain. The fabric varies from coarse to fine. At most Chalcolithic sites, Gray Ware forms a part of the coarse utilitarian pottery primarily used for storage and cooking. In the burnished variety, the upper part of the exterior is slipped and highly burnished while the plain variety bears a slip but has no burnishing. The lower part of the outer surface of vessels in both varieties is roughened by the application of sand mixed with clay. They are often covered with soot, showing that the vessels were used for cooking. The middle portion on the external surface is often decorated with incised, punctured, cut, and appliqué designs similar to those of the burnished Red Ware. The most common vessel forms in both the varieties are wide-mouth pots, small handis, lids with or without handles, and handmade tawas (griddles) used for making rotis or unleavened bread.

At Gilund, Gray Ware has either a coarse fabric, produced on a fast wheel, or it is molded with well-levigated clay mixed with fine sand, grass, and sometimes tiny mica particles. Alternatively, it has a finer fabric like that of the Fine Thin Slipped Red Ware common in the Middle Chalcolithic Phase. The surface treatment and decorative devices are aesthetically pleasing although the fabric is not the finest and the pots are intended mostly for utilitarian purpose such as storage and cooking. Sankalia very justifiably stated, "the Ahar potter, in fact, has demonstrated how a pottery even utilitarian like storage jars can be made beautiful without painting. Also remarkable is his sense, proportion and self-restraint" (1969b:18). The Coarse Gray Ware, as the nomenclature suggests, has medium fabric in the Middle Chalcolithic (based on the presence of only a few sherds) to coarse fabric in the Middle and Late Chalcolithic. It also varies from medium to thick in section and has a black or gray color due to low firing conditions and minimum oxidation. In both Coarse Red Ware and Gray Ware, large storage and cooking pots are slipped and burnished up to the shoulder. Although the body is bare of slip, burnish, or other decoration, they are decorated on the shoulder with ridging, ap-

though in some cases it has ridged and punctured designs on the shoulder. The red color of this ware ranges from shades of deep red to light orange to tan and chocolate due to variation in the oxidation available during firing. The black color ranges from black to gray to purple or blue. The shapes include everted rim globular bowls, featureless globular bowls, and everted rim, elongated straight neck globular small pots (a similar shape has been found in Burnished Black Ware as well). This ware completely disappears in the Late Chalcolithic Phase and has not been reported from any other Chalcolithic site. The technique used for manufacturing this ware could be based on double firing but this assertion needs further research. This ware is designated as Bichrome Ware.

4. Tan and Chocolate Wares. These wares are of medium thickness, with a thin light orange/tan slip, which can sometimes resemble a thick brown or chocolate color found in Kayatha Ware. The principal shapes in this ware include the dish; dish-on-stand; bowl-on-stand with considerable variations in size; large, convex-sided bowl with thick rim; globular pot with either beaded or flat projecting rim; and large basin with ledges on the neck. The prominent ledges may have been used to hold the vessels, while the low ledges may have been purely decorative. In respect to fabric and shape, this ware is identical to the sturdy Red Ware of the Gujarat Harappans and the Tan Ware of Gujarat. Unlike

pliqué, cut, and incised designs used singly or in combination. This description is based on the large sherds and complete pots found during the excavation showing all these features on the same pot. According to Deo (1969a:88), motifs like impressed circles, concentric arcs, combed designs, and sharp ridges with cut decorations are absent on the Gray Ware at Ahar, but at Gilund all of these are very carefully executed. At Ahar, the decorations are on the unburnished surface (Deo 1969a:125–28), whereas at Gilund they are on both the burnished and unburnished surfaces. Large globular cooking pots, elongated jars, and storage vessels that were found just below the surface each had a thin and severely plain body and base that was rusticated through the application of a thin coat of fine sand. Similar treatment of the base is present on cooking pots. Rustication is a common practice today in the region, where applying clay and cow dung on the rusticated surface is considered to preserve the beauty of the pots and make them last longer (personal observation). Some of the important shapes in this type

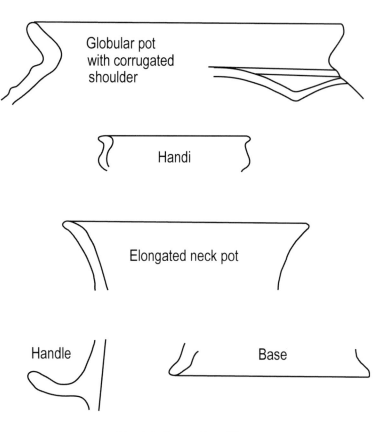

Fig. 6.4. Coarse Gray Ware.

are globular pots with everted rims, carinated elongated jars with everted or out-turned rims, and large and small basins with thick lugged, beaded rims, which served the purpose of handles. Besides these more common types, there are bowls on stands with thick stems, dishes on stands, and deep basins with handles and conical lids. An interesting shape, which seems to have had a specific purpose, is the small handi with a red band on the rim, neck, and shoulder, and carination. These handis are few in number and potentially could have been used for religious purposes.

Recent ethnographic work carried out in the region shows that the gray color with blotches of red on the exterior and interior is not produced through the use of slip. Instead, this color pattern results from firing in an oxygen-reduction atmosphere or smoky condition within the kiln (Kramer 1997). Even today, potters make similar wares using the ancient technique to produce wide-mouth globular pots for storing and carrying water. A detailed study done on the decoration techniques at Gilund shows that Gray Ware vessels have superficial decorations on the slip, which did not penetrate through to the clay and disappear when the slip flakes off the vessel. This is especially true for combed decorations, which are very common in the Mid-

dle Chalcolithic and continue into the Late Chalcolithic where they are less meticulous and more carelessly made. The superficial combed designs can perhaps be traced back to the Sothi Culture (ca. 3000–2500 BC), which may have influenced the Kayatha Combed Ware (Wakankar 1967) as they are not as chronologically distant as generally assumed. Further study may shed light on this problem.

An interesting feature at Gilund is the presence of a few thin Gray Ware sherds in the middle levels and possibly in the lower levels. The fabric of this variety is fine without gritty temper. The sherds and pots are thin to medium in section, which is similar to the Thin Slipped Red Ware where the pots are fully slipped and highly burnished on the exterior. Generally, this ware is without any decoration, and the clay has fine mica particles, which give the vessels a fine sheen. However, in some cases thin ridges on the shoulder portion are present and two sherds are painted in white with horizontal bands and dots like B&RW. The main vessel types present are the convex carinated pot and the everted-rim convex bowl. Nothing much can be said about the origin or context of this pottery except that it could have been used as a deluxe ware and that interestingly it is restricted to the eastern face of GLD-2, which also yielded the Thin Slipped Red Ware of the fine variety.

Buff and Cream Slipped Wares

At Gilund, Buff Ware similar to that mentioned in the Ahar report is completely absent, though we do have two sherds of Harappan Buff Ware with paintings in black from the middle levels of GLD-1; however, the sherds are tiny and shapes cannot be identified. Also, in the Late Chalcolithic we have three Buff Ware sherds with a buff slip and one painted in black resembling the medium fabric ware from the Malwa region. These sherds could have been imported from that area as a result of trade transactions.

Reserve Slip Ware

This ware was first recovered in the Ahar-Banas Complex at the lowest levels of Balathal Phase A (Mishra 2000). The lower levels of Gilund are also producing it, although in limited quantities. The earliest sherds are of the red-on-red variety, while the typical Harappan variety is gray-on-cream (found at Balathal in the Middle Phase but absent at Gilund).

The coarse Red Reserve Slip Ware is red and produced from fine clay with fine sand temper. It is treated with a red wash over which a thick, dark red slip is applied. When the slip is wet, various patterns are executed by scooping out the second slip possibly with a comb-like instrument. The patterns are usually found in sets or groups. The ware is fired uniformly to a high temperature and therefore the core is brick-red. The decoration, mainly on the inner surface, consists of closely spaced horizontal lines and sets of zigzag lines (Misra et al. 1995). We do not have any rim sherds from Gilund; however, at Balathal a shallow dish with a round, slightly incurved rim, cylindrical hollow stem, and stand with flared sides and short, out-turned ring is found in this ware. It is believed that the Reserve Slip Ware was originally made at Ahar-Banas Complex sites and from there spread to Harappan sites. At Gilund, however, only two sherds have been found and both precede the circumference wall which hints at the date of the early levels. However, further excavations are required before any fixed date for the origin of Ahar-Banas Complex at Gilund can be made.

Ceramics from Outside the Ahar-Banas

In addition to the typical Ahar-Banas pottery available at the sites, evidence of foreign ceramic types was recovered from all levels at Gilund. For example, in the Early Chalcolithic excavators recovered Pre-Harappan/Sothi type Combed Ware, Chalcolithic wares from Kayatha including Cream Slipped Ware and Kayatha Red-on-Red Ware, and Pre-Harappan phase Gritty Red Ware from North Gujarat. In the Middle Chalcolithic, wares recovered include Harappan Buff Ware and sturdy Red Ware in shapes like the constricted neck globular pots/jars. Malwa Ware was found in the Late Chalcolithic. Southern Neolithic Gray Ware was found in both the Late Middle Chalcolithic and Late Chalcolithic. The latter ware included the channel-spouted bowl, which was copied in the Thin Slipped Red Ware of the coarse variety. Gilund, like Navdatoli, has produced evidence of cups on stands, channel-spouted cups, and pedestal goblets, which are related to Harappan vessels on stands that seem to have continued into later phases. The site also seems to have made efforts to produce Malwa Ware types locally in the Thin Slipped Red Ware of the coarse variety.

All of these various ceramic types from Chalcolithic cultures, in addition to other artifacts (see chapters by Hanlon, Ameri, and Raczek in this volume), indicate a busy trade network, which surely contributed to the development and evolution of these cultures in various parts of western and southern India. This network may have extended throughout the subcontinent; however, we need definite and

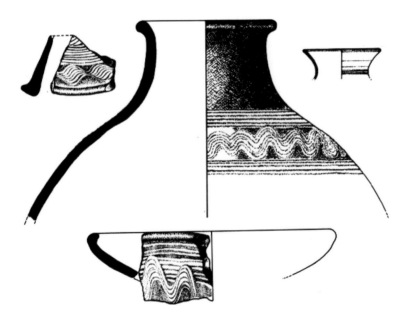

Fig. 6.5. Coarse Red Reserve Slip Ware.

conclusive data and more collaborative work among scholars to understand these intertwining interactions among cultures that are clearly neither isolated nor underdeveloped.

Distribution of Pottery on the Twin Mounds

The analysis of the distribution and spread of pottery on GLD-1 and GLD-2 helps in the analysis of site occupation. It seems that the earliest residents occupied GLD-1, since early ceramics have not been recovered from GLD-2. With growing prosperity, they seemed to have slowly spread to GLD-2; during the Middle Chalcolithic the whole site was occupied and fine pottery was used across the entire site. However, it seems that the southern extension of GLD-2 was occupied by an elite class or a more affluent section of the society during the middle of the Middle Chalcolithic, since the pottery here is finer than that from other areas of the site and includes some of the finest Thin Red Ware, Black Ware, and the Bichrome (imitation Black and Red Ware) variety of the Thin Red Ware. In the Late Chalcolithic, the occupation seems to have been reduced in size and is confined only to the northern area of GLD-2. The rest of the site is devoid of the crude, coarse pottery characteristic of Late Chalcolithic habitation. The top layers of the southern edge of GLD-2 have the late Middle pottery with the beginning signs of degradation in the ceramic assemblage and the presence of Malwa Ware. However, the surface of the whole site shows evidence of remnants of habitation in the form of coarse Red and Gray Ware pots (complete but shattered) left behind by the last inhabitants. The Early Historic deposit is restricted to GLD-1; we do not see Early Historic ceramics anywhere else at the site (for more on this, see Gullapalli and Johansen, this volume).

Besides these general observations regarding the habitation on the site, the study would be incomplete without reference to the stepped index trench that is located on GLD-1. Pottery has always been the identifying feature in archaeology, as archaeologists used it to differentiate between cultures and periods of occupation in single and multiple occupation sites throughout the world. It is the index trench on any archaeological site that gives the complete picture of the nature and periods of occupation based on the pottery, antiquity, and structural remains. At the site of Gilund the index trench is located on the higher GLD-1 mound which will provide us with the complete story of the site. However, as mentioned above, the Late Chalcolithic deposit is absent on this mound. The following is the layer-wise description of the pottery assemblage in the index

trench, Trench 4. Since the area of excavation was limited, the amount of pottery recovered was small. The layer-wise pottery distribution on GLD-1, Index Trench 4A-F (Step Trench) is provided here (see also Giorgio in this volume for a full discussion of the pottery from the index trench).

Layers 1–6 belong to the Early Historic Phase

— Layers 7–12 belong to the late Middle Chalcolithic with coarse pottery including the presence of Malwa Ware (1700-2000 BC).

— Layers 13–20 belong to the Middle Chalcolithic with a finesse in the pottery assemblage. Wares present in this phase, but not others, include Black Ware, Thin Slipped Red Ware with the everted rim globular bowls, and two sherds of the Harappan Red and Buff Ware (2000–2500 BC).

— Layers 21–24 have been associated with the contemporary Kalibangan I stage due to the presence of Polychrome Ware and a fine pottery assemblage similar to the Middle Chalcolithic.

— Layers 25–27 include the presence of Reserve Slip Ware and Tan Ware; the latter forms a very fine ware of the Ahar-Banas Complex though it is absent at the site of Gilund except for a few sherds. The former has its beginnings in the Early Chalcolithic at Balathal. Here it is of a finer variety. Hence, both of these groups can be seen as a transitional phase from Early Chalcolithic to the Middle Chalcolithic and dated between 2500–2700 BC.

— Layers 28–31 have a pottery assemblage belonging to the Early Chalcolithic Phase though a little later than the beginnings at Balathal.

— Layers 32–32A include very tiny sherds of pottery in association with microliths. The pottery is similar to that from Bagor and the other deep deposit with microliths from GLD-2.

An interesting and significant aspect gleaned from the study of the pottery of the Ahar-Banas Complex is the absence of the prolific black-painted Red Ware, which is the basis of the Early, Middle, and Late Harappan as well as the Malwa, Jorwe, and many other Chalcolithic Cultures with the exception of the Neolithic cultures of the South that appear to have had an independent ceramic culture based on Gray Wares. In addition, not only the wares but also the decorative motifs on Ahar-Banas ceramics are distinct from those of other cultural assemblages. This indicates an independent origin of the Ahar-Banas Complex as compared to the earlier view that it evolved from the Harappans, although the later developments can be attributed to contact through trade or other transactions.

Table 6.2. Index Trench Ceramics

Layer	Lot Numbers	Pottery Types/Shapes
1-6	All trenches 4A, 4B, 4C and lot numbers 4D.3001 to 4D.3009 of Trench 4D	Early Historic Sunga-Kushan ceramic assemblage with types including: Red Slipped Ware: round, short-necked globular pots, lids Red Micaceous Ware: globular pots Unslipped Red Ware: everted rim, concave and shoulder carinated small pot, cup with flared sides and a disc base, lids
7	Lot numbers 4D.3010–13 and 4D.3016	Late Middle Ahar-Banas Complex ceramic assemblage with types including: Black and Red Ware Coarse Thin: everted rim bowls, featureless rim bowls Black and Red Ware Coarse Thick: jar/pot, basin Coarse Gray Ware: wide-mouth globular pots, out-curved rim wide-mouth jar/pots Coarse Red Ware: everted rim wide-mouth jar/pots, basins, everted rim wide-mouth pots, everted rim deep bowl, out-turned rim wide-mouth jar Medium Coarse Red Ware: body sherds only Thin Slipped Coarse Red Ware: everted rim bowls, featureless rim bowls, everted rim wide-mouth small pot Cream Slipped Malwa Ware: body sherd only Malwa Ware painted in black: body sherds only
8	Lot numbers 4D.3015 and 4D.3017	Late Middle Ahar-Banas Complex ceramic assemblage with types including: Black and Red Ware Coarse Thin: everted rim bowls, featureless rim bowls Black and Red Ware Coarse Thick: everted rim pot, out-turned rim wide-mouth pot, out-curved rim wide-mouth pot Coarse Gray Ware: out-turned rim wide-mouth jar/pots, wide-mouth small pot, basin Coarse Red Ware: everted rim wide-mouth jar/pots, basins, everted rim wide-mouth pots, wide-mouth elongated neck jar, out-curved rim jar/pot Medium Coarse Red Ware: wide-mouth small pot, everted rim large bowls, featureless rim large bowls Thin-Slipped Coarse Red Ware: everted rim bowls, featureless rim bowls, everted rim wide-mouth small pot Malwa Ware painted in black: body sherds only
9	Lot numbers 4D.3018, 4D.3021–23, and 4D.3026	Middle Ahar-Banas Complex ceramic assemblage with types including: Black and Red Ware Coarse Thin: everted rim bowls, featureless rim bowls Black and Red Ware Coarse Thick: body sherds only Coarse Gray Ware: everted rim wide-mouth globular pots, out-turned rim small pot, narrow-mouth pot, featureless bowl, wide-mouth pot, basin Coarse Red Ware: everted rim wide-mouth jar/pots, basins, everted rim wide-mouth pots, out-curved rim jar Thin Slipped Coarse Red Ware: featureless rim bowls, everted rim wide-mouth small pot Thin Slipped Fine Red Ware: body sherds only Malwa Ware painted in black: 2 body sherds only
10		No pottery recovered in the Index Trench as the layer was only present in an adjacent trench.
11	Lot numbers 4E.3006, 4E.3007, and 4E.3011	Middle Ahar-Banas Complex ceramic assemblage with types including: Black and Red Ware Coarse Thin: everted rim bowls, featureless rim bowls Black and Red Ware Fine Thin: body sherds only Black-and-Red Ware Coarse Thick: body sherds only Coarse Gray Ware: out-turned rim wide-mouth pots, wide-mouth small pot Coarse Red Ware: everted rim wide-mouth pots, basins, wide-mouth elongated neck jar Medium Coarse Red Ware: body sherds only Thin Slipped Coarse Red Ware: everted rim bowl
12	Lot numbers 4E.3011	No pottery

cont'd.

Table 6.2 cont'd.

Layer	Lot Numbers	Pottery Types/Shapes
13	Lot numbers 4E.3008–10, 4E.3013, 4E.3014, and 4E.3016–18	Middle Ahar-Banas Complex ceramic assemblage with types including: Black and Red Ware Coarse Thin: everted rim bowls, everted rim wide-mouth small pot Black and Red Ware Fine Thin: body sherds only Black and Red Ware Coarse Thick: wide-mouth pot Coarse Gray Ware: wide-mouth small pot, featureless rim bowl, everted rim bowl, out-turned rim narrow neck pot Coarse Red Ware: everted rim deep basin, featureless deep bowl, basins Medium Coarse Red Ware: body sherds only Thin-Slipped Coarse Red Ware: featureless rim bowls, everted rim bowl Thin Slipped Fine Red Ware: everted rim pot
14	Lot numbers 4E.3023, 4E.3024, 4E.3029, 4E.3030	Middle Ahar-Banas Complex ceramic assemblage with types including: Black and Red Ware Fine Thin: body sherds only Black and Red Ware Coarse Thick: everted rim, triangular edge jar/pot, everted rim wide-mouth pot Coarse Gray Ware:, featureless rim bowl, out-turned rim pot Coarse Red Ware: everted rim deep basin, basins Medium Coarse Red Ware: everted rim globular pot Thin Slipped Coarse Red Ware: everted rim wide-mouth pot Thin Slipped Fine Red Ware: body sherds only
15	Lot numbers 4E.3026	Black and Red Ware Coarse Thick: everted rim bowl Coarse Gray Ware: out-turned rim pot Coarse Red Ware: basins Medium Coarse Red Ware: everted rim globular pot Thin Slipped Fine Red Ware: everted rim bowls
16	Lot numbers 4F.3003, 4F.3004, 4F.3008	Black and Red Ware Coarse Thick: everted rim bowl, wide-mouth pot Black and Red Ware Fine Thin: everted rim bowl, featureless rim bowl Coarse Gray Ware: out-turned rim pot, featureless rim bowl Coarse Red Ware: basins, wide-mouth pot Medium Coarse Red Ware: body sherds only Thin Slipped Fine Red Ware: everted rim, elongated neck pot Thin Slipped Coarse Red Ware: everted rim bowl, everted rim wide-mouth pot, everted rim, elongated neck small pot, out-turned rim pot, wide-mouth narrow neck small pot Black Ware: body sherds only
17	Lot numbers 4F.3005, 4F.3007, 4F.3011, 4F.3012	Black and Red Ware Coarse Thick: everted rim wide-mouth pot, wide-mouth pot, out-turned rim pot, everted rim, narrow neck globular pot Black and Red Ware Fine Thin: everted rim bowl, featureless rim bowl Coarse Gray Ware: out-turned rim pot, featureless rim bowl, wide-mouth pot, wide-mouth elongated neck jar Fine Gray Ware: body sherds only Coarse Red Ware: basins, everted rim wide-mouth pot, out-turned rim pot, everted rim, elongated neck jar, wide-mouth pot Medium Coarse Red Ware: everted rim wide-mouth pot, wide-mouth pot, featureless globular bowl, everted rim, narrow neck globular pot Thin Slipped Fine Red Ware: everted rim globular bowl, wide-mouth small pot Thin Slipped Coarse Red Ware: everted rim bowl, everted rim wide-mouth pot, everted rim, elongated neck small pot, featureless bowl Black Ware: body sherds only Bichrome Ware or Imitation Black and Red Ware: everted rim globular bowl Buff Ware with black painting, fine (probably Harappan) Black on Red Ware, fine (probably Harappan)

Table 6.2 cont'd.

Layer	Lot Numbers	Pottery Types/Shapes
17A	Lot numbers 4F.3008 and 4F.3012	Black and Red Ware Coarse Thick: wide-mouth pot, featureless globular bowl Black and Red Ware Fine Thin: everted rim bowl, Coarse Gray Ware: out-turned rim pot, featureless rim bowl, wide-mouth pot
17A cont'd.		Coarse Red Ware: basins, everted rim wide-mouth pot, out-turned rim pot, wide-mouth pot, featureless deep basin Medium Coarse Red Ware: everted rim wide-mouth pot Thin Slipped Fine Red Ware: everted rim globular bowl, wide-mouth small pot, wide-mouth elongated neck globular small pot Thin Slipped Coarse Red Ware: featureless bowl Malwa Ware: body sherd only
18	Lot numbers 4F.3013	Black and Red Ware Coarse Thick: body sherds only Coarse Gray Ware: wide-mouth pot Coarse Red Ware: body sherds only Medium Coarse Red Ware: everted rim wide-mouth pot Thin Slipped Fine Red Ware: body sherds only Thin Slipped Coarse Red Ware: body sherds only
19[1]	Lot numbers 4F.3016, 4F.3017, 4F.3021–23, 4F.3026	Black and Red Ware Coarse Thick: wide-mouth pot Black and Red Ware Fine Thin: everted rim bowl Coarse Gray Ware: wide-mouth pot Coarse Red Ware: basins, everted rim wide-mouth pot, dish Medium Coarse Red Ware: body sherds only Thin Slipped Fine Red Ware: everted rim globular bowl Imitation Black and Red Ware: everted rim globular bowl
20	Lot numbers 4F.3024	Black and Red Ware Fine Thin: body sherds only Coarse Gray Ware: body sherds only Coarse Red Ware: body sherds only Thin-Slipped Fine Red Ware: body sherds only
21	Lot numbers 4F.3025	Black and Red Ware Coarse Thick: body sherds only Black and Red Ware Fine Thin: body sherds only Coarse Gray Ware: out-turned rim pot Coarse Red Ware: basins Medium Coarse Red Ware: body sherds only Thin Slipped Fine Red Ware: everted rim globular bowl Thin Slipped Coarse Red Ware: everted rim bowl, everted rim narrow neck globular pot, wide-mouth pot Black Ware: body sherds only Polychrome Ware: body sherds only
22	Lot numbers 4F.3027	Black and Red Ware Fine Thin: everted rim pot Coarse Red Ware: everted rim wide-mouth pot, out-turned rim pot, featureless globular pot, wide-mouth jar Medium Coarse Red Ware: body sherds only Thin Slipped Fine Red Ware: everted rim globular bowl Thin Slipped Coarse Red Ware: everted rim bowl, everted rim bowl, wide-mouth small pot
23	Lot numbers 4F.3028	Black and Red Ware Coarse Thick: body sherds only Coarse Gray Ware: out-turned rim pot Coarse Red Ware: body sherds only Medium Coarse Red Ware: body sherds only Thin Slipped Fine Red Ware: everted rim globular bowl Thin Slipped Coarse Red Ware: body sherds only Polychrome Ware: body sherds only

cont'd.

Table 6.2 cont'd.

Layer	Lot Numbers	Pottery Types/Shapes
24	Lot numbers 4F.3029	Black and Red Ware Coarse Thick: body sherds only Black and Red Ware Fine Thin: body sherds only Coarse Gray Ware: body sherds only Coarse Red Ware: everted rim wide-mouth pot Medium Coarse Red Ware: body sherds only Thin Slipped Fine Red Ware: everted rim globular bowl Polychrome Ware: body sherds only
25	Lot numbers 4F.3030	Coarse Gray Ware: body sherds only Coarse Red Ware: wide-mouth pot Thin Slipped Fine Red Ware: body sherds only
26	Lot numbers 4F.3031	Black and Red Ware Coarse Thick: wide-mouth pot Coarse Gray Ware: wide-mouth pot, out-turned rim pot Coarse Red Ware: everted rim, elongated neck pot Medium Coarse Red Ware: body sherds only Thin Slipped Fine Red Ware: everted rim globular bowl Thin Slipped Coarse Red Ware: body sherds only Reserve Slip Ware: body sherds only Tan Ware: everted rim wide-mouth pot
27	Lot numbers 4F.3032	Black and Red Ware Coarse Thick: wide-mouth pot Coarse Gray Ware: body sherds only Coarse Red Ware: everted rim wide-mouth pot Thin Slipped Fine Red Ware: everted rim globular bowl

N.B.: The lot numbers that are missing in the list either had mixed material or belong to pit excavations.

NOTE

1. Due to the depth of the Index Trench, Layers 19 through 27 were excavated in a 1 m by 1 m area only.

7

Ceramic Sequence of Gilund (Index Trench 4F)

Lorena Giorgio

Trench 4F, situated on the western side of the higher mound of GLD-1, was excavated in part to provide an index of the pottery sequences at Gilund (see Chapter 3 for a summary of the Index Trench excavation). Studying pottery from an Index Trench can indicate the changes that took place in the life of a settlement, shifts in technology, and local and long-distance exchange. Each layer was assigned two numbers: one unique to Trench 4F, and another that connected the layers to the sequences in the rest of the mound. The lowest layers of the trench are aceramic, appear to predate the Chalcolithic occupation, and extend into the sand dune. This article describes the pottery retrieved from each layer, starting with the layer closest to the surface of the mound.

Layer 15 (Layer 2 in 4F)

The bulk of the pottery coming from this layer is represented by Coarse Red Ware including everted wide-mouth and out-turned rim pots (shapes commonly associated with Coarse Gray Ware). Body sherds carry the incised, punctured, or ridged decoration on the surface and are not slipped. Usually, the decorative motifs are located just below the upper portion of the body that has been slipped with a thick, bright red burnished slip. In this layer, the fabric of Coarse Red Ware is gritty and gray or red with large amounts of mica (found in chunks), a characteristic mostly found in the pottery belonging to the late phase of Middle Chalcolithic and Late Chalcolithic periods.

A sub-variety of Medium Coarse Red Ware was also found. The outer surface is treated with a thick red slip on the upper part, while the lower part is rusticated and unslipped and sometimes has the presence of a wash. This ware is commonly associated to the late period of Middle Chalcolithic. The fabric of this ware appears to be more compact and levigated compared to Coarse Red Ware fabrics. It normally has a gray core and a bright, burnished red slip on the outer surface. The most common shape associated with this ware is the everted rim wide-mouth pot with elongated neck. However, it is also common to find shapes that are more typical of Coarse Red Ware, such as wide-mouth pots, out-curved rim pots, and everted rim elongated neck jars. In this layer, no rims have been found. The decoration of the body sherds is executed under the slipped portion and includes incised lines, ridges, and a punctured motif.

The Black and Red Ware is present in this layer including the shape of everted rim convex bowl for the coarse thin variety and everted wide-mouth pot for the Black and Red coarse thick variety. The presence of this variety at Gilund suggests that this kind of pottery was not only used for small tablewares, such as bowls and dishes, but also for many large and medium size pots of coarse fabrics. At Gilund it appears to be both a deluxe and a utilitarian ware, in contrast to other sites. The fabric is gritty with the use of large grain (2–5 mm) tempering material of sand, quartz, quartzite, and chalcedony. The surfaces have been treated in a similar manner to those of Coarse Red Ware; they have a thick, burnished slip on the upper part, which is generally black on the upper portion of the rim and turns to a brownish red farther down the body. The lower part of the body is generally rusticated and occasionally it presents smoothed patches from contact with fire, suggesting that these vessels have been used to cook in addition to being storage vessels.

Two sherds of unburnished Black and Red Ware have been found: one body sherd and one rim of an everted rim globular bowl. This kind of ware is characterized by matte black and red surfaces; it is porous and the fabric is similar to that of the common burnished Black and Red bowls (fine with a dark gray to black core). Other sherds belonging to this variety of Black and Red Ware come from Trench 206, situated on the southwestern slope of GLD-2 mound where another step-trench has been excavated.

In Layer 15 a large number of body sherds and rims belonging to the Coarse Gray Ware were identified. The shapes are those typical of this kind of ware which is represented mostly by wide-mouth out-curved, out-turned rim pots. The surface is gray with patches due to the firing process. The thick slip is burnished and present on the upper half of the body of the vessel; the bottom part is mostly rusticated. The inner surface is unslipped and shows tracks of clay removal using a comb-like instrument. These traces are present on the inner walls of almost all the vessels made of different kinds of ware. The decoration of Coarse Gray Ware includes ridges, diamonds formed by shaping the ridges, drop-shaped punctured motifs, and incised lines.

Thin Red Slipped Ware is present in both the coarse and fine varieties, including the everted rim or featureless rim bowl made of the coarse variety and the everted rim globular bowl made of the finer one. Thin Red Slipped Ware is considered to be a deluxe ware since the clay is pure and well levigated and the vessels are well-fired. As a result they have the characteristic metallic ring and a reddish core, although it is sometimes possible to find a gray core in-between the red "borders." The color of the slip is generally plum red but occasionally tends to brownish red. The inner surface is without any slip or wash and is generally finely scraped.

Layer 16 (Layer 3 of 4F)

This layer rests above the layer with the highest pottery to soil ratio. The bulk of the pottery is represented by the Coarse Red Ware in the form of basins and pots. The ware is similar to the description above. Body sherds of Medium Coarse Ware are also present in more quantity than the Coarse Gray Ware. The Coarse Gray Ware, together with the Coarse Red Ware, is the most common ware at Gilund.

The Thin Red Slipped Coarse is present in the form of wide-mouth, narrow neck small pots, everted rim elongated neck small jars, and an out-curved pot, the latter of which is rarely associated with this kind of pottery.

Interestingly, some body sherds of Black Burnished Ware with ridges and punctured motifs are present. This ware is associated with the lower levels of Phase B at Gilund. Although this pottery has both fine and coarse varieties, the

Black Burnished Ware in this layer is fine, with little or no tempering material and with a deep black core. The surface is black slipped and highly burnished on its entire exterior surface and rim portion. The core, fabric, and surface treatment of this ware have a remarkable affinity with the Black and Red Ware. Found in the shape of bowls with convex sides and everted rims or small globular pots, this pottery can be presumed to be a deluxe ware or a ware meant for special occasions.

Layer 17 (Layer 4 of 4F)

This layer is characterized by a large amount of Black and Red Coarse Thick Ware. The shapes recognized from the rim sherds are pots with out-turned or wide-mouth rims and everted rim, narrow neck globular jars. The fabric is gritty since the clay has been mixed with small to medium size inclusions of tempering material such as sand. The core of the vessels is gray. The traces on the body sherds suggest that the body had been shaped roughly and then thinned by using tools; the excess clay on the inner surfaces has been removed by using a comb-like tool. This was a common technique to shape big vessels. The outer surfaces present a thick, light red burnished slip.

As expected, the Coarse Red variety is present in basins, pots, and jar/pot shapes, with the only exception an everted rim deep bowl, a shape not common in this ware. No differences in fabric and surface treatment have been noted. Similarly, the Coarse Gray Ware is represented by the common shapes of out-turned rim pots, everted rim, narrow neck globular pots, and wide-mouth pots. Also identified were a featureless rim and an everted rim deep bowl.

The Thin Red Slipped Ware occurs in both the fine and coarse variety. The shapes include everted rim globular bowls with ridges and punctured motifs and wide-mouth small globular pots in the fine variety, as well as featureless rim and everted rim bowls made of the coarse fabric.

Layer 17a (Layer 3a in 4F)

The only body sherd of Cream Slipped Ware recovered was found in this sub-layer. This ware, uncommon in the Ahar-Banas Complex, is treated with a thick, burnished cream slip on the outer surface and has a fine fabric with a blackish core; it produces a metallic ring similar to the Thin Red Slipped Fine Ware.

As in Layer 15 (2 of 4F), some sherds of unburnished Black and Red Ware have been found in the shape of an everted rim globular bowl and, as in Layer 3, some sherds of Black Burnished Ware.

Layer 17 (Layer 5 of 4F)

Large quantities of Black and Red Coarse Thick Ware in the form of out-turned rim and everted wide-mouth rim pots were noted in this layer. The same shape is found in the Black and Red Coarse thin variety where the only difference is the out-curved rim. Usually this variety is associated with everted rim or featureless rim bowls that present a thick, burnished slip on both the surfaces. The interior and the shoulder portion of the outer wall of the vessels are black while the rest is red or plum red, although occasionally it turns into a brownish red, tan, or chocolate. The fabric is thin, medium to fine, and with a dark gray to blackish core. The decorations are painted in white on either the interior or exterior of the vessel, possibly pre-firing. The common motifs include groups of straight and wavy lines, hatched diamonds, dots, and circles. More rarely, a solar motif has been found.

Among the common wares present in this layer are Coarse Red, Coarse Gray, and Thin Red Slipped (both fine and coarse). In addition, a sherd of Malwa Ware with black painted lines was found, indicating contact with the Deccan region.

Layer 17 (Layer 6 of 4F)

Coarse Red Ware is the most common variety in this layer, the rims of which appear to be from basins, except for one rim sherd that comes from a wide-mouth pot. As above, all the different types are encountered in this layer without any substantial difference in fabric or surface treatment. Some sherds of Black on Red have been found; the external surface is slipped with a thick, burnished deep red slip and the paintings are executed with a black pigment. The inner wall is without any slip and it presents traces of scooping clay; the fabric is coarse with a black core. The presence of these sherds indicates contact with regions to the south. In addition, this layer included two body sherds of Harappan Buff Ware painted in black. The sherds are fine in fabric with a buff core carrying a single wavy line painted in black. They indicate contact with contemporaneous Harappan sites, although it is not possible to identify which sites from visual analysis.

Layer 18 (Layer 7 of 4F)

From this layer only a few sherds have been encountered, the bulk of which are Coarse Red Ware. All types are present except for the Black and Red Coarse Thin.

Layer 19 (Layer 8 of 4F)

The pottery distribution in this layer is similar to that of Layer 18, above. In addition, two body sherds of Polychrome Ware were found. This ware is associated with the lower layers at Gilund; it is a Red Ware with a coarse fabric, but with a distinctive surface that consists of a combination of black, red, and white painted decoration mostly represented by interlaced diamonds. For this reason it is classified separately. The shapes of these vessels are difficult to identify as only body sherds have been found from the site.

Layer 20 (Layer 9 of 4F)

No pottery recovered.

Layer 21 (Layer 10 of 4F)

This layer included mostly body sherds of the common varieties of pottery. Shapes identified include basins of Coarse Red Ware; everted rim bowls with wide mouth and narrow neck, and wide-mouth small pots of Thin Red Slipped Coarse Ware; and an everted globular bowl of Thin Red Slipped Fine Ware. Two body sherds of Polychrome Ware were also found.

Layer 22 (Layer 11 of 4F)

Black and Red Coarse Thick Ware is present in the form of a rim belonging to an everted rim pot and body sherds with gritty fabric and a deep black core. The Coarse Red Ware is present mostly in the form of pots with a gritty fabric and a gray core, indicating that the vessels were low fired.

The Thin Red Slipped Ware is present in both varieties, although the common shapes, such as the everted rim globular bowl or wide-mouth small pots, do not present traces of wheel throwing.

Layer 23 (Layer 12 of 4F)

Pottery of all varieties recovered. However, only body sherds were found, so it is not possible to identify the different shapes. The sherds are not well preserved as depositional processes have almost washed out or altered the surface slip.

Layer 24 (Layer 13 of 4F)

Small quantities of pottery came from this layer. The Black and Red Coarse Thin and the Thin Red Slipped Coarse Wares were totally absent. The pottery presents the same characteristics as Layer 23 (12 of 4F), without substantial differences among the fabrics and the surface treatment. One sherd of Polychrome Ware was found.

Layer 25 (Layer 14 of 4F)

Only very small sherds of Coarse Red Ware, Coarse Gray Ware, and Thin Red Slipped Fine Ware were encountered.

Layer 26 (Layer 15 of 4F)

All common varieties of pottery were identified except the Black and Red Coarse Thin Ware. As usual, the bulk of the pottery is represented by the Red Coarse Ware with rims of an everted, elongated neck pot with incised motif. In the Coarse Gray Ware variety, the pots have out-turned and wide-mouthed rims and the fabric is coarser that that of the previous layers.

From this layer, which belongs to the earliest period of the settlement, a body sherd of Reserved Slip Ware was found. The Reserved Slip Ware is made of fine clay mixed with fine sand; it presents a buff core with a reserved slip of deep dull red. Reserved Slip Ware is also found in the lower levels at the site of Balathal, although in larger quantities than at Gilund. This may be explained by the reduced soil volume excavated at Gilund for the lower levels.

Layer 27 (Layer 16 of 4F)

No differences in pottery have been noted, as the sherds are few and not well preserved. A single sherd of Reserved Slip Ware is present.

Layers 28, 29, 30, 31, 32, 32: A small amount of pottery came from these layers. The pottery appears to be less coarse than that found in the site of Balathal.

Table 7.1. Summary of Ceramics from Index Trench

Layer	4F Layer	CRW	MCW	BRW	uBRW	CGW	TRS	BBW	MW	CSW	HBW	BORW	PW	RSW	UID
	1???														
15	2	x	X	x	x	x	x								
16	3	x	X			x	x	x							
17	3a			x				x		x					
	4???														
17	5	x		x		x	x		x						
17	6	x									x	x			
18	7	x		x		x	x								
19	8	x		x		x	x						x		
20	9														
21	10	x		x		x	x						x		
22	11	x		x			x								
23	12	x		x		x	x								
24	13	x				x							x		
25	14	x				x	x								
26	15	x		x		x	x							x	
27	16													x	

CRW: Coarse Red Ware
MCW: Medium Coarse Ware
BRW: Black and Red Ware
uBRW: unburnished Black and Red Ware
CGW: Coarse Gray Ware
TRS: Thin Red Slipped Ware
BBW: Black Burnished Ware

MW: Malwa Ware
CSW: Cream Slipped Ware
HBW: Harappan Buff Ware
BORW: Black on Red Ware
PW: Polychrome Ware
RSW: Reserve Slip Ware
UID: Unidentifiable (degraded)

Fig. 7.1. Black and Red Ware (thick) everted rim, wide-mouth pot with interior and exterior burnished slip (4F-3002a).

Fig. 7.2. Coarse Gray Ware everted rim jar/pot (4F-3002b).

Fig. 7.3. Thin Slipped Red Ware (coarse) everted rim bowl (4F-3002c).

Fig. 7.4. Coarse Red Ware, everted rim with triangular edge (4F-3002d).

Fig. 7.5. Thin Slipped Red Ware (coarse) everted rim, elongated neck jar, with interior and exterior burnished slip (4F-3002i).

Fig. 7.6. Coarse Gray Ware basin (4F-3002j).

Fig. 7.7. Coarse Red Ware jar with thick red interior and exterior slip (4F-3002k).

Fig. 7.8. Coarse Red Ware globular pot (4F-3002l).

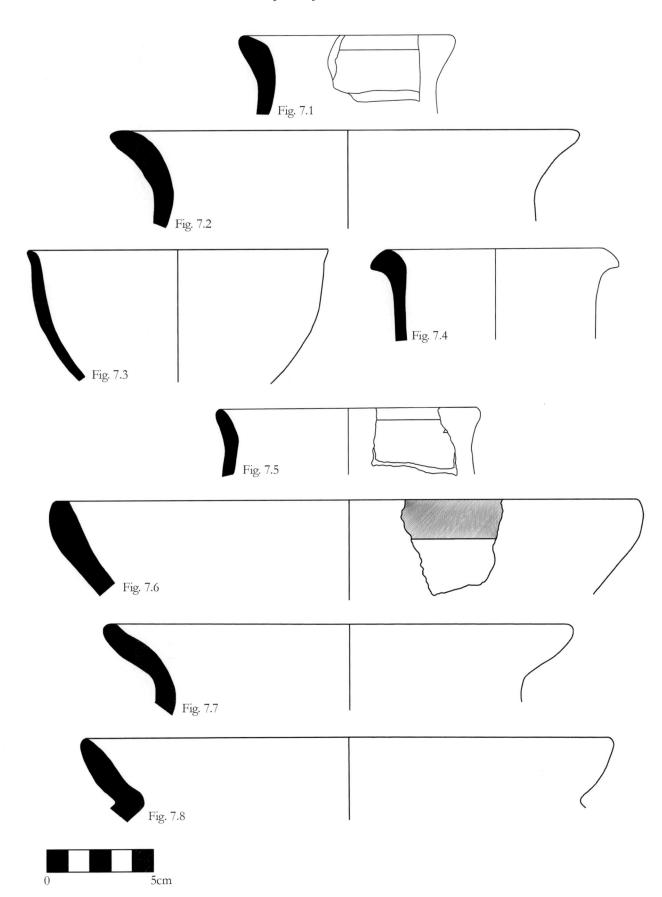

Fig. 7.1

Fig. 7.2

Fig. 7.3

Fig. 7.4

Fig. 7.5

Fig. 7.6

Fig. 7.7

Fig. 7.8

0 5cm

Fig. 7.9. Thin Slipped Red Ware (coarse) pot with interior and exterior slip (4F-3003-a).

Fig. 7.10. Coarse Gray Ware rim with thick gray slip and ridge (4F-3004a).

Fig. 7.11. Coarse Gray Ware pot with interior slip (4F-3004b).

Fig. 7.12. Thin Slipped Red Ware (coarse) small wide-mouth pot (4F-3004c).

Fig. 7.13. Coarse Red Ware stand (4F-3004e).

Fig. 7.14. Thin Slipped Red Ware (coarse) everted rim, shallow carinated bowl (4F-3005a).

Fig. 7.15. Thin Slipped Red Ware (coarse) small wide-mouth pot (4F-3005b).

Fig. 7.16. Thin Slipped Red Ware (coarse) wide-mouth pot (4F-3005c).

Fig. 7.17. Black and Red Ware everted rim pot with interior black slip and exterior red slip on upper portion; lower portion is rusticated (4F-3005e).

Fig. 7.18. Coarse Red Ware (medium) body sherd with incised and punctuated design (4F-3005f).

Fig. 7.19. Coarse Red Ware body sherd with impressions (4F-3005g).

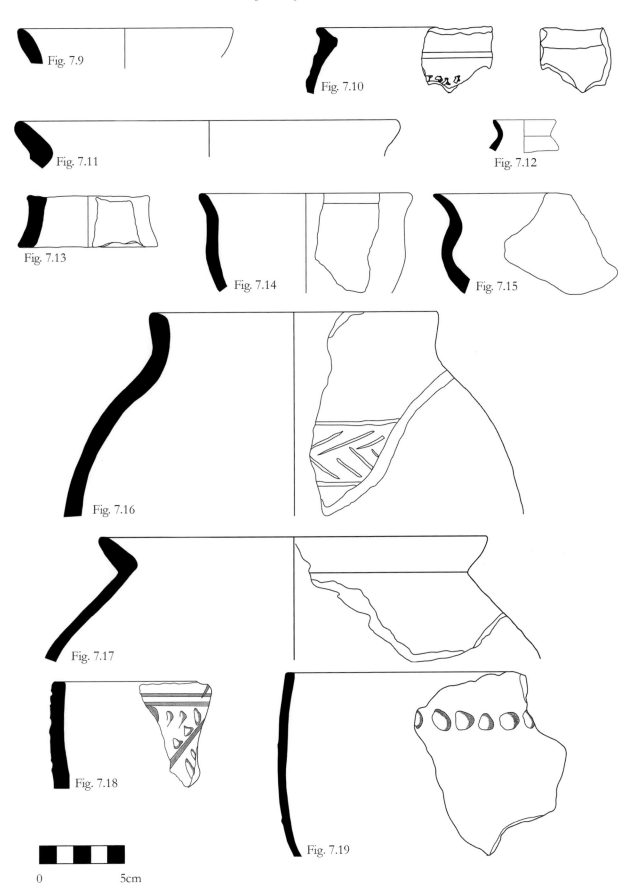

Fig. 7.9

Fig. 7.10

Fig. 7.11

Fig. 7.12

Fig. 7.13

Fig. 7.14

Fig. 7.15

Fig. 7.16

Fig. 7.17

Fig. 7.18

Fig. 7.19

0   5cm

Fig. 7.20. Black and Red Ware everted rim deep bowl with white paint (4F-3005h).

Fig. 7.21. Black and Red Ware (thin) everted rim globular pot with ridge (4F-3007a).

Fig. 7.22. Coarse Gray Ware body sherd with impressed ridge (4F-3007b).

Fig. 7.23. Coarse Gray Ware everted rim, wide-mouth pot with ridges and interior and exterior gray burnished slip (4F-3007c).

Fig. 7.24. Coarse Red Ware everted rim pot with ridges (4F-3007d).

Fig. 7.25. Coarse Red Ware basin with red burnished slip on upper portion and rusticated lower portion (4F-3007e).

Fig. 7.26. Black and Red Ware (thick) everted rim pot with ridge (4F-3007f).

Fig. 7.27. Coarse Red Ware everted rim jar with thick burnished slip (4F-3007h).

Fig. 7.28. Coarse Gray Ware pot with slip (4F-3008b).

Fig. 7.29. Coarse Gray Ware jar/pot with slip (4F-3008c).

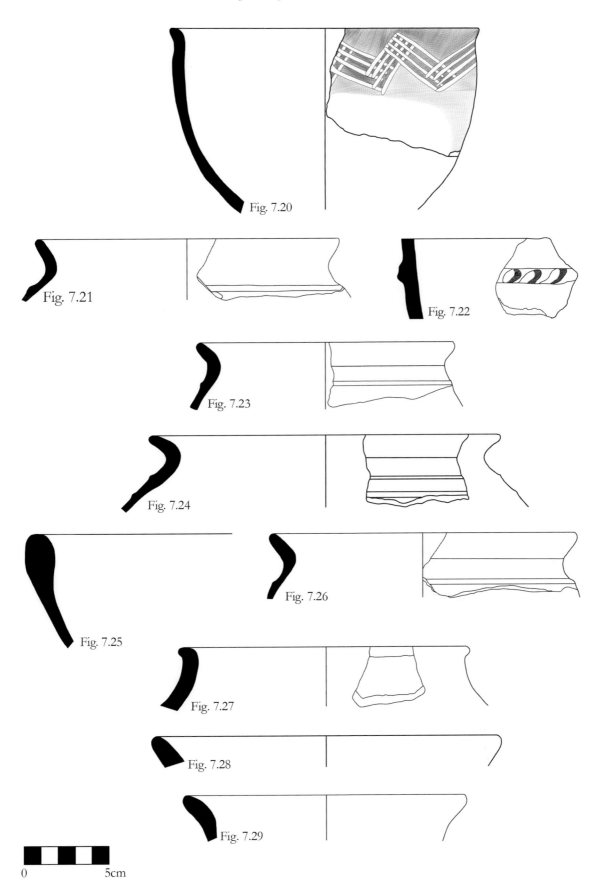

Fig. 7.20

Fig. 7.21

Fig. 7.22

Fig. 7.23

Fig. 7.24

Fig. 7.25

Fig. 7.26

Fig. 7.27

Fig. 7.28

Fig. 7.29

0 5cm

Fig. 7.30. Coarse Red Ware basin (4F-3008d).

Fig. 7.31. Coarse Red Ware (medium) everted rim globular jar/pot with interior and exterior burnished slip (4F-3008e).

Fig. 7.32. Coarse Gray Ware everted rim jar/pot with interior and exterior burnished slip (4F-3008f).

Fig. 7.33. Black and Red Ware (thick) short rimmed globular pot (4F-3009a).

Fig. 7.34. Thin Slipped Red Ware (coarse) everted rim bowl (4F-3009b).

Fig. 7.35. Thin Slipped Red Ware (coarse) bowl with ridges (4F-3009c).

Fig. 7.36. Coarse Gray Ware handle with slip on upper portion (4F-3010a).

Fig. 7.37. Black and Red Ware (thick) everted rim globular pot with ridges (4F-3010b).

Fig. 7.38. Thin Slipped Red Ware (coarse) everted rim bowl (4F-3010c).

Fig. 7.39. Coarse Red Ware everted rim globular pot (4F-3010d).

Fig. 7.40. Coarse Red Ware everted rim globular bowl (4F-3010e).

Fig. 7.41. Coarse Gray Ware everted rim bowl (4F-3010f).

Fig. 7.42. Thin Slipped Red Ware (coarse) everted rim bowl with ridge (4F-3011a).

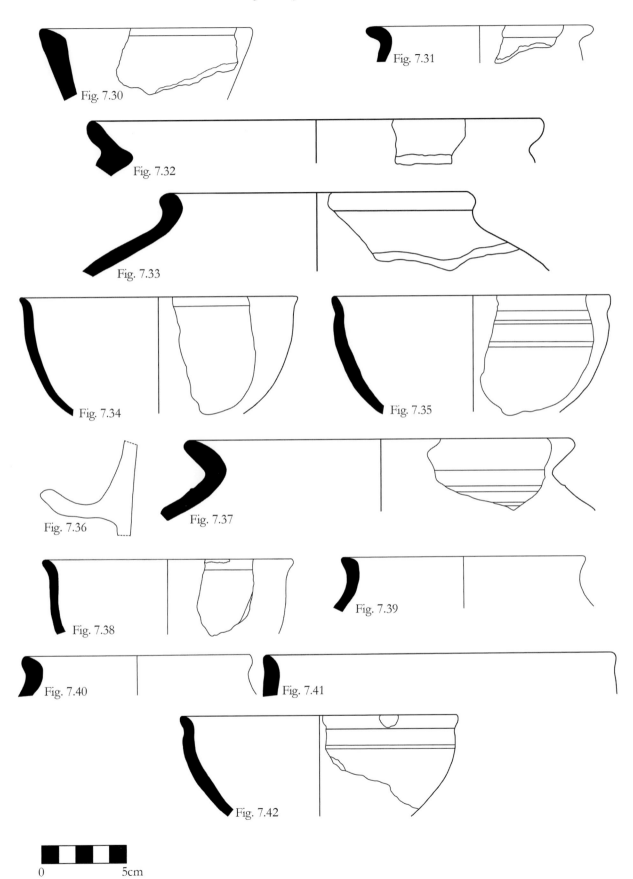

Fig. 7.30

Fig. 7.31

Fig. 7.32

Fig. 7.33

Fig. 7.34

Fig. 7.35

Fig. 7.36

Fig. 7.37

Fig. 7.38

Fig. 7.39

Fig. 7.40

Fig. 7.41

Fig. 7.42

0   5cm

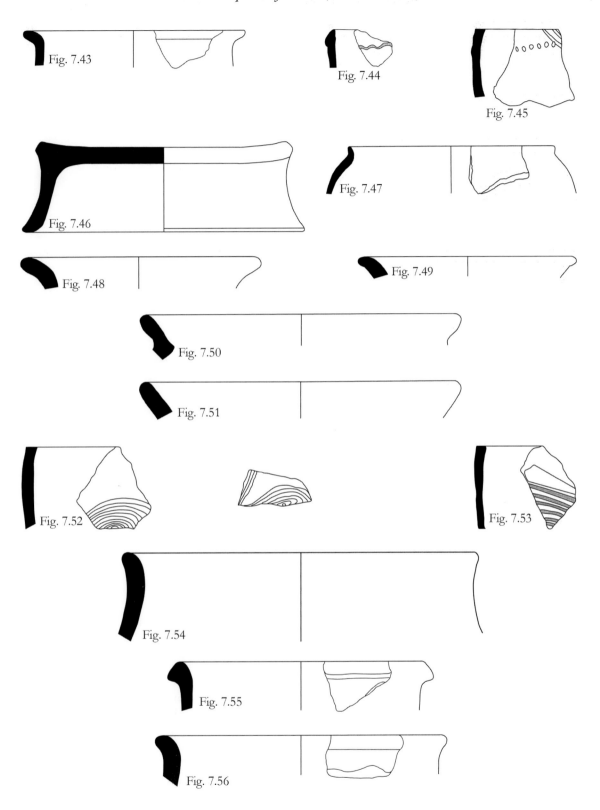

Fig. 7.43

Fig. 7.44

Fig. 7.45

Fig. 7.46

Fig. 7.47

Fig. 7.48

Fig. 7.49

Fig. 7.50

Fig. 7.51

Fig. 7.52

Fig. 7.53

Fig. 7.54

Fig. 7.55

Fig. 7.56

0   5cm

8

The Gilund Antiquities

Julie A. Hanlon

Introduction

The first excavations at Gilund conducted by B.B. Lal yielded a handful of antiquities including terracotta animal figurines and gamesmen, beads of terracotta and semiprecious stone, terracotta spheres, and stone saddle querns, and rubbers (IAR 1959–60:41-46). The 1999 to 2005 excavations unearthed a significantly larger assemblage of antiquities representing a longer range of occupation and material production at the site.

The Gilund cultural assemblage recovered during the 1999 to 2005 excavations is comprised of objects of terracotta, clay, reused pottery, stone (predominantly quartzite) and semiprecious stone, metal, shell, bone, and steatite. Terracotta and clay objects constitute the bulk of the assemblage and include figurines; personal ornaments, such as bangles and ear studs; containers of various sorts; and evidence of metallurgy and pottery technology, such as copper molds and dabbers. Antiquities of reused pottery consist of game pieces, ground discs (hopscotches), perforated discs, as well as graffiti on pottery and potter's marks.

Stone objects include beads of carnelian and other semiprecious stone, bead polishers, stone spheres (slingballs), vessel fragments, a variety of grinding stones, as well as a vast array of lithics (see Raczek, this volume). Metal objects found at Gilund include bangles, bells, chisels, coins, agricultural implements, points, nails, and rings. Shell-working is represented by bangle fragments, beads, inlay pieces, and worked shells. A number of chipped and polished bones were also uncovered. Overall, the artifacts range in antiquity from Prehistoric lithics and pottery to Medieval coins.

Methodology

The first step in the organization of these antiquities took place in the field in the midst of excavation. Antiquities were placed in paper envelopes and labeled according to their date of excavation, trench, lot number, quadrant and layer (if applicable), depth, and material. While in the field, these antiquities were logged into an antiquities register and given a two-part antiquity number comprised of the field season number and artifact number. For example, the 56th antiquity registered during the second season of excavation (2000–2001) received the number S2.056.

Organization and analysis of these artifacts continued at Deccan College Post-Graduate and Research Institute, Pune. The antiquities register was entered into an Excel spreadsheet. The artifacts were removed from their envelopes, washed, relabeled, measured, photographed, and placed into plastic boxes for permanent housing. Many of the plastic boxes were padded with Ethafoam. The labels were written with black ultra fine point Sharpie permanent markers on pieces of Tyvek and glued to the artifacts or to the Ethafoam casing. The exteriors of the boxes were also clearly labeled using black fine point Sharpie permanent markers. The boxes were additionally padded with polyester batting wrapped in Tyvek. As each artifact was measured and photographed, this information was entered into the Excel spreadsheet along with a general description of the object. At the end of the cataloguing and curation process the information available in the spreadsheet included: object classification, antiquity number, photo file name, date of excavation, mound, trench, quadrant, lot number, layer (if known), depth (from datum), period, material, measurements (length, width, height), other comments, and general description. The boxes were placed in large metal trunks along with a printed copy of an inventory and the spreadsheet.

One of the more difficult aspects in organizing the Gilund antiquities was classification. The first point of reference was the excavator's initial classification written on the envelope. A. Ghosh's An Encyclopaedia of Indian Archaeology (1990) was consulted for defining and standardizing terminology. Guidance and advice on the classification was provided by Dr. Vasant Shinde. In most cases the identification of the object is quite clear, e.g., terracotta bangle. In other cases, the use of the object is debatable or unknown. In these cases a general descriptive designation (e.g., "ground disc") was used instead of a more specific designation. Although more neutral terminology was chosen in these instances, the original designation has been retained in parenthesis (e.g., "hopscotch") to enable comparison with other sites in the region that use this classification terminology. For a comparison of the Gilund antiquities in relation to other Ahar-Banas sites in Rajasthan, see Hanlon 2010.

Terracotta Objects

Terracotta Figurines (pp. 114–121)

Like other sites associated with the Ahar-Banas culture, Gilund yielded a large number of terracotta figurines, particularly bull/cattle figurines. They are most often of fired terracotta, but there are also a number of unfired clay specimens. There is a significant variety stylistically within the entire collection, e.g., the way the face, legs, and hump are shaped; the range in size (some are quite delicate, while others are thick and heavy); and whether or not the artisan added such details as ears under the horns, or incised eyes, nose, and mouth. In particular, the humped bull figurines share stylistic affinities with those recovered at Ahar (Sankalia, Deo, and Ansari 1969: fig. 109, Nos. 1, 3, 4, 6, 7, 12), Ojiyana (Meena and Tripathi 2001; Meena and Tripathi 2001–2002: fig. 9, fig. 11), and Purani Marmi (Misra et al. 1993: fig. 1) (see also Hanlon 2010).

We are not certain of the socio-cultural, religious, or economic uses of these figurines. Only one animal figurine has signs of perforation, and no toy carts have been discovered. The majority were found in Chalcolithic habitation contexts. An analysis of the Gilund figurines is presented in the author's M.Phil thesis "The Gilund Terracottas: A New Look at the Ahar Culture in Rajasthan and Madhya Pradesh" (Hanlon 2006). Of the 63 Chalcolithic zoomorphic figurines examined in this study, 46 (73%) are damaged. Of these, 34 are missing their head and/or rear half,

while the remaining 12 consist simply of a head and/or front torso. However, none of the pieces fit together; that is, none of the heads fit the damaged bodies. Only 17 (about 27%) of the 63 figurines may be classified as "nearly complete" in that they are only missing bits of horns and legs, i.e., places of clear structural weakness.

Similar situations have been observed in the Neolithic villages of 'Ain Gazal in Jordan (ca. 8300–6000 BC), Çatal Höyük in Anatolia (ca. 7200–6400 BC), and Hajji Firuz Tepe in Iran (ca. 6000–5000 BC). In all of the above cases, scholars have suggested that the deliberate breakage and subsequent disposal of the figurines was linked to ritual (Schmandt-Basserat 1997, Hamilton 1996, Voigt 2000). The archaeological context of Chalcolithic Gilund is clearly much later (ca. 3000–1700 BC) and separated by 3,000 to 4,000 km of land. However, despite the temporal and spatial separation of these cultures, they were all early agro-pastoralists who seem to have had a preoccupation with livestock. These cross-cultural comparisons therefore provide a useful point of reference for looking at the Gilund terracottas. Furthermore, the use of hand-modeled figurines in domestic ritual has been documented in India in both historical and modern contexts (Jayaswal 1987, 1989, Jayaswal and Krishna 1986, Shah 1992).

Of the 34 headless figurines, 6 were found in pit contexts (Trenches 6 [two pits],[1] 20, 25, 305, and 310). None of the heads came from pit contexts. Of the 17 nearly complete figurines, 6 were from pit contexts (Trenches 6, 7, 8, 9, and 12). In addition, 6 of the 41 figurine horns came from pit contexts. However, we need to keep in mind that these contexts are not well defined. They may have been dug for the purpose of burying these figurines or simply as places for general refuse.

Because many of the figurines are damaged, it makes species identification slightly tenuous (see Wengrow 2003). The humped animals are easily identified as zebu, or humped cattle (*Bos indicus*), and are the most numerous, making up about 44% of the collection. Twelve humpless cattle have been identified on the basis of shape (often the rump is raised, bodies are generally stocky), length of tail, and similarity in design to the humped cattle figurines. Animal figurines, as a general category separate from bull/cattle figurines, comprise approximately 29% of the figurines. However, one must also take into account that many of these figurines are fragmentary and may represent humped cattle or humpless cattle, or some other species of quadruped such as sheep, goat, or dog. There are also 3 stylized figurines, which are reminiscent of the type found at Kayatha (Ansari and Dhavalikar 1975). Ansari and Dhavalikar (1975:130) suggest that these stylized bulls, characterized by conical bodies and large horns, were used as ritual objects.

Schmandt-Besserat (1997) notes that the horns found at 'Ain Gazal correspond well to the characteristic shape and length of the living species: "Bovine horns are represented as stocky and curving frontward; those of wild goats are accurately indicated by a marked anterior spine and sharp curvature. Ram horns are semicircular, while those of gazelles elegantly sweep backwards" (Schmandt-Besserat 1997:49–50). Unfortunately, most of the horns on the Gilund specimens have broken off. The horns found detached from their original bodies do show a variety of thicknesses and shapes. However, it is uncertain whether these shapes are reflective of species.

The distribution of figurines at Gilund is clustered on mound GLD-2 in the areas to the north and west of the parallel walls, which date from the Middle and Late Chalcolithic Phases (Fig. 8.1). Figurines are particularly concentrated in Tr. 6 (10 figurines including 1 stylized, and 1 horn), Tr. 25 (10 figurines, and 1 horn), and Tr. 35 (11 figurines plus 1 stylized, and 11 horns). As there was only 1 figurine recovered from the "burned houses" on top of GLD-2, which date to the Late Chalcolithic, it seems that the cattle figurines are most concentrated in the Middle Chalcolithic Phase. On the one hand, this concentration of figurines near the parallel walls may be a result of the intensity of excavation in this area. On the other hand, considering that much of the area around the parallel walls was already excavated by B.B. Lal during the 1959–60 excavations, the high concentrations may be more significant. Outside of this area of concentration, figurines occur sporadically. No Chalcolithic figurines were found on mound GLD-1, nor were any recovered from Area III on the western slope of GLD-2, or from Area II on the southern slope. Outside of this central area only 1 horn and 2 bulls were recovered from the five trenches excavated in Area IV (i.e., pyrotechnic or industrial area) on the far southern slope of GLD-2.

Within the trenches, the figurines occur in association with domestic objects (see Table 8.1). It is notable how often they occur alongside hammerstones or agricultural implements like grinding stones. In a few instances they occur in layers with rectilinear containers (votive tanks) and/or small lamps (votive lamps) (Tr. 7, 12, 32, and 35). Despite the aim of this exercise, no clear patterns of association stand out. The context of a layer is perhaps too broad to make any real inferences about function or direct association. However, at a very general level, we can state that figurines occur in households alongside the general assemblage of items of daily use. It is worth noting that excavations at the Ahar period site of Mahidpur (Ali, Trivedi, and Solanki 2004) revealed terracotta cattle figurines found in domestic contexts, in one instance in association with a chulha (a clay/brick hearth) and a number of pestle stones and saddle querns (Ali, Trivedi, and Solanki 2004:25, 29).

Whether these figurines were conventional household items or had ritual value, their proliferation suggests the vital role of cattle in the Ahar-Banas agro-pastoral culture. (See Tables 8.2, 8.3, and 8.4.)

Personal Ornaments
Ear Spools (pp. 120–121)

A total of eight ear spools were recovered during excavations. Of these, 7 are made from terracotta and 1 is of unfired clay. Four come from the Middle Chalcolithic, 1 from the Late Chalcolithic, and 2 from the Early Historic (Table 8.5). One is a surface find, but based on stylistic similarities it is likely from the Late Chalcolithic. The ear spools vary in length from 1.13 to 3.22 cm and in diameter from 1.26 to 2.61 cm. Several of the ear spools are perforated and therefore may have served as beads or another type of ornament. However, their classification here as ear ornaments is based on the classification of similar materials from Ahar (Sankalia, Deo, and Ansari 1969: fig. 106).

Ear Studs (pp. 122–123)

A total of six ear studs were recovered during excavations. Ear studs are differentiated from ear spools on the basis of size and shape. Ear studs are small and button-shaped, whereas ear spools resemble modern spools of thread and have an hourglass shape. Three ear studs are from the Middle Chalcolithic, and 3 are from the Late Chalcolithic (Table 8.7). All of the ear studs were recovered from Chalcolithic trenches on GLD-2 and all are made of terracotta. The ear studs vary in length from 0.58 to 1.45 cm and in diameter from 0.70 to 1.36 cm.

Bangles (pp. 122–123)

Fifteen terracotta bangle fragments were discovered during the excavations. Three come from the Middle Chalcolithic, 2 from the Late Chalcolithic, and 10 from the Early Historic (Table 8.6). Most of the bangles are plain, although 2 show signs of red paint (S2.070, S2.053), and another has a ridged design (S3.165). The fragments vary in length from 1.18 to 3.26 cm and in diameter from 0.51 to 0.89 cm for the round bangles, and in width from 0.54 to 0.82 cm for the flat/oval bangles.

Ornament (pp. 122–123)

One distinctive terracotta ornament was recovered as a surface find on mound GLD-2. It resembles a serrated

Table 8.1. Materials Associated with Figurines by Trench and Layer

Trench	Number of Figurines and Horns	Associated Materials and Contexts of Figurines and Horns
5	1 humped cattle	• 1 humped cattle found in layer with 2 hammer stones, 1 sphere, 2 terracotta beads, 1 terracotta disc
6	1 animal, 5 cattle, 4 humped cattle, 1 stylized cattle; 1 horn	• 1 animal figurine found in pit with steatite bead • 1 horn in found in pit with carnelian bead • 2 humped cattle and stylized bull found in layer with 1 shell bangle, 4 grinding stones, 5 hammer stones, 4 pounders/rubber stones, 1 copper bead, 1 shell bead, and 1 worked sherd • 1 animal, 2 cattle, and 1 humped cattle found in layer with 3 hammer stones, 1 quern fragment, 1 sphere, 1 terracotta bead, and 1 copper blade fragment • 1 cattle figurine found singly in pit • 1 humped cattle found singly in pit
7	1 animal; 3 horns	• 1 animal figurine found singly in pit • 3 horns found in layer with copper bangle, 5 pounders/rubber stones, 10 hammer stones, 6 grinding stones, 2 lithics, 1 small complete pot, 1 rectilinear container, 1 polished bone, 1 worked shell, 2 ground discs, 1 game piece
8	1 animal, 1 cattle, 1 humped cattle; 3 horns	• 1 animal found in layer with 4 grinding stones, 2 rubber stones, 3 lithics • 2 horns found in layer with 2 terracotta spheres, 3 querns, 3 grinding stones, 3 hammer stones, 4 steatite beads, 1 bone bead, 1 game piece, and 1 lithic • 1 humped cattle and 1 horn found in layer with 5 hammer stones, 4 rubber stones, 2 quern fragments, 1 piece of incised red slate, 3 game pieces, 5 steatite beads, 1 carnelian bead, 1 ground disc, and 1 perforated terracotta disc • 1 cattle figurine found in a pit with 1 hammer stone
9	3 animals, 1 cattle; 2 horns	• 1 horn found in layer with steatite bead • 1 animal figurine found in layer with terracotta gamesman • 1 cattle figurine found in pit with 3 steatite beads, 4 hammer stones, and 1 quern fragment • 1 horn found singly • 2 animal figurines found in layer with 2 hammer stones, 1 rubber stone, 1 pestle, 1 ground disc, and 5 steatite beads
11	1 horn	• 1 horn found in pit with 1 terracotta gamesman and 2 steatite beads
12	1 humped cattle; 2 horns	• 1 horn found in layer with 2 steatite beads, 1 terracotta bead, 1 hammer stone, 1 stone pendant, 1 terracotta pendant, 1 unidentified stone ornament, 4 lithics, and 1 small lamp • 1 humped cattle figurine found in pit with steatite microbead • 1 horn found in associated lot with 1 rubber stone, 1 steatite bead, 1 clay lump, and 1 stamp-shaped object of sun-dried clay with a wavy-line pattern on the bottom
13	2 humped cattle; 1 horn	• 1 horn found in section cleaning • 2 humped cattle found in layer with 1 dabber, 2 grinding stones, 3 hammer stones, and 1 terracotta sphere
18	1 humped cattle	• 1 humped cattle found in layer with 1 hammer stone
20	3 animals	• 1 animal found singly in pit, with 1 animal figurine in layer above with 1 stone sphere • 1 animal found singly
21	1 humped cattle	• 1 humped cattle found in layer with steatite bead
25	2 cattle, 8 humped cattle; 1 horn	• 4 humped cattle and 1 horn found in layer with 1 grinding stone, 1 dabber, 1 terracotta sphere, 1 stone bead, and 1 steatite microbead • 1 humped cattle found singly in pit fill • 2 cattle and 3 humped cattle found in layer with 1 perforated disc, 2 terracotta spheres, and 1 dabber
27	1 animal	• 1 animal found in layer with 17 lithics, 2 ground stone fragments, and 1 possible seal impression
30	3 animals, 1 cattle, 1 humped cattle; 1 horn	• 1 humped cattle and 1 horn found in layer with 1 game piece and 1 terracotta bead • 1 animal found in layer with 7 game pieces, 2 ground discs, 1 perforated disc, 1 stone sphere, and 1 rubber stone • 2 animals and 1 cattle found in layer with 1 hammer stone and 1 potsherd with graffiti

Table 8.1 (cont'd.)

Trench	Number of Figurines and Horns	Associated Materials and Contexts of Figurines and Horns
31	2 horns	• 1 horn found in layer with 1 carnelian bead, 1 terracotta bead, 1 decorative piece, and 1 lithic • 1 horn found in the baulk with 1 perforated stone
32	1 humped cattle	• 1 humped cattle found in layer with 2 rectilinear containers, 5 ground discs, 1 perforated disc, 2 rubber stones, 3 lithics, 1 decorative piece, 1 terracotta bead, 1 sherd of pottery with graffiti, 1 quern and 6 quern fragments
34	4 humped cattle, 1 stylized cattle; 1 horn	• 1 humped cattle found in layer with 2 worked shells, 1 shell bangle, and 1 terracotta bead • 1 humped cattle and 1 horn found together on a floor • 2 humped cattle found in layer with 1 rubber stone, 1 polisher, and 1 pot sherd with graffiti • 1 stylized cattle found in layer with 11 worked shells, 3 hammer stones, 2 steatite beads, 3 miniature vessel fragments, 1 terracotta bead, and 1 crucible
35	5 animals, 2 cattle, 2 humped cattle, 1 stylized cattle; 11 horns	• 3 horns found in layer with 4 worked shells, 1 dabber, 2 rubbers, 4 mullers, 1 polisher, 1 quern fragment, 3 hammer stones, 2 terracotta spheres, and 13 lithics • 1 animal and 6 horns found in layer with 1 carnelian bead, 4 lithics, and 1 shell inlay piece • 2 animals, 1 cattle, 1 humped cattle found in layer with 14 lithics, 1 stone bead, 2 terracotta bead fragments, 10 hammer stones, 1 ground disc, 3 steatite microbeads, 2 mullers,1 polisher, 1 rubber, 1 copper bangle fragment, 1 copper ring fragment, 1 sharpener, 1 stone sphere, 1 terracotta sphere, 2 worked shells, and 1 rectilinear container • 1 animal found singly • 1 horn found in quad scraping with 1 steatite microbead • 1 horn found in layer with 1 stone bead and 1 hammer stone • 1 animal, 1 cattle, 1 humped cattle, 1 stylized cattle found in layer with 12 lithics, 1 polisher, 1 grinding stone, 4 hammer stones, 1 rubber, 1 sharpener, 1 jar stopper, 2 stone beads, 1 complete miniature pot, 1 pot sherd with graffiti
305	1 cattle	• 1 cattle figurine in pit with steatite microbead
310	2 humped cattle; 1 horn	• 1 horn in pit with 1 worked sherd and 1 pot sherd with graffiti • 1 humped cattle figurine found singly in pit • 1 humped cattle figurine found in pit with 2 ground discs

wheel. Its function has not been determined. One possibility is that it may have been a personal ornament. The center is perforated. It is 4.65 cm long, 3.6 cm wide, and 2.25 cm thick. Although it lacks stratigraphic context, it is likely a Late Chalcolithic or Early Historic antiquity based on the production quality and its point of discovery on GLD-2.

Toys/Games

Miniature Vessels (Toy Pots) (pp. 124–125)

Nine miniature vessels and miniature vessel fragments were recovered from Chalcolithic levels at Gilund (Table 8.8). Six come from the Middle Chalcolithic and 3 from the Late Chalcolithic. They are hand-molded of both terracotta and unfired clay. All of the miniature vessels were found in domestic contexts. They range in diameter from 1.92 to 4.43 cm and in height from 1.28 to 2.73 cm.

Discs and Gamesmen (pp. 124–125)

Eight discs and 8 gamesmen were recovered during excavations. These discs differ from the ground discs in the reused pottery section because they are made entirely of terracotta and have been purposefully shaped into round discs. The conical and cylindrical gamesmen may have been used in a game similar to chess, like pachisi. Most of the conical and cylindrical gamesmen are made of red terracotta with a light slip. Nine come from the Middle Chalcolithic, 1 from the Late Chalcolithic, and 2 from the Early Historic (Table 8.9). Four were found in mixed or erosional contexts.

Perforated Terracotta Discs (Wheels) (pp. 126–127)

Eight perforated terracotta discs are similar in form and material to objects classified as "wheels" at Ahar (Sankalia, Deo, and Ansari 1969: fig. 111). Two come from the

Table 8.2. Distribution of Figurines by Period

Period	Humped Bulls	Bulls	Other Figurines/ Fragments	Horns	Trench Total
Middle Chalcolithic	13	4	18	24	59
Late Chalcolithic	18	8	9	13	48
Early Historic	1	0	1	3	5
Erosion/Surface	7	0	3	1	11
TOTALS:	39	12	31	41	123

Table 8.3. Distribution of Animal Figurines by Trench

Trench	Period	Humped Bulls	Bulls	Other Figurines/ Fragments	Horns	Trench Total
5	Late Chalcolithic	1	0	0	0	1
6	Late Chalcolithic	4	4	3	1	12
7	Late Chalcolithic	0	0	1	3	4
8	Late Chalcolithic	1	1	1	3	6
9	Middle Chalcolithic	0	1	3	2	6
11	Middle Chalcolithic	0	0	0	1	1
12	Middle Chalcolithic	1	0	0	2	3
13	Middle Chalcolithic	2	0	0	1	3
18	Middle Chalcolithic	1	0	1	0	2
20	Middle Chalcolithic	0	0	4	0	4
21	Middle Chalcolithic	1	0	0	0	1
25	Late Chalcolithic	8	2	0	1	11
27	Middle Chalcolithic	0	0	1	0	1
29	Late Chalcolithic	1	0	0	0	1
30	Late Chalcolithic	1	1	3	1	6
31	Late Chalcolithic	0	0	0	2	2
32	Late Chalcolithic	1	0	0	1	2
34	Middle Chalcolithic	4	0	1	1	6
35	Middle Chalcolithic	2	2	7	11	22
39	Middle Chalcolithic	0	0	0	1	1
69	Late Chalcolithic	1	0	0	0	1
75	Late Chalcolithic	0	0	0	1	1
105	Middle Chalcolithic	0	0	0	2	2
205	Middle Chalcolithic	0	0	1	0	1
305	Middle Chalcolithic	0	1	0	0	1
310	Middle Chalcolithic	2	0	0	1	3
4A	Early Historic	0	0	0	2	2
4B	Early Historic	1	0	1	1	3
4D	Late Chalcolithic	0	0	1	0	1
4E	Middle Chalcolithic	0	0	0	1	1
4F	Middle Chalcolithic	0	0	0	1	1
TOTALS:		32	12	28	40	112

Table 8.4. Erosion/Surface Finds*

Area	Humped Bulls	Bulls	Other Figurines/ Fragments	Horns	Trench Total
	2	0	0	0	2
GLD-2	4	0	2	0	6
4H	0	0	1	0	1
4J	1	0	0	0	1
4K	0	0	0	1	1
TOTALS:	7	0	3	1	11

The layers in which these items were discovered contained a combination of Early Historic, Late Chalcolithic, and Middle Chalcolithic materials.

Table 8.5. Distribution of Ear Spools by Trench

Trench	Period	Ear Spools
19	Middle Chalcolithic	1 (unfired clay)
203	Middle Chalcolithic	2
302	Middle Chalcolithic	1
201	Late Chalcolithic	1
4A	Early Historic	2
Surface	Late Chalcolithic?	1

Table 8.6. Distribution of Ear Studs by Trench

Trench	Period	Ear Studs
20	Middle Chalcolithic	1
35	Middle Chalcolithic	1
302	Middle Chalcolithic	1
5	Late Chalcolithic	1
69	Late Chalcolithic	1
210	Late Chalcolithic	1

Table 8.7. Distribution of Terracotta Bangle Fragments by Trench

Trench	Period	Bangles
101	Middle Chalcolithic	1
104	Middle Chalcolithic	1
105	Middle Chalcolithic	1
6	Late Chalcolithic	1
4D	Late Chalcolithic	1
4A	Early Historic	1
4B	Early Historic	2
4C	Early Historic	5
S1	Early Historic	2

Table 8.8. Distribution of Miniature Vessels (Toy Pots) by Trench

Trench	Period	Material(s)	Quantity
5	Late Chalcolithic	Unfired Clay	1
7	Late Chalcolithic	Unfired Clay	1
13	Middle Chalcolithic	TC	1
17	Middle Chalcolithic	Unfired Clay	1
34	Middle Chalcolithic	Terracotta (1), Unfired Clay (2)	3
105	Middle Chalcolithic	TC	1
4H / 4I	Late Chalcolithic	TC	1

Middle Chalcolithic contexts, 5 from the Late Chalcolithic, and 1 from the surface (Table 8.10). Some of these discs fit the typology of toy cart wheels because they are molded and have either incised spokes or raised centers around the perforation. However, we have not found any associated toy carts. If these objects were not associated with toy carts, they could have been used as ornaments, loom weights, or spindle whorls. Signs of wear around the central perfora-

tions, for example S1.388, suggest that they were indeed used for such purposes. In addition, several examples are particularly thick (approximately 1.25 cm) and have very wide perforations through the centers. These objects may have been used for a different purpose, such as net sinkers.

Votive/Ritual Objects

Small Lamps (Votive Lamps) (pp. 126–127)

Thirteen round, shallow lamps were discovered during excavations (Table 8.11). They were originally categorized as "votive lamps" due to their typological similarity with diyas (earthen lamps), which are commonly used in Indian religious practices. Three are from the Middle Chalcolithic, and 10 are from the Late Chalcolithic. All of these small lamps were discovered in habitation contexts, and it is possible that their use was not associated with ritual at all. Overall, the lamps may be divided into three types:

Table 8.9. Distribution of Discs and Gamesmen by
Trench

Trench	Period	Shape	Quantity
5	Late Chalcolithic	Disc	1
9	Middle Chalcolithic	Disc	1
11	Middle Chalcolithic	Conical	1
27	Middle Chalcolithic	Disc	1
34	Middle Chalcolithic	Conical	1
39	Middle Chalcolithic	Cylindrical	1
105	Middle Chalcolithic	Disc	1
203	Middle Chalcolithic	Disc (1), Conical (1)	2
4C	Early Historic	Disc	2
4F	Middle Chalcolithic	Disc	1
4I	Mixed	Conical	1
4K	Mixed	Conical	3
TOTAL:			16

Table 8.10. Distribution of Perforated
Terracotta Discs (Wheels) by Trench

Trench	Period	Quantity
8	Late Chalcolithic	1
25	Late Chalcolithic	2
33	Late Chalcolithic	1
39	Middle Chalcolithic	1
74	Late Chalcolithic	1
101	Middle Chalcolithic	1
Surface	?	1

Table 8.11. Distribution of Small Lamps (Votive Lamps)
by Trench

Trench	Period	Type	Quantity
5	Late Chalcolithic	2. pinched edges	1
7	Late Chalcolithic	2. pinched edges	1
12	Middle Chalcolithic	1. round with raised edges	1
25	Late Chalcolithic	2. pinched edges	1
35	Middle Chalcolithic	3. square	1
71	Late Chalcolithic	2. pinched edges	1
201	Late Chalcolithic	1. round	1
202	Middle Chalcolithic	1. round (1), round with raised edges (1)	2
203	Middle Chalcolithic	1. round	1
210	Late Chalcolithic	2. pinched edges	1
4D	Late Chalcolithic	1. round	1
S1*	Late Chalcolithic?	1. round with raised edges	1
TOTAL:			13

This lamp was found in a pit sealed by Layer 1. S1 is a trench that was opened on the side of GLD-1 to follow the circumference of the wall. It contains a mixture of Early Historic erosion, Late Chalcolithic materials, and part of the fortification wall from the Middle Chalcolithic period.

1. Round: simple round dishes, often blackened on the inside from burning. Some have a ridge around the edge and are flat in the middle.
2. Pinched Edges: these lamps are round with edges pinched into little triangles.

3. Square: there is only one of this type, and it was difficult to decide whether or not to classify it with the small rectilinear containers. However, it is quite shallow and more likely served as a lamp.

*Rectilinear Containers
(Votive Tanks) (pp. 126–129)*

At Gilund we discovered a number of small rectilinear containers with rounded insides. Many have incised graffiti on the outside. Ghosh (1990:277) defines "votive tanks" as "hand-modeled terracotta miniature tanks and/or shrines, used as popular ritual objects." However, he also notes that most of these objects come from Early Historic contexts, that is, between the 3rd century BC and the 4th century AD. At Gilund, similar objects, which we have chosen to call "rectilinear containers," were discovered in Chalcolithic contexts: 3 in the Middle Chalcolithic, and 6 in the Late Chalcolithic (Table 8.12). As such, it is possible that they may represent a different class of objects, and may not have been associated with ritual.

Table 8.12. Distribution of Rectilinear Containers (Votive Tanks) by Trench

Trench	Period	Graffiti / Decoration	Quantity
7	Late Chalcolithic	X or upside-down V (top broken)	1
25	Late Chalcolithic	Incised finger nail marks on 1 corner	1
32	Late Chalcolithic	None	1
32	Late Chalcolithic	Incised X	1
34	Middle Chalcolithic	Incised V design	1
34	Middle Chalcolithic	Incised V design in 2 horizontal bands	1
75	Late Chalcolithic	Incised V design	1
4F	Middle Chalcolithic	Incised zigzag design	1
4H	Late Chalcolithic	Upside-down incised V on 2 sides, X on 1 side, and upside-down V with row of punctured dots	1
TOTAL:			9

Table 8.13. Distribution of Molds

Trench	Period	Quantity
5	Late Chalcolithic	1
69	Late Chalcolithic	1
75	Late Chalcolithic	1
112	Late Chalcolithic	1
202	Middle Chalcolithic	1
203	Middle Chalcolithic	1
209	Late Chalcolithic	1
4B	Early Historic	1
	Late Chalcolithic	1
TOTAL:		9

Molds and Crucibles

Molds (pp. 128–129)

These antiquities were originally designated as lamps and containers based on the classification of similar materials from Ahar (Sankalia, Deo, and Ansari 1969: fig. 107, no. 6, fig. 115, nos. 1–3, pl. XVIII). Upon closer inspection, we realized that these were not lamps, but copper molds. They are similar in size and exceptionally thick to withstand the heat of molten metal. In addition, several are broken, likely as a result of removing the copper ingot. (See Table 8.13.)

Crucibles (pp. 128–129)

During excavations a number of unique cylindrical containers were discovered. These were identified as cru-cibles in the field because they resemble the shape of crucibles. However, while some show signs of burning, none of the objects appear to have been exposed to high heat. Therefore, if they indeed are crucibles associated with glass or metal work, they had not yet been put to use as such. All of these objects are from the Middle Chalcolithic and were found on the eastern slope of GLD-2, away from the potential "pyrotechnic center." One of the objects is of unfired clay, and the other 2 are of terracotta. They range in diameter from 3.11 to 5.59 cm and in height from 3.84 to 4.55 cm.

Vitrified Crucible Fragments (pp. 130–131)

A total of 6 vitrified fragments were discovered in Area III at Gilund. They are blackened to the point that the clay has become like pumice, and one of the fragments still has pieces of what appears to be copper attached to the inside. It is likely that these fragments were once part of one or more crucibles used in the smelting of copper. Reconstruction was attempted, but none of the fragments fit together. Four of the 6 come from a Middle Chalcolithic trench.

Dabbers and Stoppers

Dabbers (pp. 130–131)

A total of 8 objects were classified as dabbers on the basis of form. Dabbers were often used by potters to widen pots before firing. The objects classified as dabbers fit the characteristic shape and general description of dabbers outlined by A. Ghosh (1990:329). However, several such objects discovered at Gilund are of unfired clay, and therefore would not have been strong enough to support the vessel

Excavations at Gilund

Table 8.14. Distribution of Dabbers by Trench

Trench	Period	Material	Quantity
13	Middle Chalcolithic	Unfired clay	1
20	Middle Chalcolithic	Unfired clay	1
25	Late Chalcolithic	Unfired clay	1
25	Late Chalcolithic	Poorly fired terracotta	1
35	Middle Chalcolithic	Unfired clay	1
4A	Early Historic	Poorly fired terracotta	1
4B	Early Historic	Poorly fired terracotta	1
4D	Middle Chalcolithic	Terracotta	1
TOTAL:			8

Table 8.15. Distribution of Round Lumps

Trench	Period	Object	Material	Quantity
9	Middle Chalcolithic	Bun-shaped lump	Unfired clay	1
12	Middle Chalcolithic	Lump	Unfired clay	1
39	Middle Chalcolithic	Unidentified object	Terracotta	1
4F	Middle Chalcolithic	Roti-firing stone	Terracotta	1

Table 8.16. Distribution of Miscellaneous Unidentified Objects by Trench

Trench	Period	Material	Description
5	Late Chalcolithic	Burnt clay	10.41 x 8.92 x 6.91 cm, large rectangular piece, has depression like a door jamb, and square molded edges
31	Late Chalcolithic	Terracotta	3.58 x 3.46 x 1.14 cm, small triangular piece of micaceous red ware with evidence of a large perforation on one side
32	Late Chalcolithic	Terracotta	8.15 x 7.48 x 1.67 cm, looks like the corner of a picture frame, triangular piece of micaceous ware covered in a maroon slip, has linear depressions along length and width
204	Middle Chalcolithic	Unfired clay	4.10 x 3.55 x 1.93 cm, clay lump with incised fingernail mark design on top, curved concave bottom
302	Middle Chalcolithic	Terracotta	1.66 x 1.35 x 0.68, Red Ware fragment with appliqué in shape of a C
310	Middle Chalcolithic	Terracotta	4.62 x 3.73 x 1.67 cm, oval lump of terracotta with round indent in the middle
4A	Early Historic	Terracotta	5.48 x 4.20 x 2.30 cm, roughly triangular object with four small punched holes in a line on one side
4K	Late Chalcolithic	Clay	4.12 cm long and 1.95 cm in diameter, small conical object with a rounded point at the top and a broken and uneven bottom
S1	Middle Chalcolithic	Terracotta	4.92 x 3.10 x 1.06 cm, oval lump with impressions, look like teeth impressions, found in wall cutting
S1	Middle Chalcolithic	Clay	14 cm tall and 6.5 to 7 cm in diameter, thick and heavy object of piled of fired clay

Table 8.17. Distribution of Game Pieces by Trench

Trench	Period	Diamond	Triangle	Rectangle	Square	Other	Trench Totals
5	Late Chalcolithic	7	0	0	3	0	10
6	Late Chalcolithic	2	0	0	0	0	2
7	Late Chalcolithic	6	1	0	2	0	9
8	Late Chalcolithic	3	0	1	4	0	8
20	Middle Chalcolithic	2	0	0	0	0	2
27	Middle Chalcolithic	0	0	1	0	0	1
30	Late Chalcolithic	7	0	0	1	0	8
201	Late Chalcolithic	2	0	0	0	0	2
203	Middle Chalcolithic	0	1	3	0	0	4
4C	Late Chalcolithic/Early Historic	5	12	5	3	1 (hexagon)	26
4D	Middle Chalcolithic/Late Chalcolithic	3	27	11	3	0	44
4F	Middle Chalcolithic	1	0	0	0	0	1
S1	Middle Chalcolithic	4	0	0	0	0	4
TOTALS:		42	41	21	16	1	121

during beating and shaping. Alternatively, they may have been used as jar stoppers. Four of the 8 are of unfired clay, 1 is of terracotta, and 3 are of poorly fired terracotta. A total of 4 come from the Middle Chalcolithic, 2 from the Late Chalcolithic, and 2 from the Early Historic (Table 8.14).

Stoppers (pp. 130–131)

A total of 5 stoppers were discovered during excavations. Four are of terracotta and 1 is of unfired clay. Stoppers were used to plug the tops of jars to keep the contents fresh. All come from Middle Chalcolithic habitation levels. Similar objects have also been discovered at Ahar (for example, S5.210 is similar to Sankalia, Deo, and Ansari 1969: fig. 118, No. 1).

Terracotta Spheres (Slingballs)

See Spheres (Slingballs) section in Stone Objects.

Miscellaneous Terracotta Objects

Weight (pp. 130–131)

One terracotta weight was discovered during excavations. It comes from the Middle Chalcolithic habitation levels in Trench 204. It is rectangular in shape, slightly chipped, and has a small drilled hole to remove excess weight

Spout Fragment (pp. 130–131)

A spout was discovered in the Early Historic habitation levels in Trench 4B. It is made of coarse micaceous Red Ware and is 9.24 cm in length. Its diameter varies from 5.7 cm at the base to 1.47 cm at the narrowest end.

Decorative Tile (pp. 130–131)

A single carved decorative tile was discovered in Early Historic levels on GLD-1. It is made of highly fired terracotta. It is broken on three sides and appears to be perforated in the middle. It measures 7.79 cm long, 6.48 cm wide, and 1.25 cm thick.

Unidentified Terracotta Objects

Round Lumps

Four round objects were recovered during excavations. One was found in association with the chulha in 4F Middle Chalcolithic habitation levels. Perhaps this was a roti firing stone, as it is flat, round, and shows signs of having been fired at high temperatures. Similar round lump-like objects have also been recovered from Middle Chalcolithic levels in Trenches 9, 12, and 39 (Table 8.15). Two of these are unfired clay, and one is terracotta. Their use is unknown.

Table 8.18. Distribution of Ground Discs (Hopscotches) by Trench and Size

Trench	Period	TC 1.4–2 cm	TC 2–4 cm	TC 4–6 cm	TC 6 cm +	Stone 2.74–4 cm	Stone 4–6 cm	Stone 6 cm +	Trench Totals
5	Late Chalcolithic	0	2	4	1	0	0	0	7
6	Late Chalcolithic	0	0	1	0	0	0	0	1
7	Late Chalcolithic	0	2	0	0	0	0	0	2
8	Late Chalcolithic	1	0	0	0	0	0	0	1
9	Middle Chalcolithic	0	2	0	0	0	0	0	2
13	Middle Chalcolithic	0	1	0	0	1	0	0	2
20	Middle Chalcolithic	0	1	0	0	0	0	0	1
23	Middle Chalcolithic	0	2	0	0	0	0	0	2
30	Late Chalcolithic	1	2	2	0	1	0	0	6
32	Middle Chalcolithic	0	0	5	0	0	0	0	5
35	Middle Chalcolithic	0	1	1	0	0	0	0	2
39	Middle Chalcolithic/ Early Chalcolithic	0	1	0	0	0	0	0	1
41	Middle Chalcolithic/ Early Chalcolithic	0	1	0	0	0	0	0	1
65	Late Chalcolithic	0	1	0	0	0	0	0	1
68	Late Chalcolithic	0	2	4	0	0	0	0	6
69	Late Chalcolithic	0	0	1	0	0	0	0	1
74	Late Chalcolithic	0	1	0	0	0	0	0	1
103	Middle Chalcolithic	0	0	0	0	1	0	0	1
104	Middle Chalcolithic	0	0	0	1	0	0	0	1
105	Middle Chalcolithic	0	1	0	0	0	0	0	1
113	Late Chalcolithic	0	0	1	0	0	0	0	1
201	Late Chalcolithic	0	2	1	0	0	0	0	3
202	Middle Chalcolithic	0	1	0	0	0	0	0	1
203	Middle Chalcolithic	0	0	5	0	0	0	0	5
204	Middle Chalcolithic	0	1	0	0	0	0	0	1
209	Late Chalcolithic	0	1	1	1	0	0	0	3
210	Late Chalcolithic	0	0	3	0	0	0	0	3
211	Late Chalcolithic	0	2	1	0	0	0	0	3
310	Middle Chalcolithic	0	2	0	0	0	0	0	2
4A	Early Historic	0	3	4	0	1	0	0	8
4B	Early Historic	0	3	0	1	1	1	1	7
4C	Early Historic/ Late Chalcolithic	0	5	0	0	0	2	0	7
4D	Late Chalcolithic/ Middle Chalcolithic	1	2	0	1	0	0	0	4
4F	Early Historic/ Middle Chalcolithic	1	1	0	0	0	0	0	2
4H/4I	Erosion	0	1	0	0	0	0	0	1
4K	Erosion	0	1	0	0	0	0	1	2
S1	Erosion	0	0	1	0	0	0	0	1
TOTALS:		4	45	35	5	5	3	2	99

Table 8.19. Distribution of Ground Discs (Hopscotches) by Period and Size

Period	TC 1.4–2 cm	TC 2–4 cm	TC 4–6 cm	TC 6 cm +	Stone 2.74–4 cm	Stone 4–6 cm	Stone 6 cm +	TOTALS
Middle Chalcolithic	0	14	11	1	2	0	0	28
Late Chalcolithic	3	17	19	3	1	0	0	43
Early Historic	1	12	4	1	2	3	1	24
Erosion	0	2	1	0	0	0	1	4

Stump

A single fired clay stump was recovered from the Late Chalcolithic habitation levels in Trench 211. It has a round depression at the top and the bottom flares out. It measures 9.65 cm in height and its width varies from 6.8 cm at the top to 10.1 cm at the bottom. Its use is unknown, but perhaps it was used to hold pots in a chulha.

Miscellaneous Unidentified Objects

There are a number of objects that could not be placed definitively into any category. Their use is unknown. They are listed in Table 8.16.

Reused Pottery

Game Pieces (pp. 132–133)

Game pieces are purposefully shaped and/or broken pieces of pottery that have, as the name suggests, been reused as game tokens. Although ceramics have the ability to shatter into any number of shapes, what identifies "game pieces" from general pottery sherds is that they exhibit a somewhat limited range in size and shapes and are often found together in groups. They seem to have been most popular at Gilund around the Late Chalcolithic period. Twelve come from Middle Chalcolithic contexts, 44 from Middle/Late Chalcolithic, 39 from Late Chalcolithic, and 26 from Late Chalcolithic/Early Historic contexts (Table 8.17).

Ground Discs (Hopscotches) (pp. 134–135)

The classification of ground discs as "hopscotches" follows the definition given by A. Ghosh in An Encyclopedia of Indian Archaeology (1990:179): "flat potsherds with edges ground to a round shape or similarly shaped discs of stone or bone..." As the name suggests, their use may have been as children's toys in a game like hopscotch. However, they could have been used for any number of purposes, such as lids or tokens. A total of 99 ground discs (89 terracotta

and 10 stone) were recovered during excavations (Tables 8.18 and 8.19). Twenty-eight come from Middle Chalcolithic contexts, 43 from Late Chalcolithic, 24 from Early Historic, and 4 from erosional contexts. On average, a complete terracotta hopscotch measures 3.94 cm long, 3.81 cm wide, and 0.9 cm thick. The average terracotta hopscotch fragment measures 2.81 cm wide and 0.622 cm thick. The average stone hopscotch measures 4.48 cm long, 4.16 cm wide, and 1.23 cm thick.

Vent Plug (pp. 136–137)

One large sherd from the curved portion of a jar or bowl has been identified as a vent plug. It was found in association with the tandoor located in Structure 4, Trench 4F, in Middle Chalcolithic habitation levels. It is a large piece of Red Ware, 5.73 x 5.68 cm, slipped and burnished on one side.

Perforated Discs (pp. 136–137)

Perforated discs are similar in size and shape to ground discs, but have a small perforation in the center. The exact use of these antiquities is highly debated. It has been suggested that they may have been used as spindle whorls or as ornaments. The wear around the perforations suggests the former. A total of 25 perforated discs and 11 perforated disc fragments were discovered during excavations. All of them are made out of reused pottery. Sixteen come from the Middle Chalcolithic, 18 from the Late Chalcolithic, 1 from the Early Historic, and 1 from an erosional context. The average size of a complete perforated disc is 4.54 cm long by 4.31 cm wide and 0.76 cm thick. The average size of a perforated disc fragment is 3.98 cm long (approximate diameter) by 0.67 cm thick. The perforated discs are generally concentrated on mound GLD-2 in the Middle and Late Chalcolithic habitation levels (Tables 8.20 and 8.21).

Worked Sherds

A total of 7 worked sherds were recovered during excavations. Four come from the Middle Chalcolithic contexts,

Table 8.20. Distribution of Perforated Discs by Trench and Size

Trench	Period	2.18–4 cm	4– 6 cm	6 cm +	Trench Totals
9	Middle Chalcolithic	0	1	0	1
25	Late Chalcolithic	0	1	0	1
30	Late Chalcolithic	1	0	0	1
32	Late Chalcolithic	0	1	0	1
38	Middle Chalcolithic	0	1	0	1
57	Late Chalcolithic	0	0	1	1
68	Late Chalcolithic	0	2	0	2
71	Late Chalcolithic	1	0	0	1
74	Late Chalcolithic	0	2	0	2
102	Middle Chalcolithic	0	1	0	1
104	Middle Chalcolithic	3	1	0	4
112	Late Chalcolithic	2	1	0	3
113	Late Chalcolithic	0	1	0	1
201	Late Chalcolithic	0	1	0	1
202	Middle Chalcolithic	1	2	0	3
203	Middle Chalcolithic	4	1	0	5
209	Late Chalcolithic	0	2	1	3
211	Late Chalcolithic	1	0	0	1
4A	Early Historic	1	0	0	1
4F	Middle Chalcolithic	0	0	1	1
4I	Erosion	0	1	0	1
TOTALS:		14	19	3	36

and 3 from the Late Chalcolithic (Table 8.22). Worked sherds are pieces of reused pottery that have been deliberately ground or chipped on the edges. Unlike game pieces, ground discs (hopscotches), or perforated discs, they most likely functioned as tools, such as spoons, scrapers, or potters' implements. They average in size around 5.89 cm long by 4.43 cm wide and 1.20 cm thick.

Graffiti on Pottery

(pp. 138–139)

Twenty-two instances of graffiti on pottery were uncovered during excavations, along with one pre-firing incised line, and one stamped impression on a jar rim. The majority of the graffiti was executed by scratching the outer surface of the vessel after firing, although there are instances of marks on the inside of vessels as well. Most of the marks resemble Xs, Vs, or straight lines. There are also several more intricate designs. Fifteen come from the Middle Chalcolithic, 8 from the Late Chalcolithic, and 1 from the Early Historic (Table 8.23).

Table 8.21. Distribution of Perforated Discs by Period and Size

Period	2.18–4 cm	4–6 cm	6 cm +	Totals
Middle Chalcolithic	8	7	1	16
Late Chalcolithic	5	11	2	18
Early Historic	1	0	0	1
Erosion	0	1	0	1

Table 8.22. Distribution of Worked Sherds by Trench

Trench	Period	Size	Quantity
6	Late Chalcolithic	9.96 x 4.75 x 0.50 cm	1
12	Middle Chalcolithic	2.56 x 2.32 x 0.79 cm 7.07 x 6.00 x 1.18 cm	2
105	Middle Chalcolithic	2.61 x 2.00 x 0.99 cm	1
310	Middle Chalcolithic	3.14 x 2.26 x 0.69 cm	1
4C	Late Chalcolithic	7.73 x 6.01 x 2.29 cm	1
4D	Late Chalcolithic	8.17 x 7.66 x 1.98 cm	1

Table 8.23. Distribution of Graffiti on
Pottery by Trench

Trench	Period	Quantity
30	Late Chalcolithic	1
31	Late Chalcolithic	2
32	Late Chalcolithic	1
34	Middle Chalcolithic	1
35	Middle Chalcolithic	2
201	Late Chalcolithic	1
202	Middle Chalcolithic	1 (pre-firing incision)
203	Middle Chalcolithic	1
205	Middle Chalcolithic	2
206	Middle Chalcolithic	1
207	Middle Chalcolithic	1 (stamp)
209	Late Chalcolithic	2
310	Middle Chalcolithic	5
4C	Early Historic	1
4E	Middle Chalcolithic	1
Surface	Late Chalcolithic (?)	1

Stone Objects

Stone Tools

The wide variety of stone tools suggests that grain processing was a significant part of daily life at Gilund. This is particularly evidenced by grinding tools like ground stones, rubber stones, querns, mullers, pestles, and pounders. Stone tools were also used in bead and lithics manufacture, as well as common aspects of daily life (e.g., a hammerstone could be used for pounding a stake into the ground, as well as for knapping stone tools). Whether or not stone tools (other than lithics) were recorded as antiquities varied between and within seasons. Therefore the numbers given are only a partial representation of the entire collection of stone tools excavated at Gilund during the 1999 to 2005 excavations. In addition, the majority of stone tools from Gilund are housed in a separate collection outside of Deccan College, and were not available for individual analysis. Therefore, the classifications and calculations provided below are primarily based on information from the antiquities registers.

Ground Stones

A total of 60 ground stones (a.k.a. grinding stones) and 62 ground stone fragments were recovered during ex-

cavations. Common materials include marble and quartzite. Sixty-five come from the Middle Chalcolithic, 52 from the Late Chalcolithic, and 5 from the Early Historic.

Rubber Stones

A total of 58 rubber stones and 17 rubber stone fragments were recovered during excavations. Common materials include quartzite, sandstone, and granite. Thirty-six come from the Middle Chalcolithic, 37 from the Middle Chalcolithic, and 1 from the Early Historic.

Hammerstones

A total of 173 hammerstones and 56 hammerstone fragments were recovered during excavations. Common materials include quartz, quartzite, and granite. One hundred and twenty come from the Middle Chalcolithic, 101 from the Late Chalcolithic, 7 from the Early Historic, and 1 from an erosional context.

Composite Types

A number of composite stone tools were found: 5 ground/hammerstones and 13 rubber/hammerstones (Tables 8.24 and 8.25). Common materials include sandstone, quartzite, and granite. Seven come from the Middle Chalcolithic, 11 from the Late Chalcolithic, and 1 from the Early Historic.

Querns

A total of 8 querns and 26 quern fragments were recovered during excavations. Common materials include quartzite, granite, sandstone, and schist. Six come from the Middle Chalcolithic, 25 from the Late Chalcolithic, and 3 from the Early Historic.

Mullers

A total of 17 mullers and 5 muller fragments were recovered during excavations. Nearly all of the specimens are of quartzite. Seven come from the Middle Chalcolithic, 12 from the Late Chalcolithic, and 3 from the Early Historic.

Pestles

A total of 8 pestles and 5 pestle fragments were recovered during excavations. Common materials include sandstone and quartzite. Four come from the Middle Chalcolithic, 7 from the Late Chalcolithic, and 2 from the Early Historic.

Pounders

A total of 12 pounders were recovered during excavations. Nearly all of the specimens are of quartzite. Two come from the Middle Chalcolithic, 9 from the Late Chal-

Table 8.24. Distribution of Ground Stones, Rubber Stones, and
Hammerstones by Trench

Trench	Period	Ground Stone	Rubber Stone	Hammer Stone	Composite Types	Trench Totals
5	Late Chalcolithic	5	3	19	1	28
6	Late Chalcolithic	4	5	12	0	21
7	Late Chalcolithic	6	9	12	6	33
8	Late Chalcolithic	7	6	14	2	29
9	Middle Chalcolithic	4	16	19	2	41
10	Middle Chalcolithic	1	0	2	0	3
12	Middle Chalcolithic	0	3	6	0	9
12/13 (baulk)	Middle Chalcolithic	0	3	1	1	5
13	Middle Chalcolithic	8	2	7	1	18
17	Middle Chalcolithic	0	0	0	1	1
24	Middle Chalcolithic	19	0	20	0	39
25	Late Chalcolithic	1	0	1	0	2
27	Middle Chalcolithic	30	0	21	0	51
30	Late Chalcolithic	1	0	7	1	9
31	Late Chalcolithic	0	6	6	1	13
32	Late Chalcolithic	0	2	2	0	4
34	Middle Chalcolithic	0	2	7	0	9
35	Middle Chalcolithic	1	4	21	0	26
58	Late Chalcolithic	0	0	1	0	1
64	Late Chalcolithic	1	0	1	0	2
65	Late Chalcolithic	1	0	2	0	3
68	Late Chalcolithic	5	0	1	0	6
69	Late Chalcolithic	5	0	2	0	7
70	Late Chalcolithic	5	1	1	0	7
71	Late Chalcolithic	8	0	2	0	10
201	Late Chalcolithic	0	0	3	0	3
202	Middle Chalcolithic	0	0	7	0	7
203	Middle Chalcolithic	0	3	2	0	5
204	Middle Chalcolithic	0	0	1	1	2
205	Middle Chalcolithic	0	1	1	0	2
209	Late Chalcolithic	3	1	4	0	8
210	Late Chalcolithic	0	1	6	0	7
211	Late Chalcolithic	0	0	2	0	2
4A	Early Historic	2	0	2	0	4
4B	Early Historic	3	1	3	1	8
4C	Late Chalcolithic	0	3	1	0	4
4C	Early Historic	0	0	2	0	2
4D	Middle Chalcolithic	0	1	1	0	2
4D	Late Chalcolithic	0	0	1	0	1

cont'd.

Table 8.24 (cont'd.)

Trench	Period	Ground Stone	Rubber Stone	Hammer Stone	Composite Types	Trench Totals
4E	Middle Chalcolithic	1	0	1	0	2
4F	Middle Chalcolithic	0	1	1	1	3
4H	Late Chalcolithic/ Middle Chalcolithic	0	0	1	0	1
S1	Middle Chalcolithic	1	0	2	0	3
S1	Erosion	0	0	1	0	1
TOTALS:		122	74	229	19	444

Table 8.25. Distribution of Ground Stones, Rubber Stones, and Hammerstones by Period

Period	Ground Stone	Rubber Stone	Hammer Stone	Composite Types	Totals
Middle Chalcolithic	65	36	120	7	228
Late Chalcolithic	52	37	101	11	201
Early Historic	5	1	7	1	14
Erosion	0	0	1	0	1

colithic, and 1 from the Early Historic.

Polishers

A total of 5 polishers and 1 polisher fragment were recovered during excavations. Nearly all of the specimens are of quartzite and 1 is possibly of granite. Three polishers and the polisher fragment are clustered in Trenches 34 and 35, which date to the Middle Chalcolithic. The remaining 2 polishers were found together in Trench 7 and date from the Late Chalcolithic (Tables 8.26 and 8.27).

Chopper

One chopper was discovered in the Late Chalcolithic habitation levels of Trench 65 on the top of mound GLD-2.

Sharpeners/Whet Stones

Two sharpeners/whet stones were recovered during excavations. Both were found in the Middle Chalcolithic habitation levels of Trench 35, near the bottom of the eastern slope on mound GLD-2. One is made of granite and the other is made of quartzite.

Perforated Stones/Weights

One round cylindrical stone weight and 6 perforated stones were recovered during excavations. One hypothesis is that they were originally used as grinding stones until the center was ground completely through on both sides. They may also have been used as weights for digging sticks, with the stick placed through the perforation. The cylindrical stone weight was found in a Middle Chalcolithic context. Four perforated stones come from the Middle Chalcolithic, and the remaining 2 from the Late Chalcolithic (Table 8.28).

Bead Polishers (pp. 138–139)

Two bead polishers were recovered during excavations. One was found on the surface and bears grooves from polishing beads or other similarly sized objects. The other, found in Trench 5 on GLD-2, does not bear such grooves. It was fashioned from a piece of micaceous sandstone, which would have been a useful abrasive. Both bead polishers date from the Late Chalcolithic.

Worked Stones

A total of 11 worked stones were discovered during excavations. This category includes stones that may have been used as tools or appear battered by other tools, but do not fit into any of the above categories. One comes from the Early Chalcolithic, 3 from the Middle Chalcolithic, 2 from the Late Chalcolithic, 3 from the Early Historic, and 1 from the surface (Table 8.29).

Excavations at Gilund

Table 8.26. Distribution of Querns, Mullers, Pestles, Pounders, and Polishers
by Trench

Trench	Period	Querns/ Quern Fragments	Mullers	Pestles	Pounders	Polishers	Trench Totals
5	Late Chalcolithic	1	0	0	2	0	3
6	Late Chalcolithic	2	0	0	2	0	4
7	Late Chalcolithic	0	1	0	5	2	8
8	Late Chalcolithic	5	0	0	0	0	5
9	Middle Chalcolithic	3	0	3	1	0	7
12	Middle Chalcolithic	1	0	0	1	0	2
30	Late Chalcolithic	3	0	0	0	0	3
31	Late Chalcolithic	3	0	2	0	0	5
32	Late Chalcolithic	7	0	0	0	0	7
34	Middle Chalcolithic	0	0	0	0	1	1
35	Middle Chalcolithic	1	6	0	0	3	10
65	Late Chalcolithic	0	0	1	0	0	1
68	Late Chalcolithic	1	0	0	0	0	1
74	Late Chalcolithic	0	0	2	0	0	2
201	Late Chalcolithic	0	2	0	0	0	2
205	Middle Chalcolithic	1	0	0	0	0	1
209	Middle Chalcolithic	1	6	0	0	0	7
211	Late Chalcolithic	0	3	0	0	0	3
4A	Early Historic	0	3	0	1	0	4
4B	Early Historic	1	0	0	0	0	1
4C	Early Historic	2	0	2	0	0	4
4D	Late Chalcolithic	2	0	2	0	0	4
4I	Middle Chalcolithic	0	0	1	0	0	1
S1	Middle Chalcolithic	0	1	0	0	0	1
GRAND TOTALS:		34	22	13	12	6	87

Table 8.27. Distribution of Querns, Mullers, Pestles, Pounders, and Polishers
by Period

Period	Querns/ Quern Fragments	Mullers	Pestles	Pounders	Polishers	Totals
Middle Chalcolithic	6	7	4	2	4	23
Late Chalcolithic	25	12	7	9	2	55
Early Historic	3	3	2	1	0	9

Table 8.28. Distribution of Perforated Stones/Weights by Trench

Trench	Period	Description	Quantity
5	Late Chalcolithic	Perforated Stone, Quartz Sandstone	1
12	Middle Chalcolithic	Perforated Stone, Quartzite	1
24	Middle Chalcolithic	Round Weight, Sandstone	1
31	Late Chalcolithic	Perforated Stone, Sandstone	1
103	Middle Chalcolithic	Perforated Stone, Quartzite	1
205	Middle Chalcolithic	Perforated Stone, Sandstone	1
4E	Middle Chalcolithic	Perforated Stone, Quartzite	1

Table 8.29. Distribution of Bead Polishers by Trench

Trench	Period	Quantity
8	Late Chalcolithic	2
39	Early Chalcolithic	1
70	Late Chalcolithic	1
4A	Early Historic	2
4B	Early Historic	1
4D	Middle Chalcolithic	1
4E	Middle Chalcolithic	1
4K	Middle Chalcolithic	1
Surface		1

Ground Discs (Hopscotches)

See Ground Discs (Hopscotches) section in Terracotta Objects.

Spheres (Slingballs) (pp. 140–141)

A significant number of terracotta and stone spheres were recovered during excavations: 71 stone spheres (1.4-6.26 cm), and 56 terracotta spheres (0.89-3.54 cm). The distribution of spheres across Gilund is shown in Tables 8.30, 8.31, and 8.32. These spherical objects are characteristically identified as "slingballs". According to A. Ghosh, such spherical objects "were thrown by the complicated technique of releasing by means of slings, double-stringed bows or catapults or simply by hand" (1990:187). However, considering the amount of work necessary to round and shape the stone spheres, it is possible that the stone spheres served a different purpose from their terracotta counterparts.

Handle Fragment (pp. 140–141)

A handle fragment of sandstone was discovered on the west slope of GLD-2 near the pottery yard.

Metal Objects (pp. 140–149)

Chalcolithic Levels

There are few copper antiquities at Gilund. Over the five field seasons, only ten copper objects were discovered in Chalcolithic contexts. Six come from the Middle Chalcolithic and four from the Late Chalcolithic. Two iron objects were also discovered in Chalcolithic contexts: one from the Middle Chalcolithic and one from the Late Chalcolithic. However, it is very likely that these iron objects are dateable to the Early Historic. A list of the Chalcolithic metal antiquities is given in Table 8.33.

Early Historic Levels

The number of metal objects increases significantly in the Early Historic levels. A total of 109 metal items were recovered. These may be divided into whole iron objects (45), iron fragments (54) and other metal objects (10). Some of the iron fragments were found alone, while others were associated with iron objects (e.g. hoe fragments, rod fragments). GLD-1 is the only mound with Early Historic levels, and therefore all of the metal dating to the Early Historic period was discovered on this mound. A list of the Early Historic metal antiquities is given in Tables 8.34, 8.35, and 8.36.

Shell Objects

Bangles (pp. 148–151)

A total of 70 shell bangles were discovered during excavations at Gilund. Sixty-five of these were found on GLD-1, and the remaining five were found in Chalcolithic habitation contexts on GLD-2. Five come from the Middle Chalcolithic, two from the Late Chalcolithic, 40 from the Early Historic, 19 from Late Chalcolithic/Early Historic erosional contexts, and four from the surface (Tables 8.27 and 8.38).

Worked Shells (pp. 150–153)

A total of 73 worked shells were recovered during excavations. Fifty-six come from the Middle Chalcolithic, 12 from the Late Chalcolithic, and 5 from the Early Historic. A shell is classified as "worked" if it has evidence of deliberate rubbing or grinding on its edges. All of these shells have been worked on the bottom edge, and some have also been worked on the sides. Two shells are perforated, but this may be due to molluscan predators. Most of the shells

Excavations at Gilund

Table 8.30. Distribution of Stone and Terracotta Spheres (Slingballs)
by Trench and Size

Trench	Stone 1.4–2 cm	Stone 2–4 cm	Stone 4–6 cm	Stone 6 cm <	TC 0.89–2 cm	TC 2–3 cm	TC 3 cm <	Trench Totals
5	0	3	2	0	0	0	0	5
6	2	1	0	0	2	1	0	6
7	2	1	0	1	0	1	0	5
8	0	1	0	0	2	1	0	4
9	1	0	0	0	1	1	0	3
12	0	0	0	0	1	1	0	2
13	0	0	0	0	3	2	1	6
18	0	0	0	0	1	0	0	1
20	0	1	0	0	1	0	0	2
25	0	1	0	0	3	1	1	6
30	0	1	0	0	0	1	0	2
32	0	1	0	0	0	0	0	1
33	0	0	0	0	0	1	0	1
34	0	0	0	0	1	0	0	1
35	2	0	0	0	3	0	0	5
58	0	0	0	0	1	0	0	1
68	0	1	0	0	1	0	0	2
69	0	1	0	0	0	0	0	1
74	0	2	0	0	0	0	0	2
101	0	1	0	0	2	0	0	3
104	0	1	0	0	0	0	0	1
201	1	2	0	0	0	0	0	3
202	0	0	1	0	1	0	0	2
203	0	1	0	0	0	0	0	1
204	0	0	0	0	1	2	0	3
205	0	0	2	0	1	1	0	4
206	0	1	0	0	0	0	0	1
207	0	0	0	0	0	1	0	1
209	0	1	1	0	0	0	0	2
210	0	0	0	1	0	0	0	1
310	0	0	0	0	1	0	0	1
4A	2	2	0	0	4	0	0	8
4B	1	2	0	0	3	0	0	6
4C	2	2	1	0	3	0	0	8
4E	0	1	0	0	0	0	0	1
4F	2	1	0	0	1	0	0	4

cont'd.

Table 8.30 cont'd.

Trench	Stone 1.4–2 cm	Stone 2–4 cm	Stone 4–6 cm	Stone 6 cm <	TC 0.89–2 cm	TC 2–3 cm	TC 3 cm <	Trench Totals
4H	1	0	0	0	1	0	0	2
4I	0	1	0	0	0	0	0	1
4K	0	0	0	0	1	0	0	1
5B	0	0	0	0	1	0	0	1
S1	0	1	0	0	2	0	0	3
Surface	0	0	0	1	0	1	0	2
TOTALS:	16	31	7	3	42	15	2	116*

14 stone spheres were not available for measurement. Their distribution is given in Table 8.31.

Table 8.31. Distribution by Trench of Additional Unmeasured Stone Spheres (Slingballs)

Trench	Spheres
9	3
24	2
27	1
74	2
70	1
38	1
39	1
206	2
211	1
TOTAL:	14

Table 8.32. Distribution of Stone and Terracotta Spheres (Slingballs) by Period and Size

Period	Stone 1.4–2 cm	Stone 2–4 cm	Stone 4–6 cm	Stone 6 cm <	TC 0.89–2 cm	TC 2–3 cm	TC 3 cm <	Trench Totals
Middle Chalcolithic	5	7	3	0	18	8	1	42
Late Chalcolithic	5	16	3	2	9	6	1	42
Early Historic	5	6	1	0	11	0	0	23
Mixed	1	2	0	0	4	0	0	7
Surface	0	0	0	1	0	1	0	2
TOTALS:	16	31	7	3	42	15	2	116

Table 8.33. Chalcolithic Metal Antiquities

Object	Metal Type	Period	Trench	Mound	Qty
Bangle	Copper	Late Chalcolithic	7	GLD-2	1
Bangle Fragment	Copper	Middle Chalcolithic	35	GLD-2	1
Blade (?)	Copper	Late Chalcolithic	65	GLD-2	1
Blade Fragment	Copper	Late Chalcolithic	6	GLD-2	1
Chisel Fragment	Copper	Middle Chalcolithic	304	GLD-2	1
Fragment	Copper	Middle Chalcolithic	202	GLD-2	1
Fragment	Copper	Middle Chalcolithic	4F	GLD-1	1
Ring	Copper	Late Chalcolithic	29	GLD-2	1
Ring Fragment	Copper	Middle Chalcolithic	35	GLD-2	1
Ring Fragment	Copper	Middle Chalcolithic	305	GLD-2	1
TOTAL:					10
Blade Fragment	Iron	Late Chalcolithic	33	GLD-2	1
Nail	Iron	Middle Chalcolithic	301	GLD-2	1
TOTAL:					2

were concentrated in the Middle Chalcolithic habitation levels on mound GLD-2, particularly in Trenches 34 and 35 (Table 8.39). These trenches are located near the bottom of the northwest slope of GLD-2.

Cowries (pp. 152–153)

Seven cowries were discovered during excavations. All of the cowries were discovered on GLD-1 in Early Historic layers (Table 8.40). The cowries range in size from 1.25 to 1.87 cm long, 0.67 to 1.42 cm wide, and 0.50 to 0.70 cm in height/thickness.

Inlay Pieces (pp. 152–153)

Four inlay pieces were discovered during excavations. Two are round and 2 are diamond-shaped. Three come from the Middle Chalcolithic, and 1 is from the Early Historic (Table 8.41).

Bone Objects (pp. 152–153)

A total of 6 bone objects were recovered during excavations. Of these, 5 were found in Late Chalcolithic contexts, and 1 in the Early Historic (Table 8.42).

Steatite/Soapstone Objects

Two steatite paste antiquities (not including beads) and a handful of soapstone vessel fragments were recovered during excavations. Steatite, also known as soapstone, is a metamor-

phic rock composed largely of talc. It is very soft. It can be easily carved, or ground up into a powder and mixed with other materials to make a fine paste. This paste can be molded, shaped, or cut to create artifacts like beads and rings.

Button (pp. 152–153)

A single steatite paste button was discovered in Late Chalcolithic habitation levels on the top of GLD-2. It has a convex top and a flat bottom. A similar, if not identical, specimen was discovered at Ahar (Sankalia, Deo, and Ansari 1969: fig. 98, No. 26). Despite the wide-scale use of steatite for bead-making during the Chalcolithic, this is the only specimen of steatite discovered at Ahar.

Ring (pp. 152–153)

One steatite paste ring fragment was discovered during excavations. It comes from a section scraping in Trench 4B on GLD-1. Since all layers excavated in this trench are Early Historic, it is likely that this ring is also from the Early Historic period.

Soapstone Vessels (pp. 154–155)

A total of 12 soapstone vessel fragments were recovered during excavations. The vessel fragments have been divided into two groups based on similarity and find location. Nine of the 12 (Group 1) were found close together near the top of GLD-1, and it is very likely that they all belong to the same vessel. The vessel fragments from Group 1 all have a black wash on the exterior and a rather smoothed interior

Table 8.34. Early Historic Iron Antiquities and Fragments

Object	Metal Type	Trench	Qty
Arrow Head	Iron	4A	1
Axe	Iron	4B	1
Bell	Iron	4B	1
Bell Fragment	Iron	4A	1
Blade	Iron	4B	1
Blade Fragment (?)	Iron	4A	1
Blade Fragment (?)	Iron	4B	1
Chisel	Iron	4A	1
Chopper	Iron	4B	1
Dagger	Iron	4A	1
Hoes	Iron	4B	5
Hollow Point	Iron	4A	1
Bowl	Iron	4B	1
Rod	Iron	4B	1
Lamp Fragment	Iron	4B	1
Nail	Iron	4A	1
Nail Fragments	Iron	4A	4
Nail	Iron	4C	1
Nail Fragment (?)	Iron	4C	1
Points	Iron	4A	2
Points	Iron	4B	9
Points	Iron	4C	3
Ring Fragment	Iron	4A	1
Sickle Handle?	Iron	5B	1
Unidentified Object	Iron	4B	1
Unidentified Object	Iron	4C	1
Unidentified Object	Iron	5B	1
SUBTOTAL:			45
Fragments	Iron	4A	5
Fragment	Iron	4B	9
Fragments	Iron	4C	6
Fragments	Iron	5B	9
Hoe Fragments	Iron	4B	6
Iron Rod Fragments	Iron	4B	4
Unidentified Object Fragments	Iron	4B	7
Unidentified Object Fragments	Iron	5B	8
SUBTOTAL:			54
GRAND TOTAL IRON OBJECTS:			99

Table 8.35. Other Metal Antiquities

Object	Metal Type	Trench	Qty
Bell Fragment	Bronze	4C	1
Coin	Bronze	4F	1
Bangle Fragment	Copper	4C	1
Coin	Copper	4C	1
Ring	Copper	4B	2
Bangle Fragment	Copper/ Iron	4A	1
Bell	Copper/ Iron	4B	1
Wire Fragments	Lead	4C	2
TOTAL:			10

Table 8.36. Early Historic Metal Antiquities by Trench

Trench	Iron	Copper	Bronze	Other	Trench Total
4A	19	0	0	1 (copper/iron)	20
4B	49	2	0	1 (copper/iron)	52
4C	12	2	1	2 (lead)	17
4F	0	0	1	0	1
5B	19	0	0	0	19
TOTALS:	99	4	2	4	109

Table 8.37. Distribution of Shell Bangles by Trench and Type

Trench	Period	Plain	Incised Design	Raised Circle Design	Trench Totals
6	Late Chalcolithic	0	1	0	1
101	Middle Chalcolithic	1	0	0	1
104	Middle Chalcolithic	1	0	0	1
4A	Early Historic	8	4	5	17
4B	Early Historic	7	0	2	9
4C	Early Historic/ Late Chalcolithic	8	1	3	12
4D	Middle Chalcolithic	1	0	0	1
4E	Middle Chalcolithic	1	0	0	1
4F	Middle Chalcolithic	0	1	0	1
4H	Erosion	2	1	0	3
4H/4I	Erosion	6	0	0	6
4I	Erosion	1	0	0	1
4K	Erosion	0	1	0	1
5B	Early Historic	3	0	0	3
S1	Erosion	6	0	2	8
GLD-1	Surface	1	1	0	2
GLD-2	Surface	2	0	0	2
TOTALS:		48	10	12	70

Table 8.38. Distribution of Shell Bangles by Period and Type

Period	Plain	Incised Design	Raised Circle Design	Totals
Middle Chalcolithic	4	1	0	5
Late Chalcolithic	1	1	0	2
Early Historic	25	5	10	40
Erosion	15	2	2	19
Surface	3	1	0	4

surface, sometimes with evidence of the same black wash. It is possible that the interior was also slipped, but the wash has been eroded. The vessel appears to have been carved out of soapstone and exhibits chisel marks on the exterior. There is a thick black wash on it and an appliqué design near the rim in a black paste. Judging from S1.015, it was likely a large bowl with a diameter of 20–25 cm.

Table 8.39. Distribution of Worked Shells by Trench

Trench	Period	Quantity
7	Late Chalcolithic	1
9	Middle Chalcolithic	2
27	Middle Chalcolithic	1
30	Late Chalcolithic	2
31	Late Chalcolithic	4
34	Middle Chalcolithic	20
35	Middle Chalcolithic	13
101	Middle Chalcolithic	2
102	Middle Chalcolithic	1
103	Middle Chalcolithic	1
105	Middle Chalcolithic	1
201	Late Chalcolithic	3
203	Middle Chalcolithic	2
204	Middle Chalcolithic	1
209	Late Chalcolithic	2
4A	Early Historic	1
4B	Early Historic	1
4C	Early Historic	1
4D	Middle Chalcolithic	5
4E	Middle Chalcolithic	5
4F	Middle Chalcolithic	2
5B	Early Historic	1
S1	Early Historic	1
TOTAL:		73

Table 8.40. Distribution of Cowries by Trench

Trench	Period	Description	Quantity
4B	Early Historic	2 whole, 1 half	3
4C	Early Historic	1 whole, 1 half	2
4D	Early Historic	erosion layer on slope, teeth missing	1
4K	Early Historic	erosion layer, half	1

Table 8.41. Distribution of Inlay Pieces by Trench

Trench	Mound	Period	Shape	Quantity
35	GLD-2	Middle Chalcolithic	round	1
13	GLD-2	Middle Chalcolithic	diamond	1
4B	GLD-1	Early Historic	diamond	1
4F	GLD-1	Middle Chalcolithic	round	1

Table 8.42. Distribution of Bone Objects by Trench

Trench	Period	Object	Qty
4D	Late Chalcolithic	Worked Bone	1
4E	Late Chalcolithic	Polished Bone	1
7	Late Chalcolithic	Polished Bone	1
70	Late Chalcolithic	Ornament	1
205	Late Chalcolithic	Worked Bone	1
4A	Early Historic	Bone Point	1
TOTAL:			6

The 3 vessel fragments (Group 2) were found further down the slope. However, it is possible that the pieces in Group 2 belonged to the same vessel as those in Group 1. It may only be the effects of slope wash and heavy erosion on the Group 2 pieces which cause the differences in appearance. For example, piece S3.048 has the same chisel marks as S1.041C and S1.043. Otherwise, if they are two separate vessels, then they are both examples of a tradition of soapstone vessel carving that began as early as the Late Chalcolithic and continued into the Early Historic.

Acknowledgments

I would like to thank the several anonymous reviewers for their comments, which have helped improve this manuscript. Any inadequacies found within are, of course, the sole responsibility of the author. The bulk of this research was completed between September 2004 and May 2005 in the Department of Archaeology at Deccan College Post-Graduate and Research Institute in Pune, Maharashtra. This research was made possible through a travel grant from the University of Pennsylvania Museum of Anthropology and Archaeology. I am very grateful for the guidance and advice of Professor Vasant S. Shinde during the classification and organization of the Gilund antiquities, as well as the kind hospitality of the Deccan College faculty, students, and staff. I would also like to emphasize my sincere gratitude to the late Dr. Gregory L. Possehl for his guidance, support, encouragement, and inspiration.

NOTE

8.1. The two figurines and single horn found in pit contexts in Trench 6 all come from different pits.

Terracotta Objects

Humped Cattle Figurines

Area 1

S1.117 Humped bull of terracotta. The head and front legs are missing and the figurine has been burned. It also appears to have udders on the underbelly, which is quite significant. The back legs are pinched, and there are two punched holes in the rear back side. 3.13 cm long, 1.30 cm wide, and 2.04 cm tall. Locus: Tr. 6, habitation levels, Late Chalcolithic.

S1.181 Terracotta figurine with front legs that are joined and come to a point. It is missing its horns and half of the face is broken. The back legs are also damaged. It has a small pinched hump, delicate arched torso, and pointed snout. 4.66 cm long, 1.17 cm wide, and 3.03 cm tall. Locus: Tr. 6, habitation levels, Late Chalcolithic.

S1.326 Terracotta figurine with front legs joined and back legs pinched apart. It has a prominent hump and a long snout. 5.03 cm long, 1.80 cm wide, and 3.12 cm tall. Locus: Tr. 8, habitation levels, Late Chalcolithic.

S1.268 Nearly complete terracotta figurine. As noted above, the term "nearly complete" denotes a figurine that has most major appendages intact, but shows signs of damage at points of weakness, such as the horns. This figurine is only missing one horn and part of its hump. It has articulated front legs, rounded undefined back legs, and no tail. Its face has a rounded snout and there are ear details below the horns. It has been fired to a red color. There is also a white film, either concretion or paint on its body and face. 4.4 cm long, 1.51 cm wide, and 4.82 cm tall (including horns). Locus: Tr. 12, the parallel walls, Middle Chalcolithic.

S1.250 Terracotta figurine with missing head and damaged front legs. It has a prominent pinched hump that is broken at the tip and slightly pinched back legs. It also has a distinctive long tail with indented/pinched design, perhaps made to look like a braid. 5.15 cm long, 1.74 cm wide, and 2.9 cm tall. Locus: Tr. 13, the parallel walls, Middle Chalcolithic.

S2.043 Terracotta figurine lacking horns and rear half of torso. It has a prominent hooked hump. The front legs are joined and flare out at the bottom. 5.84 cm long, 2.85 cm wide, and 4.53 cm tall. Locus: Tr. 25, habitation levels, Late Chalcolithic.

S2.045 Terracotta figurine with only the top the half of the torso and rear remaining. It has a prominent hooked hump, raised rump, and no tail. 3.45 cm long, 1.85 cm wide, and 3.6 cm tall. Locus: Tr. 25, habitation levels, Late Chalcolithic.

S2.088 Nearly complete reduced terracotta figurine. The horns are missing and the front legs are damaged. It has a pointy hooked hump, long tail, and articulated back legs. It has a detailed face with punctured dots for the nose and eyes. 4.89 cm long, 1.83 cm wide, and 2.99 cm tall. Locus: Tr. 29, habitation levels, Late Chalcolithic.

S3.131 Nearly complete terracotta figurine. It is only missing one horn. It has a prominent round hump, and articulated front legs. The back legs are slightly damaged. 4.17 cm long, 1.32 cm wide, and 4.58 cm tall (including horns). Locus: Tr. 34, habitation levels, Middle Chalcolithic.

S3.115 Terracotta figurine with missing head and broken hump. Its front legs are articulated, and the back legs are pinched and slightly rounded. It has no tail. 5.05 cm long, 1.72 cm wide, and 3.74 cm tall. Locus: Tr. 34, habitation levels, Middle Chalcolithic.

S4.356A Terracotta figurine with a missing head and a broken hump. The front legs are joined and flared, while the back legs are articulated. 4.89 cm long, 1.94 cm wide, and 2.84 cm tall. Locus: Tr. 35, habitation levels, Middle Chalcolithic.

S3.251 Terracotta figurine missing head and rear half of torso. The front legs are joined, and the hump has broken off. 5.18 cm long, 2.09 cm wide, and 4.57 cm tall. Locus: Tr. 35, habitation levels, Middle Chalcolithic.

Area IV

S4.177 Nearly complete terracotta figurine with only horns missing. The front and back legs are joined, and there are subtle articulations for the feet. It has a rounded face, prominent hooked hump, and long tail. 6.22 cm long, 1.88 cm wide, and 4.04 cm tall. Locus: Tr. 310, habitation levels, Middle Chalcolithic.

NB: All of the photographs in this chapter were taken by the author.

Terracotta
Humped Bull Figurines

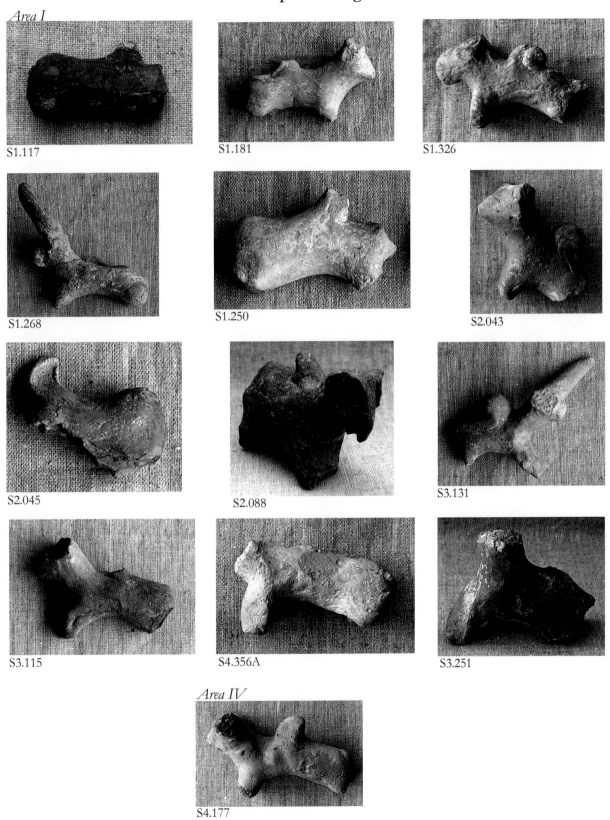

Area I

S1.117

S1.181

S1.326

S1.268

S1.250

S2.043

S2.045

S2.088

S3.131

S3.115

S4.356A

S3.251

Area IV

S4.177

Humped Cattle Figurines (*cont'd.*)

Surface

S3.160 Front half of an unfired clay figurine. The head and rear are missing, but the hump is visible. There is a small round indentation on either side of the neck. This is significant because other than S1.303 no other figurine has such marks. These may indicate that it was part of a toy cart. 2.42 cm long, 1.24 cm wide, and 2.57 cm tall. Locus: Surface find on mound GLD-2.

S5.002 Terracotta figurine with head and front legs missing. It has a prominent hooked hump, raised rump with tail, and slightly pinched back legs. There also appears to be a yellow residue on the rump. 4.9 cm long, 1.95 cm wide, and 3.75 cm tall. Locus: Surface find on mound GLD-2.

S1.018 Nearly complete terracotta figurine with only face and horns missing. The front legs are joined with a small concavity underneath, and the back legs are pinched. It has a prominent hump, a large long tail on a raised rump, and a long torso. 6.69 cm long, 1.99 cm wide, and 4.65 cm tall. Locus: Surface find.

S2.039 Nearly complete terracotta figurine with only the horns missing. All of the legs are pinched out. It has a pinched nose, prominent hooked hump, and a short stubby tail. 5.23 cm long, 1.84 cm wide, and 3.29 cm tall. Locus: Surface find.

Humpless Cattle and Animal Figurines

Area I

S1.281 Terracotta bull figurine with large, round, button snout. The front legs are joined and there is a small cavity between them. The horns and the entire torso have been broken off. 5.52 cm long, 2.18 cm wide, and 3.59 cm tall. Locus: Tr. 6, habitation levels, Late Chalcolithic.

S1.289 Terracotta bull figurine with front legs joined. The top half of the head is missing; all that remains is a small portion of the right ear. It has a thick heavy torso with no hump, and there is a raised bump on the rump. 6.72 cm long, 2.34 cm wide, and 4.72 cm tall. Locus: Tr. 6, habitation levels, Late Chalcolithic.

S1.290 Terracotta figurine with missing head and front left leg. The torso is arched and may have had a hump. It has a raised rump with a stubby tail sticking out of the back. There are also small incised lines on left side of the torso. 3.44 cm long, 1.39 cm wide, and 2.08 cm tall. Locus: Tr. 6, habitation levels, Late Chalcolithic.

S1.444 Terracotta bull figurine with front legs joined and flared at bottom. It is missing its horns, but there are pinched ears visible. It has a flat featureless face and no hump. It has a little tail and indent in the rump. 5.13 cm long, 1.41 cm wide, and 3.84 cm tall. Locus: Tr. 6, habitation levels, Late Chalcolithic.

S1.382 Nearly complete reduced terracotta figurine. The head is damaged and it is difficult to discern whether or not it had horns. All of the legs are articulated, short, and stubby. It has a pointed snout, and seems to have a hump behind the head. 3.71 cm long, 2.26 cm wide, and 3.46 cm tall. Locus: Tr. 9, habitation levels, Middle Chalcolithic.

S1.303 Nearly complete ram figurine. The top of the head and the rear right leg are broken. It has a pointed snout, articulated legs that are pointed at the bottom, and a small broken tail on the top of the rump. There are small round impressions on both sides of the torso, which may indicate that it was used in a toy cart. 4.27 cm long, 2.56 cm wide, and 4.38 cm tall. Locus: Tr. 9, habitation levels, Middle Chalcolithic.

Humped Bull Figurines (Continued)

Surface

S3.160

S5.002

S1.018

S2.039

Humpless Cattle and Animal Figurines

Area I

S1.281

S1.289

S1.290

S1.444

S1.382

S1.303

Humpless Cattle and Animal Figurines (cont'd.)

Area I (cont'd.)

S5.156 Ram figurine missing horns, front legs, and back left leg. All legs appear to have been articulated, even though they are now broken. It has a pointed snout, and looks similar to S1.303, but with lower ears/horns and a bit fatter torso, and a stubby tail on the rump. 5 cm long, 2.3 cm wide, and 4.1 cm tall. Locus: Tr. 9, habitation levels, Middle Chalcolithic.

S1.485 Terracotta figurine with front legs joined and a long snout. The back half is missing, so it is difficult to classify. 4.19 cm long, 2.03 cm wide, and 4.1 cm tall. Locus: Tr. 20, habitation levels, Middle Chalcolithic.

S2.041 Terracotta bull figurine missing horns, front legs, top of torso, and rear. The incised hair lines along the torso and the pointed snout are unique. 5.23 cm long, 2.99 cm wide, and 4.59 cm tall. Locus: Tr. 25, habitation levels, Late Chalcolithic.

S2.058 Nearly complete terracotta bull figurine. The front legs are joined, the horns are missing, and it has a flat, featureless face. There is also a raised bump on the rump and an indent on the rear. 5.17 cm long, 2.61 cm wide, and 4.77 cm tall. Locus: Tr. 30, habitation levels, Late Chalcolithic.

S5.084 Terracotta bull figurine missing front legs and head. It has a medium tail on a raised hump, and the back legs are separated. There is also an indent on the underbelly and some kind of impressions on the left side near the rear. 2.8 cm long, 1.9 cm wide, and 2.25 cm tall. Locus: Tr. 30, habitation levels, Late Chalcolithic.

S3.252 Terracotta figurine with short, fat torso. It is missing its head and the legs on the right side. It also has a prominent tail. 4.66 cm long, 1.99 cm wide, and 2.58 cm tall. Locus: Tr. 35, habitation levels, Middle Chalcolithic.

Surface

S1.463 Terracotta figurine with just rear half remaining. It has a wide fat torso, and a short tail on a raised rump. The back legs are separated. There are signs of white paint or concretion across the sides of the torso. There are also fingerprints on rump, and textured imprints (possibly from fabric) along body. 3.41 cm long, 2.06 cm wide, and 2.9 cm tall. Locus: Surface find on mound GLD-2.

GLD-1

S3.224 Well-crafted, nearly complete terracotta figurine. It has large, thick horns that are broken on the ends. The body is humpless, and the front legs are joined with a small cavity in between. The back legs are pinched out slightly, and it has a long tail. It has a detailed face with punctures for the nose and eyes, and the ears are visible below the horns. 5 cm long, 1.92 cm wide, and 4.98 cm tall. Locus: Tr. 4E, habitation levels, Middle Chalcolithic.

Other Figurines

Area I

S4.223 Nearly complete stylized bull figurine. One horn is broken and the other is missing. It has a flat featureless face, and a columnar body that flares out with a concave bottom. 3.85 cm tall, 2.67 cm wide (at the top), and 1.34 cm thick. Locus: Tr. 35, habitation levels, Middle Chalcolithic.

S5.212 Broken bear or bull figurine. The front legs are joined and flare out at the bottom. It has a pinched ear, and incised lines indicating hair. These incised lines are concentrated on the front and are more spaced apart on the bottom. 3.7 cm long, 2.5 cm wide, and 4.2 cm tall. Locus: Tr. 35, habitation layers, Middle Chalcolithic.

S3.183 Head of a terracotta figurine. It resembles a pig, but could represent any number of different animals. It has no horns and one ear is broken. It has a longer and more pronounced button snout than most of the other figurines. It also appears to be coated with an orange substance. 2.37 cm long, 2.62 cm wide, 1.86 tall. Locus: Tr. 35, habitation levels, Middle Chalcolithic.

Humpless Cattle and Animal Figurines (Continued)

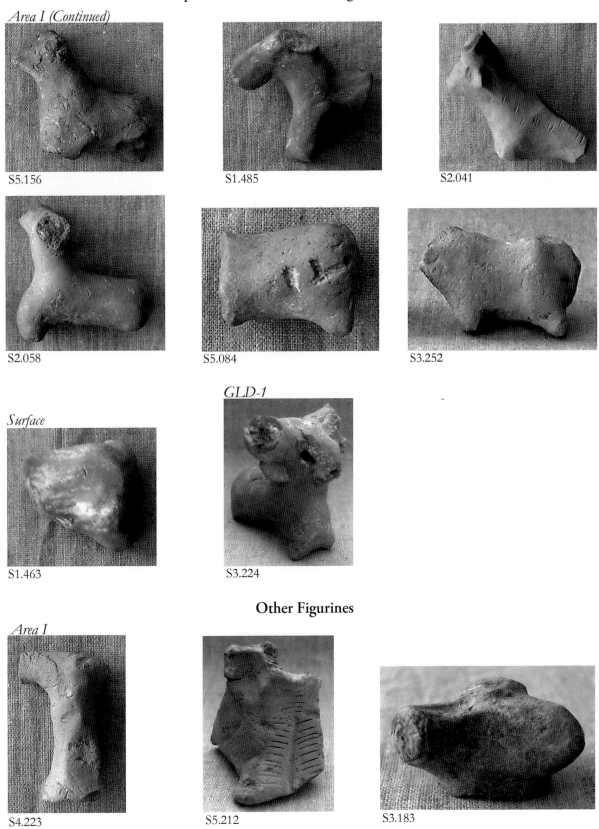

Area I (Continued)

S5.156

S1.485

S2.041

S2.058

S5.084

S3.252

Surface

GLD-1

S1.463

S3.224

Other Figurines

Area I

S4.223

S5.212

S3.183

Other Figurines *(cont'd.)*

Area III

S3.383 Seated bird figurine. It lacks any legs on the underside and is made of medium-coarse terracotta. 3.7 cm long, 2.37 cm wide, and 3.4 cm tall. Locus: Tr. 205, habitation levels, Middle Chalcolithic.

Surface

S3.161 A modeled piece of coarse ware with a red wash/slip. It resembles a snake, and was identified as a snake figurine by the excavator. 5.18 cm long, 1.84 cm wide, and 1.36 cm thick. Locus: Surface find on mound GLD-2.

GLD-1

S1.178 Seated bull figurine with gold/red color paint/slip. The bottom is concave and unpainted. The tail is wrapped and lying atop the back and the hump is right behind the head. It has short horns, appliqué eyes with tiny holes punched for pupils, nostril holes, and a small indent for the mouth. 3.68 cm long, 1.95 cm wide, and 2.39 cm tall. Locus: Tr. 4B, habitation levels, Early Historic.

S1.172 Elephant trunk. It is curled at the bottom and is very light in weight. It is slipped/washed in a pinkish-orange color. 3.8 cm long, 1.9 cm wide, and 2.1 cm thick. Locus: Tr. 4B, habitation levels, Early Historic.

S3.297 Arm from a human figurine. It is broken at both ends. It has a band around the middle with punched dots on it and is slipped in an orange/cream/pink color. 8.73 cm long, 3.06 cm wide, and 2.63 cm thick. Locus: Tr. 4H, erosional layers, possibly Early Historic.

S3.325 Humped bull figurine with perforated neck design. The front legs and left back leg are missing, and so it is uncertain whether it was meant to be seated or standing. The remaining right leg is articulated and flares outward. The rump is damaged. The hump is located directly behind the head. It does not appear to have had horns. It has a perforated design around the neck and slight facial features. 7.14 cm long, 4.01 cm wide, and 5.12 cm tall. Locus: Tr. 4J, erosional layers, possibly Early Historic.

Personal Ornaments

Ear Spools

Area III

S4.026 Ear spool of coarse fired clay. It has an hourglass shape and is flared at both ends. 2.76 cm long with diameter varying from 2.61 to 1.91 cm. Locus: Tr. 201, habitation levels, Late Chalcolithic.

S4.124 Ear spool of coarse fired clay. It is similar to S4.026, but with a more pronounced hour-glass shape. It is bright red and flared at both ends, with one end slightly wider than the other. Both ends are concave. 2.40 cm long with diameter varying from 2.49 cm on the widest end, to 1.26 cm in the middle. Locus: Tr. 203, habitation levels, Middle Chalcolithic.

Area IV

S4.039 Ear spool of coarse terracotta/fired clay. It has a conical/cylindrical shape and is perforated in the middle. It may have been longer; there are signs of breakage at the more slender end. 1.93 cm long with diameter varying from 1.72 to 2 cm. Locus: Tr. 203, habitation levels, Middle Chalcolithic.

Surface

S4.198 Broken cylindrical ear spool with button-like ends. Thumb-/fingerprints are visible on the unbroken end. 3.22 cm long with diameter varying from 1.99 cm on the wider ends to 1.73 cm in the center. Locus: Surface find on GLD-2, likely Late Chalcolithic.

GLD-1

S1.023 Perforated hourglass-shaped ear spool with flared ends. The wider end has an incised design depicting a triangle with rows of dots around it. The other end is plain. 1.49 cm long and 1.94 cm in diameter at the widest end with the design. Locus: Tr. 4A, habitation levels, Early Historic.

S1.252 Ear spool with ridge in the middle. It is made of fine clay that has been fired to a red color. It has a wide perforation in the center. 1.13 cm long and 1.48 cm in diameter. Locus: Tr. 4A, habitation levels, Early Historic.

Other Figurines (Continued)

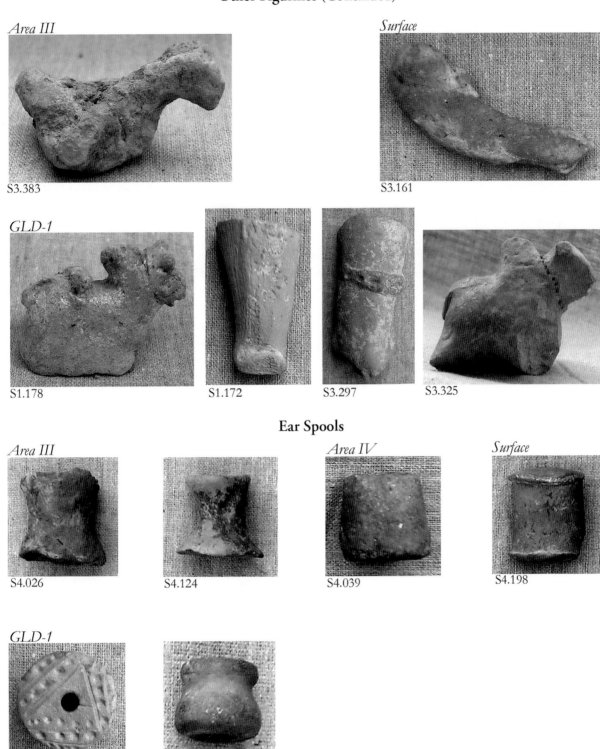

Area III

S3.383

Surface

S3.161

GLD-1

S1.178

S1.172

S3.297

S3.325

Ear Spools

Area III

S4.026

S4.124

Area IV

S4.039

Surface

S4.198

GLD-1

S1.023

S1.252

Ear Studs

Area I

S1.422 Button-type ear stud of coarse red terracotta. One end is smaller in diameter than the other. The smaller end may have some red paint on it, while the larger end appears plain, but has a faint hint of red. 0.79 cm in length and 0.70 cm in diameter on the widest end. Locus: Tr. 20, pit in habitation levels, Middle Chalcolithic.

S4.102 Button-shaped ear stud. The larger of the two ends has an incised design of concentric circles. The other, smaller end is plain. The shape is the same as S1.422 and S4.209. 0.79 cm in length with diameter varying from 1.36 cm on the widest end (with incised design) to 0.79 cm on the other end. Locus: Tr. 35, pit in habitation levels, Middle Chalcolithic.

S5.127 Ear stud of fine clay/terracotta with finial-like shape. 1.45 cm in length and 0.9 cm in diameter at the widest point. Locus: Tr. 69, habitation levels, Late Chalcolithic.

Area III

S4.209 Ear stud of Buff/Tan Ware. It is similar in shape and size to S1.422, but it shows no signs of slip or painted decoration. 0.63 cm in length with diameter varying from 1.16 cm to 0.80 cm. Locus: Tr. 210, habitation levels, Late Chalcolithic.

Area IV

S4.022 Cylindrical ear stud of coarse terracotta with concave ends. 1.40 cm long with diameter varying from 1.36 cm on the ends to 1.23 cm in the middle. Locus: Tr. 302, habitation levels, Middle Chalcolithic.

Bangles

Area II

S2.053 Coarse Red Ware bangle with red paint/slip. This red paint/slip is much thinner than that on S2.070. There are also signs of white paint on the bangle. 2.34 cm in length and 0.58 cm in diameter. Locus: Tr. 101, habitation levels, Middle Chalcolithic.

S2.070 Flat bangle, oval rather than circular in profile, made of medium to fine terracotta. It is covered with a red paint or slip, which is now cracking with age. It is painted on all sides, but the paint is almost completely worn away on one side. 2.66 cm in length, 0.82 cm wide, and 0.66 cm thick. Locus: Tr. 104, habitation levels, Middle Chalcolithic.

S2.219 Plain cream/orange colored bangle of fine terracotta. 3.0 cm in length and 0.64 cm in diameter. Locus: Tr. 105, habitation levels, Middle Chalcolithic.

GLD-1

S1.317 Slipped and burnished bangle of fine terracotta. 2.0 cm in length and 0.54 cm in diameter. Locus: Tr. 4B, habitation levels, Early Historic.

S3.204, 1 of 2 Plain bangle of fine terracotta. 3.26 cm in length and approximately 0.64 cm in diameter. Locus: Tr. 4C, pit in habitation levels, Early Historic.

S3.204, 2 of 2 Plain bangle of fine terracotta. 2.42 cm in length and 0.55 cm in diameter. Locus: Tr. 4C, pit in habitation levels, Early Historic.

S3.165 Tan/orange slipped bangle. Flat/oval in shape and made of fine terracotta. 2.24 cm in length, 0.77 cm wide, and 0.50 cm thick. Locus: Tr. 4D, habitation levels, Late Chalcolithic.

Ornament

S5.004 This ornament may depict a sun or a floral motif. It is fashioned of medium terracotta and when whole would have had 15–16 "rays" or "petals." The area around the perforation is raised and bulges out. 4.65 cm in length, 3.6 cm wide, and 2.25 cm thick. Locus: Surface find on GLD-2.

Ear Studs

Area I

S1.422

S4.102

S5.127

Area III

S4.209

Area IV

S4.022

Bangles

Area II

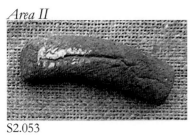
S2.053

S2.070

S2.219

GLD-1

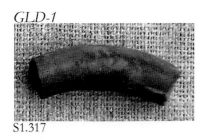
S1.317

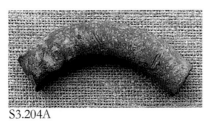
S3.204A

S3.204B

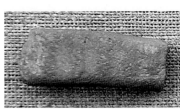
S3.165

Ornament

S5.004

Toys/Games

Miniature Vessels (Toy Pots)

Area I

S1.169 Miniature vessel of similar shape and size as S3.214A. It is made of medium-coarse unfired clay. It is quite shallow with a rounded bottom. One can easily feel where the original artisan pulled up the clay on the outside of the pot with his or her fingers, as the grooves are still preserved (each approximately 1.0 cm wide or less). It has an interior diameter of 3.3 cm and is approximately 1.3 to 1.5 cm deep. Locus: Tr. 5, habitation levels, Late Chalcolithic.

S1.223 Miniature vessel of coarse unfired clay. It is over half of the original vessel, and has raised edges and a slightly rounded bottom. It has an interior diameter of ca. 2.75 cm and a depth of 1.5 cm. Locus: Tr. 7, habitation levels, Late Chalcolithic.

S1.518 Terracotta miniature vessel with signs of burning on the inside and bottom. The edges are pinched and raised, and the bottom is rounded. 2.0 cm in diameter and 1.1 cm deep. Locus: Tr. 13, habitation levels near parallel walls, Middle Chalcolithic.

S1.491 Miniature vessel of unfired clay. It appears to have been made by rolling the unfired clay into a round ball and then pushing a finger into the middle to make an impression. It has uneven rounded edges and bottom. 1.20 cm in diameter and 0.70 to 0.80 cm deep. Locus: Tr. 17, habitation levels, Middle Chalcolithic.

S3.214A Miniature vessel of fine unfired clay. It has a slightly rounded bottom, probably from being molded in the palm of the hand, and raised edges that flare out slightly near the top. It is reconstructed from two pieces. It has an interior diameter of 3.1 cm and a depth of 2.0 cm. Locus: Tr. 34, habitation levels, Middle Chalcolithic.

Area II

S2.067 Miniature vessel of medium-coarse terracotta. The edges have been smoothed out into a cylindrical shape. It has flat, straight sides and a flat bottom. 1.5 cm in diameter and 0.7 cm deep. Locus: Tr. 105, habitation levels, Middle Chalcolithic.

GLD-1

S4.074 Miniature vessel of coarse Red Ware. It appears to have been made in the same manner as S1.491. 1.0 cm in diameter and ca. 0.60 cm deep. Locus: Tr. 4H/4I, erosional layers at the base of GLD-1.

Discs

Area I

S1.299 Hand-molded disc of reduced ware. 4.8 cm long, 4.21 cm wide, and 1.16 cm thick. Locus: Tr. 5, habitation levels, Late Chalcolithic.

Area III

S4.088 Thick round disc. It is quite eroded and may have once been slipped. 2.76 cm in diameter and 1.42 cm thick. Locus: Tr. 203, habitation levels, Middle Chalcolithic.

GLD-1

S3.217 Two cylindrical clay discs. One is cut diagonally and the second is broken on its top. Both are approximately 2.5 cm in diameter and 1.3 to 1.5 cm thick. Locus: Tr. 4C, habitation levels, Late Chalcolithic.

S3.401 Disc fragment with small incised dots along the border. The other side is plain. 2.14 cm long, 1.40 cm wide, and 0.64 cm thick. Locus: Tr. 4F, habitation levels, Late Chalcolithic.

Gamesmen

Area I

S1.160 Miniature conical gamesman of fine clay with a rounded top and flat bottom. It is slightly eroded and not perfectly round. 0.93 cm in diameter and 1.21 cm tall. Locus: Tr. 11, habitation levels, Middle Chalcolithic.

S3.159 Conical gamesman of coarse clay with concave bottom. Top diameter of 0.95 cm and bottom diameter of 1.9 cm. Locus: Tr. 34, habitation levels, Middle Chalcolithic.

S5.208 Conical gamesman with red slip. It has a curved top with eroded slip. Diameter of 1 to 1.65 cm. Locus: Tr. 39, habitation levels, Early Chalcolithic.

GLD-1

S3.334 Three conical gamesmen found together near the base of GLD-2 and GLD-1, close to the Street trenches. From left to right: the first has a slightly concave bottom and is slipped in red; base diameter of 2.12 cm and a height of 3.66 cm. The second is slightly damaged at the top and bottom; base diameter of 2.38 cm and a height of 3.54 cm. The third has a relatively flat bottom and its top is broken off; base diameter of 1.74 cm and a height of 2.07 cm. Locus: Tr. 4K, erosional levels, likely Early Historic.

Miniature Vessels (Toy Pots)

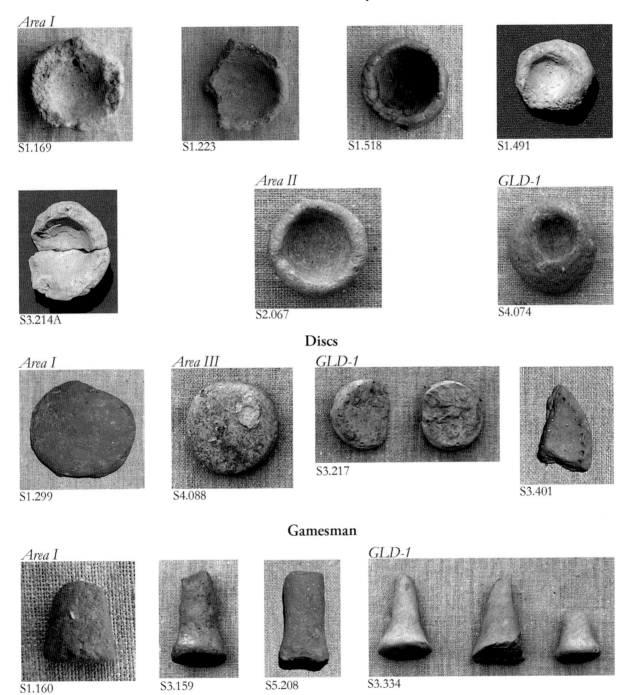

Area I

S1.169

S1.223

S1.518

S1.491

S3.214A

Area II

S2.067

GLD-1

S4.074

Discs

Area I

S1.299

Area III

S4.088

GLD-1

S3.217

S3.401

Gamesman

Area I

S1.160

S3.159

S5.208

GLD-1

S3.334

Perforated Terracotta Discs (Wheels)

Area I

S1.380 Red perforated terracotta disc. It appears to have been wheel-made with well-levigated clay. The top and bottom are coarse, but the sides have been worn smooth. It is likely a spindle whorl. 5.57 cm in diameter and 1.26 cm thick. Locus: Tr. 8, habitation levels, Late Chalcolithic.

S1.346 Hand-molded terracotta disc of medium-coarse unfired clay, refit from two pieces. The area around the perforation is raised on one side. 4.62 cm in diameter and 2.32 cm thick. Locus: Tr. 25, habitation levels, Late Chalcolithic.

S1.388 Eroded, reduced terracotta disc with broken edges and a scratch mark on one side near the perforation. The perforation widens near the edges and narrows inside. It is relatively heavy. A line near the perforation suggests that it may have been hung by a string and/or used as a loom weight. 6.76 cm long, 5.6 cm wide, and 1.92 cm thick. Locus: Tr. 25, habitation levels, Late Chalcolithic.

S5.179 Perforated disc of coarse red terracotta. Approximately 3.5 cm in diameter and 0.85 cm thick. Locus: Tr. 39, habitation levels, Early Chalcolithic.

S5.048A This perforated terracotta disc has a significant amount of chaff in the clay. It is red with an uneven perforation. 5.0 cm in diameter and 1.25 cm thick. Locus: Tr. 74, habitation levels, Late Chalcolithic.

Area II

S2.207 Perforated disc of fine terracotta with three lines on one side radiating from the center. The bottom is plain. Its thickness tapers at the edges and it is light and delicate. 3.72 cm in diameter and 0.85 cm thick. Locus: Tr. 101, habitation levels, Middle Chalcolithic.

Area III

S4.091 Perforated reduced terracotta disc. The top is slightly convex with a small raised area around the perforation. The thickness tapers at the edges. Approximately 3.8 cm in diameter and 1.36 cm thick. Locus: Tr. 203, habitation levels, Middle Chalcolithic.

Votive/Ritual Objects

Small Lamps (Votive Lamps)

Area I

S5.213 Hand-molded lamp of unfired clay (type 1). 4.75 by 4.15 cm wide and 1.65 cm in height. Locus: Tr. 12, habitation levels, Middle

Chalcolithic.

S1.347 Miniature lamp shaped with pinched edges (type 2). 2.60 by 2.12 cm wide and 1.40 cm in approximate height. Locus: Tr. 25, habitation levels, Late Chalcolithic.

S4.371 Half of a broken square lamp (type 3). It is made of coarse Red Ware with a thin red slip. Approximately 2.5 cm wide and 1.15 cm in height. Locus: Tr. 35, habitation levels, Middle Chalcolithic.

S5.068 Terracotta lamp with pinched edges (type 2). 3.3 cm in diameter and about 1.4 cm in height. Locus: Tr. 71, habitation levels, Late Chalcolithic.

Area III

S3.061 Two Black and Red Ware lamps slipped with black on the inside (type 1). The backs are plain. One is broken in half. Both are approximately 7 cm in diameter and 1.65 to 1.94 cm in height. Locus: Tr. 201, habitation levels, Late Chalcolithic.

S4.060 Hand-molded lamp of Red Ware (type 1). 3.5 cm in diameter and 1.84 cm in height. Locus: Tr. 202, habitation levels, Middle Chalcolithic.

GLD-1

S3.111 Wheel-thrown lamp with white concretions along the inside (type 1). 5.32 by 5.0 cm wide and 1.49 cm in height. Locus: Tr. 4D, habitation levels, Late Chalcolithic.

Rectilinear Containers (Votive Tanks)

Area I

S1.118 Broken base of a Red Ware rectilinear container with an upside-down V design on one side. 3.25 by 3.22 cm wide and 1.78 cm tall. Locus: Tr. 7, habitation levels, Late Chalcolithic.

S2.084 Broken base of a Red Ware rectilinear container with fingernail impressions on one corner. 3.8 by 3.75 cm wide and 2.65 cm tall. Locus: Tr. 25, habitation levels, Late Chalcolithic.

S3.026 Nearly complete Red Ware rectilinear container. Broken around the top edges and cracked down the center. Approximately 2.9 cm square and 3.5 cm tall. Locus: Tr. 32, habitation levels, Late Chalcolithic.

S3.308 Rectilinear container fragment with incised X design. One side of a four-sided Red Ware container. 2.65 cm long and 1.55 cm wide. Locus: Tr. 32, habitation levels, Late Chalcolithic.

Perforated Terracotta Discs (Wheels)

Area I

S1.380   S1.346   S1.388   S5.179

Area II   *Area III*

S5-048   S2.207   S4.091

Small Lamps (Votive Lamps)

Area I

S5.213   S1.347   S4.371   S5.068

Area III   *GLD-1*

S3.061A   S4.060   S3.111

Rectilinear Containers (Votive Tanks)

Area I

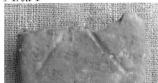

S1.118

S2.084

S3.026

S3.308

Rectilinear Containers (Votive Tanks) (cont'd.)

Area I (cont'd.)

S3.245A Corner of rectilinear Red Ware container fragment with incised V design on the sides. 2.05 cm wide and 2.65 cm tall. Locus: Tr. 34, habitation levels, Middle Chalcolithic.

S3.245B Red Ware rectilinear container fragment with incised V design on both sides. The pattern consists of sideways Vs aligned in horizontal rows. 4.65 cm wide and 4.2 cm tall. Locus: Tr. 34, habitation levels, Middle Chalcolithic.

S5.228 Red Ware rectilinear container fragment with incised lines design. 5.1 cm wide and 2.6 cm tall. Locus: near Tr. 75, surface find, likely Late Chalcolithic.

GLD-1

S3.275 Complete Red Ware rectilinear container with zigzag design on the sides. The outer layers are beginning to crackle and chip off. 2.95 cm square and 3.65 cm tall. Locus: Tr. 4F, pit at top of Deep Trench, likely Late Chalcolithic.

Molds and Crucibles

Molds

Area I

S5.219 Shallow, coarse slipped Red Ware mold 1.5 to 2 cm deep. The edges are broken and one side is badly damaged. 9.0 cm long, 6.45 cm wide, and 3.7 cm in height. Locus: Tr. 69, Late Chalcolithic.

S5.227 Coarse, heavy brick-like mold. It is relatively shallow, less than 1.3 cm deep. 7.8 cm long, 5.1 cm wide, and 3.55 cm in height. Locus: Tr. 75, Late Chalcolithic.

Area II

S5.229 Heavy mold with evidence of cracking from the heat. It is brittle and crumbling with concretions on the bottom. It is about 1 cm deep with white residue on the inside. 8.75 cm long, 4.2 cm wide, and 3.1 cm in height. Locus: Tr. 112, Late Chalcolithic.

Area III

S4.053 Heavy, brick-like mold. The top is very shallow and shows evidence of burning. 10.42 cm long, 7.29 cm wide, and 5.16 cm in height. Locus: Tr. 202, Middle Chalcolithic.

S4.118 Large coarse mold with concretions covering the top and sides. The interior is black and the bottom is red. There appear to be seed impressions on the bottom (shown). It is broken on both ends. 10.57 cm long, 9.83 cm wide and 5.03 cm in height. Locus: Tr. 203, Middle Chalcolithic.

GLD-1

S1.034 Reduced black slipped mold. The shallow interior is slipped and burnished and about 1 to 1.5 cm deep. There is an incised V design on the remaining end. 7.3 cm long, 6.2 cm wide, and 5.2 cm in height. Locus: Tr. 4B, Late Chalcolithic or Early Historic.

Crucibles

Area I

S1.457 Hand-molded crucible with flat bottom and thick walls (roughly 1.3 cm thick). It is rather heavy, constructed of unfired clay, and broken on one side. The object has no signs of burning. 5.59 cm in diameter, approximately 3 cm deep and 3.84 cm tall. Locus: Tr. 20, habitation levels, Middle Chalcolithic.

S4.109 Wheel-thrown crucible of coarse fabric. It has thin walls and is burned black all over. Roughly one-third of the original remains. It was found in a round structure. Base diameter 3.11 cm, approximately 4 cm deep and 4.55 cm tall. Locus: Tr. 27, habitation levels, Middle Chalcolithic.

S4.131 Complete cylindrical crucible with flat base. It appears to be of medium-coarse Red Ware, and shows signs of burning on the inside. 3.19 cm in diameter, 4.18 cm tall, approximately 3.4 cm deep, with walls 0.3 to 0.4 cm thick. Locus: Tr. 34, habitation levels, Middle Chalcolithic.

Rectilinear Containers (Votive Tanks) (Continued)

Area I (Continued)

S3.245A

S3.245B

S5.228

GLD-1

S3.275

Molds

Area I

S5.219

S5.227

Area II

S5.229

Area III

S4.053

S4.118

GLD-1

S1.034

Crucibles

Area I

S1.457

S4.109

S4.131

Vitrified Crucible Fragments

Area III

S4.019 Burned container fragment with what appears to be copper still attached. It measures 4.96 cm long, 3.22 wide cm, and 2.51 cm thick. Locus: Tr. 201, Layer 1, Late Chalcolithic.

S4.137 Four vitrified crucible fragments. They are blackened and coarse like pumice. Two have pieces of what appears to be copper still attached. From left to right the measurements are: (1) 8.41 x 7.42 x 2.34 cm; (2) 6.66 x 5.52 x 2.03 cm; (3) 7.06 x 4.93 x 3.34 cm; (4) 5.01 x 4.36 x 2.44 cm. Locus: Tr. 203, SW/SE Quadrant, Layer 1, Late Chalcolithic.

S4.219 Burned mold fragment, blackened and coarse like pumice. It measures 5.80 cm long, 5.09 cm wide, and 2.58 cm thick. Locus: Tr. 209, SW Quadrant, Layer 1, Late Chalcolithic.

Dabbers and Stoppers

Dabbers

Area I

S1.421 Dabber of unfired coarse clay. It is conical with a flat bottom and finger grooves along the sides. 3.26 by 3.08 cm wide and 3.13 cm tall. Locus: Tr. 20, habitation layers, Middle Chalcolithic.

S2.196 Poorly fired clay dabber. 4.86 by 4.18 cm wide and 4.57 cm tall. Locus: Tr. 25, habitation layers, Late Chalcolithic.

S4.073 Pear-shaped dabber of unfired clay. It is relatively heavy and composed of fine to medium clay. It was refit from two pieces. 6.21 by 5.26 cm wide and 6.54 cm tall. Locus: Tr. 35, habitation layers, Middle Chalcolithic.

Stoppers

Area I

S5.210 Stopper with round knob-like top with pinched edges. 3.5 cm wide and 3.7 cm long. Locus: surface near Tr. 12, likely Middle Chalcolithic.

S4.138 Conical red terracotta stopper. It is hand-molded with visible fingerprints on the sides. 3.26 to 3.31 cm wide and 3.53 cm long. Locus: Tr. 13, above wall, Middle Chalcolithic.

S4.100 Eroded knob-shaped stopper of buff-colored terracotta. 2.69 to 2.91 cm wide and 3.44 cm long. Locus: Tr. 35, habitation levels, Middle Chalcolithic.

S4.353 Stopper of coarse terracotta with concave bottom. 2.7 to 3.45 cm in diameter and 5.54 cm long. Locus: Tr. 35, habitation levels, Middle Chalcolithic.

Area III

S4.161 Stopper of fine unfired clay with pinched design at the top. 2.75 to 3.19 cm wide and 3.75 cm long. Locus: Tr. 204, habitation levels, Middle Chalcolithic.

Miscellaneous Terracotta Pieces

Weight

Area III

S3.216 Slightly chipped rectangular block of terracotta. It may have been used as a unit of measurement. It has a small hole drilled into the side. This hole may have been drilled after the unit was fired in order to make the unit the correct weight. 5.34 cm long, 3.32 cm wide, and 1.52 cm thick. Locus: Tr. 204, habitation levels, Middle Chalcolithic.

Spout Fragment

GLD-1

S1.519 Spout fragment of coarse micaceous Red Ware. It is slipped on the lip and inside, but not on the outside. It has been refit from two pieces. 1.47 to 5.7 cm in diameter and 9.24 cm long. Locus: Tr. 4B, habitation layers, Early Historic.

Decorative Tile

GLD-1

S1.057 Carved decorative tile of highly fired terracotta. It is broken on three sides. It appears to be perforated in the middle and has carved decorative marks. 7.79 cm long, 6.48 cm wide, and 1.25 cm thick. Locus: Tr. 4A, habitation levels, Early Historic. Re-used Pottery

Vitrified Crucible Fragments

Area III

S4.019

S4.137

S4.219

Dabbers

Area I

S1.421

S2.196

S4.073

Stoppers

Area I

Area III

S5.210

S4.138

S4.100

S4.353

S4.161

Miscellaneous Terracotta Objects

Weight

Area III

Spout Fragment

GLD-1

Decorative Tile

GLD-1

Game Pieces

Area I

S1.501 Group of 2 diamond-shaped game pieces. Left to right: (1) 6.95 x 5.22 x 0.82 cm; (2) 4.74 x 3.67 x 0.70 cm. Locus: Tr. 6, habitation levels, Late Chalcolithic.

S1.495 Group of four game pieces: two diamonds, one square, and a diamond/triangle. Left to right: (1) 6.88 cm tall x 5.32 cm wide x 1.10 cm thick; (2) 6.76 x 4.61 x 0.71 cm; (3) 4.28 x 4.43 x 3.06 cm; (4) 3.66 x 3.06 x 0.54 cm. Locus: Tr. 7, habitation levels, Late Chalcolithic.

Area III

S4.086 Triangular game piece. 3.84 cm in height, base of 7.18 cm, and 0.84 cm thick. Locus: Tr. 201, habitation levels, Late Chalcolithic.

S4.140 A single rectangular game piece. It is made of Black and Red Ware and its edges have been rounded. 7.0 cm long, 5.01 cm wide, and 0.61 cm thick. Locus: Tr. 203, habitation levels, Middle Chalcolithic.

GLD-1

S3.108 Group of three game pieces: one triangle and two diamonds. The triangle is 4.11 cm tall, 3.57 cm wide at the base, and 0.62 cm thick. The diamonds are 4.10 x 3.39 x 0.62 cm and 3.45 x 2.76 x 0.58 cm. Locus: Tr. 4D, habitation levels, Middle Chalcolithic.

S3.122 Group of nine game pieces: seven triangles and two squares. The triangles range in size from 1.84–3.07 cm tall, 1.59–2.73 cm wide at the base, and 0.38–0.75 cm thick. The squares are 2.37 x 2.75 x 0.72 cm and 2.02 x 1.73 x 0.64 cm. Locus: Tr. 4D, habitation levels, Middle Chalcolithic.

S3.033 Group of six game pieces: two diamonds, one hexagon, one square, and two rectangles. The diamonds measure 4.32 x 3.75 x 0.62 cm and 3.42 x 2.03 x 0.57 cm. The hexagon is 3.19 x 2.55 x 0.61 cm. The square is 2.56 x 2.42 x 0.47 cm. The rectangles are 2.12 x 1.72 x 0.46 cm and 3.30 x 2.14 x 0.49 cm. Locus: Tr. 4C, habitation levels, Late Chalcolithic.

Reused Pottery

Game Pieces

Area I

S1.501

S1.495

Area III

S4.086

S4.140

GLD-1

S3.108

S3.122

S3.033

Terracotta Ground Discs (Hopscotches)

Area I

S1.373 Large, thick ground disc made from a Black and Red Ware sherd. 6.54 cm in diameter and 1.32 cm thick. Locus: Tr. 5, habitation levels, Late Chalcolithic.

S1.493A Ground disc made from a Black and Red Ware sherd. Found with S1.493B in a pit. 4.50 cm in diameter and 0.70 cm thick. Locus: Tr. 5, pit, Late Chalcolithic.

S1.493B Ground disc made from a Black and Red Ware sherd. It has jagged edges with signs of chipping. It was found in a pit together with S1.493A. 4.86 cm in diameter and 0.49 cm thick. Locus: Tr. 5, pit, Late Chalcolithic.

S2.035 Ground disc made from a Gray Ware sherd with red slip. One edge is ground smooth and the others are chipped. There is a round indent in the center that is likely a sign of attempted perforation. 4.0 cm long, 3.57 cm wide, and 0.75 cm thick. Locus: Tr. 23, habitation levels, Middle Chalcolithic.

S3.029 Group of 5 ground discs: 2 Buff Ware (A, C), 1 Black and Red Ware (B), and 2 Red Ware (D, E). Ground disc B was made from a Black and Red Ware sherd with a painted design (checked diamonds). The sides show evidence of both chipping and grinding. The 5 ground discs range in length from 4.30–4.65 cm, in width from 4.23–4.59 cm, and in thickness from 0.89–1.38 cm. Locus: Tr. 32, habitation levels, Late Chalcolithic.

GLD-1

S1.451 Ground disc made from a Red Ware sherd. It is slipped on both sides and bears an incised design (pre-firing) near the top. The edges have been ground smooth. 3.3 cm in diameter and 0.87

cm thick. Locus: Tr. 4B, habitation levels, Early Historic.

S3.038 Ground disc made from a Black and Red Ware sherd with painted stripes in maroon/brown. It is slipped on both sides and the edges are ground and chipped. 2.72 cm in diameter and 0.54 cm thick. Locus: Tr. 4C, habitation levels, Late Chalcolithic.

S3.266 Miniature ground disc about the size of a button. It is made from a Black and Red Ware sherd and has jagged chipped edges. 1.40 cm in diameter and 0.45 cm thick. Locus: Tr. 4F, habitation levels, Middle Chalcolithic.

Stone Discs (Hopscotches)

Area I

S1.432 Sandstone ground disc with one convex top and rounded bottom. There is evidence of both chipping and grinding around the edges. 3.12 cm in diameter and 1.43 cm tall. Locus: Tr. 13, habitation levels, Middle Chalcolithic.

GLD-1

S1.186 Sandstone ground disc that is chipped around the edges and along the top and bottom. It was found in a pit on GLD-2. 6.36 cm in diameter and 1.8 cm thick. Locus: Tr. 4B, pit, Early Historic.

S1.277 Ground disc made from a green-tinted stone, possibly serpentinite. It has jagged chipped edges and a film on one side. Both sides are relatively flat. 4.54 cm in diameter and 1.3 cm thick. Locus: 4B, habitation levels, Early Historic.

S3.072 Schist ground disc with chipped and ground edges. Both sides are relatively flat. 4.49 cm long, 4.26 cm wide, and 0.95 cm thick. Locus: Tr. 4C, habitation levels, Late Chalcolithic.

Terracotta Ground Discs (Hopscotches)

Area I

S1.373

S1.493A

S1.493B

S2.035

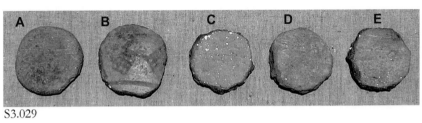

S3.029

GLD-1

S1.451

S3.038

S3.266

Stone Discs (Hopscotches)

Area I

S1.432

GLD-1

S1.186

S1.277

S3.072

Vent Plug

GLD-1

S3.272 Vent plug made from reused pottery. The concave bottom is cream color. The convex top is slipped and burnished, and fading in color from black to red. The slip is now cracking. The edges are very jagged. It is thickest in the middle and tapers out to 0.1 mm on the ends. It was found in a pit near the tandoor structure on GLD-1. It measures 5.73 cm long, 5.68 cm wide, and 0.89 cm tall. Locus: Tr. 4F, pit near tandoor structure, Late Chalcolithic.

Perforated Discs

Area I

S5.152 A square-shaped perforated disc made from a thick, coarse Black and Red Ware sherd. The perforation is very straight. On the bottom side of the disc there is erosion around the perforation. The perforation is approximately 0.5 cm in diameter. The disc is relatively flat. It measures 4.5 cm by 4.5 cm, and is 0.95 cm thick. Locus: Tr. 9, habitation levels, Middle Chalcolithic.

S5.039 Perforated disc made from a Black and Red Ware sherd, slipped on both sides and burnished on the inside. The slip has eroded from the area around the perforation. The perforation is approximately 0.6 cm in diameter. The disc measures 5.75 cm long, 5.4 cm wide, and 0.85 cm thick. Locus: Tr. 68, habitation levels, Late Chalcolithic.

S5.034 Perforated disc made from a thin Black and Red Ware sherd of fine fabric. The edges are ground smooth and the disc is slightly concave. The perforation is approximately 0.2 cm in diameter. The disc measures 3.2 cm long, 3.1 cm wide, and 0.55 cm thick. Locus: Tr. 71, habitation levels, Late Chalcolithic.

S5.048B Perforated disc made from a micaceous Red Ware sherd slipped on both sides. The perforation (approximately 0.5 cm in diameter) is eroded on the top. The disc has uneven edges which are now smooth as a result of grinding or erosion. It is slightly concave. 4.15 cm long, 4.0 cm wide, and 0.75 cm thick. Locus: Tr. 74, habitation levels, Late Chalcolithic.

Area II

S2.063 Perforated disc made from a Red Ware sherd, slipped on both sides. One side is highly eroded and on the top the slip has eroded from the area around the perforation. The perforation is approximately 0.5 cm in diameter. 5.64 cm long, 5.42 cm wide, and 0.99 cm thick. Locus: Tr. 104, habitation levels, Middle Chalcolithic.

S2.149 Perforated disc made of Tan Ware. The edges are well ground and the disc is very flat. The perforation is slightly oval and is approximately 0.45 cm wide. There is little erosion around the perforation. The disc measures 2.50 cm in diameter and is 0.78 cm thick. Locus: Tr. 104, habitation levels, Middle Chalcolithic.

Area III

S4.186 Perforated disc made from a thin red micaceous ware. The disc is badly eroded and was found in a pit sealed by Layer 3. There is erosion around the perforation, which is perfectly round and measures 0.4 cm in diameter. The disc measures 3.72 cm long, 3.55 cm wide, and 0.57 cm thick. Locus: Tr. 203, habitation levels, Middle Chalcolithic.

S4.257 Perforated disc made from a thin micaceous Red Ware sherd. It appears to be badly eroded and was reconstructed from three pieces. It is relatively flat with an oval perforation of 0.75 cm x 0.65 cm. The disc is round with ground edges. It is 6.78 cm long, 6.43 cm wide, and 0.61 cm thick. Locus: Tr. 209, habitation levels, Late Chalcolithic.

GLD-1

S2.028 Perforated disc fragment made from a Red Ware sherd, slipped red on one side. The exterior edge is well ground. The perforation may have been as wide as 1 cm. The remaining fragment measures 3.30 cm in length, 2.20 cm wide, and 0.78 cm thick. Locus: Tr. 4A, habitation levels, Early Historic.

S3.323 Perforated disc made from a coarse Black and Red Ware sherd. The perforation measures approximately 0.6–0.7 cm in diameter and is chipped around the edges. The disc is heavy and slightly concave. 6.60 cm long, 6.23 cm wide, and 1.21 cm thick. Locus: Tr. 4F, Deep Trench, Middle Chalcolithic.

Vent Plug

GLD-1

S3.272

Perforated Discs

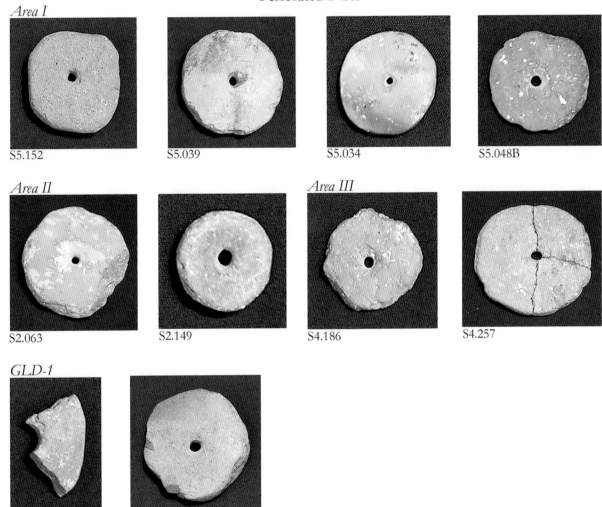

Area I

S5.152   S5.039   S5.034   S5.048B

Area II   *Area III*

S2.063   S2.149   S4.186   S4.257

GLD-1

S2.028   S3.323

Graffiti on Pottery

Area I

S3.225 Triangle-shaped graffiti on interior of a Black and Red Ware sherd. 3.52 cm long, 2.64 cm wide, and 0.57 cm thick. Locus: Tr. 31, NE quadrant, Late Chalcolithic.

S3.130 Graffiti on exterior of a Black and Red Ware sherd. Pipal leaf design. 3.80 cm long, 2.39 cm wide, and 0.57 cm thick. Locus: Tr. 34, NW quadrant, Layer 1 on slope, Middle Chalcolithic.

S3.400 Three lines on interior of a medium coarse Red Ware rim. 9.16 cm long, 5.25 cm wide, and 1.05 cm thick. Locus: Tr. 35, NE quadrant, Middle Chalcolithic.

S3.416 Double X's scratched onto the exterior of a coarse Red Ware sherd. 2.14 cm long, 3.95 cm wide, and 0.75 cm thick. Locus: Tr. 35, SE quadrant, Middle Chalcolithic.

Area III

S3.062 Graffiti on exterior of a Black and Red Ware rim sherd (slipped black on interior). 3.67 cm long, 3.33 cm wide, and 0.82 cm thick. Locus: Tr. 201, Layer 1 on slope, Late Chalcolithic.

S3.415 Exterior incised design on the mouth of a thin, coarse Red Ware globular jar. It was found inside a larger storage jar at the base of a pit. The fragment of globular jar is 10.86 cm tall, 9.54 cm wide, and 0.47 cm thick. Locus: Tr. 205, NE quadrant, Pit 1 sealed by the surface, Middle Chalcolithic.

S3.289 Lines of graffiti on exterior of a thick Black and Red Ware sherd. 8.11 cm long, 3.27 cm wide, and 0.75 cm thick. Locus: Tr. 206, NE/SE quadrants, Pit 1 sealed by surface, Middle Chalcolithic.

S4.369 Graffiti on exterior of a thin, white-painted Black and Red Ware rim sherd. The graffiti depicts a box with lines. 7.90 cm long, 5.19 cm wide, and 0.67 cm thick. Locus: Tr. 209, NW/SW quadrants, Late Chalcolithic.

S4.370 Incised design on exterior of an eroded Black and Red Ware rim. 4.31 cm long, 3.75 cm wide, and 0.65 cm thick. Locus: Tr. 209, NW quadrant, Late Chalcolithic.

Area IV

S4.342a One of two X-shaped graffiti on exterior of thin, coarse Red Ware sherds. 6.66 cm long, 3.95 cm wide, and 0.52 cm thick. Locus: Tr. 310, SW/NW quadrants, in pit sealed by Layer 1, Middle Chalcolithic.

S4.342b Second of two X-shaped graffiti on exterior of thin, coarse Red Ware sherds. 4.37 cm long, 3.50 cm wide, and 0.49 cm thick. Locus: Tr. 310, SW/NW quadrants, in pit sealed by Layer 1, Middle Chalcolithic.

S4.345 Series of short lines on the inner side of a thin, coarse Red Ware rim sherd. 4.40 cm long, 3.16 cm wide, and 0.44 cm thick. Locus: Tr. 310, NW quadrant, in Pit 2 sealed by Layer 4, Middle Chalcolithic.

GLD-1

S3.074 Square-shaped graffiti on exterior of a Red Ware sherd. 4.94 cm long, 2.90 cm wide, and 0.89 cm thick. Locus: Tr. 4C, NW/SW quadrant, Late Chalcolithic.

S3.399 X-shaped graffiti on exterior of a Red Ware sherd. 4.25 cm long, 3.00 cm wide, and 0.49 cm thick. Locus: Tr. 4E, Middle Chalcolithic.

Stone Objects

Bead Polishers

Area I

S1.139 Bead polisher fragment of micaceous sandstone broken on three sides. It does not exhibit any grooves. Like S4.001 the top edge is very straight. 6.46 cm long, 4.14 cm wide, and 2.46 cm tall. Locus: Tr. 5, habitation levels, Late Chalcolithic.

Surface

S4.001 Bead polisher fragment of micaceous schist. A number of grooves created from bead polishing are visible on one side. One of the grooves is approximately 2.0 mm deep. The opposite side has battering marks. 7.82 cm long, 6.42 cm wide, and 3.09 cm tall. Locus: Surface find, possibly Late Chalcolithic.

NB: The line drawings of the graffiti on pottery are by the author.

Graffiti on Pottery

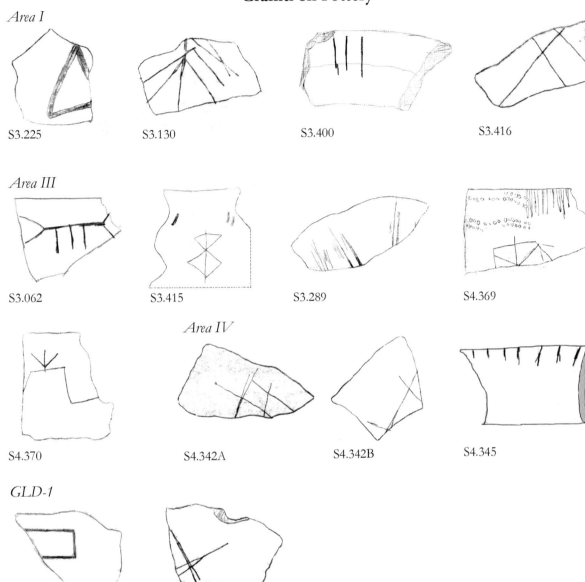

Area I

S3.225   S3.130   S3.400   S3.416

Area III

S3.062   S3.415   S3.289   S4.369

Area IV

S4.370   S4.342A   S4.342B   S4.345

GLD-1

S3.074   S3.399

Stone

Bead Polishers

Area I

S1.139

Surface

S4.001

Spheres (Slingballs)

Area I

S1.253 Large, quartz sandstone sphere with a bluish tint. It appears weathered and is well-rounded in shape. 5.19 cm in diameter. Locus: Tr. 5, habitation levels, Late Chalcolithic.

S1.330 Large, very heavy, sandstone sphere. The ball is completely round and its surface is pitted. 5.76 cm in diameter. Locus: Tr. 5, habitation levels, Late Chalcolithic.

S1.085 Small quartzite sphere with a single battering mark. 1.4 cm in diameter. Locus: Tr. 9, habitation levels, Middle Chalcolithic.

S3.256 Quartzite sphere with a smooth surface. One end is rather flat. It measures 2.92 cm long, 2.80 cm wide and 2.80 cm tall. Locus: Tr. 30, habitation levels, Late Chalcolithic.

S5.138 Quartz sandstone sphere with rough surface. It has a round shape. 2.55 cm in diameter. Locus: Tr. 69, habitation levels, Late Chalcolithic.

Area II

S2.209 Quartz sandstone sphere with rough pitted surface. 2.03 cm in diameter. Locus: Tr. 101, habitation levels, Middle Chalcolithic.

S2.007 Quartzite sphere with a battered surface. Its shape is more like a rounded cube than a sphere. It measures 3.53 cm long, 3.35 cm wide and 3.30 cm tall. Locus: Tr. 104, habitation levels, Middle Chalcolithic.

Area III

S3.065 Very smooth sandstone sphere. Its shape is a nearly perfect sphere with minimal scratches and pits. 1.88 cm in diameter. Locus: Tr. 201, habitation levels, Late Chalcolithic.

S4.037 Larger quartzite sphere. It is almost perfectly round. Approximately 4.59 cm in diameter. Locus: Tr. 202, habitation levels, Middle Chalcolithic.

S3.253 Large sphere of banded quartz sandstone. Its surface is pitted, weathered, and covered in concretions. Its shape is more rounded and cube-like than spherical. It measures 4.03 cm long, 3.98 cm wide and 3.87 cm tall. Locus: Tr. 206, habitation levels, Middle Chalcolithic.

GLD-1

S3.018 Very smooth quartz sphere with battering marks on one end. Its shape is rather uneven and lumpy rather than spherical. It measures 1.94 cm long, 1.86 cm wide and 1.80 cm tall. Locus: Tr. 4C, habitation levels, Late Chalcolithic.

S3.234 Large, sandstone sphere. It has a very smooth surface and its shape is almost perfectly spherical. There is also a black pitted area, which may indicate burning. Approximately 4.00 cm in diameter. Locus: Tr. 4E, habitation levels, Middle Chalcolithic.

Handle Fragment

Surface

S1.153 Broken sandstone handle. It measures 9.99 cm long, 4.40 cm wide and 3.55 cm thick. Locus: Surface find, possibly Late Chalcolithic.

Metal Objects – Copper and Bronze

Blades

Area I

S1.376 Blade or knife fragment. It is broken on three sides, and only the wide end opposite the point is an original edge. Therefore, it is possible that the object is something other than a blade. It appears to have been fashioned from a thin flat sheet of copper. 2.63 cm long, 2.02 cm wide, and 0.31 cm thick. Locus: Tr. 6, habitation levels, Late Chalcolithic.

S5.121 Unidentified copper object, possibly a flat blade or knife. One end is triangular, and the other end is flat and narrowed for hafting. 4.9 cm long, 2.9 cm at widest point, and 0.4 cm thick. Locus: Tr. 65, habitation levels, Late Chalcolithic.

Chisel

Area IV

S4.185 Chisel fragment. The top end is broken. It is heavy and well made. 4.42 cm long, 2.81 cm wide, 0.50 cm thick. Locus: Tr. 304, habitation levels, Middle Chalcolithic.

Spheres (Slingballs)

Area I

S1.253   S1.330   S1.085   S3.256   S5.138

Area II   *Area III*

S2.209   S2.007   S3.065   S4.037   S3.253

GLD-1

S3.018   S3.234

Handle Fragment

Surface

S1.153

Copper and Bronze

Blades   ### Chisel

Area I   *Area IV*

S1.376   S5.121   S4.185

Metal Objects – Copper and Bronze (cont'd.)

Bangles

Area I

S1.260 Copper bangle broken into two pieces. It has a heavy white film on the surface. Each piece is between 3.13 to 3.13 cm long and 0.35 cm in diameter. Locus: Tr. 7, habitation levels, Late Chalcolithic.

GLD-1

S2.109 Corroded bangle fragment. One end appears recently broken, and the other end is corroded. 3.78 cm long and 0.40 cm in diameter. Locus: 4A, habitation levels, Early Historic.

Kohl Stick

GLD-1

S3.069 Kohl stick fashioned from a thin strip of copper. The thickness varies from 0.1 to 0.5 cm. The thin end is jagged, perhaps from a recent break. The thick end is a rounded square. 4.90 cm in length, 0.54 cm in width, and 0.51 cm thick. Locus: Tr. 4C, habitation levels, Late Chalcolithic.

Rings

Area I

S4.085 Thin copper wire bent into the shape of a ring. It is very fragile. 2.08 cm long, 1.76 cm wide, and 0.15 cm thick. Locus: Tr. 29, habitation levels, Late Chalcolithic.

Area II

S4.134 Bronze ring fragment. The break is visible on one end and the other end is corroded. The ring bears a slight ridge running along the band. 1.59 cm long, 0.45 cm wide, and 0.12 cm thick. Locus: Tr. 305, habitation levels, Middle Chalcolithic.

Bell

GLD-1

S3.218 Handle of a bronze bell. It is finely crafted and is rust-ing green. It appears to have been made in a mold. 2.00 cm long, 1.81 cm wide, and 2.98 cm thick. Locus: Tr. 4C, habitation levels, Early Historic.

Coins

Area IV

S4.084 Bronze coin, roughly dated to the 15th century (786 Muslim Era, AD 1408). 1.94 cm in diameter and 0.70 cm thick. Locus: Tr. 310, fill, Tughluq.

GLD-1

S3.091 Heavily corroded copper coin. 1.57 cm long, 1.53 cm wide, and 0.59 cm thick. Locus: Tr. 4C, erosional layers, Early Historic.

Surface

S4.251 Plain heavy coin found on the surface. 1.24 cm in diameter and 0.56 cm thick. Locus: surface, period unknown.

Metal Objects – Iron

Hollow Points

GLD-1

S1.005 Hollow iron point reconstructed from two pieces. The interior diameter at the widest point is 1.8 cm. The thickness of the metal is 2–3 mm. The point itself is 7.5 cm long, 2.58 cm wide, and 2.25 cm thick. Locus: Tr. 4A, habitation levels, Early Historic.

S3.035B Hollow iron point. The thickness of the metal is approximately 1 mm. It was found together with S3.035A. 7.21 cm long, 1.52 cm wide, and 1.12 cm thick. Locus: Tr. 4C, habitation levels, Early Historic.

Points

GLD-1

S2.104 Iron point. 7.29 cm long, 1.35 cm wide, and 1.19 cm thick. Locus: Tr. 4A, habitation levels, Early Historic.

S1.029 Very corroded pointed iron piece. 3.22 cm long and 0.88 cm wide. Locus: Tr. 4A, habitation levels, Early Historic.

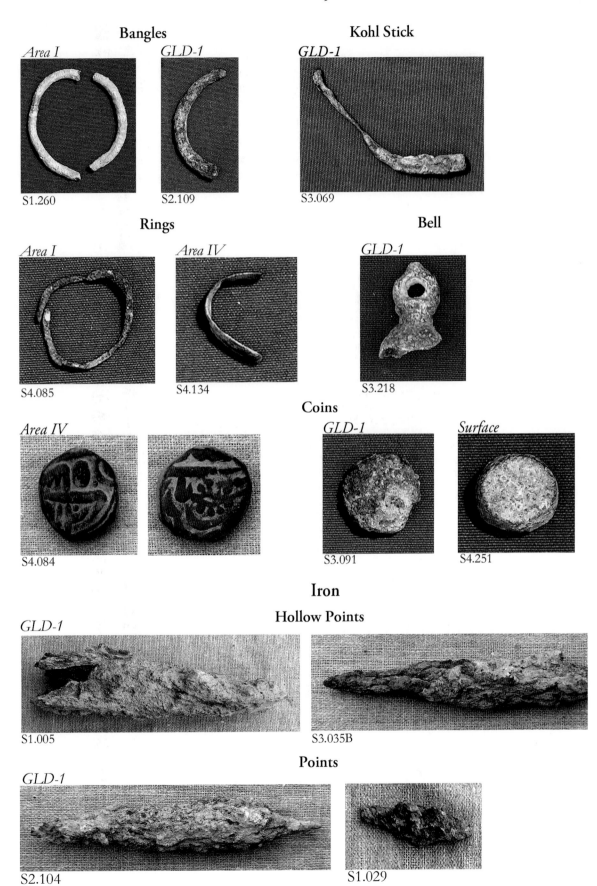

Bangles

Area I
S1.260

GLD-1
S2.109

Kohl Stick

GLD-1
S3.069

Rings

Area I
S4.085

Area IV
S4.134

Bell

GLD-1
S3.218

Coins

Area IV
S4.084

GLD-1
S3.091

Surface
S4.251

Iron

Hollow Points

GLD-1
S1.005

S3.035B

Points

GLD-1
S2.104

S1.029

Metal Objects – Iron (cont'd.)

Points (cont'd.)

GLD-1 (cont'd.)

S1.293 Point or a nail with its top missing. It is thick and broken at both ends. 3.72 cm long and 0.97 cm wide. Locus: Tr. 4B, habitation levels, Early Historic.

S1.342 Point or a nail found in Pit 3. 4.59 cm long and 0.83 cm wide. Locus: Tr. 4B, pit, Early Historic.

S1.343 Thick iron point. Found in Pit 4/5. 4.44 cm long and 1.21 cm wide. Locus: Tr. 4B, Pit 4/5, Early Historic.

S1.455 Thick iron point. Found in Pit 1. 4.45 cm long and 1.30 cm wide. Locus: Tr. 4C, Pit 1, Early Historic.

S3.035A Thick, heavy iron point. Found together with S3.035B. 6.19 cm long, 1.96 cm wide, and 1.89 cm thick. Locus: Tr. 4C, habitation levels, Early Historic.

Nails

Area IV

S4.117 Nail or point. It is broken on both ends. 4.28 cm long, 1.31 cm wide, and 1.28 cm thick. Locus: Tr. 301, habitation levels, Middle Chalcolithic.

GLD-1

S2.089 Complete nail with rounded head. 4.80 cm long, 1.83 cm wide, and 1.37 cm thick. Locus: Tr. 4A, habitation levels, Early Historic.

S3.199 Possible nail. It is broken on both ends. 3.57 cm long, 0.72

cm wide, and 0.64 cm thick. Locus: Tr. 4C, habitation levels, Early Historic.

S3.203 Flat rectangular nail fragment with both ends broken. Like S3.199, it has dusty orange rust. It was found in Pit 7, sealed by the surface. 2.00 cm long, 0.97 cm wide, and 0.63 cm thick. Locus: Tr. 4C, Pit 7, Early Historic.

Arrow Head

GLD-1

S2.217 Iron arrow head. Pointed at both ends, or one end pointed and the other narrowed for a shaft. 4.49 cm long, 1.96 cm wide, and 0.89 cm thick. Locus: Tr. 4A, habitation levels, Early Historic.

Axe

GLD-1

S1.310 Very large, heavy axe head. The edge is still quite sharp despite corrosion. It is thin at the cutting edge and then thickens to about 5.5 cm at the other end, which is broken. The axe as a whole seems to be disintegrating into flaking iron sheets. It measures 10.28 cm long, 10.09 cm wide, and 5.26 cm thick. Locus: Tr. 4B, habitation levels, Early Historic.

Chopper

GLD-1

S1.103 Thin, light chopping blade. It was fashioned from a thin sheet of iron. 9.31 cm long, 6.43 cm wide, and 0.35 cm thick. Locus: Tr. 4B, habitation levels, Early Historic.

Points (Continued)

GLD-1 (continued)

S1.293

S1.342

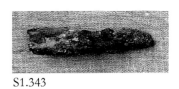

S1.343

S1.455

S3.035A

Nails

Area IV

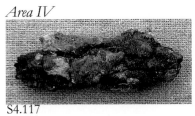

S4.117

GLD-1

S2.089

S3.199

S3.203

Arrowhead

GLD-1

S2.217

Axe

GLD-1

S1.310

Chopper

GLD-1

S1.103

Metal Objects – Iron (cont'd.)

Dagger

GLD-1

S2.057A Iron dagger with thick curved handle. It was reconstructed from two pieces and is fairly heavy. The tip is broken off of the blade. 11.96 cm long, 3.30 cm wide, and 1.61 cm thick. Locus: Tr. 4A, habitation levels, Early Historic.

Blades

Area I

S2.031 Blade fragment consisting of a thin strip broken at both ends. It was found in the back fill of Layer 1. 3.16 cm long, 1.71 cm wide, and 0.35 cm thick. Locus: Tr. 33, context unknown, Late Chalcolithic (or later).

GLD-1

S1.174 Possible blade. It is a relatively thin strip of iron. It appears to be a complete specimen with both ends intact. There is a visible but corroded perforation at one end approximately 0.3 cm in diameter. 10.92 cm long, 1.95 cm wide, and 0.87 cm thick. Locus: Tr. 4B, habitation levels, Early Historic.

Rod

GLD-1

S1.459A Rectangular iron rod broken on both ends. 9.82 cm long, 1.6 cm wide, and 1.81 cm thick. Locus: Tr. 4B, habitation levels, Early Historic.

Chisel

GLD-1

S1.195 Iron chisel. One end is rectangular and the other end is pointed. It appears to be a complete specimen. 4.89 cm long, 2.12 cm wide, and 1.21 cm thick. Locus: Tr. 4A, habitation levels, Early Historic.

Sickles

GLD-1

S2.054 Sickle or iron plough. It is crescent shaped with a wider base (2.15 cm at base vs. 0.7 cm at tip). It is flat and appears to be separating into layers. On the inner edge there is a groove where a sharp blade could fit. 9.53 cm long, between 2.34 and 0.88 cm wide, and 1.93 cm thick. Locus: Tr. 5B, habitation levels, Early Historic.

S2.172A Unidentified object, possibly a sickle or hoe. One end is triangular with a pointed tip (now broken). It has an S-like curved shape. It is flat and is flaking off in layers. 12.31 cm long, between 1.77 and 2.83 cm wide, and 1.52 cm thick. Locus: Tr. 5B, habitation levels, Early Historic.

Hoes

GLD-1

S1.105 Possible hoe fragment. In profile it looks as if it was made from layers of metal. It is triangular and becomes thinner towards the wider end, decreasing from roughly 4 to 2 cm. It is flat on both sides. 7.78 cm long, 3.69 cm wide, and 2.6 cm thick. Locus: Tr. 4B, habitation levels, Early Historic.

S1.309A Heavy iron hoe. The central opening may have held a wooden stick or rod. This opening is 0.7 to 2 cm in diameter. It widens at one end and narrows at the other. The hoe was found near S1.310 (axe), close to the floor. It measures 8.89 cm long, 5.29 cm wide, and 5.3 cm tall. Locus: Tr. 4B, habitation levels, Early Historic.

S1.437 Pear-shaped heavy iron hoe fragment. 5.58 cm long, 4.01 cm wide, and 3.53 cm thick. Locus: Tr. 4B, habitation levels, Early Historic.

Dagger

GLD-1

S2.057A

Blades

Area I

S2.031

GLD-1

S1.174

Rod

GLD-1

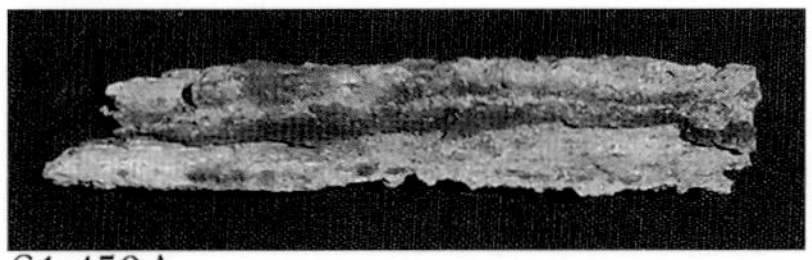

S1.459A

Chisel

GLD-1

S1.195

Sickles

GLD-1

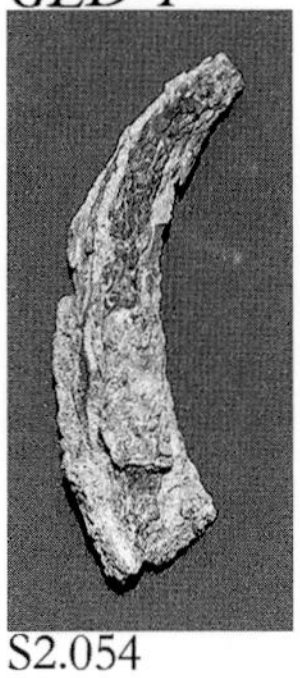

S2.054

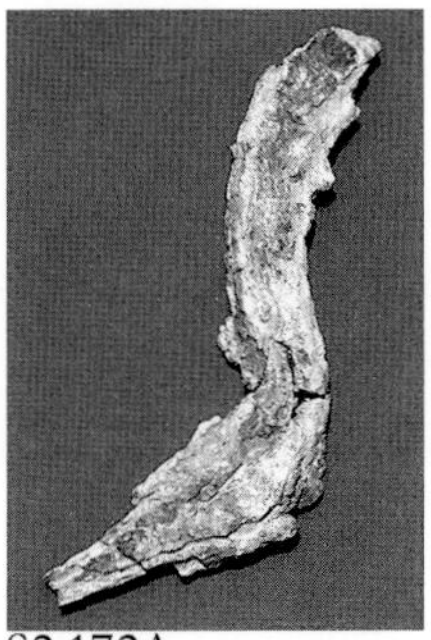

S2.172A

Hoes

GLD-1

S1.105

S1.309A

S1.437

Metal Objects – Iron (cont'd.)

Bowl

GLD-1

S1.179A Round iron bowl about 1.6 cm deep. It has V-shaped indentations on opposite sides. The metal is about 3-4 mm thick. The bowl is 12.6 cm long, 12.5 cm wide and 2.65 cm tall. Locus: Tr. 4B, habitation levels, Early Historic.

Lamp

GLD-1

S1.413 Lamp with pipal leaf–shaped base (approximately 4–6 mm thick). It is flat with a small hook extending upwards, which is now broken. The piece was found in Pit 3. It measures 5.3 cm long, 4.2 cm wide, and 4.11 cm tall. Locus: Tr. 4B, Pit 3, Early Historic.

Bells

GLD-1

S2.106 Handle of an iron bell. Similar in form to S1.296. 3.78 cm long, 2.56 cm wide, and 3.38 cm thick. Locus: Tr. 4A, habitation levels, Early Historic.

S1.284 Iron bell reconstructed from 9 pieces. It is rusting orange, green, and yellow. The metal from which it is shaped is between 1 to 2 mm thick. The handle is approximately 3 mm thick. The clapper is still inside. The clapper is made of iron and looks like a string tied in a knot. The bell is 6.15 cm tall, 4.29 cm wide, and 2.91 cm thick. Locus: Tr. 4B, habitation levels, Early Historic.

S1.296 Iron bell. The handle is round with a hole in the middle. The handle is attached to a square piece, and then a round piece. 4.82 cm long, 4.18 cm wide, and 4.18 cm thick. Locus: Tr. 4B, habitation levels, Early Historic.

Ring

GLD-1

S1.026 Hook or ring fragment. One end is broken and the other end is corroded. 2.04 cm long and 0.35 to 0.71 cm thick. Locus: Tr. 4A, habitation levels, Early Historic.

Metal Objects – Lead

Wire Fragments

GLD-1

S3.052 Two wire fragments. Both have one broken end and one rounded end. They are likely part of the same wire. The first measures 1.13 cm long and 0.18 cm in diameter. The second measures 1.07 cm long and 0.23 cm in diameter. Locus: Tr. 4C, habitation levels, Early Historic.

Shell Objects

Bangles

Area I

S1.079 Small fragment of a bangle with lines running lengthwise along the edge. 1.25 cm long, 0.95 cm wide, 0.32 cm thick. Locus: Tr. 6, habitation levels, Late Chalcolithic.

GLD-1

S1.028 Bangle fragment, nearly half of the original, reconstructed from two pieces. It has incised lines along the length of the band and a deep diagonal incision and line design across the center. 5.50 cm long, 1.12 cm wide, and 0.33 cm thick. Locus: Tr. 4A, habitation levels, Early Historic.

S1.036 Wide bangle fragment with a channel running along the length of the band. 2.60 cm long, 1.47 cm wide, 0.45 cm thick. Locus: Tr. 4A, habitation levels, Early Historic.

Bowl

GLD-1

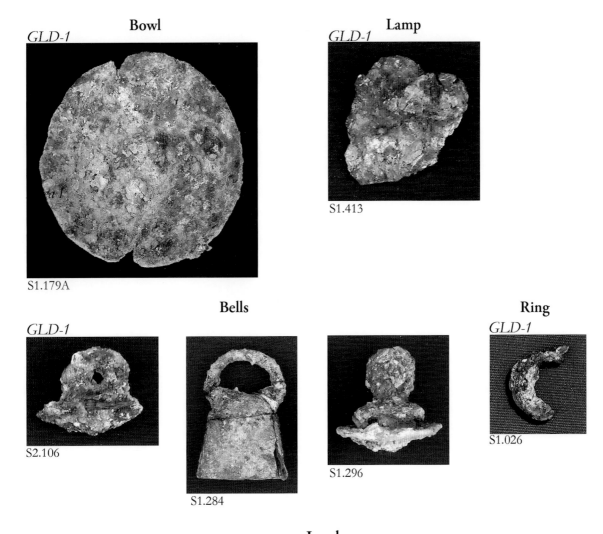

S1.179A

Lamp

GLD-1

S1.413

Bells

GLD-1

S2.106

S1.284

S1.296

Ring

GLD-1

S1.026

Lead

Wire Fragments

GLD-1

S3.052

Shell

Shell Bangles

Area I

S1.079

GLD-1

S1.028

S1.036

Bangles (cont'd.)

GLD-1 (cont'd.)

S1.051 Bangle fragment with raised circle design. 2.90 cm long, 1.17 cm wide, and 0.67 cm thick. Locus: Tr. 4A, habitation levels, Early Historic.

S1.168 Fragment of plain wide bangle. 2.05 cm long, 1.48 cm wide, 0.29 cm thick. Locus: Tr. 4A, habitation levels, Early Historic.

S1.276 Bangle fragment with raised circle design in the center and incised design on the band. The band has three circles inscribed in a rectangle. This design probably continued further down the band. 4.66 cm long, 1.13 cm wide, and 0.56 to 1.11 cm thick. Locus: Tr. 4A, habitation levels, Early Historic.

S2.076 Well-crafted bangle fragment with incised design: diagonal lines and small squares along the edge of the band. 5.03 cm long, 0.87 wide, and 0.54 cm thick. Locus: Tr. 4A, habitation levels, Early Historic.

S2.098 Fragment of a plain bangle reconstructed from two pieces. 5.78 cm long, 0.63 cm wide, and 0.55 cm thick. Locus: Tr. 4A, habitation levels, Early Historic.

S2.110 Nearly complete bangle reconstructed from three pieces. It has a raised circle design in the center and incised lines cut vertically across the band. Approximately 5 cm in diameter, 0.72 cm wide, and 0.47 cm thick. Locus: Tr. 4A, habitation levels, Early Historic.

S1.327 Bangle fragment with raised circle design, reconstructed from two pieces. 4.87 cm long, 0.65 to 0.81 cm wide, and 0.38 cm thick. Locus: Tr. 4B, habitation levels, Early Historic.

S1.410 Bangle fragment with incised V designs running the length of the band. It also has a raised circle design in the center. 4.36 cm long, 0.65 cm wide, and 0.5 to 0.76 cm thick. Locus: Tr. 4B, habitation levels, Early Historic.

S1.237 Bangle fragment with raised circle design. 4.80 cm long, with width varying from 0.5 to 0.83 cm, and thickness varying from 0.6 to 1.0 cm. Locus: Tr. 4C, habitation levels, Early Historic.

S3.220 Plain wide bangle, nearly half of the original. 5.94 cm long, 1.08 cm wide, 0.52 cm thick. Locus: Tr. 4C, habitation levels, Early Historic.

S3.391 Small fragment of a bangle with incised lines running diagonally across the band. 2.21 cm long, 0.51 cm wide, and 0.36 cm thick. Locus: Tr. 4F, deep trench, Middle Chalcolithic.

S3.332 Bangle fragment with raised line running along the length of the band. 3.85 cm long, 0.89 cm wide, and 0.45 cm thick. Locus: Tr. 4K, erosional context.

S2.049 Nearly 3/4 of a flat plain bangle reconstructed from two pieces. 5.94 cm top to bottom, 4.84 cm across, and 0.64 cm thick. Locus: Tr. 5B, habitation levels, Early Historic.

Surface

S4.023 Bangle fragment with a shallow channel running along the length of the band and a perforation on one end. 4.45 cm long, 0.92 cm wide, and 0.66 cm thick. Locus: surface find GLD-1, date unknown.

Worked Shells

Area I

S1.145 Bivalve worked on bottom edge and perforated near the center. It is not clear if the perforation is natural, i.e., from a molluscan predator, or from human actions. Locus: Tr. 9, habitation levels, Middle Chalcolithic.

S1.146 Bivalve worked on bottom edge with two perforations near the center. One of the perforations is larger than the other. Locus: Tr. 9, habitation levels, Middle Chalcolithic.

S2.178 Bivalve heavily worked along the bottom edge. Locus: Tr. 30, from eroded top layer, likely Late Chalcolithic.

S3.350 Burned bivalve. Locus: Tr. 31, habitation levels, Late Chalcolithic.

S3.365 Bivalve worked on bottom and sides. Bottom edge is nearly straight. This shell may have been used as a scraper. Locus: Tr. 31, habitation levels, Late Chalcolithic.

S3.374 Bivalve worked along bottom, blunted at one end and pointed at the opposite. It was likely used as a spoon. Locus: Tr. 31, habitation levels, Late Chalcolithic.

S3.357 Bivalve worked on bottom edge. Locus: Tr. 34, habitation levels, Middle Chalcolithic.

S3.373 Burned bivalve, worked on the bottom edge. Locus: Tr. 34, habitation levels, Middle Chalcolithic.

Area II

S2.189 Bivalve worked on bottom edge. Locus: Tr. 105, habitation levels, Middle Chalcolithic.

Shell Bangles (Continued)

GLD-1 (Continued)

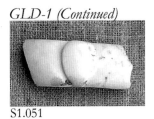
S1.051

S1.168

S1.276

S2.076

S2.098

S2.110

S1.327

S1.410

S1.237

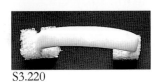
S3.220

S3.391

S3.332

S2.049

Surface

S4.023

Worked Shells

Area I

S1.145

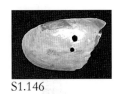
S1.146

S2.178

S3.350

S3.365

Area II

S3.357

S3.373

S2.189

S3.374

Worked Shells (cont'd.)
GLD-1

S2.200 Bivalve worked on bottom edge. Locus: Tr. 5B, habitation levels, Early Historic.

S4.057 Shoulder waste fragment from a conch shell. Locus: Tr. S1, erosional layer, Early Historic.

Cowries
GLD-1

S1.110 Cowrie with top broken off and teeth missing. 1.84 cm long and 1.42 cm wide. Locus: Tr. 4B, habitation levels, Early Historic.

S3.198 Whole cowrie. 1.46 cm long, 1.08 cm wide, and 0.70 cm in height. Locus: Tr. 4C, habitation levels, Early Historic.

S3.309 Cowrie with teeth missing. 1.25 cm long, 0.88 cm wide, and 0.58 cm in height. Locus: Tr. 4D, erosional layer, Early Historic.

S3.331 Cowrie broken in half. 1.42 cm long, 1.36 cm wide, and 0.60 cm in height. Locus: Tr. 4K, erosional layer, Early Historic.

Inlay Pieces
GLD-1

S2.071 Diamond-shaped inlay piece. 1.25 cm long, 1.20 cm wide, and 0.24 cm thick. Locus: Tr. 4B, habitation levels, Early Historic.

S3.260 Round inlay piece. 1.34 cm long, 1.19 cm wide, and 0.23 cm thick. Locus: Tr. 4F, deep trench, Middle Chalcolithic.

Bone Objects
Bone Point
GLD-1

S2.027 Bone point with visible manufacture marks. It is smooth and well-polished. 3.89 cm long, 0.60 cm wide, and 0.52 cm thick. Locus: Tr. 4A, habitation levels, Early Historic.

Worked Bone
Area III

S3.395 Worked bone found against a pit. It has a worked design on the edge. 4.81 cm long, 2.32 cm wide, and 0.83 cm thick. Locus: Tr. 205, habitation levels, Middle Chalcolithic.

GLD-1

S3.311 Hollow worked bone. 3.91 cm long and 2.05 to 2.11 cm in diameter. Locus: Tr. 4D, habitation levels, Middle Chalcolithic.

Unidentified Bone Object
Area I

S5.031 Bone disc with six perforations. 3.3 cm in diameter and 0.3 cm thick. Locus: Tr. 70, pit, Late Chalcolithic.

Steatite/Soapstone Objects
Button
Area I

S5.206 Steatite paste button with convex top and flat bottom. 2.2 cm in diameter and 0.95 cm in height. Locus: Tr. 68, habitation levels, Late Chalcolithic.

Ring
GLD-1

S1.520 Half of a broken steatite paste ring. It was recovered during a section scraping of 4B. It measures 1.34 cm in length, and between 0.33 and 0.38 cm in diameter. Locus: Tr. 4B, section scraping, Early Historic.

Worked Shell (Continued)

GLD-1

S2.200

S4.057

Cowries

GLD-1

S1.110

S3.198

S3.309

S3.331

Inlay Pieces

GLD-1

S2.071

S3.260

Bone

Point

GLD-1

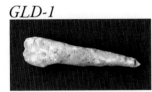

S2.027

Worked Bone

Area III

S3.395

GLD-1

S3.311

Unidentified Bone Object

Area I

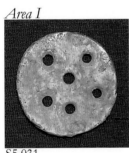

S5.031

Steatite

Button

Area I

S5.206

Ring

GLD-1

S1.520

154 *Excavations at Giland*

Soapstone Vessels

Group 1 Vessel Fragments

GLD-1

S1.015 Soapstone rim fragment reconstructed from 3 pieces. It appears to be part of the same vessel as S1.041A–C and S1.043. The inner side is very smooth, but the outer side has a black paste with incised hash marks going diagonally across it. 28 cm long, 4.86 cm tall, and 0.9 cm thick. Locus: Tr. 4A, habitation levels, Early Historic.

S1.041A Rim fragment of soapstone vessel reconstructed from three pieces. It appears to be part of the same vessel as S1.015 and S1.043. It has a black wash on both sides and an angular rim. The outer side has hash marks and the appearance of appliqué in black paste. 9.46 cm wide, 5.56 cm tall, and 0.94 cm thick. Locus: Tr. 4A, habitation levels, Early Historic.

S1.041B Base fragment of soapstone vessel reconstructed from 7 pieces. Forms part of the same vessel as S1.015 and S1.043. Has same black wash on both sides with a white film or concretion on the inside. The outer side has chisel marks on it, similar to S1.041C. 12.5 cm long, 2.14 cm tall, and 0.54–0.86 cm thick. Locus: Tr. 4A, habitation levels, Early Historic.

S1.041C Group of 3 soapstone vessel fragments, likely part of the same vessel as S1.041A,B, S1.015, and S1.043. (1) is the smallest, and is likely a body or a base piece. It is flat and has a black wash and chisel marks on one side. (2) is flat with black wash and chisel marks on one side. The interior side (not shown) has a white concretion or film. (3) is flat with a black wash and chisel marks. The inside is plain. Outer sides of vessel fragments with the chisel marks are shown. No measurements were taken for these pieces, but a 10 cm scale is shown in the picture, with each black or white box representing 1 cm. Locus: Tr. 4A, habitation levels, Early Historic.

S1.043 Soapstone vessel fragment that likely forms part of the same vessel as S1.015 and S1.041A–C. It is flat with black wash on one side and signs of appliqué in black paste near the top. It also has chisel marks. The wide grooves measure approximately 1.7–1.8 cm wide and the crests in-between measure approximately 0.15–0.2 cm wide. There also appears to be some black wash on the inner side (not shown). The fragment is 12.14 cm long, 6.06 cm wide, and 0.73 cm thick. Locus: Tr. 4A, habitation levels, Early Historic.

Group 2 Vessel Fragments

GLD-1

S1.019 Rim fragment from a soapstone vessel. There are some traces of black film on the interior (shown) and the back is completely black. The rim is very angular. The entire fragment was reconstructed from 3 pieces. It is made of the same blue/green/gray soapstone as S3.336 and S3.402. 6.57 cm long, 5.97 cm wide, and 1.03 cm thick. Locus: Tr. 4B, habitation levels, Late Chalcolithic.

S3.402 Rim fragment from a soapstone vessel. Like S1.019 and S3.336 the top of the rim is angular. There are some incised hash marks on the outer side. The inside (shown) is quite smooth. 8.40 cm long, 4.14 cm tall, and 0.85 cm thick. Locus: Tr. 4C, habitation levels, Late Chalcolithic.

S3.048 Soapstone vessel fragment. One side has chisel marks, and the other side is flat and smooth. 5.38 cm long, 3.35 cm wide, and 0.89 cm thick. Locus: Tr. 4C, habitation levels, Late Chalcolithic.

S3.336 Rim fragment from a soapstone vessel. The top of the rim is angular, similar to S1.019. It is likely part of the same vessel as S3.048, S3.402, and possibly S1.019. It does not have any black wash, but the stone is the same texture and color as S1.019. 3.65 cm long, 1.91 cm tall, and 0.80 cm thick. Locus: Tr. 4K, pile sealed by Layer 1, Late Chalcolithic or Early Historic.

Soapstone Vessels
Group 1

GLD-1

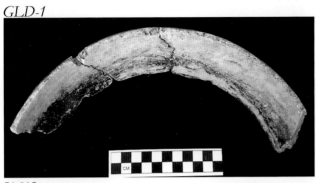

S1.041A

S1.015

S1.041B

S1.041C

Group 2

GLD-1

S1.019

S3.402

S3.048

S3.336

9

Report on the Seal Impressions and Related Small Finds

Marta Ameri

Introduction

In the 1960s, Indian archaeologists began to more intensively explore and define the areas to the east of the Indus heartland. In the early stages of exploration, the consensus among South Asian scholars had been that the geographical barrier imposed by the Thar Desert and the Aravalli mountain range was too great to allow contact between eastern cultures such as those of the Ahar River Basin, and areas further to the west. In fact, in describing the area around the site of Ahar in his 1969 excavation report, H.D. Sankalia wrote that "unlike many of the other regions in India where civilization has developed, this region, particularly around Ahar, is so girt by hills—the spurs of the Aravallis—that one feels as if one has reached one of the dead ends of the world, from which there is no exit" (Sankalia 1969: vii). In general, excavation evidence has tended to support this view; few artifacts that can be attributed to Harappan and post-Harappan spheres have been found to the east of the Aravallis. These include a small number of etched carnelian beads found in Layers 1b and 1c at Ahar (Deo 1969b:165), as well as some pottery types, especially Tan Wares, found at Balathal (Misra 1997).

More recently, however, the discovery of a large cache of sealings impressed by stamp seals at the Ahar-Banas site of Gilund has challenged the view of this area as an isolated backwater. The motifs on these seal impressions closely resemble those found in Central Asia and Iran, but bear little resemblance to local or Harappan materials. This exceptional find calls for a re-examination of past interpretations of the site, the archaeological complex to which it belongs, and its contacts with cultures in Southern and Central Asia from the end of the 3rd to the beginning of the 2nd millennium BC. The initial reaction to the seals and seal amulets found at Gilund connected them to material, particularly

seals, excavated at sites belonging to the Bactria Margiana Archaeological Complex and found at sites as far afield as Iran, Mesopotamia, and the Gulf (Possehl, Shinde, and Ameri 2004, Shinde, Possehl, and Ameri 2005). However, a more thorough examination of the comparative material (Ameri 2010) suggests that the iconography found on the seals and seal amulets from Gilund was in fact in existence throughout Middle Asia as early as the middle of the 3rd millennium BC, and likely made its way to India at this time.

The discovery of seal impressions at Gilund places the site squarely within an administrative tradition that existed throughout the Near East and Asia as early as the 6th millennium B.C.[1] The fact that the Gilund seal impressions were discovered in a specially constructed bin in a building that appears to have been used for storage further emphasizes their importance. In many societies where seals were used in administration, broken impressions were kept as a record of a transaction or possibly to prevent the counterfeiting of seals.[2] The presence of what appears to be a well-developed system of administration at Gilund raises important questions about its political organization, its relationship with other Ahar-Banas sites, and its possible interaction with "foreign" lands. The size of the site, as well as the presence of large-scale, seemingly public architecture, suggests that the political organization at Gilund exceeded that of a simple village economy, and conceivably included ruling elites who controlled the resources that were available to the community.

The first part of this chapter presents the glyptic materials found at Gilund, examining their form, function, and iconography as well as the contexts in which they were discovered. The final part analyzes the chronological implications of the contexts in which the administrative material was found. The examination of these contexts suggests that the use of sealing was not a short-lived phenomenon in the

Ahar-Banas, but rather that, once adopted, sealing became a strong tradition with a long lifespan within this culture.

Definition of Terms

The terminology used in the study of seals and sealing is highly specific and often misunderstood.[3] Thus, before describing the material found at Gilund, it will be useful to provide the reader with a general definition of the descriptive terms. The first assumption that is made in a study of seals and sealings such as this one is that these artifacts are the remnants of an administrative system where goods or documents were sealed to maintain their integrity. The act of sealing refers to the closing or labeling of a container or document in such a way that its integrity is guaranteed by the person (or office) that seals it. In antiquity, this integrity was usually guaranteed by the use of a decorated seal on a malleable surface such as clay or wax.[4] For the purpose of this discussion we are interpreting seals as markers of authority or ownership belonging to an individual or office which are used to guarantee the integrity of a package, room, or document. This is a simplistic explanation, but sufficient for the present purpose.[5]

In the following discussion, the term *sealing* will be used to refer to a piece of clay that would have been used to close or lock a container or door. Ideally a sealing retains a negative impression of the object it secured (on the reverse), as well as of the decorated seal that provided the guarantee for the product (on the obverse). However, the vagaries of archaeology mean that sometimes much of this information is lost, and a sealing may preserve only part of an impression on either its obverse or reverse. Some sealings do not preserve any of this information, and are referred to as sealings solely on the basis of the type of material from which they are made[6] or the contexts in which they are found.[7] Sealings that retain no negative impressions are sometimes also referred to simply as sealing clay, or "lumps of sealing clay." In the case of Gilund, many of the clay lumps with no impressions on either side are referred to as sealings based on the fact that they were found in the same cache as the impressed sealings.

The term *seal* is used to refer to an object, usually incised or decorated in relief, which is used to make an impression on the malleable surface of the sealing. The decoration on the seal is considered the positive, while that which is found on a sealing (the seal impression) is the negative. Seals are generally made from a hard material such as stone, metal, or terracotta and can be used repeatedly over a long period of time. It has been suggested that seals functioned as a badge of authority and were often worn so as to be

clearly visible to others. The fact that many seals are pierced so they can be carried around on a string seems to encourage this view. In addition, images of women from Early Dynastic Mesopotamia (see for example Aruz et al. 2003: cat. no. 104a) show them wearing seals attached to the pins used to fasten the shoulders of their garments.

Finally, the term *seal impression* is used to refer to the negative impression made by the carved or decorated surface of the seal onto a malleable surface. In the following discussion, the surface on which a seal impression is made is generally a lump of clay used to seal a container, thus a sealing. However, impressions of seals can also been found on pottery and possibly also on architectural elements.

The sealings at Gilund were not given antiquity numbers when they were first excavated and have since been given G.S. (Gilund Sealing) numbers. The first digit in the G.S. number reflects the season during which the sealing was excavated, while the second set of numbers gives each artifact a unique identity. The sealings were cleaned and consolidated by a team of conservators from the Smithsonian Center for Material Research and Education in the fall of 2004 and are now housed in specially outfitted containers at Deccan College in Pune, India.[8]

The Sealings

The corpus of sealings found at Gilund is made up of 249 fragments of sealing clay, many of which had been impressed by stamp seals. The sealings were found primarily in contexts that can be dated to the Middle Ahar-Banas period. The majority (G.S. 4.001–4.214) of the 249 sealings from Gilund were unearthed during the fourth season (2002–2003) in Trench 13, in a bin[9] located in a room subsidiary to the structure with the parallel walls (Fig. 3.2).[10] This small bin, located in the space between walls NS7 and NS8, appears to be contemporary with the later phase of the parallel-wall complex. The bin is located in a corner of the room, about 20 cm to the west of Wall EW7 and 10 cm to the south of the unnamed northern wall. The location of this bin reflects common practice in contemporary village houses where storage bins are still often located in the corners of rooms (Ansari 2000).

The bin itself is about 85 cm deep[11] and 70 cm wide at its widest point (Fig. 9.1). Both the interior and exterior were carefully lined with a thick layer of light-colored plaster. The uppermost part of the bin had a lining of bricks around the perimeter. Two bricks were also found on the lip of the pit, but not over the remainder of the top. It is not clear whether the entire bin was originally sealed with bricks or if they were only placed around the edges. In ad-

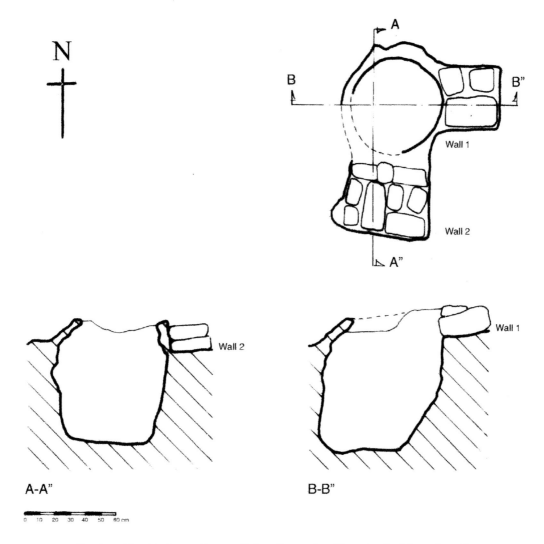

Fig. 9.1. Clay bin located in parallel-wall complex. (Drawing by Marta Ameri)

dition to the brick lining, there are also two low brick walls associated with the bin, one to its south and a second one to the east, connecting it to wall NS7. The wall to the south, labeled Wall 2 in Figure 9.1, is preserved to a depth of 2 bricks and placed against the plaster wall of the bin. The bricks are of varying sizes but carefully laid. It is possible that this low wall functioned as a step up to the edge of the bin. Wall 1, to the east, is preserved to a depth of only 1 brick and may articulate with Wall NS7, though this is still uncertain.[12] Here too the bricks are of different sizes but appear to be carefully laid.

The first impressed sealings were found when the brick lining around the edge of the bin was removed (Fig. 9.2). Two were identified and photographed in situ, one on the northern edge of the opening and another one on

the western edge. The uppermost portion of pit fill was composed of "mixed ... brick material [and] sandy crumbly soil with some ash,"[13] while the fill of the lower portion (30 to 90 cm) was "completely gray ash with a lot of charcoal, bones—completely white as to an excess of heating, small pebbles, lumps of clay, brick pieces, pottery." The majority of the sealings were found in this lower part of the pit, on the northwest side. The eastern and southern sides of the pit were filled mostly with bricks, possibly part of the later brick lining or covering of the bin.[14]

A second, smaller set of sealings (eight) was found in a large pit (lot 1014) in Trench 11, just outside the parallel-wall structure, during the first season of excavation (1999–2000). Other impressions were found singly throughout the excavated areas of GLD-2, but rarely in sig-

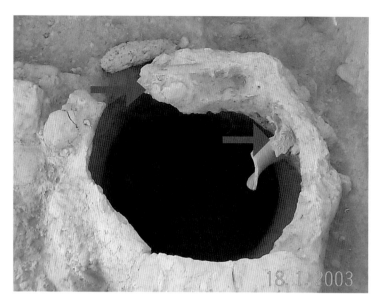

Fig. 9.2. Clay bin located in parallel-wall complex.

nificant contexts. Most of the sealings found during season 5, for example, were found in contexts that can best be characterized as slope wash. However, G.S. 5.007 was found in the same pit as most of the sealings unearthed during season 1 (this pit was excavated as lot 5120029 in 2005[15]).

The sealings themselves appear to have been used primarily to close storage vessels (see Table 9.1). Of the sealings with readable backs, most have a double curvature which suggests that they were pressed onto the shoulder of a jar or other closed vessel. String or rope impressions are visible on a few of these, while others have visible textile impressions. A second group of sealings with flat backs may have been used to seal boxes or other flat-topped containers. One sealing (G.S. 1.008) preserves a positive impression of the seal that impressed it on its reverse, suggesting that this lump of clay was placed over an existing sealing, which had been in some

way invalidated (possibly by having been broken or smudged). The most extraordinary sealing, however, is a large jar stopper (G.S. 4.060) that was preserved whole and retains the negative impression of the entire mouth of the jar that it sealed. Unfortunately, due to the fragile nature of unbaked clay, the backs of many sealings are badly damaged and cannot be read. In addition, the fragmentary nature of many of the sealings, as well as the fact that the Gilund pottery and the sealings have been stored in different places, made it impossible to analyze whether there was any direct relationship between the two. Nonetheless, the presence of incised markings that seem to resemble the incised decoration on some of the vessels was noted on the reverse of at least two sealings (G.S. 4.090 and G.S. 4.150).

In general, each sealing was impressed, often multiple times, by a rectilinear or round stamp seal. The large jar stopper (G.S. 4.060), for example, was impressed at least eight times with a single rectangular seal. Of all the sealings found at Gilund, only G.S. 1.014 and possibly G.S. 1.015 were impressed by more than one seal, which suggests that as a rule only one person (or office) was responsible for each container.

The clay of the sealings ranges in texture from very clean and fine, to coarse with fairly large inclusions. In general, the clay is not as finely textured and levigated as that traditionally used for sealing in other regions, particularly in contemporaneous Mesopotamia. While on a macroscopic level the clay appears to be similar to the fabric of local wares, future analyses will hopefully enable us to determine whether the sealings were made on local or imported clay. A study of this type (Blackman 1999) was conducted on the

Table 9.1. Readable Impressions on Backs of Sealings

	Concentric Circle	Flower	Cross-hatch	Spiral & Ladder	Spiral	Sunburst	"Fish"	Other	Total
Shoulder of vessel	7	5		3		3		14	32
Rim of Vessel	7	9	1	4	1	3	2	24	50
Neck of vessel	5	6		4				10	25
Flat	3	9		2	4	1		10	29
Rope impression	2	4		1	1			7	15
Textile impression	1					1		2	4
Vessel decoration	3	3		1				4	11

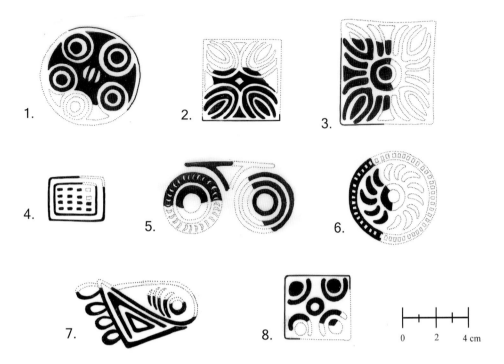

Fig. 9.3. Reconstructed seal designs. (Drawings by Julia Jarrett)

sealings from the Turkish site of Hacinebi. The author examined the chemical composition of clays used in sealings in an attempt to determine the sources of the sealing clay and thus of the products which they guaranteed.

Reconstructed Seals

While many of the impressions are too badly damaged to allow us to recognize all the seals that made them, it has been possible to substantially reconstruct at least eight of the seals that were used on the sealings found at Gilund. It is still too early to tell whether the sealings were impressed at Gilund or elsewhere. None of the seals or seal-type objects found at the site matches exactly the impressions on the sealings, but future excavations may provide more information.

Most of the impressions found at Gilund were made by stamp seals, both circular and rectilinear in shape. The designs are all geometric and some are very complex, but there is no evidence of writing. None of the seals has the typical motifs, such as human or animal figures under a line of script, that are found on the seals of the Harappan civilization. There are, however, parallels with seals and impressions found in Early and post-Harappan contexts at sites in the Greater Indus Valley (for example, seals found at Kunal [J.S. Khatri, and M. Acharya 1997] and in the Jukhar levels at Chanhudaro [Mackay 1943: pls. XLIX, L]), as well as at

other sites throughout Western and Central Asia—from copper/bronze stamp seals found at Bactria Margiana Archaeological Complex (BMAC) sites like Togolok 21 (Sarianidi 1998: no. 1350) and Gonur Tepe (Hiebert 1994: fig. 9.15) to impressions of seals pressed onto jars found in the cemetery at Shahdad (Hakemi 1997: pl. Ia).[16]

While more than half of the impressions are too badly damaged to allow us to fully reconstruct the seals that made them or have no visible impressions, it has been possible to make out and partially reconstruct at least eight of the seals that were used on the sealings found at Gilund (see Fig. 9.3). The eight seals that could be reconstructed with a certain degree of certainty from the evidence of the Gilund sealings include:

1. Circle of concentric circles seal (Fig. 9.3, no. 1): The one seal that is found on the largest number of impressions (at least 28 of the 249 extant sealings) is a circular seal with five bulls-eyes arranged around a round central element with two raised lines. The best impressions of this seal can be seen on G.S. 4.071, 4.078, 4.079, and 4.081. It is not clear whether the deep impression on G.S. 4.080 is made by the same seal or a second, similar one. Two seal-amulets found in excavations of Ahar-Banas sites have surface decorations that closely resemble the impression made by this seal. The first of these is a terracotta "ornamental piece" found in the excavations at Ahar (Deo 1969c:190, n. 9). It is circular in

shape and has a round hole in the center. Six circles appear to have been cut out of the outer border of the piece, leaving a deeply scalloped edge. A raised border that runs along their edges further defines the scalloping and central circle. If this piece were to be pressed onto a lump of wet clay, the resulting impression would be very similar to that of the "circle of concentric circles" seal used on the Gilund sealings. The second related seal amulet was found at Gilund itself. This fragmentary piece (S5.216) preserves the traces of two concentric circles and the triangular element between them.[17]

2.   Flower with diamond center seal (Fig. 9.3, no. 2): At least two separate square seals with a four-petal flower design were used on the sealings from Gilund. The first of these, seen on G.S. 4.089, 4.090, and 4.091, among others, has four petals made by delicate nested tear-shaped lines and a central diamond-shaped element created to fill the voids left by the petals.

3.   Flower with round center seal (Fig. 9.3, no. 3): The second flower seal has a round bulls-eye-shaped center and very thick lines. The seal itself, which is seen most clearly in G.S. 4.092 and 4.093, seems to have been larger than the flower seal with the diamond center. Together, the two seals with flower designs are found on about 20% of the sealings, making this the most common design found at Gilund.

4.   Rectilinear/crosshatch design (Fig. 9.3, no. 4): This design is most clearly visible on G.S. 4.060. This large jar stopper was impressed multiple times with a rectangular seal about 3.6 x 3.0 cm in size. The decoration of the seal consists of a crosshatched rectangle within a simple rectangular frame. Crosshatch designs are also found on G.S. 4.004 and G.S. 4.020, but it is not possible to tell if they were made by the same seal.

5.   Spiral and ladder seal (Fig. 9.3, no. 5): G.S. 4.064 has two concentric circles. The outermost of these has short lines projecting from the outer ring, creating a pattern similar to that of a seashell. This motif, which may be the same as the one impressed on G.S. 4.070, is often associated with a second pattern that consists of three large concentric circles. Close examination of a number of the sealings found at Gilund suggest that these two elements together formed a single seal, which represents a slightly different take on the double spiral motif and is reconstructed in Figure 9.3.

6.   Sunburst seal (Fig. 9.3, no. 6): At least one seal with a sunburst motif was impressed on the sealings from Gilund. The seal which can be reconstructed most easily was probably round (although the outer edges are not preserved) and consists of a circular center with short curved lines radiating out from it. An outer ring decorated with a ladder-like

design made by slanted parallel lines frames this sunburst. Impressions of this seal are found on G.S. 4.067, 4.068, and 4.069. Other fragmentary impressions that seem to have been made by this seal are found on G.S. 1.130 and 4.145. These two impressions show the edge of the seal and support the hypothesis that it was originally round.

7.   Teardrop/"Fish" seal (Fig. 9.3, no. 7):[18] The clearest "fish" motif is found on the impression on G.S. 4.061. The design on this seal seems to consist of a teardrop shape with a round "eye". Four curved parallel lines that seem to be continuations of the circular "eye" articulate the interior of the teardrop-shaped body. The lower line of the teardrop joins two other lines to form the outermost of three nested triangles that form the left side of the seal. Farthest to the left are four deeply impressed half-ovals which seem to form a sort of tail. The way in which this seal is impressed on G.S. 4.061 suggests that it may have been a cylinder seal rather than a stamp, but the fact that we have only one impression of it makes it impossible to be certain.

A second "fish" seal, which was not preserved well enough to attempt a reconstruction, can be identified on two of the sealings found during the first season in the pit in Trench 11. These sealings, G.S. 1.005 and 1.006, have an impression of a large oval or tear-shaped figure with an "eye" made up of concentric circles on one side and possible zigzag patterns defining the upper and lower edges.

8.   Square concentric circle seal (Fig. 9.3, no. 8): The last seal that can be reconstructed is a square seal with a round central element and four sets of incomplete concentric circles, one in each of the four corners. This seal was impressed onto G.S. 1.014, which is also the only sealing where we can definitively attest to the use of two different seals on a single sealing.

Common Elements in the Iconography of the Gilund Sealings

In addition to the eight seals that can be reconstructed, the analysis of all the sealings with visible seal impressions identified a number of basic elements that are repeated and reinterpreted from seal to seal and make up the visual vocabulary of the sealings found at Gilund. The elements discussed below are not motifs that are found on individual seals, but rather elements that are used repeatedly within the glyptic corpus of the site. Some of the elements mentioned below are found on multiple seals, while certain seals combine more than one element. Breaking the iconography on the seals down into individual elements allows us to gain a better understanding of the artistic tradition that these seals belong to, and the way in which different decorative elements are used to create a style that is then reflected in other Ahar-Banas material.

1.   Concentric circle: This motif, made by three to five concentric circles and a central dot, is found on many of the sealings from Gilund. In fact, the use of nested elements, whether circles, squares or triangles, is one of the most common stylistic features found in the Gilund material.

2.   Parallel lines: In addition to the concentric circles, many of the impressions from Gilund have parallel lines which are either straight or curved. In general the seals from Gilund seem to show an emphasis on the repetition of design elements.

3.   Spirals: Spiral elements are also found on a number of the seal impressions. Unfortunately, these tend to be fragmentary so that it is extremely difficult to identify what the original seal looked like, and most importantly, how many spirals it had. However, double spirals can be clearly identified on several impressions, including G.S. 4.062 and G.S. 4.063. The impression on G.S. 4.074, although faint, consists of two double spirals that mirror each other, forming a quadruple spiral.

4.   Flowers or leaves: At least two separate square seals with a four-petal flower design were used on the sealings from Gilund (see below), and individual petal elements can be identified on some of the other impressions (for example, G.S. 4.114).

5.   Solar elements: Several of the sealings have a motif of straight lines emanating from a round central element, suggesting a sunburst or solar motif. A very elaborate version of this motif can be seen on G.S. 4.068 and G.S. 4.069, while a simpler version is found on G.S. 5.018.

6.   Crosshatch: The most obvious occurrence of the crosshatch motif is on the rectangular seal impressed on the large jar stopper G.S. 4.060. However, traces of crosshatching can also be found on some of the other sealings, including G.S. 4.004 and G.S. 4.020

7.   Ladder/fenestration: A few of the impressions from Gilund have a ladder-like or fenestrated motif that often plays a framing role. This element can be seen most clearly surrounding the solar motif on G.S. 4.068 and G.S. 4.069, but also appears on G.S. 5.007 and G.S. 4.129

8.   Frames: Finally, it should be mentioned that many of the designs on the Gilund sealings have a framing element of some sort. This tendency can be seen in the simple rectangular frame around the crosshatched seal impressed on G.S. 4.060, as well as in the more elaborate fenestrated frame that encircles the solar motif on G.S. 4.068. The parallel lines of G.S. 1.004 are also enclosed within a triangular frame.

Related Small Finds

To further explore the question of sealing at Gilund, it will be useful to examine one other class of material found both at Gilund and at other Ahar-Banas sites, a set of decorated terracottas that may have been used to make impressions on wet clay or other materials. These objects can be divided into two groups: the seal amulets, which are flat and mostly round in shape, and the stamps, which are distinguished by the fact that they have a knob or handle on the undecorated side. Both groups are decorated with carved intaglio designs and vary widely in decoration. The one clear exception to this observation is S5.215, a rounded seal amulet whose decoration appears to have been made with a mold rather than incised. The poor state of preservation of S5.184 makes it difficult to determine how it was decorated, but it also appears to have been incised. In addition, the two star-shaped stamps, S1.246 and S1.345, were modeled by hand and not incised.

The seal amulets and stamps found at Gilund were collected as antiquities and as such were each given an individual antiquity number. The antiquity numbers from Gilund consist of a first number preceded by an S which denotes the excavation season when an artifact was found, and a second number that gives each object a unique identity.

As mentioned above, the seal amulets (Fig. 9.4) are flat. Most of the examples found at Gilund are decorated on one side and smooth on the other. Only one example (S2.061) is decorated on both sides.[19] In addition, several of the amulets are pierced. The holes in two round amulets (S1.114 and S5.216) are placed not in the center of the object, but towards the top, suggesting that they may have been worn as pendants. A square amulet (S3.025) has four symmetrically placed round holes that go all the way through. It is unclear whether their function was more than simply decorative. The last pierced amulet (S1.114) is cruciform in shape and pieced by a round hole in the centre. The function of this piercing is also unclear, but it may have functioned as a hole for a wooden handle or knob.

I have referred to these objects as seal amulets because this term is the most commonly used for materials of this type, although there is, in fact, little evidence that they were ever used for sealing. None of the seal impressions found at Gilund appear to have been made by the seal amulets found at the site. This may be due in large part to the fact that the seal amulets were excavated from much later contexts than the sealings (see discussion below). Nonetheless, the similarities between the designs on at least two of the amulets and the impressed motifs on some of the sealings cannot be

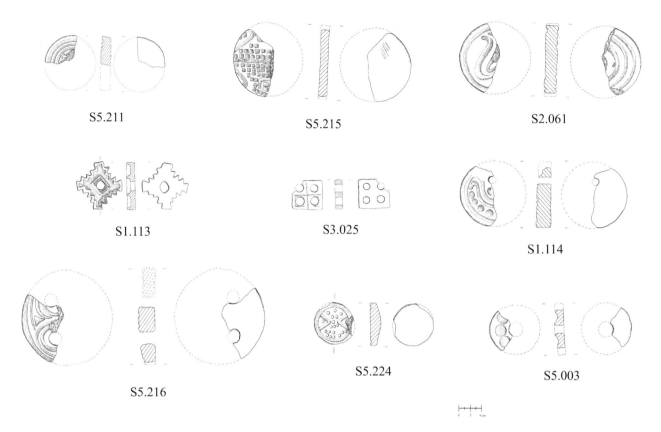

S5.211

S5.215

S2.061

S1.113

S3.025

S1.114

S5.216

S5.224

S5.003

Fig. 9.4. Reconstructed seal-amulets. (Drawings by Julia Jarrett)

ignored. The most interesting of these is the resemblance between the fragmentary concentric circle motif on S5.216 (Fig. 9.4) and the circle of concentric circles impression found on a large number of the sealings from Gilund (Fig. 9.2, no. 1). While the seal is clearly not the same as the one that made these impressions, the similarity in the design suggests that it is simply a different rendering of the same motif. The existence of multiple seals with the same or similar motifs is shown also in the two different flower seals identified on the sealings (Fig. 9.2, nos. 2, 3). It has also been suggested that the lack of a handle or knob would have made it difficult to use these seal amulets for sealing. However, seals from Shahr-i Sokhta, which are also flat and have no knob, were undoubtedly used for sealing, as is documented by the fact that impressions of some of these very seals were also found at the site (Tosi 1968: figs. 96a, b).

The designs on the seal amulets are principally geometric, though a few fragmentary examples may have had figural designs. Both S1.114 and S2.061, for example, have a swooping element that resembles the bucrania (ornament in the form of an ox's skull) found on some Harappan pottery. The most remarkable of these objects, howev-

er, is a terracotta amulet (S1.114) in the shape of a stepped cross that was found at Gilund. A second seal amulet in the same shape was found at Ahar during the excavations conducted by the Archaeological Survey of India in 1959–60.[20] This motif has strong associations with the sites of Bactria and Margiana and both of these amulets can be interpreted as imitations in clay of the copper-bronze amulets produced by the inhabitants of the desert oases of Central Asia.

The stamps, in contrast to the amulets, are three dimensional in shape (Fig. 9.5). They are distinguished by the fact that they have protrusions that can function as handles. To date, only four stamps have been identified among the material excavated at Gilund. Two of these (S1.256 and S1.345) are in the shape of many-pointed stars with an indent in the center. Both also have a small pointed handle in back. The third stamp (S5.184) is round and it has a thick rounded knob at the back. Although it is badly worn, the decoration on this piece also seems to represent a star with multiple points. In this case, however, the decoration is incised with multiple lines on the round surface of the stamp and not shaped as on the two stamps

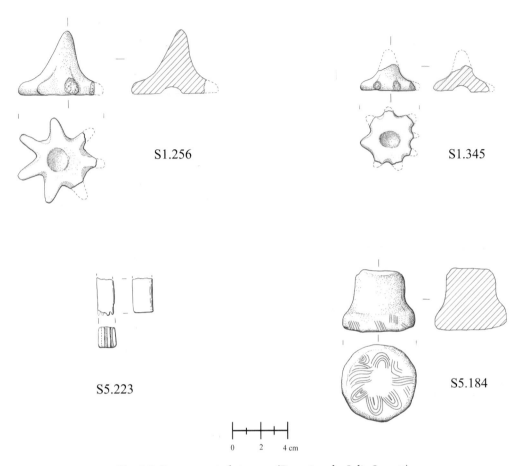

Fig. 9.5. Reconstructed stamps. (Drawings by Julia Jarrett)

mentioned above.[21] However, the fact that this last object is made of unbaked clay calls into question its possible use for sealing.

The last stamp found at Gilund (S5.223) is a long squared-off cylinder with a very small sealing surface consisting of several parallel lines incised on the short side. The sealing surface measures only about 1.5 by 1.5 cm. The most striking thing about this seal, however, is the fact that it resembles a design seen on a sealing (G.S. 5.004) that was unearthed during the fifth season of excavation. This sealing has two impressions of boxes made up of four parallel lines each, the same impression that would have been made by S5.223.

The Chronology and Contexts of the Seals and Sealings

A close examination of the contexts in which the seals and sealings were found, both at Gilund and at other Ahar-Banas sites, shows that these materials are part of a tradition that was in existence as early as the Middle Ahar-Banas period (ca. 2500–2000 BCE) and continued until the end of the Late Ahar-Banas period (2000–1700 BCE). As discussed above, the majority of the sealings from Gilund were found in a pit and a bin associated with the parallel-wall structure. This building is dated to the Middle Ahar-Banas period based on ceramic comparisons to the well-dated material from Balathal (see Chapter 3). The evidence for at least three reconstructions suggests that this structure was in use for an extended period of time. However, the extensive erosion in this area of the mound makes it difficult to ascertain whether its use continued into the Late Ahar-Banas period.[22] The remaining sealings from Gilund were found in contexts that can best be described as slope wash and give very little insight into the objects' original context or date. A confirmation of the early date for the Gilund sealings, however, is provided by a small number of sealings found at Balathal. These sealings were found in Layers 14, 15, and 16, all of which have been firmly dated to the Middle Ahar-Banas period. Published C-14 dates for these layers range from 3130–2750 BCE at the earliest to

2570–1660 BCE at the latest (Misra 2005).

On the other hand, the majority of the terracotta stamps and seal amulets from Gilund were found in habitation contexts at the top of the mound. Most of these have been dated to the Late Ahar-Banas period. Two radiocarbon samples from these uppermost layers of GLD-2 (Area I) give dates of 1630–1440, and 1690–1510 2Σ cal BCE (see Appendix 1). This later date for the terracotta stamps and amulets seems to be confirmed by the amulets from Ahar, most of which were also found in later (Ib or Ic) contexts (Deo 1969a). The supposition that the sealings and the seals may not be contemporary is also supported by the fact that there is so little overlap in the designs found on the two sets of material. The one exception to this assertion is the seal-amulet S5.216, whose resemblance to the circle of concentric circles seal was discussed above. In addition, it can be suggested that the designs found on the sealings were too fine to have been made by terracotta seals, and that perhaps they were made by seals made of different materials that were either not preserved or have not yet been identified.

In addition to the discrepancy in the dating of the seals and the sealings there is also a significant difference in the contexts in which they were found. This variation may be important in terms of the ways in which the seals functioned at Gilund. While the seal amulets and stamps were found primarily in habitation contexts in the uppermost, central part of GLD-2, the sealings were found in features (a pit and a bin) associated with a large structure that was almost definitely public in function. This suggests that seals may have been kept in the home, but were used in areas associated with public structures. Unfortunately, at Gilund there is no physical connection between the houses at the top of the mound and the building with the parallel walls. The area of the parallel-wall structure, on the eastern slope of GLD-2, was badly damaged by years of slope wash and does not seem to have preserved any Late Ahar-Banas remains, a fact that makes it difficult to ascertain both whether this area continued to have monumental architecture in the Late Ahar-Banas and whether sealings continued to be used in similar contexts in the later period. Similarly, the Late Ahar-Banas houses at the top of the mound were carefully exposed, but no excavation was carried out below them. One significant vertical excavation carried out on GLD-2 took place in Trenches 5 and 6. This area exposed an extension of the parallel-wall building, but no Middle Ahar-Banas houses. Thus, just as the absence of sealings in the Late Ahar-Banas levels may be explained by the lack of large-scale public structures dated to this period, the absence of seals in the Middle Ahar-Banas may be due to the

lack of excavated domestic contexts. On the other hand, it is also possible that, as in Central Asia and parts of Iran, we see a decline in the use of seals for administrative sealing at the beginning of the 2nd millennium BCE. In other words, while seals continue to be produced and probably worn or carried as markers of status or identity, they nonetheless cease to be used for administrative purposes, thus explaining the absence of sealings in the later periods both in the Ahar-Banas and elsewhere in the ancient world.

Conclusions

The seals and sealings found at Gilund and the other sites of the Ahar-Banas present evidence of a fully formed, if limited, administrative system that seems to have existed over a long period of time. Material found at Gilund included both sealings and two different classes of stamp seals. In addition to the observation that seals and sealings were found in different contexts at Gilund, it is also clear that the material from this site cannot be viewed in a vacuum. While Gilund has by far the largest corpus of administrative material among the Ahar-Banas sites, similar artifacts were found at both Ahar and Balathal, and will most likely be found at other sites in this area. This suggests that the Ahar-Banas Culture as a whole appropriated elements of both the sealing technology and the iconography known further to the west. The presence of seals or sealings at all these sites suggests that sealing played an important role throughout the culture.

The presence of seal impressions at Gilund calls for a reconsideration of the external contacts of the inhabitants of the area. The seals may have been used to guarantee local products, but sealing technology does not appear to have been well known in this area.[23] In addition, the designs of the seals impressed onto the Gilund sealings do not belong to the iconography of the area which is thus far known only from animal figurines, primarily bulls, and designs on painted pottery. Curiously, they also do not resemble the indigenous iconography of the nearby Harappan Civilization. Seals with similar iconography, for example, a stamp seal in the shape of a stepped cross found at Harappa (Joshi and Parpola 1987:205, H-166), were found in Harappan contexts, but are generally considered to be imports. In fact, the iconography of the seals used on the Gilund impressions most resembles that of material found in Central Asia and in southeastern Iran throughout the 3rd millennium BC.[24]

As a group, these finds call for a re-examination and possibly a redefinition of the Ahar-Banas Culture and its relationship with the world beyond its borders. The use of seals at Gilund demonstrates the presence of a complex administrative system of a type that was unexpected in this area. Even in Harappan contexts (aside from Lothal) there is very little evidence of the use of seals for guaranteeing goods. In addition, it is curious that when we do find evidence of contact with cultures outside Mewar Plain, it is not only with the nearby cultures of the Indus Valley, but also with the distant cultures of Central Asia and Iran, which have a distinct material culture characterized by an emphasis both on geometric shapes and on fantastical representations of animals and the superhuman. Taken together, this material suggests that Gilund and other sites in western India were in fact somehow involved with the large-scale web of interactions that is being increasingly documented throughout Asia in the late 3rd and early 2nd millennia BC. Further discoveries and studies of Gilund material will hopefully allow us to better define interconnections within the Middle Asian Interaction Sphere.

NOTES

9.1. The use of seals to guarantee the integrity of packages is first documented at Tell Sabi Abyad in northern Mesopotamia at the beginning of the 6th millennium BC (Duistermaat 2000). In South Asia, seals are documented at the site of Mehrgahr as early as the 4th millennium (Jarrige 1981:112), but the best-known example of administrative sealing is the cache of seal impressions found in the 3rd millennium warehouse at Lothal (Rao 1979, Frenez and Tosi 2005).

9.2. Fiandra and Pepe (2000), Fiandra (1981). Zettler (1987) suggests that sealings and tablets may also have been kept separately from other trash in order to recycle the fine sealing clay.

9.3. Much of the terminology and theory used in the study of seal-based administrative systems comes from Mesopotamian archaeology, where these materials have long been known and have been extensively studied. As a result, many of my comparisons will be to material or behaviors known from this area of the world. It is hoped that studies such as this one will help to expand the study of sealing practices in South Asia and enable us to develop more geographically specific models.

9.4. This, however, is not always the case. There are also instances, for example at Lothal (see Frenez and Tosi 2005), where finger or nail marks also seem to play an important role in the act of sealing.

9.5. The use of seals and sealings is a topic that has been much discussed in the literature of Mesopotamia and the Aegean. For a good general introduction see Gibson and Biggs 1977 and Perna 2000.

9.6. Sealing clay tends to be much cleaner and more finely levigated than clay used for other purposes.

9.7. Lumps of finely levigated clay found in contexts where many other sealings were found will generally be identified as sealings as well.

9.8. The Smithsonian conservation team consisted of Harriet F.

(Rae) Beaubien (SCMRE senior objects conservator and Archaeological Conservation Program Manager) and Claudia Chemello (post-graduate fellow, Archaeological Conservation Program). The author and Julie Hanlon also assisted with the housing of the sealings.

9.9. The bin was originally identified as lot 13.4006. The brick coping and some of the other material around the outer edge of the pit was removed as lots 13.4031, 13.4033, and 13.4034. The fill of the pit, which contained the sealings and other materials, was removed as lot 13.4039.

9.10. See Chapter 3 in this volume for a detailed description of the parallel-wall structure and its surroundings.

9.11. The original depth of the bin was probably closer to 1 m, but the removal of the bricks lining the opening and erosion left a slightly shallower dimension.

9.12. The fact that Wall NS7 is preserved to a deeper level than Wall 1 suggests that the two walls were not built together, but examination from the top seems to suggest that they were.

9.13. Excavator's observation (Ambica Dhaka and Rohit Viswanath).

9.14. Excavator's observations.

9.15. The pit in question is located between Trenches 11 and 12 and was excavated as part of Trench 11 in the first season of excavation and as part of Trench 12 in the fifth.

9.16. Some of these parallels have already been discussed in Shinde, Possehl, and Ameri 2005 and Possehl, Shinde, and Ameri 2004.

9.17. See below for a complete description of this seal-amulet.

9.18. These two seals are termed "fish" seals because of their use of a teardrop-shaped element with a single round "eye." There are some similarities between the second "fish" seal and painted fish motifs found on the early pottery from Rehman Dheri (Joshi and Parpola 1987: Rhd 254–60).

9.19. Deo (1969c:176) recorded at least one other double-sided amulet at Ahar, but it was not illustrated in the publication.

9.20. Ahar museum no. AC-5.

9.21. The use of multiple lines to define a shape is also seen in a stone seal amulet found at Rangpur. See Bhattacharyya 1991.

9.22. G. Possehl, pers. comm. 2005.

9.23. More extensive excavation of Ahar-Banas sites may in the future refute this claim, but the fact that so few sealings have been found in the far-reaching researches carried out in the Indus does suggest that the use of seals for sealing was in fact unusual in this area. However, it should also be noted that unbaked sealings are extremely difficult to identify in excavation, and may be easily overlooked or damaged in post-depositional processes.

9.24. Not all the glyptic evidence found at Gilund has foreign parallels. There is, in fact, a small but significant subset of material that can be related to the iconography found on the painted pottery of the Ahar-Banas. See Ameri 2010 for a more extensive discussion of the iconographic parallels for the seals and sealings.

1.001
Height: 3.36 cm, Width: 3.82 cm, Thickness: 2.99 cm
Obverse: The sealing has two fragmentary impressions of concentric circles coming together. The surface is very flat. The impression may be part of a flower motif, or more likely part of a concentric circle seal. There is no evidence of a central motif, suggesting it might also be an impression of a double spiral seal.
Reverse: The reverse shows the possible shoulder of a vessel, almost at right angles to the seal-impressed surface. The angle is slightly different at the two sides and there is a possible rope impression, or impression of vessel decoration, on a diagonal across the reverse (this and the fact that the two edges appear to have different angles suggests we have a diagonal section of the sealing).

1.002
Height: 5.1 cm, Width: 5.67 cm, Thickness: 2.07 cm
Obverse: The sealing has an impression of concentric semi-circles emanating from a central straight line. Only about half of the impression is preserved. The design is not clear in the center. The right side of the impression is very worn. This seal is interesting in that the central element is linear, not round.
Reverse: No impression is visible.

1.003
Height: 2.82 cm, Width: 2.88 cm, Thickness: 1.76 cm
Obverse: The sealing has two very fine and very light impressions of concentric circles. The surface impressions are fairly faint.
Reverse: The reverse shows the rim of a pot, which is at a near 90 degree angle to the back of the sealing. The seal impression is at a 45 degree angle to the rim impression.

1.004
Height: 4.02 cm, Width: 4.21 cm, Thickness: 2.32 cm
Obverse: The sealed surface is very flat. The design consists of curving parallel lines within a second set of curving lines which form a triangular funnel shape. There may be other lines outside those that form the funnel. The design almost looks like the central element between two spirals, in which case the original seal would have been extremely large.
Reverse: There is no visible impression on the reverse. There is, however, an edge, which may have been the neck of a vessel, connected to the sealed surface.

1.005
Height: 4.12 cm, Width: 4.74 cm, Thickness: 1.29 cm
Obverse: The sealing has two impressions of a "fish" design. The original seal may have been oval. The "eye" consists of central knob and two concentric circles. There is an incised zigzag line within a crescent shaped "fin" above the eye. The other markings are hard to read. Of the two impressions, one is almost complete, while the second consists of only the border and a zigzag line.
Reverse: No impression is visible.

1.006
Height: 4.7 cm, Width: 4.51 cm, Thickness: 2.28 cm
Obverse: The sealing has two impressions of a "fish" seal: Impression 1 is the same as G.S. 1.005, and is almost complete. The outer edges of the lower zigzag may be striated with very thin parallel lines. This may be an impression of wood grain on a wooden seal, but is probably just the smoothing of the wet clay. Impression 2 shows just the eye and fragments of concentric circles around it. A third fragment of an impression is also visible, but unclear. It looks as if the impression was made on very wet clay.
Reverse: The reverse has negative impressions of two arcs or rims, possibly from a box. It seems too uneven to be a vessel.

1.007
Height: 2.45 cm, Width: 3.24 cm, Thickness: 1.41 cm
Obverse: The design shows sections of three concentric circles, one with impressed dots. The central circle is impressed, not raised. Three dots are preserved.
Reverse: Possible shoulder of a vessel.

1.008
Height: 2.73 cm, Width: 3.36 cm, Thickness: 1.13 cm
Obverse: This sealing has impressions on two sides. Side 1 is an impressed concentric circle with dots in negative. Side 1 is not very clear. The central circle is not preserved. Rays seem to emanate from the third circle. It looks as if the vessel was first impressed with G.S. 1.007. The sealing was then covered with more clay and sealed again. G.S. 1.008 preserves what appears to be a negative impression of G.S. 1.007 on side 2, and the new impression is of the same seal on side 1. The original sealing (G.S. 1.007) may have been broken.
Reverse: Side 2 has an impression of an impressed concentric circle with dots in positive. Four dots and most of the first circle are preserved. Side 2 almost looks as if it could be the positive for the impression on G.S. 1.007. The surfaces are shallow.

1.009
Height: 5.4 cm, Width: 5.24 cm, Thickness: 1.83 cm
Obverse: The obverse has concentric finger impressions with some overlapping.
Reverse: The reverse is a slightly curved surface.

1.010
Height: 4.82 cm, Width: 5.27 cm, Thickness: 2.02 cm
Obverse: The sealing has approximately nine fingertip impressions, some of which are overlapping, some of which are pulled through.
Reverse: The reverse is a slightly curved surface.

1.011
Height: 3.36 cm, Width: 5.2 cm, Thickness: 2.36 cm
Obverse: The obverse has some pulling of clay, but no obvious impressions.
Reverse: The reverse has some pulling of clay, but no obvious impressions.

1.012
Height: 3.8 cm, Width: 3.9 cm, Thickness: 1.81 cm
Obverse: The obverse has a partial impression of concentric circles, one central dot, and part of an outer circle. The rest is smoothed away.
Reverse: The reverse has a slightly convex surface.

1.013
Height: 4.08 cm, Width: 2.78 cm, Thickness: 2.23 cm
Obverse: The obverse has a very faint impression of parallel curved lines. These may be concentric circles from a central line, similar to G.S. 1.002. There are also some triangular elements at the top edge.
Reverse: The reverse has a possible rim impression, but is not very clear.

1.014
Height: 6.56 cm, Width: 11.3 cm, Thickness: 6.33 cm
Obverse: The obverse has three partial impressions of at least two different seals. Impression 1 shows a square seal with a central circle and four quarter circles at the edges. Impression 2 shows the corner of a square seal, possibly the same one as above. Impression 3 shows what seems to be a rectangular seal with a herringbone pattern. The lower register is made up of crescents facing right, while the middle register is made up of straight diagonals in the other direction. The third register seems to be crescents facing left, but only the lower edge is preserved.
Reverse: The reverse may have the impression of the neck and shoulder of a pot.

1.015
Height: 8.3 cm, Width: 7.2 cm, Thickness: 4.78 cm
Obverse: The impression is very worn and hard to read. It seems to have a central circular element surrounded by four concentric circles, but these might also be spiral elements. The impression may be cut by a second impression.
Reverse: The reverse has a flat surface that may be the shoulder of a jar.

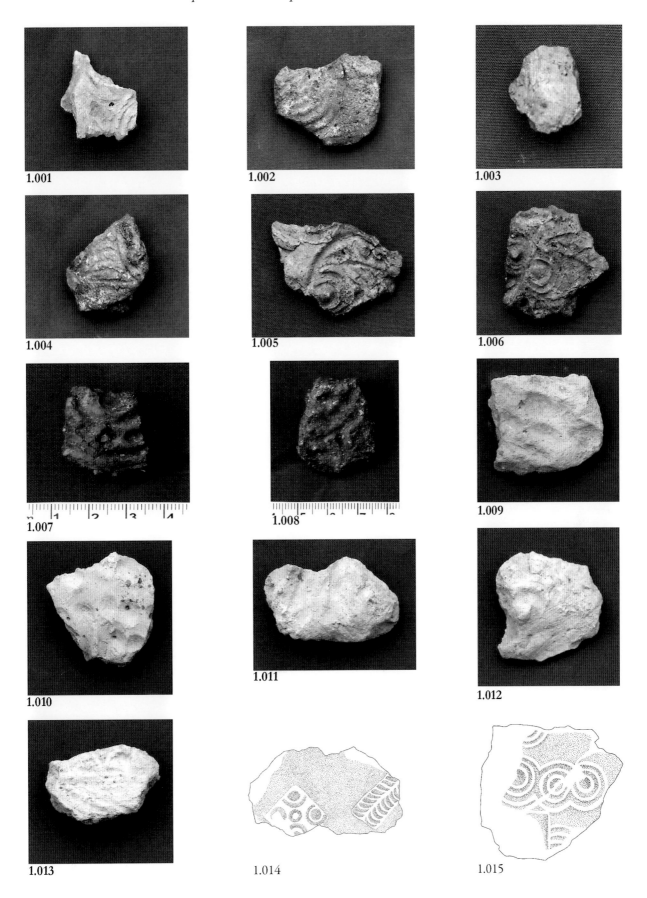

1.001

1.002

1.003

1.004

1.005

1.006

1.007

1.008

1.009

1.010

1.011

1.012

1.013

1.014

1.015

4.001
Height: 5.8 cm, Width: 7 cm, Thickness: 3.7 cm
Obverse: The sealing has two lines in one corner, but these may be modern toolmarks.
Reverse: The reverse may have the impression of the shoulder and neck of a vessel.

4.002
Height: 5.5 cm, Width: 8.9 cm, Thickness: 2.7 cm
Obverse: No impression is visible.
Reverse: The reverse has an impression of the neck and rim of a jar.

4.001

4.002

4.003
Height: 4.9 cm, Width: 5.9, Thickness: 3.9 cm
Obverse: The sealing has two impressions. Impression 1 shows concentric circles and a central diamond. Impression 2 shows half of a circle.
Reverse: The reverse has two flat surfaces at a 90 degree angle. There may also be a third surface. The sealing almost looks as if it were placed in a corner.

4.004
Height: 6 cm, Width: 4.8 cm, Thickness: 3.3 cm
Obverse: The obverse has an impression of a flat surface with crosshatched lines, all of which are very shallow and faint. It is not certain if this is a cloth or seal impression. There are also several lines left by chaff, and a square hollow off to one side. These may be two overlapping impressions.
Reverse: There is a round mark on the bottom of the sealing. This is possibly just chaff in the clay, or perhaps a rope impression. There is also what may be a straight edge, with no curvature, at an angle with the impression.

4.005
Height: 5.5 cm, Width: 5.1 cm, Thickness: 2.7 cm
Obverse: The obverse has what may be a badly made impression of a square seal.
Reverse: The sealing has a curved edge and an unclear edge at right angles. There is also a whitish deposit on the edges. The impressions on the obverse and reverse are similar, but are not at the same angle. The curved edge seems to be a pot rim. The second edge is uneven, on two levels, and has a small square hole inside the central area that would be in the middle of a sealing.

4.006
Height: 5.4 cm, Width: 4.9 cm, Thickness: 5 cm
Obverse: The impression shows the corner of square flower seal, with one petal visible. The outer edge of the impression is fairly deep, but the motif is shallow and faint. There is also what looks like the corner of a second impression.
Reverse: The reverse seems to be squared off at a strange angle to the rest of the sealing, perhaps showing a jug rim. If this is the case, it is interrupted on the inner rim, not by a break, but by a deposit of clay.

4.007
Height: 6.2 cm, Width: 7.1 cm, Thickness: 3.1 cm
Obverse: The sealing seems to have been impressed on both sides. There are two impressions of a circular or spiral design. Impression 1 is broken by a shell in the clay matrix, while impression 2 has three curved parallel lines.
Reverse: No impression is visible.

4.008
Height: 5.3 cm, Width: 6.1 cm, Thickness: 4.1 cm
Obverse: The impression is broken, but has shallow and flat concentric ovals. It may relate to G.S. 4.004.
Reverse: No impression is visible.

4.009
Height: 5.1 cm, Width: 4.9 cm, Thickness: 3.6 cm
Obverse: The sealing may have two separate designs, but they are very shallow and hard to distinguish. One seems to be of concentric circles, while the other is a braided design, or possibly a very broken flower seal.
Reverse: The reverse has one curved edge. It is unclear if this is the impression of a vessel or just finger smoothing.

4.010
Height: 3.7 cm, Width: 5 cm, Thickness: 3.8 cm
Obverse: The sealing has a very shallow fragment of an impression, probably the corner of a flower seal, set on an angle. The visible elements include

a central tear shape flanked by two lines.
Reverse: The sealing has a rope impression on its side edge. The rope was 0.6 cm high and possibly made of two strands. There is a small flat surface on the bottom, possibly representing a jug.

4.011
Height: 3.4 cm, Width: 5.5 cm, Thickness: 2.7 cm
Obverse: The sealing was deeply impressed by what appears to be a circular stamp seal. The visible elements are two curved parallel lines, perhaps circles.
Reverse: The sealing has a possible string impression on the side.

4.012
Height: 3.8 cm, Width 0.5 cm, Thickness: 2.3 cm
Obverse: The sealing has an impression of a fairly deep, fragmentary straight edge with parallel lines emanating from it that looks like the edge of flower seal. There might be a second impression, but only a straight edge is preserved.
Reverse: The reverse has a flat bottom, but no visible rim. The sealing does not appear to have been pressed on tightly.

4.013
Height: 4.2 cm, Width: 2.4 cm, Thickness: 3.2 cm
Obverse: The impression is medium in depth, but very hard to read. It looks like two left-facing arrows and a flat, straight edge. There is a possible second impression, but it is not clear and may only be a fingerprint.
Reverse: The reverse shows the edge and shoulder of a pot. The edge is almost carinated. There is some evidence of etched parallel lines on the inner side, but they are very faint.

4.014
Height: 3.1 cm, Width: 4.2 cm, Thickness: 1.7 cm
Obverse: The impression is very shallow and has a straight edge, a triangular shape, and parallel curved lines. It is possible that it was made by a flower seal. There is also a second impression, but all that is left is an edge. It is not clear if this is the edge of a pot or the edge of a deeply impressed seal as the sealing is broken at this point.
Reverse: The sealing has a compacted lower edge, but it is not smooth. It has no clear edge and is slightly bumpy.

4.015
Height: 6.5 cm, Width: 3.3 cm, Thickness: 3.3 cm
Obverse: The sealing has two shallow impressions of a square seal, probably with a flower design. Impression 1 is deeply impressed in the corner of the sealing, but the design itself is not very visible. Impression 2 is very shallow. It is broken at an angle and has curved parallel lines. The design seems to be the same as on Impression 1.
Reverse: The lower edge of the sealing is flat, but not very smooth.

4.016
Height: 4.6 cm, Width: 4.1 cm, Thickness: 2.8 cm
Obverse: The impression is very shallow and only partly visible. There is a straight edge, probably belonging to a square seal, and curved parallel lines. It looks like a fragment of a flower seal.
Reverse: The reverse has a possible rope impression, but it is not at all clear.

4.017
Height: 6.2 cm, Width: 3.7 cm, Thickness: 2.3 cm
Obverse: The sealing has a very shallow impression of three straight parallel lines.
Reverse: The reverse is very hard to read. It has one straight somewhat square edge which may be a rim. There is a possible rope impression below. The sealed surface is convex and there is a slightly concave surface next to it.

4.003

4.004

4.005

4.006

4.007

4.008

4.009

4.010

4.011

4.012

4.013

4.014

4.015

4.016

4.017

4.018

Dimensions unknown

Obverse: The sealing has two deep impressions. Impression 1 has curved parallel lines in two rows and is similar to G.S. 4.013. Impression 2 has just an edge.

Reverse: The sealing has a squared-off edge, but it is too small to be analyzed.

4.019

Height: 3.9 cm, Width: 3 cm, Thickness: 1.8 cm

Obverse: The sealing has one flat surface with possible evidence of sealing, but it is not at all clear.

Reverse: No impression is visible.

4.020

Height: 5.2 cm, Width: 4.5 cm, Thickness: 1.8 cm

Obverse: The impression is very coarse and has crosshatched lines. It seems to be related to the impression on G.S. 4.004 and may be a basket impression. It is also possible that this is the same seal as G.S. 5.007.

Reverse: The sealing has a smooth, uneven surface, possibly from leather or cloth. It may be an impression of a hand pressing down clay.

4.021

Height: 4.0 cm, Width: 4.6 cm, Thickness: 2.1 cm

Obverse: The impression is extremely shallow. It consists of a straight edge and curved parallel lines.

Reverse: The sealing has a slightly curved edge on the underside.

4.022

Height: 3.6 cm, Width: 1.9 cm, Thickness: 1.3 cm

Obverse: The impression is of medium depth with well-defined forms. The design is the same as the circle of concentric circles seal. Two fragmentary circles and part of the central element are preserved.

Reverse: The reverse is flat and slightly rounded, but the piece is very small.

4.023

Height: 5.1 cm, Width: 3.7 cm, Thickness: 2.4 cm

Obverse: No impression is visible.

Reverse: The reverse is slightly rounded with some visible striations. It may have an impression of the surface of a vessel with concentric circles and small picks. It looks like the "diamond puncture" decoration usually found on coarse gray wares.

4.024

Height: 4.9 cm, Width: 5.4 cm, Thickness: 2.9 cm

Obverse: The sealing is very worn. It has no visible impressions.

Reverse: The reverse has a strong rim and a thick string impression. The string has 3–4 strands, but the visible striations on the impression suggest it may be reed rather than string.

4.025

Height: 3.9 cm, Width: 3.7 cm, Thickness: 2.2 cm

Obverse: There is a fragment of a possible impression near the smoothed edge, as well as a scalloped edge below the possible impression.

Reverse: No impression is visible.

4.026

Height: 3.4 cm, Width: 2 cm, Thickness: 1.5 cm

Obverse: No impression is visible.

Reverse: The sealing has two smooth sides, but they are both convex rather than concave.

4.027

Height: 3.4 cm, Width: 3.7 cm, Thickness: 2.5 cm

Obverse: No impression is visible.

Reverse: The sealing looks as if it was pressed into the bottom of a bowl with a flat bottom and straight sides.

4.028

Height: 3.5 cm, Width: 4.2 cm, Thickness: 3 cm

Obverse: No impression is visible.

Reverse: The reverse has the impression of the side of a jar with a molded edge and some evidence of raised decoration that is 0.4 cm in width; this may be a rope impression, but it looks more like a molding.

4.029

Height: 3 cm, Width: 2.9 cm, Thickness: 1.7 cm

Obverse: No impression is visible.

Reverse: The reverse is a flat surface with no visible impression.

4.030

Height: 4.3 cm, Width: 3.3 cm, Thickness: 1.5 cm

Obverse: No impression is visible.

Reverse: The reverse shows an uneven surface with thin parallel striations, which may be cloth. Perpendicular striations are also visible under magnification.

4.031

Height: 4 cm, Width: 2.9 cm, Thickness: 2.4 cm

Obverse: The impression is very shallow and faint. It may be a solar motif, though the rays almost look like fingernail marks.

Reverse: No impression is visible.

4.032

Height: 3.3 cm, Width: 4 cm, Thickness: 2.7 cm

Obverse: No impression is visible, but there is some smoothing of the clay.

Reverse: The reverse shows the neck of a vessel and may be a very fragmentary string impression. There is a square spot on the rim area which may be part of a diamond pattern.

4.018

4.019

4.020

4.021

4.022

4.023

4.024

4.025

4.026

4.027

4.028

4.029

4.030

4.031

4.032

4.033
Height: 3.8 cm, Width: 3.6, Thickness: 2.5 cm
Obverse: The sealing has a curved edge and some possible horizontal striations. There are vertical striations on the surface of the sealing, which may be the edge of a square seal. A small fragment of a curved edge is visible in the corner. The surface of the sealing is slightly convex.
Reverse: No impression is visible.

4.034
Height: 4.9 cm, Width: 3.1 cm, Thickness: 2.1 cm
Obverse: The impression is very shallow and has two parallel lines. There are striations and unshaped bits on the upper surface.
Reverse: The reverse is flat, but slightly convex.

4.035
Height: 3 cm, Width: 3.2 cm, Thickness: 1.3 cm
Obverse: The sealing has two possible impressions. Both are just slightly curved edges. One consists of a break on the edge with two parallel lines above.
Reverse: The reverse is a flat, slightly convex surface.

4.036
Height: 4 cm, Width: 2.8 cm, Thickness: 1.8 cm
Obverse: The obverse has striations, probably signs of smoothing by hand, but no impression is visible.
Reverse: The reverse shows the shoulder and rim of a vessel as well as an impression of the design on the rim of vessel.

4.037
Height: 2.9 cm, Width: 2 cm, Thickness: 2 cm
Obverse: The surface shows smoothing with striations and a curved edge, but it is unclear if this is a break or if it continues.
Reverse: No impression is visible.

4.038
Height: 3.4 cm, Width: 2.2 cm, Thickness: 1.6 cm
Obverse: There is one flat edge, but it is not clear if it is the obverse or reverse.
Reverse: No impression is visible.

4.039
Height: 3.0 cm, Width: 2.8 cm, Thickness: 2.6 cm
Obverse: The sealing has three smoothed surfaces at angles to each other and one modern tool mark, but no visible impressions.
Reverse: The sealing has a concave edge.

4.040
Height: 3.0 cm, Width: 2.1 cm, Thickness: 1.6 cm
Obverse: No impression is visible.
Reverse: No impression is visible.

4.041
Height: 3.6 cm, Width: 2.1 cm, Thickness: 1.3 cm
Obverse: No impression is visible.
Reverse: The reverse has a groove that could be rope, but the angle seems wrong.

4.042
Height: 3.6 cm, Width: 2.7 cm, Thickness: 1.8 cm
Obverse: The surface is smooth and convex in shape, but no impression is visible.

Reverse: The reverse is an uneven surface with possible rope marks or impressions of pottery decoration. There is a second set of possible smaller rope or string marks above the larger ones.

4.043
Height: 3.2 cm, Width: 2.6 cm, Thickness: 1.9 cm
Obverse: The sealing has three smoothed surfaces, but no impression is visible.
Reverse: No impression is visible.

4.044
Height: 3.3 cm, Width: 2.3 cm, Thickness: 2.3 cm
Obverse: The sealing has a flat surface with some relief and some incised elements, but no legible shapes.
Reverse: The sealing may have been a bottle stopper. There is a small fragment of a ridge on one side. It is heavily covered with white deposits.

4.045
Height: 3 cm, Width: 2.1 cm, Thickness: 2.1 cm
Obverse: No impression is visible.
Reverse: No impression is visible.

4.046
Height: 3.2 cm, Width: 2.3 cm, Thickness: 1.5 cm
Obverse: No impression is visible.
Reverse: No impression is visible.

4.047
Height: 3 cm, Width: 2.8 cm, Thickness: 1.9 cm
Obverse: The sealing has a convex surface, but no impression is visible. Its shape is similar to G.S. 4.036.
Reverse: The reverse is flat but not compressed and the surface is uneven. It may be the rim and shoulder of a jar.

4.048
Height: 3.7 cm, Width: 2 cm, Thickness: 2.4 cm
Obverse: No impression is visible.
Reverse: The sealing has a convex surface with a possible rope impression.

4.049
Height: 3.28 cm, Width: 2.82 cm, Thickness: 1.87 cm
Obverse: The sealing has a smooth surface, but no impressions are visible.
Reverse: No impression is visible.

4.050
Height: 2.5 cm, Width: 2.2 cm, Thickness: 1.7 cm
Obverse: The sealing has flattened surfaces, but no impressions.
Reverse: No impression is visible.

4.051
Height: 3.2 cm, Width: 3.1 cm, Thickness: 1.6 cm
Obverse: No impression is visible.
Reverse: The reverse shows the rim of a pot.

4.052
Height: 2.7 cm, Width: 3.4 cm, Thickness: 1.3 cm
Obverse: The surface has striations and evidence of smoothing, but no impression is visible.
Reverse: The reverse appears to be the impression of the inside of a bowl.

4.033   4.034   4.035   4.036

4.037   4.038   4.039   4.040

4.041   4.042   4.043   4.044

4.045   4.046   4.047   4.048

4.049   4.050   4.051   4.052

4.053
Height: 2 cm, Width: 2.2 cm, Thickness: 1.1 cm
Obverse: No impression is visible.
Reverse: The reverse has a flat surface.

4.054
Height: 3.27 cm, Width: 1.6 cm, Thickness: 1.56 cm
Obverse: The impression is of the edge of a seal, consisting of a straight edge and two parallel lines.
Reverse: The reverse shows a straight surface with a single raised straight line, maybe a box.

4.055
Height: 4 cm, Width: 2.9 cm, Thickness: 2.1 cm
Obverse: No impression is visible.
Reverse: No impression is visible.

4.056
Height: 2.8 cm, Width: 2.6 cm, Thickness: 2.4 cm
Obverse: The surface is smoothed, but no impression is visible.
Reverse: No impression is visible.

4.057
Height: 2.4 cm, Width: 2.7 cm, Thickness: 1.4 cm
Obverse: The surface is smoothed, but no impression is visible.
Reverse: No impression is visible.

4.058
Height: 2.9 cm, Width: 2.4 cm, Thickness: 1.7 cm
Obverse: No impression is visible.
Reverse: The reverse shows possible rim or stick impression.

4.059
Height: 3.8 cm, Width: 2.4 cm, Thickness: 2.1 cm
Obverse: No impression is visible.
Reverse: No impression is visible.

4.062
Height: 5.3 cm, Width: 4.1 cm, Thickness: 2.9 cm
Obverse: The impression is very worn. It shows one side of a double spiral with two joining threads. In addition, there are three lines above the spiral element.
Reverse: The reverse has a small fragment of a flat surface.

4.063
Height: 4 cm, Width: 3.6 cm, Thickness: 3.2 cm
Obverse: The impression is one side of double spiral with two joining threads. There are three lines above the spiral. The impression is very similar to G.S. 4.062, but seems to be smaller in size. However, this may be due to the way it was sealed or the drying of the clay after the seal was impressed.
Reverse: The reverse has a small fragment of flat surface.

4.064
Height: 5 cm, Width: 8.8 cm Thickness: 3.2 cm
Obverse: The sealing has two impressions, both very worn. Impression 1 shows a large spiral or a series of concentric circles whose inner rings have been worn away. Impression 2 shows a small spiral with projections from

the outer ring. The pattern looks vaguely like a snail shell and is also worn. The two impressions may have been made by two different seals, but close analysis of this and similar impressions suggest that they are in fact the product of a single seal with two distinct decorative elements.
Reverse: The reverse shows the neck and rim of a vessel.

4.065
Height: 5.8 cm Width: 4.1 cm, Thickness: 2.5 cm
Obverse: The sealing has two impressions that seem to have been made when the clay was very wet. The second impression looks as if it might have been made merely by pulling a stylus through wet clay. Impression 1 shows concentric half circles. The lines are very thin. It looks like the eye element from S1.005 and S1.006, the "fish seal." Impression 2 has several wavy lines.
Reverse: No impression is visible.

4.066
Height: 4.7 cm, Width: 4.3 cm, Thickness: 2.0 cm
Obverse: The impression is made up of two straight parallel lines with three rounded parallel lines below. It looks like the central area of the double spiral motif. The design is similar to G.S. 4.062 and 4.063, but the lines are finer. The sealing has a smoothed area in the lower part of the impression.
Reverse: The reverse shows a flat edge with a curve or rim. There is a depression right at the rim that may be rope. There is also no visible vertical curvature, suggesting a straight-sided or very large vessel.

4.067
Height: 4 cm, Width: 8.5 cm, Thickness: 4.1 cm
Obverse: The sealing has two deep impressions of a single seal. The design is a solar pattern or sunburst motif with a chevron pattern or slanted parallel lines around the edge. The solar motif is made up of curving lines emanating from central circular element. The outer ring with slanting lines is very faint.
Reverse: The reverse is very confusing. There is a flat surface with a slight curvature underneath, which is slightly flattened at one end. It is not very smooth, but there is a strong return, possibly from the rim of a jar. A small piece of rim impression is visible.

4.068
Height: 6.1 cm, Width: 5.0 cm, Thickness: 2.5 cm
Obverse: The sealing has a nearly complete impression of a circular seal, and a small fragment of a second impression of the same seal overlapping the first. The second impression seems to be going in the same direction as the main impression. The design is a central circle surrounded by sunbursts (curved lines) with an outer frame of parallel lines. The twelve rays emanating from the central circle are very deeply impressed.
Reverse: The reverse shows the shoulder and rim of a vessel. There are some very shallow grooves on the shoulder, maybe string.

4.069
Height: 5.5 cm, Width: 3.5 cm, Thickness: 2 cm
Obverse: The sealing has a single impression of the sunburst seal. About half of the deep impression is preserved. The details are clearly visible, and there are some chaff impressions on the surface.
Reverse: The reverse shows the shoulder of a vessel, but no visible rim. This sealing has a triangular shape typical of most impressions from Gilund.

4.053

4.054

4.055

4.056

4.057

4.058

4.059

4.062

4.063

4.064

4.065

4.066

4.067

4.068

4.069

4.070
Height: 4.2 cm, Width: 4.3 cm, Thickness: 2.8 cm
Obverse: The sealed surface is flat and deeply impressed. The design is of two overlapping concentric circles. The first is made up of parallel lines between two circles with a smaller concentric circle and a dot in the center. The second is a set of concentric circles or perhaps a spiral. It is not at first clear whether these two elements form a single seal or represent two individual seals, but the presence of this same arrangement on other impressions suggests that this is a single seal, not two overlapping seals.
Reverse: The reverse has a concave edge with a possible rope or reed impressions. It seems like an odd place for rope, as there is no outer edge.

4.071
Height: 6.2 cm, Width: 10 cm, Thickness: 3.4 cm
Obverse: The sealing has two impressions of the same seal, a round seal with five concentric circles separated by triangular elements arranged around a central circular element with two parallel lines. The sealing is deeply impressed, but the lower edge is a bit faint. The first impression is almost complete, while the second is just one circle and a triangular element.
Reverse: The reverse shows the shoulder or rim of a large pot (possibly a large shallow bowl). There are strange impressions that almost look like finger marks on the bottom. This may be dirt, but the sealing has been consolidated so it is difficult to tell. However, it seems clear that the fabric of this lump is different from the rest of the sealing.

4.072
Height: 6.6 cm, Width: 6.4 cm, Thickness: 3.2 cm
Obverse: The sealing has a very worn partial impression of the circle of concentric circles seal with two circles visible.
Reverse: The reverse shows the shoulder and neck of large vessel, or perhaps shallow bowl.

4.073
Height: 4.5 cm, Width: 5.5 cm, Thickness: 3.5 cm
Obverse: The sealing has a single impression of a circular, or maybe lenticular, seal with two sets of concentric semi-circles facing opposite directions. There is also a very faint veined impression (ca. 1 cm by 1 cm) that may be a leaf.
Reverse: The reverse has a clear impression of the neck and rim of a jar. The sealing clay overhangs the rim. There is also a modern tool impression right along the rim.

4.074
Height: 4.4 cm, Width: 6.9 cm, Thickness: 2.8 cm
Obverse: The sealing has a single, very shallow impression of a round seal with concentric circles. This impression seems different than the impression on G.S. 4.071. It has a border around the edge and looks as if it may have had only four circles rather than five, but this might also be due to the poor preservation of the piece.
Reverse: The reverse shows the neck and shoulder of a large vessel. The neck and shoulder are almost perpendicular to each other.

4.075
Height: 4.1 cm, Width: 3.0 cm, Thickness: 2.1 cm
Obverse: The sealing has a deeply impressed partial impression of the circle of concentric circles seal. Parts of two circles are preserved.
Reverse: The reverse has a slightly curved surface.

4.076
Height: 3.2 cm, Width: 5 cm, Thickness: 1.2 cm
Obverse: The sealing has a partial impression of a stamp seal. A very faint impression suggests that the design is a bilaterally symmetrical image of concentric circles or spirals along a straight edge. This may be a quadruple spiral motif.
Reverse: The reverse has a flat surface, but it is not smooth enough to be ceramic.

4.077
Height: 3 cm, Width: 2.5 cm, Thickness: 1.3 cm
Obverse: The sealing has a fragmentary impression of the circle of concentric circles seal. The edge and part of one circle are preserved.
Reverse: The reverse shows the neck and possible shoulder of a vessel, but the sealing is really quite small.

4.078
Height: 6.2 cm, Width: 4.4 cm, Thickness: 2.6 cm
Obverse: The sealing has a deep partial impression of the circle of concentric circles seal which preserves two and a half circles and the central element.
Reverse: The reverse is a convex surface, maybe the neck of a vessel.

4.079
Height: 6.2 cm, Width: 5.7 cm, Thickness: 3.4 cm
Obverse: The sealing has two partial overlapping impressions of the circle of concentric circles seal. The larger impression appears to have been slightly mashed. Impression 1 preserves two and a half circles and the central element. Impression 2 has one and a half circles and overlays impression 1.
Reverse: The reverse shows the shoulder of a jar and a possible rope impression. The lower surface does not seem smooth enough to be pottery; it may be cloth over pottery.

4.080
Height: 5.8 cm, Width: 7.6 cm, Thickness: 3 cm
Obverse: The sealing has two partial impressions of the circle of concentric circles seal. Both are deeply impressed. There is also a possible 3rd impression, but it lies right at the break. Impression 1 preserves one and a half circles and part of the central element. Impression 2 has one and a half circles and the triangular element between them.
Reverse: The reverse shows the shoulder and rim of a jug. Some very light impressions, possibly of diagonal incisions, may reflect decoration on the body of the jar, but they are very hard to see. The width of the rim is 2.2 cm.

4.081
Height: 8.8 cm, Width: 8.7 cm, Thickness: 2.4 cm
Obverse: The sealing has three partial impressions of the circle of concentric circles seal. Impression 1 preserves four circles and the central element to medium depth. Impression 2 has two circles preserved, both very deeply impressed. Impression 3 has shallow impressions of two and a half circles and a modern tool mark.
Reverse: The reverse shows the rim and side of a vessel which looks like a shallow bowl. The inner surface is smooth.

4.082
Height: 5.9 cm, Width: 5.9 cm, Thickness: 2.5 cm
Obverse: The sealing has two partial impressions of the circle of concentric circles seal. Impression 1 is very shallow and preserves three and a half circles and the central element. Impression 2 is also very shallow and preserves half of a circle.
Reverse: The reverse shows the side and rim of a vessel, but is not very smooth or well packed.

4.083
Height: 5.8 cm, Width: 5 cm, Thickness: 2.8 cm
Obverse: The sealing has a partial impression of the circle of concentric circles seal. Two circles and part of the central element are preserved. There is a rectangular hole in the middle of the impression. The uppermost circle appears to have been smudged or to have gotten wet.
Reverse: The reverse shows the side and rim of vessel, possibly a shallow bowl. The surface is not very smooth or compact.

4.084
Height: 11 cm, Width: 6.1 cm, Thickness: 5.1 cm
Obverse: The sealing has two very shallow impressions of the flower seal with a round central element. The sealing is very worn and may have gotten wet at some point.
Reverse: The reverse has some flat surfaces, but they are unclear.

4.070

4.071

4.072

4.073

4.074

4.075

4.076

4.077

4.078

4.079

4.080

4.081

4.082

4.083

4.084

4.085
Height: 6.6 cm, Width: 10.6 cm, Thickness: 4.8 cm
Obverse: The sealing has three impressions of the flower seal. The surface is very smooth and worn. Impression 1 has the central element and two and a half petals preserved. Impression 2 has a straight edge and two petals. Impression 3 has a fragment of one petal preserved. Part of the surface was broken off and there are two grooves visible in the clay matrix. The edges of the grooves are smooth and do not look like string. They may have been caused by water or insect damage.
Reverse: The reverse shows the side and rim of large vessel. The rim width is 2 cm. The side is also visibly concave.

4.086
Height: 7.7 cm, Width: 6.6 cm, Thickness: 4.3 cm
Obverse: The sealing has a fragmentary impression of the corner of a flower seal and joins with G.S. 4.087. It also preserves an impression of another edge, probably of the same seal. Finally, there are two very worn impressions on the other side.
Reverse: The reverse is extremely hard to read. It looks like half of a jar stopper, but is also sealed on the side.

4.087
Height: 4.7 cm, Width: 6.2 cm, Thickness: 4.2 cm
Obverse: The sealing has a fragmentary impression of the corner of a flower seal and joins with G.S. 4.086. It also preserves an impression of another edge, probably of the same seal. Finally, there are two very worn impressions on the other side.
Reverse: The reverse is extremely hard to read. It looks like half of a jar stopper, but is also sealed on the side.

4.088
Height: 5.4 cm, Width: 5.3 cm, Thickness: 2.3 cm
Obverse: The sealing has partial impressions of what appears to be a flower seal. The impression appears to have been made when the clay was very wet (or possibly by hand).
Reverse: The reverse shows the shoulder and possibly the rim of a jug. There is a possible impression of incisions on the rim of the jug, but it is very faint.

4.089
Height: 6.7 cm, Width: 4.5 cm, Thickness: 3.2 cm
Obverse: The sealing has a somewhat shallow impression of a flower seal and possibly some fingerprints.
Reverse: The reverse shows two straight edges on two sides of a rectangular element; one edge is slightly concave. This may be the top for a box. There are some grooves and one raised element on the concave side.

4.090
Height: 5.6 cm, Width: 5.2 cm, Thickness: 3.2 cm
Obverse: The sealing has a partial impression of a flower seal with a central diamond element. It seems to have been deeply impressed originally, but is now badly worn. There are wear marks on the surface of the sealing.
Reverse: The reverse has a small fragment of a flat edge which is not smooth and may have an impression of an incised design from a vessel. The two unsealed surfaces are at right angles to each other, but it is not clear if this is fabricated or just the line of the break.

4.091
Height: 8 cm, Width: 8 cm, Thickness: 2 cm
Obverse: The sealing has two partial impressions of the flower seal with a central diamond. The second impression slightly overlaps the first at a 45 degree angle. Impression 1 is almost complete, but worn away in some parts. Impression 2 preserves the corner of the seal and overlaps impression 1.
Reverse: The reverse shows a rounded surface that is not very smooth. There are possible string impressions on the upper and side edges.

4.092
Height: 4.8 cm, Width: 5.8 cm, Thickness: 4.2 cm
Obverse: The sealing has a very deeply impressed fragmentary impression of the flower seal with a round central element.
Reverse: The reverse shows the rim and shoulder of a pot with a very short neck. The rim is about 1.6 cm wide.

4.093
Height: 7.4 cm, Width: 8.9 cm, Thickness: 3.3 cm
Obverse: The sealing has four partial impressions of the flower seal with a round central element. The original seal seems to have slightly incurving sides. Impression 1 preserves about half of the seal and has two petals. Impression 2 preserves one petal and the side elements, as well as part of the central element. Impression 3 preserves just one petal, while the last impression has just one quarter of the edge of the seal.
Reverse: The reverse shows the rim and shoulder of a large jar. There are faint impressions on the surface. The rim of the jar would have been about 1.9 cm wide.

4.094
Height: 4.7 cm, Width: 6.2 cm, Thickness: 3.8 cm
Obverse: The sealing has a very faint impression of a flower seal. The central element is not visible. The impression is smaller than G.S. 4.093, suggesting that it is the seal with the diamond-shaped center, or perhaps a third version of the flower seal. The impression is almost complete but very shallow and worn.
Reverse: The reverse is very worn and has no clear edges. There is one possible neck surface (perpendicular to the sealed surface), but it is not clear.

4.095
Height: 3.3 cm, Width: 3.7 cm, Thickness: 2 cm
Obverse: The sealing may have two impressions. One is a straight edge with parallel lines and looks like a chevron pattern with a square central element. The second possible impression above is unclear.
Reverse: The sealing is triangular in shape and the reverse has a small fragment of a concave surface.

4.096
Height: 5 cm, Width: 7.5 cm, Thickness: 2.7 cm
Obverse: The sealing has two impressions of the flower seal with a central diamond element. The impressions are side by side, but do not seem to overlap. Impression 1 is very shallow and worn while impression 2 is better preserved.
Reverse: No impression is visible.

4.097
Height: 5.1 cm, Width: 4.9 cm, Thickness: 1.8 cm
Obverse: The sealing has one partial, very shallow impression of a flower seal with a central diamond.
Reverse: The reverse shows part of a shoulder and part of the rim of a vessel, with the area between broken off. However, the angle seems to be slightly off for the rim of a jar.

4.098
Height: 4.7 cm, Width: 5.27 cm, Thickness: 2.08 cm
Obverse: The impression is very worn and hard to read. There are some parallel lines, but the central area is worn away.
Reverse: The reverse has a very compact, smooth flat surface.

4.099
Height: 5 cm, Width: 6.41 cm, Thickness: 2.4 cm
Obverse: The sealing has a smoothed, worn surface, but no impressions.
Reverse: The reverse has reed and chaff and possible finger marks. They are mostly parallel, but there is one at an angle. The clay at one end looks different, with a possible chevron or concentric circle impression. Perhaps this sealing was placed over an existing sealing.

4.100
Height: 4.09 cm, Width: 4.09 cm, Thickness: 2.52 cm
Obverse: The sealing has a very mashed and worn impression of a possible double spiral seal with only one spiral preserved.
Reverse: The reverse is a flat surface.

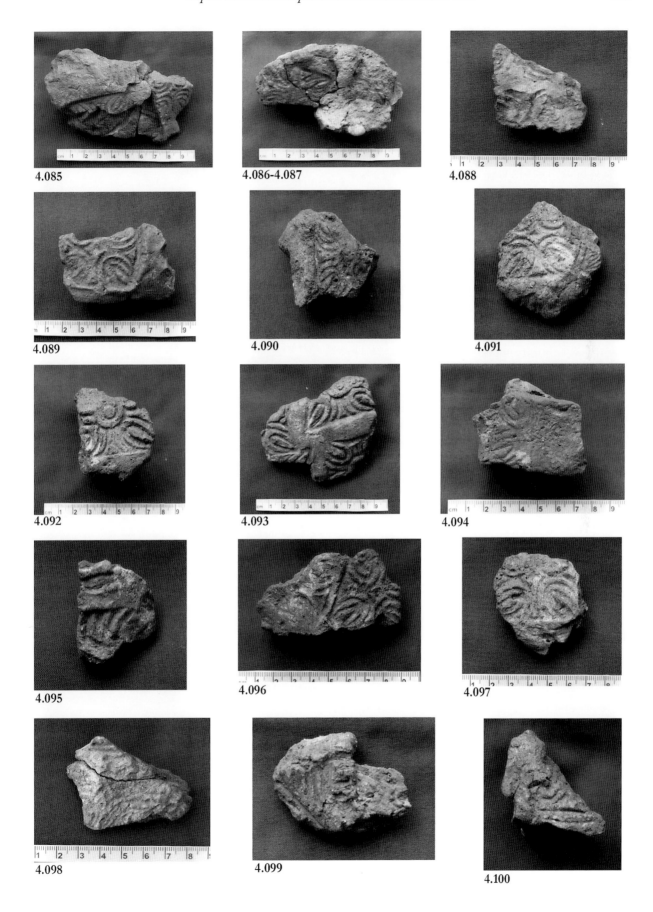

4.085

4.086-4.087

4.088

4.089

4.090

4.091

4.092

4.093

4.094

4.095

4.096

4.097

4.098

4.099

4.100

4.101

Height: 4.52 cm, Width: 4.57 cm, Thickness: 2.75 cm

Obverse: The sealing has a worn impression of a double circle seal, possibly the same as G.S. 4.064. Part of the circle with the spiral is preserved, but not very visible. Some of the surface of the impression seems to have flaked off.

Reverse: No impression is visible.

4.102

Height: 4.7 cm, Width: 8.8 cm, Thickness: 3.67 cm

Obverse: The sealing has a very worn and flattened impression of a square or rectangular seal, possibly the flower seal. Some parallel curved lines are visible, but they are very faint and some of the surface has flaked off.

Reverse: No impression is visible.

4.103

Height: 5.94 cm, Width: 7.9 cm, Thickness: 3.75 cm

Obverse: The sealing has two worn, but visible, impressions of the flower seal with a diamond center. Both impressions are oriented at more or less the same angle.

Reverse: No impression is visible.

4.104

Height: 5.20 cm, Width: 4.46 cm, Thickness: 2.36 cm

Obverse: The sealing has two impressions of a square seal. Impression 1 preserves the corner of the flower seal. One petal and part of a second are visible. Impression 2 is made by a square seal (probably the flower seal), but no design is preserved. Only the corner, impressed over the first impression, is visible.

Reverse: The reverse has a possible impression of rope or a very fine jar rim, but it is very hard to tell.

4.105

Height: 4.29 cm, Width: 4.18 cm, Thickness: 3.6 cm

Obverse: The sealing has one very worn impression of the corner of the flower seal. One petal is preserved. There is a small rectangular hole in the middle of the impression.

Reverse: No impression is visible.

4.106

Height: 3.28 cm, Width: 4.97 cm, Thickness: 2.66 cm

Obverse: The sealing has a partial impression of the flower seal with a diamond center. Two petals and part of the central diamond are preserved.

Reverse: No impression is visible.

4.107

Height: 3.04 cm, Width: 4.55 cm, Thickness: 2.46 cm

Obverse: The sealing has two impressions of a square seal. Impression 1 shows the corner of the flower seal. One very deeply impressed petal with very fine lines is preserved. Impression 2 shows the corner of a square seal, but no image is preserved.

Reverse: No impression is visible.

4.108

Height: 3.58 cm, Width: 2.89 cm, Thickness: 1.81 cm

Obverse: The sealing has one impression of the corner of a flower seal. Part of a petal and a triangular spacer element are preserved.

Reverse: No impression is visible.

4.109

Height: 4.03 cm, Width: 3.32 cm, Thickness: 1.85 cm

Obverse: The sealing has a very worn partial impression of the flower seal with the diamond central element. The impression is very faint.

Reverse: The reverse shows the shoulder and neck of a vessel.

4.110

Height: 3.74 cm, Width: 4.07 cm, Thickness: 2.55 cm

Obverse: The sealing has a partial impression of the flower seal with the diamond central element. This sealing shows that the central diamond is hollowed out (or full in original seal).

Reverse: No impression is visible.

4.111

Height: 3.69 cm, Width: 2.86 cm, Thickness: 1.7 cm

Obverse: The sealing has a faint partial impression of a flower seal. Parts of a petal and of the triangular element between petals are preserved.

Reverse: The reverse has a flat surface with small bump (possible carination).

4.112

Height: 2.14 cm, Width: 3.46 cm, Thickness: 1.51 cm

Obverse: The sealing has a very worn partial impression of a flower seal. Two partial petals are preserved. There may also be spiral or concentric circles, but it is very hard to tell.

Reverse: No impression is visible.

4.113

Height: 3.10 cm, Width: 2.45 cm, Thickness: 1.67 cm

Obverse: The sealing has a partial impression of the flower seal. A fragment of petal and trumpet elements are preserved.

Reverse: No impression is visible.

4.114

Height: 3.31 cm, Width: 3.34 cm, Thickness: 1.45 cm

Obverse: The sealing has a very worn partial impression of a flower seal. One petal and parts of two side elements are preserved as well as possibly one trumpet. The impression is slightly flattened.

Reverse: No impression is visible.

4.115

Height: 2.83 cm, Width: 3.67 cm, Thickness: 2.11 cm

Obverse: The sealing has one definite impression of the corner of a square seal, probably a flower seal. The second impression is unclear, but also seems to be the corner of a flower seal.

Reverse: The reverse has a fragment of a concave surface and a fragment of a flat surface at approximately a 30 degree angle to each other. The rest is broken off. Possibly the shoulder and neck of a vessel.

4.101

4.102

4.103

4.104

4.105

4.106

4.107

4.108

4.109

4.110

4.111

4.112

4.113

4.114

4.115

4.116
Height: 2.43 cm
Width: 3.41 cm
Thickness: 0.91 cm
Obverse: The sealing has a very faint fragmentary impression of a flower seal. The corner and part of petal are preserved. The lines are not crisp.
Reverse: No impression is visible.

4.117
Height: 3.51 cm
Width: 2.48 cm
Thickness: 2.37 cm
Obverse: The sealing has a very worn fragmentary impression of a flower seal. The central diamond element and two petals are preserved.
Reverse: No impression is visible.

4.118
Height: 1.95 cm
Width: 1.8 cm
Thickness: 1.65 cm
Obverse: The sealing has a tiny fragmentary impression of a petal from the flower seal.
Reverse: The reverse has a tiny flat surface.

4.119
Height: 2.8 cm
Width: 2.11 cm
Thickness: 1.4 cm
Obverse: The sealing has a fragmentary impression of a flower seal. The trumpet element and parts of two petals are preserved. The impression is fairly deep and detailed. The round edge suggests that this may be yet another version of a flower seal.
Reverse: The reverse has a tiny fragment of a flat surface.

4.120
Height: 3.86 cm
Width: 2.63 cm
Thickness: 2.04 cm
Obverse: The sealing has a very faint, worn partial impression of a flower seal. The central diamond element, a trumpet, and parts of petals are preserved. The impression seems to have been mashed.
Reverse: No impression is visible.

4.121
Height: 3.31 cm
Width: 2.75 cm
Thickness: 1.99 cm
Obverse: The sealing has a very deep partial impression of a flower seal, probably the one with a round central element.
Reverse: The reverse shows what looks like the lip of a vessel. This suggests that the sealing may be a jar stopper, although it seems too small.

4.122
Height: 3.31 cm
Width: 2.94 cm
Thickness: 0.69 cm
Obverse: The sealing has a partial impression of a flower seal. A triangular element and parts of two petals are preserved.
Reverse: The reverse is flat with one (seemingly applied) clay strip. The sealing as a whole is very thin.

4.123
Height: 2.02 cm
Width: 1.68 cm
Thickness: 1.51 cm
Obverse: The sealing has an impressed curving line, perhaps the outer edge of a round seal.
Reverse: No impression is visible.

4.124
Height: 2.68 cm
Width: 2.77 cm
Thickness: 1.24 cm
Obverse: The sealing has a partial impression of a flower seal. It is a bit worn and mashed. A triangular element and parts of two petals are preserved.
Reverse: No impression is visible.

4.125
Height: 1.6 cm
Width: 1.9 cm
Thickness: 0.81 cm
Obverse: The sealing has a tiny curved line. It is not clear if this is the edge of a round seal or just a rounded element.
Reverse: No impression is visible.

4.126
Height: 2.06 cm
Width: 2.53 cm
Thickness: 0.97 cm
Obverse: The sealing has a partial impression of a flower seal. The bottom of a triangular element and part of a petal are preserved. The triangular element is somewhat mashed.
Reverse: The reverse is a flat surface.

4.127
Height: 3.57 cm
Width: 3.12 cm
Thickness: 1.53 cm
Obverse: The sealing has two possible impressions. Impression 1 shows parallel curving lines in a rectilinear seal. Impression 2 has two parallel lines and a third line at an angle. It almost looks like impressed matchsticks.
Reverse: No impression is visible.

4.128
Height: 4.08 cm
Width: 3.72 cm
Thickness: 2.08 cm
Obverse: The sealing has two very narrow curved parallel lines. The clay may have been impressed when very wet.
Reverse: The reverse shows the rim of a vessel.

4.129
Height: 4.0 cm
Width: 3.5 cm
Thickness: 2.4 cm
Obverse: The sealing has an impression of a ladder design enclosed by two curved lines.
Reverse: The reverse shows the rim of a vessel.

4.130
Height: 3.44 cm
Width: 3.43 cm
Thickness: 1.2 cm
Obverse: The sealing has a partial impression of a round seal with an outer "ladder" frame. It is probably an impression of the sunburst seal seen in G.S. 4.067–69.
Reverse: The reverse is a convex surface.

4.116

4.117

4.118

4.119

4.120

4.121

4.122

4.123

4.124

4.125

4.126

4.127

4.128

4.129

4.130

4.131
Height: 2.9 cm, Width: 3.0, Thickness: 2.37 cm
Obverse: The sealing has a fairly deep impression of a triangular element flanked by curved parallel lines. It was probably part of a flower seal.
Reverse: The reverse shows a concave edge, possibly the neck of a jar, but it is not very smooth or clean.

4.132
Height: 2.23 cm, Width: 3.58 cm, Thickness: 2.44 cm
Obverse: The sealing has a partial impression of a round seal. A triangular element and a flanking curved line are visible. There is also a mountain-shaped element (with two peaks) below the triangle.
Reverse: The reverse shows the rim of a vessel.

4.133
Height: 3.0 cm, Width: 3.32 cm, Thickness: 2.04 cm
Obverse: The sealing has a partial impression of a round seal, possibly the circle of concentric circles seal. A triangular element and two curved lines are preserved.
Reverse: The reverse may show the neck and shoulder of a vessel, but the curvature seems a bit off. It looks like the bottom of a bowl, or possibly a jar stopper.

4.134
Height: 3.88 cm, Width: 4.54 cm, Thickness: 1.63 cm
Obverse: The sealing has an uneven impression of a double spiral where the lines of circles do not join. Most of one spiral and part of a second are visible. There may be a faint ladder design on the second spiral. It seems to be an impression of the same seal as G.S. 4.064 and 4.070 (the spiral and ladder seal). The whole design seems to consist of a concentric circle and spiral on one side and a circle with a ladder design or rays on the other.
Reverse: The reverse is a rough, almost flat surface, but there is no clear negative of a vessel.

4.135
Height: 3.54 cm, Width: 3.74 cm, Thickness: 1.39 cm
Obverse: The sealing has a very worn and mashed impression of the spiral and ladder seal, which seems to have been partially rubbed away. The lines are all mashed together. The impression shows part of one spiral with circles that do not match up (same as G.S. 4.134). There are modern toolmarks or chaff marks on the sealed surface, which is almost concave.
Reverse: The reverse has a slight double curve. There are some very faint raised lines that are almost parallel and possibly show decoration on the pot.

4.136
Height: 2.64 cm, Width: 4.33 cm, Thickness: 2.79 cm
Obverse: The sealing has an impression of three large concentric circles and possibly a central dot.
Reverse: No impression is visible.

4.137
Height: 2.93 cm, Width: 3.82 cm, Thickness: 1.5 cm
Obverse: The sealing has an impression of three concentric circles of which the central one is very small and almost looks like a yin-yang. One side of the middle circle seems to split. The upper part of the impression is worn away.
Reverse: The reverse is a concave surface with three faint parallel lines, possibly decoration from a pot. The third line is very faint.

4.138
Height: 4.22 cm, Width: 3.38 cm, Thickness: 2.13 cm
Obverse: The sealing has a deep impression of three concentric circles of which the smallest is very wide, wider on one side. There is one crack on the outer edge of the impression, and another one along the edges of the second circle.
Reverse: The reverse is a straight surface, maybe the neck or shoulder of a vessel.

4.139
Height: 2.70 cm, Width: 3.85 cm, Thickness: 1.32 cm
Obverse: The sealing has an impression of concentric circles, probably the same as G.S. 4.138. The smallest circle is very thick and larger on one side. The impression is very worn and only the central circle is well preserved.
Reverse: The reverse is a flat surface, maybe the shoulder of a vessel.

4.140
Height: 3.91 cm, Width: 3.2 cm, Thickness: 1.5 cm
Obverse: The sealing has two or three concentric circles and a possible ladder motif.
Reverse: The reverse shows the rim of a vessel.

4.141
Height: 3.91 cm, Width: 3.6 cm, Thickness: 2.50 cm
Obverse: The sealing has an impression of a very high (0.46 cm) central circular element. Only half of the element is preserved and it is surrounded by a very faint ladder motif.
Reverse: The reverse shows a concave surface, probably the curved side of a vessel, but it is not clear if it is an interior or exterior.

4.142
Height: 4.5 cm, Width: 5.3 cm, Thickness: 2.77 cm
Obverse: The sealing has one set of three concentric circles as well as a possible second set. It may be an impression of a double spiral type or a spiral and ladder seal. The central circle is very high (0.27 cm) as is the dividing element between the two sets of circles.
Reverse: The reverse shows neck and rim of a large pot.

4.143
Height: 3.92 cm, Width: 4.24 cm, Thickness: 2.58 cm
Obverse: The sealing has a partial impression of the circular element with a surrounding ladder design from the spiral and ladder seal.
Reverse: The reverse shows the shoulder and rim of a small jug-like vessel.

4.144
Height: 3.76 cm, Width: 5.4 cm, Thickness: 2.8 cm
Obverse: The sealing has a very faded and worn impression of a circular motif surrounded by a ladder motif.
Reverse: The reverse shows the neck of a larger vessel.

4.145
Height: 2.15 cm, Width: 3.61 cm, Thickness: 1.51 cm
Obverse: The sealing has two partial impressions of the outer edge of the sunburst seal. Impression 1 shows the ladder design. On impression 2 a curved edge is visible, but there are no visible elements of design.
Reverse: The reverse is flat, but there is a visible impression of a vessel.

4.131

4.132

4.133

4.134

4.135

4.136

4.137

4.138

4.139

4.140

4.141

4.142

4.143

4.144

4.145

4.146

Height: 2.76 cm, Width: 2.95 cm, Thickness: 1.52 cm

Obverse: The sealing has a partial impression of the outer ladder design of the sunburst seal.

Reverse: The reverse shows the shoulder and neck of a vessel, but there is an odd angle in part of it, which may be a spout. There are also some strips of raised clay, possibly cloth impressions.

4.147

Height: 2.2 cm, Width: 3.52 cm, Thickness: 1.65 cm

Obverse: The sealing has a partial impression of a curved line.

Reverse: No impression is visible.

4.148

Height: 2.83 cm, Width: 3.9 cm, Thickness: 1.38 cm

Obverse: The sealing has a very flat partial impression of a circle of concentric circles or a double spiral seal. Two small concentric circles or spirals are preserved.

Reverse: The reverse is a flat surface with some modern tool marks and a possible rope impression.

4.149

Height: 4.08 cm, Width: 4.31 cm, Thickness: 1.8 cm

Obverse: The sealing has a partial impression of the circle of concentric circles seal. Two circles and the central element are preserved.

Reverse: The reverse has a flat bottom and a possible partial rim impression with thick light-colored accretions.

4.150

Height: 3.86 cm, Width: 4.87 cm, Thickness: 1.8 cm

Obverse: The sealing has a partial impression of the circle of concentric circles seal. The central element and three circles are preserved. The central element is faint, while the circles are deeply impressed.

Reverse: The reverse is a concave surface and has what seem to be impressions of incised lines on a vessel.

4.151

Height: 4.76 cm, Width: 4.95 cm, Thickness: 2.66 cm

Obverse: The sealing has two partial impressions of a circle of concentric circles seal. Impression 1 has just the edge of the seal, but it is deeply impressed. Impression 2 has part of one circle and a triangular dividing element.

Reverse: The reverse is a slightly concave surface with some modern tool marks.

4.152

Height: 3.08 cm, Width: 4.18 cm, Thickness: 1.82 cm

Obverse: The sealing has two or three partial impressions of a circle of concentric circles seal. Only the outer edge of the seal is preserved on all three. All the impressions are fairly deep. The third impression is preserved only as a break at the edge of the sealing.

Reverse: No impression is visible.

4.153

Height: 3.26 cm, Width: 3.20 cm, Thickness: 2.13 cm

Obverse: The sealing has one partial impression of a circle of concentric circles seal. Most of one circle and a triangular element are preserved. The break at the edge of the sealing looks as if it might be a second impression.

Reverse: The reverse has part of a flat surface with some impressions of incisions on a pot and some modern tool marks.

4.154

Height: 3.5 cm, Width: 4.0 cm, Thickness: 2.31 cm

Obverse: The sealing has a very worn partial impression of a circle of concentric circles seal. Two circles and part of the central element are preserved. It is not clear if this is the same concentric circle seal found on most of the sealings as the triangular element is not as big or as well made, and the circles appear to be closer and thinner. The design of the central element is uncertain. The sealing is broken at the edge of the impression.

Reverse: The reverse shows the rim of a vessel.

4.155

Height: 3.56 cm, Width: 3.60 cm, Thickness: 2.4 cm

Obverse: The sealing has a very flat partial impression of a circle of concentric circles seal. The central element and parts of five circles are preserved. The central element is slightly worn.

Reverse: The reverse is a concave surface.

4.156

Height: 3.18 cm, Width: 2.33 cm, Thickness: 0.91 cm

Obverse: The sealing has two partial impressions of a circle of concentric circles seal, one deep and one extremely faint. Both show the edge of the seal and part of circles.

Reverse: The reverse is a slightly concave surface.

4.157

Height: 2.12 cm, Width: 1.26 cm, Thickness: 2.3 cm

Obverse: The sealing has a tiny fragment of an impression of a circle of concentric circles seal. A triangular element and part of a circle are preserved.

Reverse: No impression is visible.

4.158

Height: 2.7 cm, Width: 2.0 cm, Thickness: 1.61 cm

Obverse: The sealing has a partial impression of a circle of concentric circles seal. One circle is preserved.

Reverse: No impression is visible.

4.159

Height: 1.76 cm, Width: 1.85 cm, Thickness: 1.4 cm

Obverse: The sealing has a fragmentary impression of a circle of concentric circles seal. The triangular element and part of a circle are preserved.

Reverse: No impression is visible.

4.160

Height: 2.5 cm, Width: 2.35 cm, Thickness: 1.8 cm

Obverse: The sealing has a partial impression of a circle of concentric circles seal. Two circles and part of the central element are preserved.

Reverse: No impression is visible.

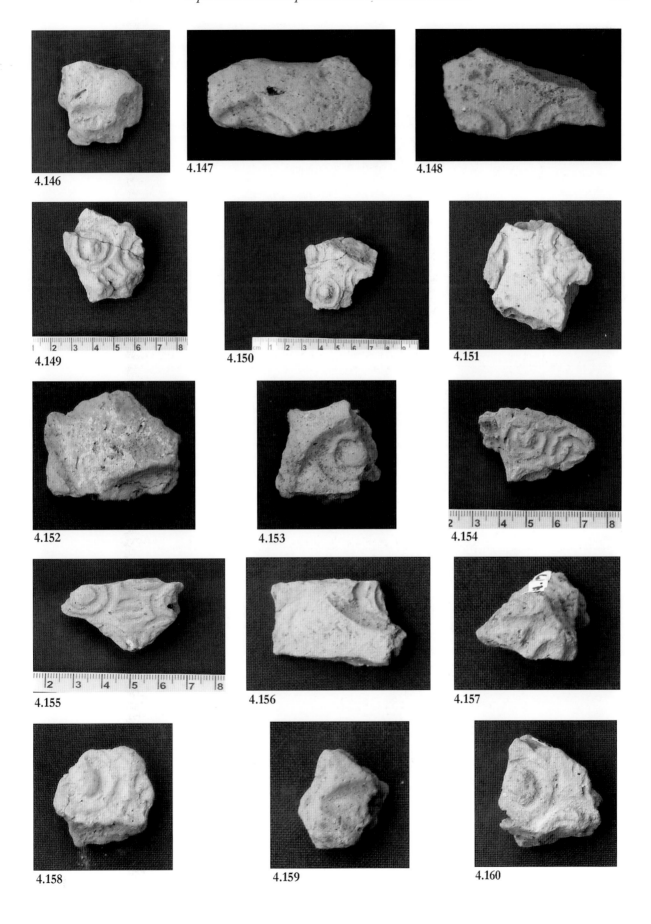

4.146

4.147

4.148

4.149

4.150

4.151

4.152

4.153

4.154

4.155

4.156

4.157

4.158

4.159

4.160

4.161
Height: 4.0 cm, Width: 2.9, Thickness: 1.13 cm
Obverse: The sealing has a deep impression of concentric circles. The impression seems to have been made on wet clay. The outer edge is not very well defined.
Reverse: The sealing is very thin and concave.

4.162
Height: 2.5 cm, Width: 2.3, Thickness: 1.4 cm
Obverse: The sealing has a partial impression of a circle of concentric circles seal. One circle and one triangular element are preserved. There is a modern tool impression across the circle.
Reverse: No impression is visible.

4.163
Height: 2.7 cm, Width: 2.31 cm, Thickness: 1.83 cm
Obverse: The sealing has two partial impressions of a sunburst seal. Impression 1 preserves parts of a ladder motif while impression 2 shows just the edge.
Reverse: No impression is visible.

4.164
Height: 3.1 cm, Width: 2.46 cm, Thickness: 2.05 cm
Obverse: The obverse has a very faint impression that is unclear. It looks like parallel lines that lie at an angle to the edge of the seal. Possibly part of the "fish" seal.
Reverse: No impression is visible.

4.165
Height: 2.76 cm, Width: 1.5 cm, Thickness: 1.06 cm
Obverse: The impression has fragments of concentric circles and other lines, but it is very hard to read.
Reverse: No impression is visible.

4.166
Height: 3.1 cm, Width: 2.4 cm, Thickness: 1.4 cm
Obverse: The obverse of the sealing has chaff impressions.
Reverse: No impression is visible.

4.167
Height: 2.60 cm, Width: 2.8 cm, Thickness: 1.2 cm
Obverse: The sealing has an impression of a small corner of a circle of concentric circles seal.
Reverse: No impression is visible.

4.168
Height: 3.0 cm, Width: 2.6 cm, Thickness: 1.2 cm
Obverse: The sealing has an impression of what look like large concentric circles.
Reverse: No impression is visible.

4.169
Height: 3.9 cm, Width: 1.6 cm, Thickness: 1.5 cm
Obverse: The sealing has an impression of parallel lines.
Reverse: No impression is visible.

4.170
Height: 3.3 cm, Width: 2.7 cm, Thickness: 1.7 cm
Obverse: The obverse is a flat surface.
Reverse: No impression is visible.

4.171
Height: 2.6 cm, Width: 1.4 cm, Thickness: 2.25 cm
Obverse: No impression is visible.
Reverse: No impression is visible.

4.172
Height: 2.85 cm, Width: 2.4 cm, Thickness: 1.45 cm
Obverse: The sealing has a possible impression of concentric circles.
Reverse: No impression is visible.

4.173
Height: 3.3 cm, Width: 2.1 cm, Thickness: 1.1 cm
Obverse: The impression seems to show a design of two interweaving lines, but it is very worn.
Reverse: No impression is visible.

4.174
Height: 2.0 cm, Width: 1.4 cm, Thickness: 2.1 cm
Obverse: The sealing has a fragmentary impression of concentric circles.
Reverse: No impression is visible.

4.175
Height: 2.4 cm, Width: 1.9 cm, Thickness: 1.4 cm
Obverse: The sealing has a fragmentary impression of three parallel lines.
Reverse: No impression is visible.

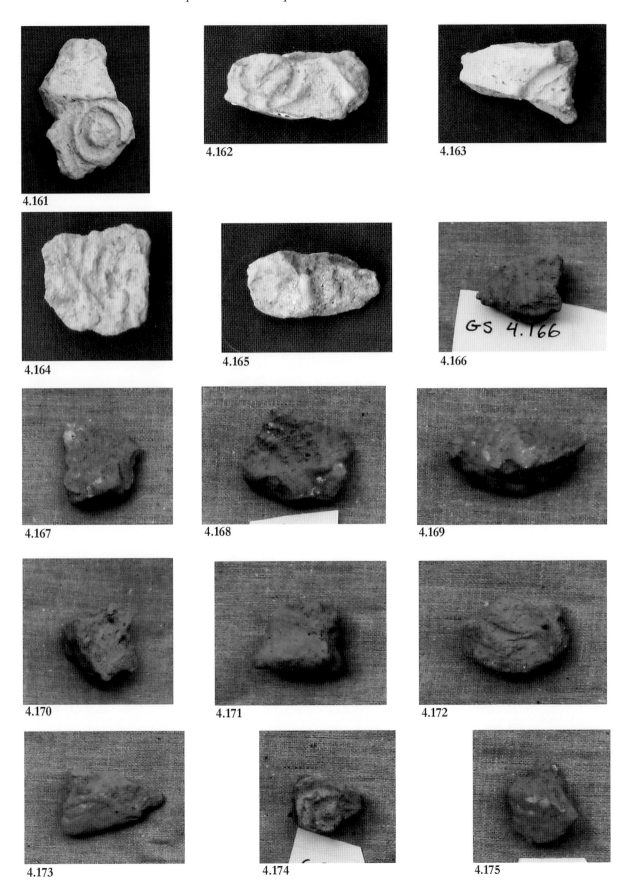

4.161

4.162

4.163

4.164

4.165

4.166

4.167

4.168

4.169

4.170

4.171

4.172

4.173

4.174

4.175

4.176
Height: 2.6 cm, Width: 1.9 cm, Thickness: 1.2 cm
Obverse: No impression is visible.
Reverse: No impression is visible.

4.177
Height: 1.7 cm, Width: 1.6 cm, Thickness: 1.8 cm
Obverse: No impression is visible.
Reverse: No impression is visible.

4.178
Height: 2.5 cm, Width: 2.0, Thickness: 1.0 cm
Obverse: The sealing has a partial impression of a very mashed concentric circle.
Reverse: No impression is visible.

4.179
Height: 2.5 cm, Width: 1.4 cm, Thickness: 1.3 cm
Obverse: The sealing has a partial impression of part of concentric circles or perhaps the middle of a spiral.
Reverse: No impression is visible.

4.180
Height: 1.9 cm, Width: 1.8 cm, Thickness: 1.6 cm
Obverse: The sealing is too small to read properly, but it appears to have a circular edge.
Reverse: No impression is visible.

4.181
Height: 2.3 cm, Width: 2.15 cm, Thickness: 1.6 cm
Obverse: The sealing has an impression of mashed parallel lines.
Reverse: No impression is visible.

4.182
Height: 2.7 cm, Width: 1.7 cm, Thickness: 1.7 cm
Obverse: The sealing has a smoothed surface and appears to be broken at the edge of a round seal impression.
Reverse: No impression is visible.

4.183
Height: 2.75 cm, Width: 3.3 cm, Thickness: 1.5 cm
Obverse: No impression is visible.
Reverse: No impression is visible.

4.184
Height: 2.5 cm, Width: 2.4 cm, Thickness: 1.6 cm
Obverse: The sealing may have a fragmentary impression of a circle of concentric circles seal.
Reverse: No impression is visible.

4.185
Height: 2.4 cm, Width: 2.45 cm, Thickness: 2.15 cm
Obverse: No impression is visible.
Reverse: No impression is visible.

4.186
Height: 2.1 cm, Width: 1.35 cm, Thickness: 1.3 cm
Obverse: No impression is visible.
Reverse: No impression is visible.

4.187
Height: 2.25 cm, Width: 2.15 cm, Thickness: 1.15 cm
Obverse: No impression is visible.
Reverse: No impression is visible.

4.188
Height: 2.1 cm, Width: 1.6 cm, Thickness: 1.1 cm
Obverse: No impression is visible.
Reverse: No impression is visible.

4.189
Height: 2.2 cm, Width: 1.9 cm, Thickness: 1.8 cm
Obverse: No impression is visible.
Reverse: No impression is visible.

4.190
Height: 2.1 cm, Width: 1.6 cm, Thickness: 0.95 cm
Obverse: No impression is visible.
Reverse: No impression is visible.

4.191
Height: 2.2 cm, Width: 2.0 cm, Thickness: 1.1n cm
Obverse: No impression is visible.
Reverse: No impression is visible.

4.192
Height: 2.4 cm, Width: 1.5 cm, Thickness: 1.6 cm
Obverse: No impression is visible.
Reverse: No impression is visible.

4.193
Height: 1.8 cm, Width: 1.6 cm, Thickness: 1.55 cm
Obverse: No impression is visible.
Reverse: No impression is visible.

4.194
Height: 1.9 cm, Width: 1.5 cm, Thickness: 0.9 cm
Obverse: No impression is visible.
Reverse: No impression is visible.

4.195
Height: 1.8 cm, Width: 1.3 cm, Thickness: 1.3 cm
Obverse: No impression is visible.
Reverse: No impression is visible.

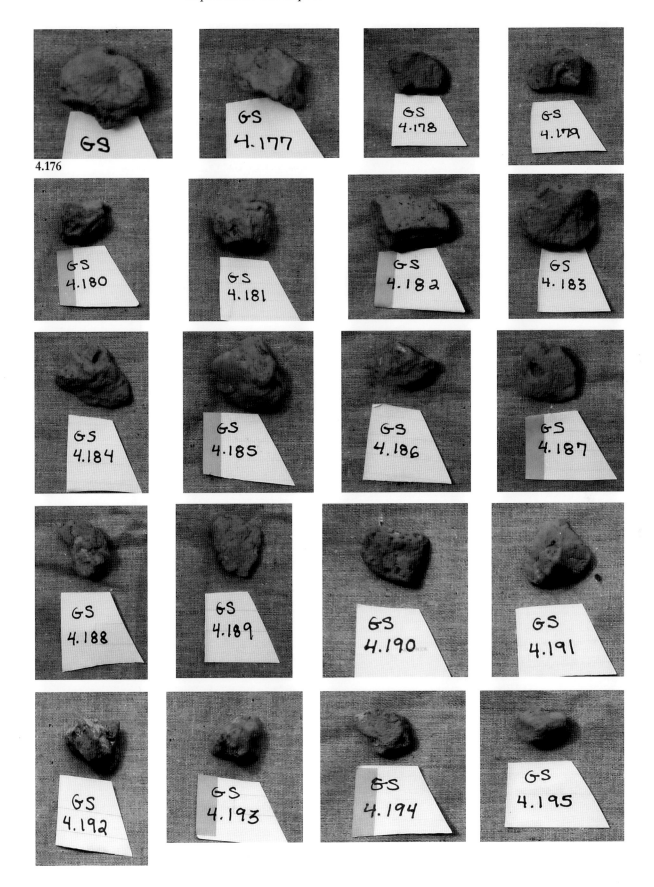

GS 4.176

GS 4.177

GS 4.178

GS 4.179

GS 4.180

GS 4.181

GS 4.182

GS 4.183

GS 4.184

GS 4.185

GS 4.186

GS 4.187

GS 4.188

GS 4.189

GS 4.190

GS 4.191

GS 4.192

GS 4.193

GS 4.194

GS 4.195

4.196
Height: 2.45 cm, Width: 2.0 cm, Thickness: 1.65 cm
Obverse: The sealing may have a fragmentary impression of the corner of a flower seal.
Reverse: No impression is visible.

4.197
Height: 2.5 cm, Width: 1.75 cm, Thickness: 1.95 cm
Obverse: The sealing may have a fragmentary impression of concentric circles.
Reverse: No impression is visible.

4.198
Height: 2.7 cm, Width: 2.95 cm, Thickness: 2.0 cm
Obverse: The surface of the sealing is broken, no impressions are preserved.
Reverse: No impression is visible.

4.199
Height: 3.55 cm, Width: 2.8 cm, Thickness: 1.85 cm
Obverse: No impression is visible.
Reverse: No impression is visible.

4.200
Height: 4.8 cm, Width: 3.0 cm, Thickness: 3.5 cm
Obverse: The sealing has an impression of a straight and a curving line, maybe part of a spiral seal.
Reverse: No impression is visible.

4.201
Height: 4.8 cm, Width: 3.0 cm, Thickness: 3.5 cm
Obverse: No impression is visible.
Reverse: No impression is visible.

4.202
Height: 5.0 cm, Width: 4.0 cm, Thickness: 2.94 cm
Obverse: The sealing has a partial impression of a large concentric circle or double spiral seal.
Reverse: The reverse is a convex surface with a possible impression of rope or decoration on pottery. This impression is a 1.4 cm wide strip with parallel diagonal striations that follow the curve of the sealing.

4.203
Height: 5.25 cm, Width: 4.2 cm, Thickness: 3.3 cm
Obverse: No impression is visible.
Reverse: No impression is visible.

4.204
Height: 5.7 cm, Width: 4.2 cm, Thickness: 3.3 cm
Obverse: The sealing has a very worn impression with a possible chevron pattern.
Reverse: No impression is visible.

4.205
Height: 3 cm, Width: 3.65 cm, Thickness: 2.2 cm
Obverse: No impression is visible.
Reverse: No impression is visible.

4.206
Height: 3.65 cm, Width: 3.6 cm, Thickness: 3.1 cm
Obverse: No impression is visible.
Reverse: No impression is visible.

4.207
Height: 3.6 cm, Width: 3.05 cm, Thickness: 2.05 cm
Obverse: No impression is visible.
Reverse: No impression is visible.

4.208
Height: 3.8 cm, Width: 3.7 cm, Thickness: 2.5 cm
Obverse: The sealing has a distorted impression of a flower seal.
Reverse: No impression is visible.

4.209
Height: 3.25 cm, Width: 3.65 cm, Thickness: 1.9 cm
Obverse: No impression is visible.
Reverse: No impression is visible.

4.210
Height: 4.1 cm, Width: 4.3 cm, Thickness: 2.7 cm
Obverse: The obverse of the sealing is a flat surface.
Reverse: No impression is visible.

4.211
Height: 4.9 cm, Width: 4.3 cm, Thickness: 3.6 cm
Obverse: No impression is visible.
Reverse: No impression is visible.

4.212
Height: 4.8 cm, Width: 3.2 cm, Thickness: 2.4 cm
Obverse: The sealing has a possible impression of the edge of a seal.
Reverse: No impression is visible.

4.213
Height: 6.2 cm, Width: 3.5 cm, Thickness: 3.2 cm
Obverse: The sealing has a poorly made impression of a circular seal. It is worn and mashed.
Reverse: No impression is visible.

4.214
Height: 3.35 cm, Width: 2.85 cm, Thickness: 1.65 cm
Obverse: The sealing has a partial impression showing the edge of rounded seal and portions of two or three curved lines.
Reverse: The reverse is a convex surface, possibly the neck and shoulder of a jar. The lower portion shows a very slight curvature, perhaps reflecting the roundness of vessel.

4.215
Height: 6.82 cm, Width: 6.9 cm, Thickness: 4.15 cm
Obverse: The sealing has two shallow impressions of a flower seal with a diamond center. It is mashed in sections.
Reverse: The reverse has a knob coming down, as if it were placed over a hole, but no clear impression.

GS 4.196

GS 4.197

GS 4.198

GS 4.199

GS 4.200

GS 4.201

GS 4.202

GS 4.203

GS 4.204

GS 4.205

GS 4.206

GS 4.207

GS 4.208

GS 4.209

GS 4.210

GS 4.211

GS 4.212

GS 4.213

4.214

4.215

4.216
Height: 3.5 cm, Width: 4.3 cm, Thickness: 2.32 cm
Obverse: The sealing has a fairly deep partial impression of two curving lines (concentric circles) and the edge of the seal.
Reverse: The reverse shows the shoulder and rim of a vessel, but no real neck is visible.

5.001
Height: 4.31 cm, Width: 5.78 cm, Thickness: 2.38 cm
Obverse: The sealing has two impressions of a seal with two figure eights, or four impressions of a single figure-eight seal. It is not clear if this is a single large seal or multiple impressions of a smaller one. The different angles of the two sets of figure-eight designs suggest that there are multiple impressions of the same seal. The second impression is at the break and slightly warped.
Reverse: No impression is visible.

5.002
Height: 2.88 cm, Width: 2.81 cm, Thickness: 1.46 cm
Obverse: The sealing has a deep impression of a cross in a circle within a second circle. The second circle is fairly deeply impressed.
Reverse: The sealing is triangular as if it was placed on the shoulder of a jar, but there is no rim impression.

5.003
Height: 3.56 cm, Width: 3.86 cm, Thickness: 2.2 cm
Obverse: The sealing has a partial impression of two concentric circles and an outer design that is very hard to read but which may have some ladder elements.
Reverse: The reverse shows the shoulder and rim of a vessel.

5.004
Height: 2.05 cm, Width: 2.99 cm, Thickness: 1.8 cm
Obverse: The sealing has two impressions, or a single impression of two squares made up of four parallel lines each. The second impression is badly worn.
Reverse: No impression is visible.

5.005
Height: 3.22 cm, Width: 3.72 cm, Thickness: 1.9 cm
Obverse: The sealing has an impression of a rectangle within a rectangle, and also some other marks which cannot be clearly identified as ancient impressions or trowel marks.
Reverse: The reverse is a flat surface with some chaff.

5.006
Height: 3.76 cm, Width: 2.96 cm, Thickness: 1.73 cm
Obverse: The sealing has two impressions of a small oval seal with 3 lines inside. The second impression is very deep and not very clear.
Reverse: The reverse is a concave surface.

5.007
Height: 6.41 cm, Width: 6.9 cm, Thickness: 3.5 cm
Obverse: The sealing has two impressions with a linear design. There are five parallel lines perpendicular to a ladder-like design. The second impression has only fragments of rectangles and fragments of ladder.
Reverse: The reverse shows the shoulder and rim of a large vessel. The vessel has a double rim. There is some material on the lower surface which may be dirt that was not fully removed.

5.008
Height: 1.83 cm, Width: 2.89 cm, Thickness: 1.3 cm
Obverse: The sealing has a partial impression of a circular seal, possibly the circle of concentric circles seal.
Reverse: No impression is visible.

5.009
Dimensions unknown.
Obverse: No impression is visible.
Reverse: The reverse shows a somewhat square rim with two lines, maybe string.

5.010
Height: 3.24 cm, Width: 2.64 cm, Thickness: 2.01 cm
Obverse: No impression is visible.
Reverse: The reverse is a concave surface. It may be the shoulder of a jar, but no rim is visible.

5.011
Height: 2.7 cm, Width: 3.5 cm, Thickness: 1.75 cm
Obverse: No impression is visible.
Reverse: The reverse shows the rim and possibly the neck of a vessel, but it is very broken and fragmentary.

5.012
Height: 3.12 cm, Width: 4.69 cm, Thickness: 2.37 cm
Obverse: No impression is visible.
Reverse: The reverse shows the rim of a vessel.

5.013
Height: 1.6 cm, Width: 3 cm, Thickness: 2.08 cm
Obverse: No impression is visible.
Reverse: The reverse is slightly convex and has a flat edge.

5.014
Dimensions unknown.
Obverse: The sealing has no visible impression, but some fingerprints are preserved.
Reverse: The reverse shows the rim of a pot and is mashed at the center.

4.216

5.001

5.002

5.003

5.004

5.005

5.006

5.007

5.008

5.009

5.010

5.011

5.012

5.013

5.014

5.015
Height: 5.1 cm
Width: 4.9 cm
Thickness: 3.2 cm
Obverse: No impression is visible.
Reverse: The reverse shows the neck of a large jar.

5.016 (shown with 5.001, previous page)
Height: 2.52 cm, Width: 3.44 cm, Thickness: 1.53 cm
Obverse: The sealing has a partial impression of the seal with two figure eights.
The impression is at the break and thus slightly warped. It joins G.S. 5.001.

Reverse: No impression is visible.

5.017 (not shown)
Height: 1.72 cm, Width: 2.4 cm, Thickness: 0.83 cm
Obverse: The sealing has an impression of the seal with two figure eights.
Reverse: No impression is visible.

5.018
Height: 6.09 cm, Width: 5.25 cm, Thickness: 4.03 cm
Obverse: The sealing has half of an impression of rays emanating from the center. No edge of a seal is visible.
Reverse: The reverse is a flat surface.

4.060
Height: 11.5 cm, Width: 10.5 cm, Thickness: 7 cm
Obverse: The sealing has a rounded surface with nine or more impressions of a rectangular stamp with crosshatched decoration. The crosshatch/weave design has three lines by three lines in a rectangular frame. The seal is impressed indiscriminately over the surface of the jar stopper, but the impressions overlap in only one spot.
Reverse: The sealing shows the inner rim of a jug/jar. The rim diameter of the jar is 7.5 cm. The sealing overhangs the rim of the jar on one side. The wall of the jar seems to have been more vertical on one side than on the other.

4.061
Height: 10.9, 6.9 cm, Width: 7.5, 5.5 cm, Thickness: 3.5, 3.9 cm
Obverse: The sealing has a well smoothed surface and an impression of a single, very large seal, possibly a cylinder. The impression seems to repeat, but is broken. The design is an eye or teardrop motif, maybe a fish, with curved parallel lines inside. This is followed by four very deep gouges with curved ends and a concentric triangle motif that seems to curve back up into the teardrop.
Reverse: The reverse of the sealing shows a lower rim and wall of a large jar or bowl. The sealing seems to have continued over the rim. The sealed vessel seems to have had a wide, flat rim and nearly vertical sides.

5.015

5.018

4.060

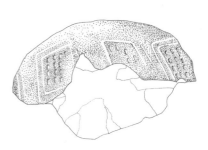

4.061

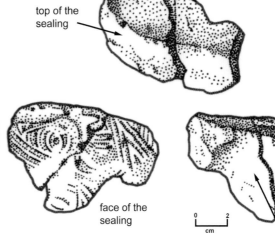

top of the
sealing

face of the
sealing

back of the
sealing

S1.113

Seal-amulet

Seal-amulet in the shape of a stepped cross. The center has a round piercing in a square frame. The back is solid and undecorated. There are some white incrustations along the edges. H. 7.38 cm, W. 7.44 cm, D. 1.4 cm

S1.114

Seal-amulet

Round seal-amulet. The seal is broken, only about half is preserved. It is decorated on one side and smooth on the other. It appears that the seal was originally pierced by a single off-center hole. The design is a U-shaped border containing a semicircular arrangement of four dots that get progressively smaller and curving line that may represent half of bucrania or a possible tulip shape. A fragment (about half) of a circular element is preserved in the curve of U, directly below the piercing. H. 6.3 cm, W. 3.9 cm, D. 1.6 cm

S1.256

Stamp

Broken terracotta stamp. The piece consists of a stub handle and 7 points, with a round dimple in center. It is hand modeled, not molded or incised. H. 4.6 cm, W. 6.2 cm, D. 5.9 cm

S1.278

Seal-amulet?

Fragment of round seal-amulet? The object is poorly incised with a possible sunburst? The design consist of a triangle with slightly outcurving sides and two diagonal lines emanating from it within a circular frame. H. 4.0 cm, W. 5.0 cm

S1.345

Stamp

Fragment of terracotta stamp. All the edges are broken. The piece has remnants of a stub handle and four or five points. There is a dimple in the center between the points. H. 3.65 cm, W. 3.60 cm, D. 1.8 cm

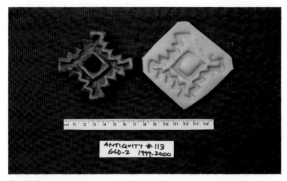 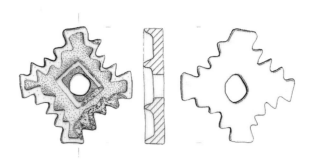

S1.113

S1.114

 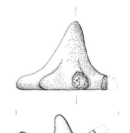 

S1.256

 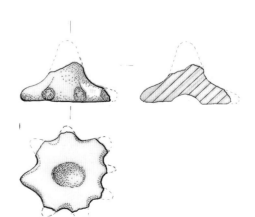

S1.345

S2.061
Seal-amulet
Round seal-amulet that is decorated on both sides. About half of seal is preserved.
Side 1 has four concentric circles and a hollow center. Side 2 has a circular border and a swooping tulip or bucrania design. H. 7.2 cm, W 4.5 cm, D. 1.35 cm

S3.025
Seal-amulet
Square seal-amulet. About 3/4 of seal is preserved. Two incised lines divide the amulet into quadrants, each of which is pierced with a round hole. The holes get slightly narrower towards the back. There are traces of a square border or frame, but it was either not very well preserved or not very well made to begin with. H. 4.6 cm, W. 5.0 cm , D. 1.2 cm

S4.087
Seal-amulet?
Corner fragment of pierced square or rectangular piece. The object has one complete hole and parts of three others preserved. One side is smooth, while the other appears to have been cut out. The walls of the hole are preserved, but not area around them. H. 4.11 cm, W.22 4.10 cm, D. 1.86 cm

S5.003
Seal-amulet?
Fragment of round seal-amulet (?). About one third preserved. The object is pierced in the center. It is decorated on one side and smooth on the other. The design is round depressions, of which three (one complete, two partial) are preserved, that seem to go around perimeter of object. H. 4.06 cm, W 2.48 cm, D. 1.13 cm

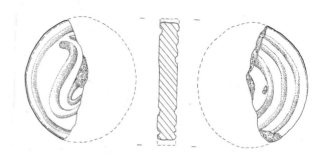

S2.061

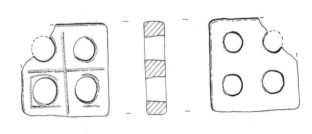

S3.025

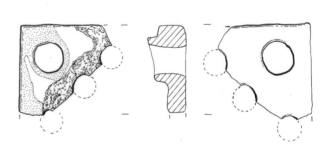

S4.087

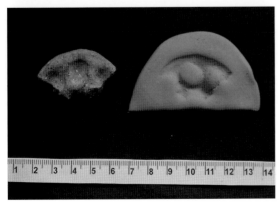

(Drawing Not Available)

S5.003

S5.184
Stamp seal
Stamp seal? Clay object in the shape of an inverted mushroom. The clay is very fine and dense, but not fired, making it unlikely that this object could have been for sealing. The design consists of wiggly lines making a star-like shape. The decoration extends from the bottom onto the sides (ca. .75 cm), and looks as it has been redone in some spots. H. 4.4 cm, W. 5.35 cm.

S5.211
Seal-amulet
Fragment of seal-amulet. About 1/4 preserved. The seal is decorated on one side, smooth on the other. The design consists of two concentric circles around exterior and a mosaic/ patched pattern in center. The raised "squares" in center are not carefully made or arranged. H. 3.83 cm, W 4.3 cm, D. 1.47 cm.

S5.215
Seal-amulet
Round seal-amulet (?). About 1/3 preserved. The object is decorated on one side, smooth on the other. The design consists of cross-hatching and two diagonal lines. The design seems to be impressed rather than incised, suggesting that this is an impression rather than seal, but the object seems to have been intentionally baked, suggesting that it was meant to be preserved. It looks like the original design was symmetrical, consisting of a base crosshatched decoration with at least four diagonal lines forming a diamond shape around the edges. Striations on the clay suggest that the object that made the impression was made of wood (or reed?). H. 6.88 cm, W. 4.45 cm, D. 089 cm.

S5.216
Seal-amulet
Pierced round seal-amulet. About 1/3 preserved. One side is decorated, the other is smooth. The design consists of two broken concentric circles made up of two lines each and a triangular element between them. There is also a circular frame that follows shape of seal. The lines are gouged out, seemingly with pointy, possibly triangular instrument. H. 4.45 cm, W. 7.0 cm, D. 1.75 cm.

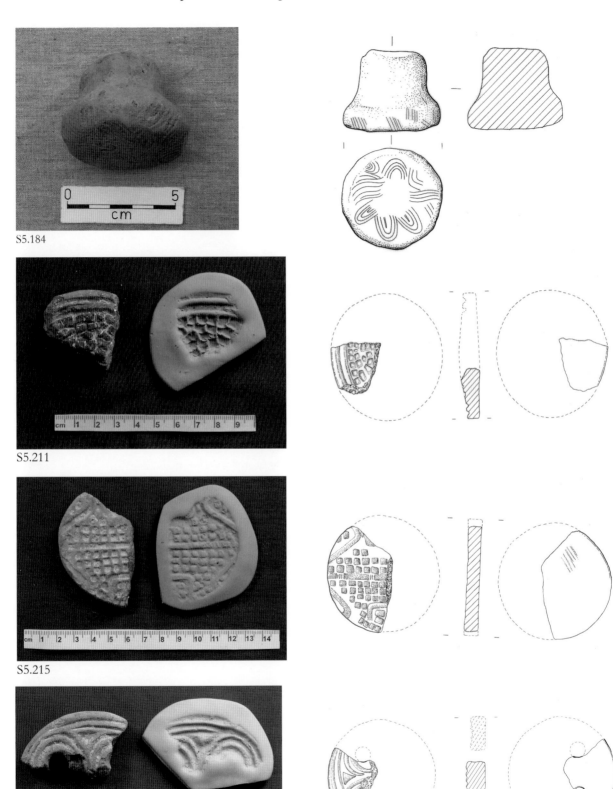

S5.184

S5.211

S5.215

S5.216

S5.220

Seal-amulet

Round seal-amulet. About one third preserved. Decorated on one side, smooth on the other. The design consists of three concentric circles that follow the shape of the object. The center contains a set of square (?) punchmarks that seem to be randomly placed. The seal is coarsely made. It is not perfectly round and the decoration is crudely executed. The lines are lines incised, but not cleaned up or smooth. Clay is dark brown/burnt. H. 4.75 cm, W. 4.44 cm, D. 1.58 cm.

S5.223

Stamp seal

Small stamp seal in the shape of a squared off rod. The design consists of four parallel lines, of which only two are fully preserved. The others have broken off. The lines were made by gouging. The object may be a piece of reused pottery. H. 2.78 cm, W. 1.58 cm, D. 1.3 cm.

S5.224

Amulet?

Unbaked clay disk with a rounded back. The design on the front is an incised circular border with two triangles pointing inward and many small round punch marks haphazardly filling the remaining surface. The fabric of the piece is very micaceous. H. 4.4 cm, W. 4.4 cm, D.1.1 cm

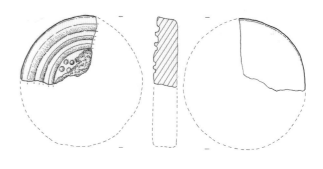

S5.220

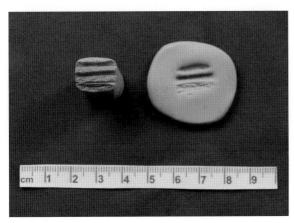
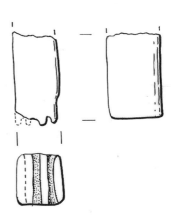

S5.223

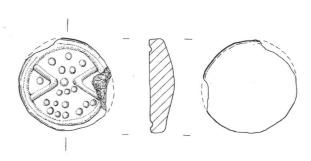

S5.224

10

Lithics at Gilund

Teresa P. Raczek

Introduction

Lithics of the 3rd and 2nd millennium BC have been well documented and analyzed in many parts of South Asia including the Indus region, the Deccan, and Southern India. In contrast, until recently little was known about the lithics from the early farming settlements of southeastern Rajasthan. However, tens of thousands of chipped stone artifacts were recovered during the 1999–2005 excavations at Gilund. The unexpected presence of such a high number of lithics provided the unique opportunity to study the lithic technology used during the early farming days of southeastern Rajasthan. A thorough analysis of the Gilund lithics was undertaken in spring 2004, summer 2005, and fall 2006.

Prior to the excavations at Gilund, the only excavated sites in the region with published lithic reports were Ahar (Ansari 1969) and Bagor (Misra 1973). Few lithics were collected from Ahar, including six fluted cores (four chert and two quartz), one chalcedony backed blade, and several tools classified as Middle Stone Age (MSA). While the Ahar report does not provide the exact number of MSA specimens, it illustrates a variety of scrapers (hollow, side, convex, and borer-cum-hollow) and borers. Although scrapers were used in the Paleolithic, they have also been found in many Holocene contexts throughout the world. The Ahar assemblage had fewer chert and chalcedony lithics compared to Gilund. This result may derive from the use of regular screening at Gilund which allowed excavators to recover the tiniest of microliths. Comparing the quartz lithics between Ahar and Gilund is challenging. The Ahar report states that 16,194 quartz nodules were collected in roughly equal proportions from phases Ia, Ib, and Ic. Because quartz is plentiful in the region and found in the mud bricks at Ahar, Ansari attributed the presence of most of the Ahar quartz to depositional processes and the nodules

were not analyzed. Some part of the quartz at Gilund may also come from similar processes as indicated by the high counts of shatter (chips and chunks), as well as medial and distal flakes (presented below). However, the Gilund assemblage also includes plentiful quartz tools as well as quartz blades and flakes with prepared platforms and multiple ridges. This indicates that the inhabitants of Gilund did regularly produce quartz lithics.

In contrast to Ahar, vast quantities of lithics were recovered from the small habitation of Bagor. Bagor varies greatly from the other excavated sites of the Mewar Plain since it consists largely of a lithic scatter and it has no evidence of permanent features such as architecture. The site has been described most commonly as a temporary occupation of pastoralists and hunter-gatherers. V.N. Misra's analysis of the Bagor collections demonstrated that a wide variety of microlith types were present (1973, 1982), while Khanna's analysis indicated a range of raw materials were used, including quartz, chert, and chalcedony (1993).

In addition to lithics collected from excavations at Ahar and Bagor, microliths were also noted in association with Ahar Black and Red Ware during multiple surface surveys in the region. V.N. Misra's research in the Berach basin was the first to make this observation (1967). Rima Hooja's survey also identified dozens of sites where both microliths and Ahar Black and Red Ware had been found together (1988). Dasgupta's survey in the area immediately surrounding Gilund also found such sites (2006a, 2006b, and see this volume). Thus, it appears that lithics were used throughout southeastern Rajasthan during the Ahar-Banas time period, a fact which prompted Hooja to remark, "the whole issue of the lithic industry of the Ahar Culture sites needs a re-appraisal" (1988:76). The excavations at Gilund presented the perfect opportunity to rise to this challenge and perform the first comprehensive analysis of lithics from early farming settlements of this region and time period.

Lithic Studies

In many parts of the world, lithics continued to be used after copper became commonly available (Eriksen 2010, Kardulias 2003, Rosen 1997). In South Asia, sites such as Harappa and Inamgaon, as well as many others used lithics in concert with copper, and lithic use did not sharply decline until the introduction of iron (Cleland 1986). Cleland hypothesized that the increased allocation of resources towards copper production in the Late Harappan led to restructured strategies for lithic raw material procurement and tool production (1986). Copper also changed blade production methods when it was manufactured into punch tips for the production of blades (Anderson-Gerfaud et al. 1989, Lechevallier 2003, Méry et al. 2007). In sum, even with the advent of copper tools, lithics remained an important technology in the 3rd and 2nd millennium BC in South Asia (Raczek 2010b).

The study of technologies, such as lithic production, provides valuable insight into ancient societies (Bhan, Vidale, and Kenoyer 2002, Miller 2007, Wright 1991, 1993) because technology is culturally embedded (Lemonnier 1986, Pfaffenberger 1992). The production and use of lithics was woven into the fabric of everyday life since lithics were used to accomplish common tasks. As a result, common practices, strategies, and skills shared by inhabitants of a site or region can be identified by studying lithic production through typology and attribute analysis. In addition, material procurement and social and economic networks can be documented through stone raw material analysis.

In order to pursue some of these lines of inquiry, it is necessary to go beyond simple typologies and study multiple lithic attributes including production scars, measurements, and raw material. In addition, a full analysis studies the full assemblage including cores and "debitage" along with tools and worked blades since cores and debitage carry multiple signatures of production methods. These analyses provide essential data for determining procurement and production sequences, as well as skill and knowledge.

Spatial Distribution and Selection of Sample

Overall, most lithics at Gilund were found in layers associated with the Early and Middle Ahar-Banas phases. Very few lithics were found in association with Early Historic and

Table 10.1. Count of Study Sample Lithics per Trench at Gilund

Trench	Count	
	Primary study sample	Secondary study sample
4D	0	4
6	1	1
7	1	0
8	2	0
9	57	693
10	0	3
12	3	10
13	6	9
16	9	19
18	50	66
19	1	0
24	3	116
25	2	7
27	950	3196
31	1	0
32	1	0
33	2	2
34	1	0
35	30	40
38	391	1463
39	475	2502
40	309	1844
41	509	2259
64	2	3
65	11	11
68	3	0
69	4	18
70	2	0
201	3	0
202	1	0
301	0	5
Grand Total	2830	12271

Late Ahar-Banas phases (the upper layers) of either mound. While lithics were recovered from all areas of the site, the vast majority were collected from GLD-2 (see Fig. 10.1 and Table 10.1, lithics included in samples analyzed). Trenches

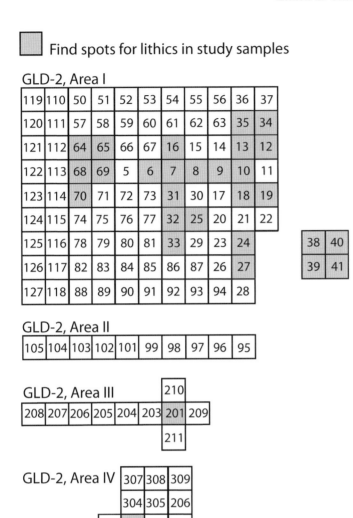

Fig. 10.1. *Location of lithics included in study sample.*

24, 27, and 38–41, which were laid in a line that was perpendicular to and south of the parallel-wall structure, proved to be a rich source for lithics. These trenches were lower in elevation than the parallel-wall structure and contained the terminating ends of three mudbrick walls unrelated to the parallel-wall structure. Although the upper layers were highly disturbed and largely comprised debris which eroded from the top of GLD-2, the middle layers were intact and located in association with the mudbrick walls, while the lowest layers approached sterile soil. Only lithics from the middle and lower layers were included in the study sample presented here.[1]

A high density of lithics was also encountered in Trench 18, a test pit cut into the space between Walls NS4 and NS5 of the parallel-wall complex located on the eastern side of GLD-2. Although only 116 lithics were recovered

here, the soil volume excavated was minimal, so the ratio of lithics to soil volume was quite high. These lithics presumably pre-date the construction of the parallel walls. The abundance of lithics from Trench 9, located immediately to the west of the parallel walls, postdate the walls. Thus, lithic production and use continued through multiple time periods.

The concentration of lithics under and around the parallel walls indicates that the use of lithic tools was an important part of the activities that were conducted in this part of the site and may be related to the parallel walls. However, as many of the lithics recovered here predate or postdate the walls, alternative explanations must be considered. One possibility is that the edge of the site may have been an attractive area for discarding sharp household refuse. Ethnographic research has shown that sharp lithic waste products are sometimes carefully discarded away from habitation areas since they can be dangerous to bare feet and small children (Clark 1991). Thus, it would not be unusual to find lithic materials concentrated in non-residential parts of the site. This pattern seems to play out at Gilund, where very few lithics were found in association with houses.

Methods of Analysis

During excavation, screens with a small mesh (slightly less than 1/8") were employed which allowed for the collection of all but the smallest microchips. All visible lithics were collected by the screeners and placed in paper or plastic envelopes according to lot number. All lithics were then counted in the field before being washed and placed in storage. Most of the lithic analysis took place at Deccan College, Pune, although some preliminary sorting occurred in camp and at the dig house in Gilund village.

Because of the immense number of artifacts recovered and time constraints on analysis, a sampling strategy was undertaken. Only lithics from GLD-2 were sampled, including lithics recovered from strata 2, 3, 12, 21, 30, and 31 and all strata located in association with the parallel walls. In all, over 23,000 chipped stone artifacts were analyzed. Of these, 15,101 were determined to have come from well-stratified archaeological contexts and were included in this summary report.

The artifacts were divided into primary and secondary study samples. The primary study sample comprised all artifacts that were analyzed individually, including complete artifacts, all proximal pieces, and the medial and distal parts of tools, backed pieces, truncated pieces, and retouched pieces (see Table 10.2, Methods of Analysis). Complete artifacts were recorded and analyzed individually and a full set of data was collected for each. With the exception of metric measurements, complete data was also collected for all broken artifacts in the primary study sample. The secondary study sample included shatter and all medial and distal lithics with the exception of tools and backed, truncated, or retouched pieces. These lithics were separated by type, fragment (medial or distal), raw material, and lot, then counted and weighed as a group. All data was entered into a database using Entrer Trois archaeological software designed by Shannon McPherron and Simon Holdaway. All measurements were taken to the .01 mm with Mitutoyo absolute digimatic calipers which quickly and accurately entered the measurement directly into the database through a USB port. Weights were measured to the .1 gram on an Acculab GSI-200 scale and then hand entered into the database.

Data collected is shown in Table 10.3 (General Attributes Recorded). All artifacts were assigned a type according to a modified version of Misra's typology for Bagor (1973). The definition of blades, burins, and microburins differs slightly from Misra's original typology in response to changes in type definitions during the intervening decades. For the purposes of this study a piece was identified as a blade if it had parallel sides (or nearly parallel sides in the case of quartz), even if the length was not twice the width. Since it appeared that many parallel-sided blades fell just short of the 2:1 ratio, it was decided to record only the presence or absence of parallel sides. As artifact length and width were also recorded, it is possible to determine which of these artifacts are longer or shorter than the 2:1 ratio by querying the database.

A number of attributes were recorded for complete and proximal flakes and blades including descriptions of platforms, backing, truncation, retouch, dorsal scars, and raw material. Platform descriptions were recorded as part of the investigation into core production techniques. Location and type of backing were recorded in order to provide information on hafting techniques. Many attributes in this study were recorded in part to provide a basis of comparison for future researchers. In addition, a series of attributes were recorded on a sample of cores in order to answer a series of questions about core production, blade removal, and reduction (Raczek 2010a).

Metric attributes recorded for all complete artifacts included length, width, thickness, and weight. For flakes and blades, length was measured from the point of percussion to the farthest possible point on the artifact. Width was measured at the halfway point of the length, as was thickness. For core measurements, length was taken on the side of the longest blade or flake removal in the direction of the blade or flake removal. Width of the core was taken at a point that was perpendicular to and at the halfway point of the length. Thickness was measured by rotating the artifact 90° from the width. For many cores, this resulted in the thickness being larger than the width. However, this positioning strategy was used because many cores were worked from front to back in a single direction. Thus, width and thickness measured in this way reflected the way that the core may have been positioned during production. The length of tools—both broken and whole—was measured along their longest edge. Width and thickness were then taken at the halfway point, with the exception of triangles, where the width was measured at the apex. Proximal, medial, and distal pieces of flakes and blades were not measured (with the exception of backed, truncated, or retouched

Table 10.2. Methods of Analysis

	Primary Study Sample			Secondary Study Sample
	Complete	Proximal	Medial worked Distal worked	Medial unworked Distal unworked Shatter
Analysis	Artifacts analyzed individually	Artifacts analyzed individually	Artifacts analyzed individually	Sorted into groups by lot number, type, fragment, raw material
Data Collected	Typology, attributes, raw material attributes	Typology, attributes, raw material attributes	Typology, attributes, raw material attributes	Count for each group
Measurements	Length, Width, Thickness, Weight	Weight only	Weight only	Weight for each group

Table 10.3. General Attributes Recorded

General Data	Options	Conditions
Lot number	Assigned in the field by excavators	All artifacts
Suffix	Consecutive numbers assigned to each artifact within a given lot, beginning with 0001	All artifacts
General type	Blade, flake, tool, core, shatter	All artifacts
Broken fragment	Complete, proximal, medial, distal, fragment	All artifacts
Tool type	Burin, microburin, scalene-triangle, isosceles-triangle, trapeze, trapezoid, point, drill, lunate, rhomboid, transverse-arrowhead, scraper, oblique-blunted point, notch-on-blade, notch-on-flake, other	Tools only
Scraper type	End-straight, end-concave, end-convex, side-straight, side-concave, side-convex, double-straight, double-concave, double-convex, on-core	Scrapers only
Core type	Blade, flake	Cores only
Retouch	Absent, one-edge, two-edges	Flakes, blades only
Backing	Absent, one-edge, two-edges	Flakes, blades only
Type of backing[1]	Inverse, obverse, inverse-obverse, obverse-notch, inverse-notch, both-notch, burin	Backed flakes and blades only
Location of backing[2]	Full, proximal, distal, medial, proximal-to-distal retouch	Backed flakes and blades only
Truncations	Absent, straight, angle, notch, convex, other	Flakes, blades
Dorsal features	1-ridge, 2-ridges, 3+ ridges, flake scars, unprepared, crested ridge	Flakes, blades
Platform type	Unprepared, cortical, flat, dihedral, multifaceted, punctiform, edge-flaked	Complete and proximal blades and flakes only
Length	Measured with electronic calipers	Complete, proximal
Width	Measured with electronic calipers	Complete, proximal
Thickness	Measured with electronic calipers	Complete, proximal
Weight	Measured with electronic scale	Complete, proximal

NOTES
1. Recorded twice for those pieces with backing on both edges.
2. Recorded twice for those pieces with backing on both edges.

pieces), but were weighed.

Finally, the raw material type and a number of raw material attributes were recorded for each lithic as well as for samples from the survey sites. Raw material was recorded for two reasons. First, raw material influences lithic production in multiple ways, not the least of which is the size of the artifact. Second, through the recording of raw material, it was possible to begin to match the artifacts to raw material samples collected from potential quarry sites identified in a separate survey (Raczek 2007). Basic raw material designations and interpretations of this data are presented below (and see Raczek 2011 for more details on this analysis).

Results

Types

Table 10.4 and Figure 10.2 present the distribution of simple lithic classes for Gilund. Clearly, shatter comprises the majority of analyzed artifacts from Gilund, followed by flakes and blades. The abundance of shatter reflects the common use of locally available quartz which has irregular fracture planes and breaks unpredictably. Stone-tool makers who worked in quartz were likely to produce a large amount of shatter in the process of making any oth-

Table 10.4. Distribution of Broken and Complete Lithic Types

	Complete	Broken				
		Proximal	Medial	Distal	Subtotal	Total
Blade	515	539	826	691	2056	2571
Flake	961	267	1668	1974	3909	4870
Tool	76	0	1	14	15	91
Core	184	0	0	0	6	190
Shatter	0	0	0	0	7379	7379
Total	1736	806	2495	2679	13365	15101

NOTE: Shatter is not separated into "Complete" or "Broken"

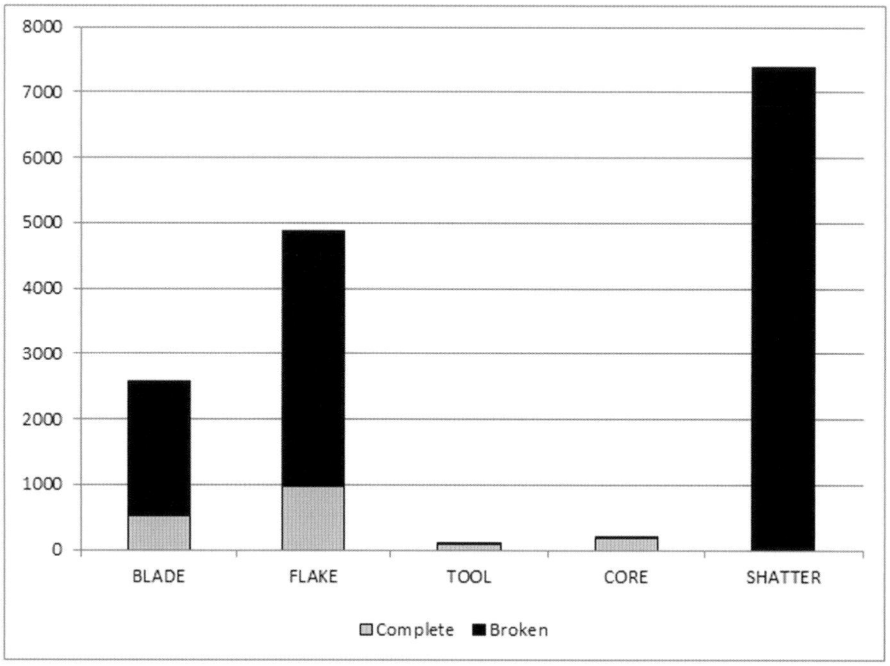

Fig. 10.2. Distribution of complete and broken lithic types at Gilund.

er product such as a flake or blade. The high amount of quartz at the site may also play a role in the ratio of complete to broken flakes and blades. Alternatively, the high percentage of shatter and broken pieces may reflect any number of depositional processes including trampling and erosion.

Flakes and Blades

Overall, the collection at Gilund is mainly composed of flakes and blades with very few formal tools, or backed pieces. The greater proportion of flakes over blades and the low number of tools indicate that informal or expedient technologies were heavily used in addition to the more formal blade technologies. As flakes are sharp they can be used for many tasks without hafting. They can also be made by almost anyone with little training. When a simple cutting implement was needed quickly, the residents at Gilund seem to have relied mainly on flakes. In New World contexts, the presence of highly informal or expedient collections has been explained by sedentism (Parry and Kelly 1987), emphasis on particular activities (Odell 1998), and raw material quality and quantity (Andrefsky 1994, Brantingham et al. 2000). At Gilund, all three of these influences are at work.

Cores

In the initial analysis, cores were divided into two categories: blade or flake. Most cores were blade cores (N=118, 62.1%), although flake cores comprised a substantial minority (N=72, 37.9%). Many blade cores had multiple platforms and were worked on multiple faces. In addition, there is evidence that many blade cores were initiated with a burin blow, instead of a crested ridge. The cores at Gilund are somewhat unique for this time period compared to many areas in South Asia, although they greatly resemble the cores from nearby Bagor (Raczek 2010a).

Tools

In general, there are very few tools at Gilund. In total, 76 complete tools and 15 broken tools were analyzed following Misra's typology for the Bagor collection (see Table 10.5). A total of ten tool types were identified including four non-geometric types and six geometric types. Non-geometric tools included microburins, burins, points, and scrapers. Two of the scrapers were side scrapers (one straight, one convex) and five were end scrapers (three straight and two convex). Geometric tools identified included isosceles and scalene triangles, lunates, rhomboids, trapezes, and trapezoids.

Of the complete tools, the majority were burins (N=29, 32%). Previous studies have shown that blade cores can be initiated with a burin blow (Barton, Olszewski, and Coinman 1996, Chazan 2001, Crabtree 1968). In many cases

burin spalls and initial blades are indistinguishable (Barton, Olszewski, and Coinman 1996). The core study at Gilund suggests that many of the blade cores were initiated with a burin blow, which complicates the category of "burin" at this site. Although it is possible that the burins at Gilund are the result of the production of a single blade-like burin spall, it is equally likely that the Gilund burins are cores that were discarded after a single removal.

The frequency of burins is followed by two geometrics: lunates (N=22, 24%) and scalene triangles (N=14, 15%). The specific form of the geometric creates ease in hafting; as a result, different shapes are amenable to different hafts or different positions within the same haft. However, with minor modification, it is easy to turn one geometric tool into another (Neeley and Barton 1994, Subbarao 1955). For example, by removing a few chips it is possible to turn a triangle into a lunate. Thus, it is difficult to say to what extent the variation among these shape-defined tools results from hafting techniques, tool function, or technological tradition. As a result, interpreting the meaning of the varying percentages of geometric tools at Gilund is difficult.

Very few microburins were identified at Gilund (N=4). Microburins are the waste products that remain after snapping blades when creating geometric tools. The ratio of microburins to geometric tools at Gilund is approximately 1:11. However, the ratio of microburins to geometric tools at nearby Bagor is almost 1:1 (Raczek 2007). The lack of microburins is puzzling and requires further investigation. Two possible explanations are proposed here. First, if tools were made at some other location, then the microburins would be discarded elsewhere and would not be part of the collection. Alternatively, the Gilund knappers used some other method of creating geometric tools.

In contrast to other lithic types, very few tools were broken (N=22, 15%), with the exception of points. The low percentage of broken points may indicate that repairs of broken tools occurred offsite (and therefore the broken pieces were also discarded offsite). In contrast to other tools, more broken (N=9) than non-broken (N=2) points were recovered. Of the broken points, 100% were the distal piece, which contained the pointed end. This concentration of distal pieces may partly be explained by the form of the point. The proximal, medial, and distal portions of points each take a different form. When broken, the proximal and medial portions cannot be distinguished from backed blades or sometimes plain blades. As a result, it is likely that any proximal or medial portions of points were categorized as blades.

Table 10.5. Distribution of Tool Types

	N	%
Microburin	4	4.4%
Burin	29	31.9%
Point	7	7.7%
Scraper	7	8.0%
Non-geometrics subtotal	47	52.0%
Isosceles triangle	4	4.4%
Lunate	22	24.2%
Rhomboid	1	1.1%
Scalene triangle	14	15.4%
Trapeze	2	2.2%
Trapezoid	1	1.1%
Geometrics subtotal	44	48.4%
TOTAL	91	100.0%

Table 10.6. Dorsal Features on Blades

	N	%
One ridge	478	45.4%
Two ridges	300	28.5%
Three or more ridges	48	4.6%
Flake scars or crested ridges	132	12.5%
Unprepared	94	8.9%
Total	1052	100%

NOTE: Medial and distal blades not included.

Table 10.9. Location of Backing

	Blades		Flakes	
	N	%	N	%
Full	235	89.4%	17	89.5%
Proximal	7	2.7%	2	10.5%
Medial	1	0.4%	0	0%
Distal	16	6.1%	0	0%
Proximal to distal retouch	4	1.5%	0	0%
TOTAL	263	100.0%	19	100.0%

Attributes

In addition to type, a number of attributes were also recorded for artifacts in the primary study sample. Particular attention was given to platform preparation and dorsal ridges (or other dorsal preparation). These attributes were recorded because of the nature of the local quartz at

Table 10.7. Blade and Flake Retouch

	Blades		Flakes	
	N	%	N	%
Edge retouch	20	2%	4	0%
End retouch	1	0%	1	0%
No retouch	1034	98%	1223	100%
TOTAL	1055	100%	1228	100%

Table 10.8. Blade and Flake Backing

	Blades		Flakes	
	N	%	N	%
One-edge	244	92.8%	18	94.7%
Two-edges	19	7.2%	1	5.3%
TOTAL	263	100.0%	19	100.0%

Gilund. Because quartz was so plentiful, it was used for a variety of purposes. For example, slingballs, grinders, and querns, among other artifacts, were sometimes made of the same quartz as lithic artifacts. When these items break in the course of use or as a result of depositional processes, the fragments may resemble flakes, broken flakes, or shatter. For this reason, platform preparation and dorsal features were recorded. Quartz flakes with no platform preparation and no dorsal preparation may, in fact, be broken fragments of

Table 10.10. Type of Backing (pieces backed on one edge only)

	Blades		Flakes	
	N	%	N	%
Inverse	4	1.6%	1	5.6%
Obverse	203	83.2%	3	16.7%
Inverse-Obverse	12	4.9%	0	0.0%
Vertical	25	10.2%	14	77.8%
TOTAL	244	100.0%	18	100.0%

other artifacts. Such lithics represent 14.3% (N=176) of flakes in the primary study sample.

Approximately 2% (N=20) of the blades and fewer than 1% of flakes (N=4) exhibited signs of retouch. In addition, only one retouched blade (and no retouched flakes) also had backing on the opposite edge. It is possible that light retouch along one edge of a blade or flake may have served the same purpose as backing. This hypothesis is supported by the identification of four blades where the backing was steep on the proximal end, but faded into light retouch on the distal end.

Both blades and flakes were backed. Backing is a technique in which one edge of a blade or flake is thickened through the removal of several microflakes or chips. Backing allows blades and flakes to be hafted more readily. Significantly, more blades (20%, N=263) than flakes (1.5%, N=19) were backed. For most blades, the backing extended the full length of the blade. However, some artifacts were backed on only one portion of the blade (proximal, medial, or distal portions). In addition, as mentioned above, there are a few examples of blades where the backing faded into retouch on the distal end. These anomalies may relate to the specific haft for which the blade was being prepared.

Four methods of backing were observed. Obverse backing was the most common backing encountered

Table 10.11. Summary of Truncations on Blades

	N	%
Non-truncated Total	1219	92.5%
Truncated Total	99	7.5%
TOTAL	1318	100.0%

Table 10.12. Truncations on Backed and Non-backed Blades

	No Backing	One Edge	Two Edges	Total	
	N	N	N	N	%
Angle	12	44	6	62	62.6%
Convex	1	1		2	2.0%
Notch	11	2	2	15	15.2%
Straight	12	4		16	16.2%
Other	2	2		4	4.0%
TOTAL	38	53	8	99	100.0%

(83.2%, N=219). In contrast, inverse backing was present only 1.6% of the time (N=4). A combination of inverse and obverse backing was also identified in just under 5% of the collection (N=12). Vertical backing was the second most common backing choice (10.2%, N=42). Vertical backing is a burin technique where a blow is struck on the edge of the platform to remove a sliver of material along one edge of the blade, thus blunting the blade (Cleland 1977:187–88). The effect is a blunted edge with the same thickness as a traditionally backed blade.

The presence or absence of truncations was recorded for all complete blades. In all, 7.5% of blades (N=99) were truncated. In addition, four types of truncations were noted: angle, convex, notch (concave), or straight. Four observed truncations that did not fit these categories were recorded as "other." Truncations were identified on both backed and non-backed blades. Angle truncation was by far the most common technique, with straight truncation the second most common. There were a small number of double-backed blades with truncations.

The method of platform preparation was recorded for all complete and proximal blades and flakes (see Table

Table 10.13. Platform Preparation

	Blades		Flakes	
	N	%	N	%
Dihedral	91	8.7%	121	9.9%
Edge flaked	122	11.6%	129	10.5%
Flat	487	46.3%	363	29.6%
Missing	33	3.1%	50	4.1%
Multifaceted	96	9.1%	122	9.9%
Punctiform	40	3.8%	50	4.1%
Unprepared	183	17.4%	392	31.9%
TOTAL	1052	100.0%	1227	100.0%

10.13). Platform preparation as represented on flakes and blades provides information about core preparation and flake and blade removal techniques. Platforms must be prepared in specific ways in order to use pressure debitage (Pelegrin 1994) which was used at the nearby site of Bagor (Inizan and Lechevallier 1990, 1995). Raw material also influences platform preparation.

The majority of blade platforms were flat, prepared by the removal of a single flake (46.3%, N=487). This was followed by unprepared platforms (17.4%, N=183) and edge-flaked blades (11.6%, N=122), where the only platform preparation consisted of tiny flake removals along the edge (see also Hoffman and Cleland 1977). In contrast to blades, the majority of flakes had unprepared platforms (31.9%, N=392), with flat platforms making up 29.6% of the collection (N=363). The greater number of flakes with unprepared platforms as compared to blades is not surprising, since most blades were removed from formal cores, while many flakes were either produced from an informal core or were used to prepare or rejuvenate formal blade cores. Setting up a proper platform for flakes may have been less important than doing so for blades, since the preservation of the core shape is much more important for blade production and pressure debitage requires careful platform preparation. In fact, the flakes may be the product of blade core preparation.

Size

Each complete artifact was measured individually for length, width, thickness, and weight. Table 10.14 presents information on the size of the lithic artifacts, and is broken down by raw material. Lithics made of quartzite were the largest in size, which tipped the "other" category of lithics into the largest spot for both flakes and blades for all measurements. Although quartz cores and flakes were longer than chert and chalcedony on average, quartz blades were shorter. The average length of chert blades and cores

Table 10.14. Average Artifact Size by Raw Material (complete artifacts only)

		Length		Width		Thickness		Weight	
		Mean	StD	Mean	StD	Mean	StD	Mean	StD
Blade	Chalcedony	11.93	11.48	4.21	4.06	1.39	1.57	0.4	0.89
	Chert	14.08	26.72	7.16	18.78	3.38	18.19	0.51	1.77
	Other	21.09	16.34	11.07	8.1	5.09	4.83	4.93	10.81
	Quartz	10.96	10.9	9.11	5.1	3.32	2.25	1.2	2.18
Combined Blade		11.54	13.82	8.81	8.0	3.31	6.47	1.18	2.65
Core	Chalcedony	13.92	N/A	12.03	N/A	5.72	N/A	1.4	N/A
	Chert	21.24	2.69	15.73	4.87	11.13	2.71	5.6	1.87
	Other	N/A	N/A	N/A	N/A	N/A	N/A	N/A	N/A
	Quartz	27.33	11.49	23.35	11.6	18.73	11.05	23.66	29.05
Combined Core		27.1	12	23.09	16.08	18.46	11.28	23.06	24.23
Flake	Chalcedony	14.69	6.7	11.63	5.75	3.48	2.36	1.13	1.43
	Chert	13.84	7.91	10.86	6.28	3.1	2.41	1.32	2.43
	Other	25.15	16.85	19.8	13.45	6.93	5.45	10.72	22.57
	Quartz	14.93	10.59	12.08	6.85	4.18	3.04	2.46	5.87
Combined Flake		15.16	10.67	12.21	7.19	4.16	3.46	2.61	7.01

NOTE: *Length, width, and thickness in mm; weight in grams.*

was longer than that of chalcedony. However, the average length of chalcedony flakes was longer than that of chert.

There is great variation in the length of lithics made from "other" raw materials. The category of "other" raw materials includes those materials that were found in very small quantities: quartzite, basalt, and garnet. While quartzite and garnet are available in the immediate vicinity of the site in small quantities, the nearest source of basalt is the Deccan Traps, located about 50 km to the south and beyond. In general, the quartzite lithics are quitev large while the garnet lithics are very small; the length of basalt lithics falls in-between. The length of chert blades also varies greatly (SD=26.72). The reason for this anomaly is unclear.

Average blade length is smaller than average blade core length for all materials. A full analysis of the cores from Gilund suggests that they were not rejuvenated by the removal of the platform, as is common with bullet cores. Because the cores are worked from front to back, instead of in-the-round, the core appears to have been turned when a new platform was desired. This sometimes had the effect of shortening the blade-producing face each time a new platform was initiated. Alternatively, cores were discarded instead of rejuvenated when the platform was worn.

As with length, lithics of "other" raw materials are the

widest, most likely because the quartzite is difficult to knap. Quartz follows "other" as the second widest. Chert blades are wider than chalcedony blades on average. However, the average width of chert flakes is less than chalcedony flakes. There is a great deal of variation of width within chert blades and "other" flakes.

Average thickness followed trends for length and width for cores and flakes. However, quartz blades were thinner than chert blades on average. The ranking of average weight for cores followed the trends for other measurements. However, the average weight of blades and flakes differed somewhat; "other" lithics were heaviest followed by quartz, chert, then chalcedony.

Raw Material

The majority of lithics at Gilund are made of locally available quartz, with the remainder made of chert, chalcedony, agate, quartzite, garnet, and fine-grained basalt. Quartz can be found in several low-lying outcrops within a kilometer of Gilund and in several larger deposits within 5 km. It is generally of variable quality, but knappable and sharp. As a result, the material is useful for cutting, scraping, and drilling activities and there was no need for the occupants of Gilund to develop complex systems for importing

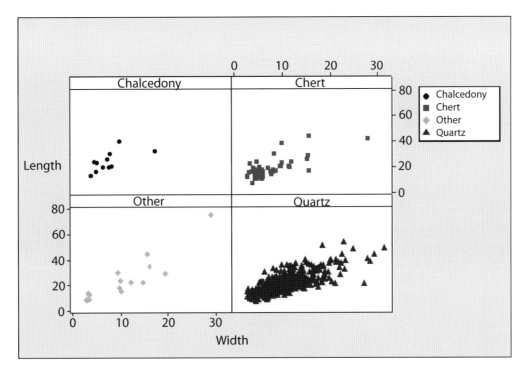

Fig. 10.3. Scatterplot of complete blades.

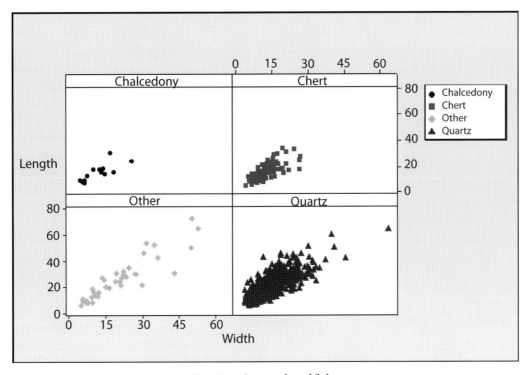

Fig. 10.4. Scatterplot of flakes.

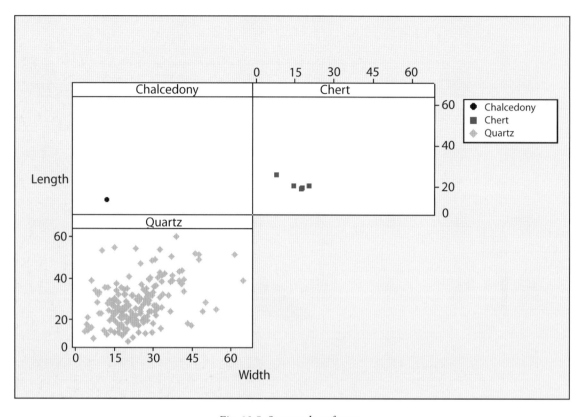

Fig. 10.5. Scatterplot of cores.

quantities of stone for these purposes.

The cherts at Gilund come in a variety of colors with various inclusions. Various shades of red and brown are the most common, but yellows, pinks, creams, and blue-grays are also present. Thin quartz veins are the most common inclusions in the cherts, but tiny quartz geodes, bands, and other minerals are present in some.

Some cherts can be found in very small quantities in the Banas River, about 1 km away from Gilund. The chert found in the Banas is usually a conglomerate with chert inclusions and washes down from the Nathdwara area or other unidentified areas in the Aravalli Mountains. The chert conglomerate is generally of better quality than the local quartz, but poorer than plain chert. Four lithics from the primary study sample match the Nathdwara chert. Some of the artifacts at Gilund appear to have been river-rolled prior to knapping, confirming that they came from a riverine source. However, other artifacts have cortex that had not been rolled. Some chert sources have been found approximately 50–80 km to the south and east of Gilund at the sites of Berugati, Bhagwanpura, Chitauriya, and Semara (Raczek 2011). A number of Gilund cherts do not resemble known chert deposits and come from sources that have not yet been located.

The chalcedonies also come in multiple varieties including clear, milky, and smoky. Some

Table 10.15. Distribution of Chalcedony Colors

	Blades	Cores	Flakes	Tools	Total	%
Clear	24		11		35	68.6%
Milky	5	1	3		9	17.6%
Orange/Red	3		1	1	5	9.8%
Smoky	1		1		2	3.9%
TOTAL	33	1	16	1	51	100.0%

Table 10.16 Distribution of Chalcedony Inclusions

	Blades	Cores	Flakes	Tools	Total	%
None/Plain	23	1	6	0	30	58.8%
Moss/Other inclusions	4	0	4	1	9	17.6%
Bands	6	0	6	0	12	23.5%
TOTAL	33	1	16	1	51	100.0%

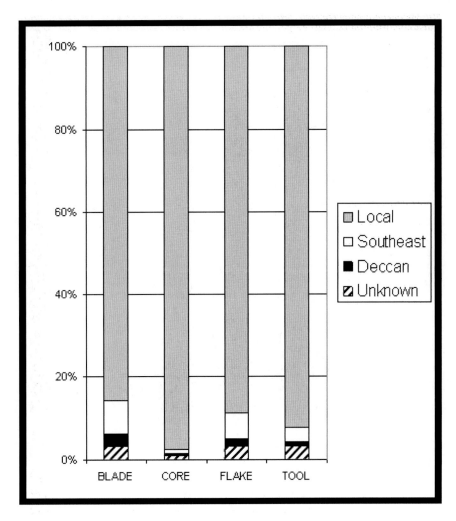

Fig. 10.6. Distribution of raw material sources (primary study sample, based on visual analysis).

pieces have river-rolled exteriors, while others have non-river-rolled cortex, which indicates that some chalcedonies came from rivers and others did not. A number of the chalcedonies have been heat-treated and appear as yellow, orange, or brilliant red. In this analysis, agate and chalcedony have been grouped together, as some lithics are smaller than the gap between bands in some agates. Thus, small lithics made from some agates appear to be made of chalcedony, blurring the distinction between these two categories. Banded inclusions were noted where present so that agates can be grouped together in the database by those who wish to examine these categories separately.

Conclusion

Compared to other excavated contemporaneous sites (Ahar, Balathal, Chatrikhera, and Ojiyana), Gilund is rich

in lithics. The results from the lithic analysis, which employed a two-tiered sampling strategy, suggest that most of the lithic materials were locally procured and formed, while some were obtained from distant sources. Although the most abundant local material was poor quality quartz, the residents did not develop complex trade networks to import good quality material. Instead, they appear to have procured raw material in the course of their normal activities. The small amounts of chert and chalcedony present may have been obtained during periodic travels or through incidental trade and exchange with members of more mobile communities (Raczek 2010a, 2011).

Overall, the technology at Gilund is fairly informal. That is, the residents of Gilund primarily produced unmodified blades and flakes and rarely produced formal microlithic tools or backed pieces. The emphasis on informal technology is consistent with the practice of sedentism

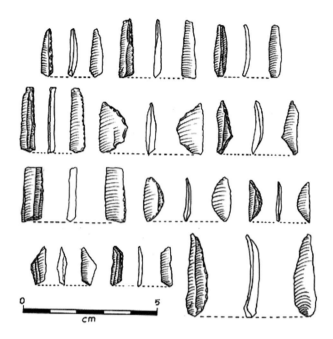

Fig. 10.7. Assorted lithics. (Drawings by Bharat Dighe, Deva-datta Phule, and Shrikant Pradhan)

and farming (Odell 1998 Parry and Kelly 1987), as well as the availability of high quantities of poor quality raw material (Andrefsky 1994). Such simple technology also required little training to master and could have been used by most residents of the site. Thus, there is no indication that lithic production at Gilund was a specialized craft (Raczek 2013). Instead, it is most likely that lithic production and use was a widespread activity for the residents of Gilund.

Acknowledgments

I am grateful to the Archaeological Survey of India for granting permission to study the Gilund collection and to the project directors, Dr. V. Shinde and Dr. G. L. Possehl, for inviting me to excavate at Gilund and analyze the lithic collections. I am also grateful for the support of Deccan College during the analysis phase. I would like to thank Professor V.N. Misra for providing helpful advice on questions of typology and the anonymous reviewers for helping to strengthen the original paper. Funding was provided in part by the William J. Fulbright Foundation and the Zwicker Fund. Logistical assistance was provided by the American Institute of Indian Studies.

NOTE

10.1. Lithics from the disturbed upper layers were also analyzed in order to provide a comparison sample. However, the results of that analysis are not presented here.

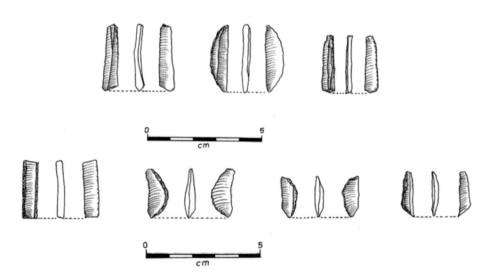

Fig. 10.8. Assorted lithics. (Drawings by Bharat Dighe, Devadatta Phule, and Shrikant Pradhan)

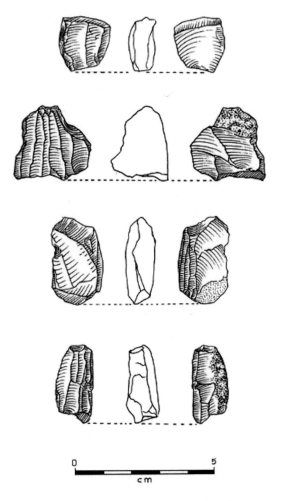

Fig. 10.9. Assorted lithics. (Drawings by Bharat Dighe, Devadatta Phule, and Shrikant Pradhan)

11

Faunal Remains from Gilund

Matthew J. Landt

Introduction

Between 1999 and 2005, numerous bone, teeth, and shell fragments were recovered during excavations at the Chalcolithic site of Gilund. As the faunal remains were being recovered from both GLD-1 and GLD-2, they were placed in paper bags and marked with the appropriate unit and level information. At the end of each excavation season these bags were gathered and cached in burlap sacks that were then stored with other artifacts recovered during the Gilund excavations. The collection is currently housed in trunks at Deccan College.

In 2005 the burlap bags containing faunal material were opened and their contents inventoried. During this process, a representative sample of bags was opened and the faunal material more closely scrutinized and counted. Because time constraints prohibited a full analysis of the remains, the 2005 inventory focused on providing an approximate number of faunal remains for the site and supplying an initial assessment of taphonomic factors that might influence the analysis of the material. While not a complete faunal report, this assessment is expected to provide sufficient details for a zooarchaeologist to appropriately plan the necessary logistics for future analysis. Further, this preliminary report indicates the way in which the differential use and discard of animal and food units at Gilund may inform discussions regarding interactions within sociocultural landscapes of the Ahar-Banas Chalcolithic.

Inventory

During the 2005 excavation season, 519 of the 1304 (40%) individual unit/level bags were inventoried. Of the total bags, 967 were labeled as containing bone and bone fragments, 248 containing shell remains, and 89 were la-beled as containing both bone and shell remnants. Of the 519 inventoried bags, 252 (26% of the 967 bone bags) were labeled bone or bone fragments and 200 (80% of the 248 shell bags) were labeled shell or shell fragments. Of the 89 bags labeled "bone and shell," 67 (75%) were opened and their contents counted.

From the 519 bags that were opened, a total of 24,852 bones/bone fragments (bones), 535 teeth/tooth fragments (teeth), and 1716 shells/shell fragments (shells) were identified. Although somewhat imperfect, this data can be utilized to generate an approximate figure for the number of bones recovered from the site and to provide a rough guide for zooarchaeologists who may be interested in whether or not the faunal collection can be utilized to ask more detailed questions of past lifeways. Based on relative percentages of sampled and unsampled envelope counts, projected NISP totals are roughly 66,078 bones, 1474 teeth, and 2220 shells for the Gilund faunal assemblage (Table 11.1). However, because the preservation of faunal remains is not likely to be consistent over the entire site (Lyon 1970, Meadow 1978, Nicholson 1998, Nielsen-Marsh and Hedges 2000), these numbers should be used only as a rough guide in consideration of the amount of bone and shell recovered during excavations.

Taphonomic Influences

The ability of zooarchaeologists to interpret faunal remains is influenced by bone altering forces that may include natural transport and weathering processes, carnivore/omnivore modification, human butchering practices, as well as excavation handling and post-excavation storage practices (Andrews and Nesbit Evans 1983, Behrensmeyer 1978, Binford 1981, Fisher 1995, Grayson 1989, Oliver 1993, White and Hannus 1983). As such, the analysis of faunal remains from archaeological sites should include the recording of

Table 11.1. Gilund 2005 Fauna Estimates

Area	No. of Trench Units	No. of Lots with Fauna			Estimated NISP		
		Bone	B/S	Shell	Bone	Tooth	Shell
Index Trench	11	53	1	27	4,573	85	266
I	34	575	57	176	48,864	1,166	1,646
II	5	1	0	27	0	1	149
III	11	80	6	15	7,706	167	140
IV	30	28	2	0	4,593	51	14
Unprove-nienced	ND	0	2	0	342	3	5
Totals	91	737	68	245	66,078	1,474	2,220

postmortem damage and modification to bone in an effort to document and understand the way in which these destructive forces influence interpretations of past cultural activities.

Various types of modification were noted in the sample of bones during inventory of the Gilund faunal assemblage. The modifications include evidence of burning, butchering marks, carnivore damage, calcium deposits, cultural modifications, and green fractures, as well as some post-burial fracturing. The majority of the faunal collection exhibits pre-excavation fracturing and a considerable amount of calcium carbonate concretions. As with the above NISP counts, the types of taphonomic influences listed here provide a preliminary, qualitative view of the Gilund faunal assemblage. These taphonomic processes do not discount an in-depth analysis of the Gilund faunal material, but the nature of the collection will emphasize some analytical techniques over others. For instance, calcium deposits are likely to preclude a number of taphonomic investigations that focus on the surface of the bone matrix (i.e., toothmarks, cutmarks, percussion fractures, etc.). However, the same concretions are not likely to impact spatial analysis or overall species identification of the faunal remains across the site.

Animal Representation

Many animal species were noted during the excavation and preliminary inventory of recovered faunal remains from the excavations at Gilund (Table 11.2). Since quantitative recordation of species composition across the site has not been undertaken, Table 11.2 is necessarily non-specific.

However, with regard to temporal and spatial patterns of animal remains, it is worth noting that the type(s) of trash, utilization practices, and the location(s) of disposal are often aggregates of social identifiers (Stein and Lekson 1992). For example, shell remains were ambiguous across the site, though fish remains were discretely located around

either the parallel walls or the units associated with the southern portion of GLD-2 that was originally identified as a possible "smelting" area (Shinde and Possehl 2005, Shinde, Possehl, and Ameri 2005). By focusing on such intraspatial distributions of faunal remains, it is possible to better understand the way in which people market and display themselves within specific socio-cultural landscapes.

More recently, during the 2005 excavations, two depressions with large concentrations of bones were uncovered on GLD-2. One of these depressions was located in front of a domestic structure on top of GLD-2 and is preliminarily associated with a Late Chalcolithic or Early Historic occupation. The other trash-filled depression was situated above the western portion of the parallel walls (see Fig. 11.1) and is more likely associated with a Middle Chalcolithic occupation. Both concentrations seemed to contain a relatively high number of Bos sp. and Bubalus bubalis bones and are large enough to suggest that consumption and disposal patterns at the household level may be distinguishable. A comparison of the two discrete, aggregate assemblages may provide diachronic information regarding prehistoric agro-pastoral practices and discard patterns at Gilund.

Table 11.2 Species Inventory from the Gilund Faunal Assemblage

Common Name	Scientific Name
Water Buffalo	*Bubalus bubalis*
Cow	*Bos indicus*
Pig	*Sus sp.*
Sheep	*Ovis aries*
Goat	*Capra hircus*
Blackbuck	*Antilope cervicapra*
Antelope/Deer	non sp.
Rabbit	*Lepus* sp.
Rodent	non sp.
Snake	non sp.
Bird	non sp.
Fish	non sp.
Bivalve	non sp.
Snail	non sp.

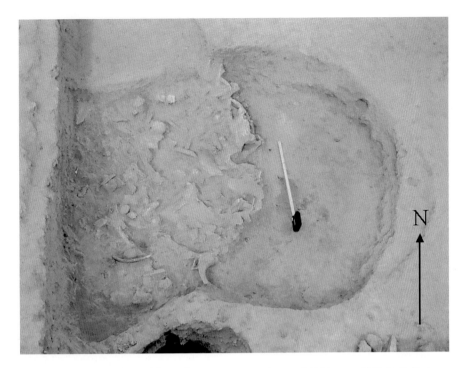

Fig. 11.1.Concentration of faunal remains, ceramics, and lithics on GLD-2. Pulled tape is 0.5 m in length.

Discussion

Explanations of large-scale, interregional social networks are important but are often hindered by inadequate understandings of local cultural entities. The major occupation of Gilund is contemporaneous with, and peripheral to, the Harappans of the Indus region, allowing archaeologists to place Gilund within a larger Middle Asian Interaction Sphere (Possehl, Shinde, and Ameri 2004). While extra-local population dynamics are certainly important to an understanding of regional networks, a focused understanding of local traditions and cultural developments (e.g., shifting agro-pastoral practices or market dynamics) cannot be understated as the foundation for all later regional interactions. While current evidence remains preliminary, the faunal remains from Gilund offer many opportunities to improve our understanding of social interactions within the Ahar-Banas Chalcolithic while focusing on local cultural developments.

The Early Chalcolithic marks a time of economic and social transition from semi-nomadic pastoralism to settled agro-pastoralism for those who dwelled in the Banas River basin (Hooja 1988, Kajale 1996, Meena and Tripathi 2001, Shinde and Possehl 2005, Thomas and Joglekar 1996). By the Middle Chalcolithic (3rd and 2nd millennia BC), do-

mesticated animal utilization characterizes agricultural and urban sites such that, as with the Harappan faunal material, domestic stock account for greater than 80% of the Chalcolithic faunal assemblages with little change in herd stock composition during the Late Chalcolithic (Hooja 1988, Meadow and Patel 2002, 2003, Thomas 2002). The shifting social milieu that is likely to have occurred during the pre-agriculture to agricultural economic shift provides a greater potential for conflict from social tension and subsistence risk during the Chalcolithic (Hegmon 1994).

As one of the largest excavated Ahar-Banas Chalcolithic sites, the recovered faunal materials are likely to shape our understanding of local interactions among sites along the Banas River as well as our knowledge of large-scale interregional social networks within a greater Asian interaction sphere (Possehl, Shinde, and Ameri 2004). The 2005 inventory of faunal remains sets the stage for understanding economic shifts and the ways in which communities perceive different social strategies (Landt 2010). By asking and addressing questions that relate to shifting economic activities during these transitional periods, we will be better able to ask questions that actually address the social growth and development of a large Chalcolithic village community and the lifeways of its human occupants.

12

Synthesizing Gilund: A Summary and Discussion of Excavation Finds

Vasant Shinde, Teresa P. Raczek, and Gregory L. Possehl

Prior to re-excavating the site at Gilund, the joint research team from the University of Pennsylvania and Deccan College posed a series of questions about early sedentism, early social complexity, and economic interaction in the Mewar region, as well as transitions between the Ahar-Banas and Early Historic periods (see Chapter 1). Through five seasons of excavation and several additional years of artifact analysis, the excavators and analysts have been able to address various aspects of these questions and enhance our understanding of social life in this region in the first few millennia BC. This chapter brings together the finds presented in the previous 11 chapters and presents a synthetic analysis of the research at Gilund.

The Rise of Sedentism and Early Farming Villages

Prior to the Ahar-Banas period, the Mewar region was inhabited by highly mobile people who practiced a range of subsistence strategies that included foraging and pastoralism. The subsequent rise of sedentism and agriculture is usually depicted as an indigenous development, not one that resulted from a migration of farmers (Deshpande and Shinde 2006, Shinde, Deshpande, and Yasuda 2004). The excavations at Gilund support this point of view, as the site has some evidence of a transition from a temporary occupation to a permanent settlement. A non-structural occupation with dense deposits of microliths was identified below the earliest excavated structures, in the deepest layers of excavation. It resembles other earlier temporary occupations in the region and bolsters this argument. The emphasis on horizontal excavation provided a modest investigation into the deepest layers of the site. However, although limited, these finds are the strongest indication yet of this transition. (For a further discussion see also Shinde 2010a, 2010b.)

The subsistence economy during most phases at Gilund was based largely on agro-pastoralism. Excavation across the site unearthed a variety of food-processing equipment including saddle querns, rubber stones, and mullers. The presence of multiple prepared underground storage silos and a large storage structure allowed the inhabitants to store agricultural products over long periods of time and to potentially offset poor agricultural years in the case of drought, failed monsoons, or pest damage. Although not systematically studied, chaff and grain impressions were identified in some pottery sherds, as well as in daub samples collected from multiple household contexts. Finally, the discovery of a number of nearby sites that may have served as farmsteads (Chapter 5) suggests that both nearby and distant land may have been cultivated to feed the inhabitants of Gilund.

Landt's faunal analysis (Chapter 11) shows that animal husbandry contributed greatly to the subsistence regime. The identification of cattle, sheep, goat, buffalo, and pig was not unexpected as these domestic species are common throughout South Asia during this time period. However, the faunal analysis also indicated that the occupants of Gilund consumed wild animals such as blackbuck, antelope/deer, and rabbit along with high quantities of fish. The pairing of animal husbandry, hunting, and fishing with crop cultivation provided the opportunity for the occupants of Gilund to consume a diverse diet.

Early Social Complexity

Identifying and explaining social and political practices and processes through archaeological data is a difficult challenge. Pointing to architectural and burial evidence, as well as a site-size hierarchy, several scholars have argued that a chiefdom society emerged around 2500 BC in central India and around 2000 BC in the Deccan region (Deshpande 1999, Dhavalikar 1984, Dhavalikar, Sankalia, and Ansari 1988, Shinde 1991). This characterization includes sites with an identified Ahar-Banas phase including Navdatoli, Nagda, and Eran in central India (Banerjee 1986, Sankalia, Deo, and Ansari 1971, Sankalia, Subbarao, and Deo 1958), as well as sites without Ahar-Banas material, such as Inamgaon and Daimabad in the Deccan (Dhavalikar, Sankalia, and Ansari 1988, Sali 1986, Shinde and Pappu 1990). In applying these models, most scholars draw from evidence in the form of burial data, regional settlement patterns, and architectural plans. Unfortunately, no burials have been located at Gilund, and burials are rare in the region, with the exception of Balathal (Robbins, Mushrif, and Walimbe 2005) and Bagor (Lukacs, Misra, and Kennedy 1982). However, the architectural remains discussed in Chapter 3 and the survey presented in Chapter 5 provide a suitable basis for discussion of community organization and hierarchy.

As the largest Ahar-Banas site, and geographically located in the center of the Banas basin, Gilund most likely played an important role in the region's political and economic life. To date, over 100 settlements with Ahar-Banas material culture have been identified in the Banas-Berach Basin and the Malwa Plateau. There are potentially other unidentified settlements because many areas have not yet been systematically surveyed. Unfortunately, due to intensive farming and construction in the region, it may no longer be possible to identify all Ahar-Banas sites. However, the two most recent surveys carried out by Ghosh around the site of Gilund (Chapter 5) and Dibyopama (2006, 2010) around the site of Balathal, along with the previous surveys of Hooja (1988) and Misra (1967), indicate the presence of different sizes and categories of sites including farmsteads, herding units, and camps for exploitation of the local sources of raw material, among other activities. Together, these studies illustrate a landscape rich in social and economic diversity.

The excavations at Gilund unearthed extensive architectural remains including domestic structures, large storage facilities, workshops, and a circumference wall. The domestic structures are generally larger than those found at other sites in the region. Some houses had multiple rooms and storage facilities, as well as kitchen areas that included a hearth. They demonstrate multiple construction methods including wattle and daub, mud brick, and stone. Most Middle Chalcolithic structures are made of mud brick with the exception of the workshop structures exposed in Area IV on the south part of GLD-2, which may have been made of burnt brick. Due to evidence of general burning in that area, further excavation is recommended in order to determine the manufacturing techniques used in the production of the bricks.

While some storage facilities were constructed at the household level, at least one appears to be communal in nature. The storage building surrounded by a vermin-impeding ash-filled trench located in Area I of GLD-2 (Chapter 3) is exponentially larger than household storage bins at Gilund. Such a large storage structure indicates that some storage activity was communally based. The administration of communally stored agricultural products marries political and economic organization at the site, points to hierarchical structures, and may indicate the presence of a type of redistributive economic system.

Multiple workshops were exposed including workshops that showed evidence of pyrotechnology. Such evidence indicates the presence of craft production at a larger scale than that of the household, and therefore a division of labor in this society. The workshops do not appear to be exceedingly large-scale operations, and there is no evidence that the entire site focused on the production of a single product for export. Instead, the workshops likely produced a variety of products, some of which were utilized by those who lived at Gilund and others that may have been exploited for trade and exchange.

The most compelling evidence for social organization and complexity comes in the form of the mudbrick parallel wall complex that resembles structures that are sometimes referred to as public granaries or storage houses (Shinde, Possehl, and Ameri 2005). The construction and maintenance of such a large and significant building indicates the presence of community leadership and social stratification. Like the large storage facility above, this facility may indicate communal storage or, if privately owned, the concentration of wealth in the hands of a few individuals. Although no other parallel-walled complex has been identified at any other Ahar-Banas site, a large stone and mud building (30 m E-W by 20 m N-S) was uncovered in the center of Balathal (Misra et al. 1995, Misra 1997). The function of that building is unclear, but similarly indicates pooling of labor and communal construction, as well as some form of central administration and social stratification.

In addition to the parallel wall complex, a small segment of a very large wall made of mud and mud brick was excavated. The wall resembles circumference walls identified at other sites like Balathal and may encircle GLD-1. The Balathal wall, located on the eastern periphery of the settlement, is made of mud bricks with a stone foundation.

Both the Gilund and Balathal walls are about 7 m wide at the top. As with the parallel wall complex, the presence of this wall indicates large-scale administration of labor and associated centralized authority.

Further evidence of administrative activities comes from the Middle Chalcolithic sealings found in an underground silo between two walls (NS6 and NS7) of the parallel wall complex and Late Chalcolithic seals and seal-amulets as discussed in Chapter 9. Such seals and sealings are often used to mark goods for ownership or to ensure their authenticity and purity before shipping. The concentration of sealings in the large parallel wall complex indicates the administrative nature of the activities that occurred there.

Together, the seals and sealings, communal storage structure, parallel wall complex, and circumference wall indicate a complex economic and political system, administration of labor, and hierarchical organization. Centrally located and larger than other settlements in the Mewar Plain, the site of Gilund clearly served an important political administrative and economic role in the region by the Middle Chalcolithic. Many of the features of early social complexity appeared in the Early Chalcolithic at Gilund and expanded in the Middle Chalcolithic.

Trade, Exchange, and Economic Interaction

Although many residents of Gilund pursued agro-pastoralism, others practiced craft production. Most of the structures excavated in Area IV of GLD-2 appear to have been associated with manufacturing activities. The identification of multiple workshops in one area points to some level of craft specialization and a robust artisanal community. For example, the complex on GLD-2 included a large oval furnace with vitrified material, along with other kilns, a dumping area with kiln wasters, and a large immovable quern. In addition to this pyrotechnological craft manufacturing workshop, several metal molds and crucibles were identified in other areas of the site (Chapter 8). Although a few copper objects were recovered in Early Chalcolithic deposits, the remains of items used in copper production point to the presence of copper manufacturing during the Middle Chalcolithic.

Although no potter's workshop was found, a number of pieces of evidence suggest that pottery was manufactured on site (Ghosh 2010). Suitable clay is locally available (Chapter 5), and some vitrified potsherds and kilns were identified. In addition, the quantity of recovered pottery, along with the large settlement size suggest that the pottery was manufactured on-site. An examination of the pottery indicates that open-air firing may have been used. Although no open-air kilns were identified, such kilns are often located away from habitations and are therefore difficult to detect archaeologically (Kramer 1997).

Evidence for trade and exchange was found through the formal analysis of multiple material classes including figurines, seals and seal impressions, pottery, and lithics. As Hanlon presented in her contribution, a large number of terracotta animal figurines found at Gilund are formally similar to those found throughout the region of the Ahar-Banas and indicate a shared iconographic tradition. The location of figurine manufacture is not clear and some unique figurine styles may have been manufactured at particular locales. For example, the upright bull figurines may have been imported from Marmi, which has been identified as a place for the manufacture of this particular type of figurine (Misra et al. 1993). Similarly, the painted figurines and cow figurines may have come from Ojiyana, where such styles are common (Hanlon 2010).

The iconography used in the seals and seal impressions found in the parallel-walled complex also indicates interaction across wide regions. As Ameri argues in Chapter 9, with some few exceptions the Middle Chalcolithic Gilund sealings differ significantly from the iconography used in contemporaneous Harappan seals and instead more closely resemble motifs found in Central Asia, including southeastern Iran. The shared iconography points to the possibility that the Ahar-Banas was tied into the 3rd millennium Middle Asian Interaction Sphere (MAIS) (Possehl 2007).

Stylistic analysis of the Gilund pottery also indicates trade and exchange with other regions including the Indus, central India, and southern India. Non-local wares found in Early Chalcolithic levels include Pre-Harappan/Sothi Combed Ware, Pre-Harappan Gritty Red Ware (north Gujarat style), Kayatha Cream Slipped Ware, and Kayatha Red-on-Red Ware. In addition, several sherds of Reserve Slip Ware, first produced towards the end of the 4th millennium BC in this region, were identified. This pottery has also been identified at Harappan and Ganeshwar-Jodhpura sites, indicating some level of interaction with those regions (Chapter 6 and Rizvi 2010). Non-local Middle Chalcolithic wares include two sherds of Harappan Buff Ware with black painting found in the Index Trench on GLD-1, sturdy constricted neck globular pots/jars of Red Ware, and Southern Neolithic Gray Ware. Three Malwa Ware sherds from central India were found in Late Chalcolithic contexts along with channel-spouted bowls of Southern Neolithic Gray Ware.

Finally, the visual raw material analysis of lithics by Raczek (Chapter 10) suggests that some of the lithics made of chert and chalcedony may have come from the southeastern margins of the Ahar-Banas area (Raczek 2013) or potentially from the Deccan (Khanna 1993). As most lithics were made of locally procured quartz, there is no evidence of a large systematic procurement network for non-local stone. Instead, these non-local materials represent incidental trade and exchange or possibly travel and direct embedded procurement. Beyond the chipped stone, other raw materials found at Gilund that were procured from non-local sources include copper and copper ore, steatite, shell, and turquoise. Although the exact sources of these items have not yet been identified, most probably lie outside of the area where Ahar-Banas sites are found. Together, they point to engaged interaction in multiple directions.

Transition between Ahar-Banas and Later Periods

The settlement at Gilund shrank dramatically in the Late Chalcolithic and was largely confined to parts of GLD-1 and the northern part of GLD-2; a small occupation survived until approximately 1500 BC. A number of changes in material culture also occurred in the later occupation. For example, although the most common construction material for the Middle Chalcolithic and the beginning of the Late Chalcolithic was mud brick, later houses were made of wattle and daub or mud. In addition, although most pottery forms and manufacturing techniques continue, three substantial changes in pottery production occurred. First, the habit of painting Ahar-Banas Black and Red Ware with white paint was largely discontinued. Second, a coarser temper in the form of sand, grass, and rice husks was introduced. Finally, vessels were less evenly fired compared to earlier phases, indicating a change in firing techniques. Such changes in the ceramic assemblage may point to changes in diet and feasting, organization of pottery production, and the introduction of vessels made from other materials (such as various metals).

Although there are a number of Early Historic sites in the Mewar region, evidence for the transition from the Chalcolithic to Early Historic periods has not yet been clearly identified. The Historic period occupations at Gilund are limited to a small area on GLD-1 and include domestic structures with hearths and storage facilities, coarse Red and Gray pottery, and iron implements including a sickle, ploughshare, dagger, nail, chisel, arrowhead, and spearhead. The reduced population size and domestic na-

ture of the occupation suggests that the Historic period settlement did not share many of the administrative features of the Chalcolithic period. However, the presence of iron indicates contact with other sites in the region including possibly Dariba (located roughly 15 km to the west) where there is a thick deposit of iron ore, or alternatively, the iron-producing site of Iswal (20 km west of contemporary Udaipur), where the Early Historic pottery is very similar to that at Gilund. The presence of stamped pottery in the latest occupational levels indicates the continuous use of the site until the Kushan period. The excavations suggest that there is an urgent need for further archaeological investigation of the Early Historic and later time periods in Rajasthan.

Areas for Further Research

The five seasons of excavation at Gilund produced a wealth of information about this ancient site. Careful excavation and meticulous curation of the small finds ensures that the artifacts and antiquities can be easily accessed and restudied by future researchers. In addition, extensive documentation through both field journals and lot forms ensured that the data collected at Gilund will be available for researchers for years to come. Full analysis of the surrounding landscape, architecture, and five data classes to date have provided a complete picture of the daily life of these early villagers. In sum, the excavations have greatly helped to answer the initial research questions. However, as is the case with every archaeological project, this excavation raised as many questions as it answered. It is a positive sign that the team ends this research phase by opening the door to future research in a number of areas.

One of the areas that would benefit from additional research is specific environmental data for the various time periods. A number of excellent climate studies in Pakistan and northern Rajasthan have provided useful data, but the specific local variation on documented climate swings is unknown. For example, documenting the status of the nearby lakebed, which is currently dry, would help illuminate the extent to which the residents used that body of water as a resource. In addition, the extent to which the Banas River was perennial during each phase remains to be determined. Since fish comprised a large portion of the village diet and the river most likely served as a transportation conduit, the loss of the river on a seasonal basis would entail a significant modification of day-to-day activities. Finally, understanding monsoonal variation will help in the formation of explanations for shifting population patterns over the millennia.

Second, excavation has demonstrated that mound

formation at Gilund was exceedingly complex. It appears that GLD-2 was abandoned before GLD-1. However, due to the small scale of the excavations, the team was not able to answer specific questions about the pattern and pace of growth of particular areas of each mound. In addition, other than understanding the parallel wall structure and surrounding features, as well as the industrial area, no clear neighborhoods have been identified at Gilund. Further horizontal excavation would shed additional light on this aspect of daily life.

Third, the survey conducted by Ghosh identified all of the remaining neighboring settlements in the immediate area. This important work clearly situates Gilund at the center of a complex society. However, the full relationship between Gilund and its immediate neighbors remains to be investigated through excavation of these smaller sites. Small site excavation in the Mewar region would undoubtedly be greatly productive, as has been previously demonstrated in the Deccan (Dhavalikar, Shinde, and Atre 1990). Unfortunately, the current expansion of agriculture and other development practices currently threaten many small sites. The need to conduct test excavations at these neighboring sites before they disappear grows more urgent with every passing year.

Fourth, a number of architectural questions were raised by the excavation. Are the parallel-wall complex and the large storage facility the only communal buildings at Gilund, or do others lay beneath the surface? How extensive is the circumference wall? Does it encircle both mounds? How many gateways are there? A number of workshops were identified, including an intriguing one on the east side of GLD-2 that has not yet been excavated, but clearly shows a thick deposit of vitrified sand. Finally, we have only begun to understand the range of house forms built by the inhabitants of Gilund.

Lastly, much has been learned about the multiple phases of Gilund and the transitions between them. However, a fine tuning of the resolution on these transitions still remains. The excavations uncovered thick layers of microliths and degraded pottery underneath the oldest architectural remains of the deepest layers of three separate trenches. However, because of the emphasis on horizontal excavations, the soil volume recovered for this first occupational phase was minimal. A larger sample of the initial occupation will reveal much about early sedentism and early farming in the Mewar region.

These questions can only be articulated because of the research that has been accomplished at Gilund. The new excavations elaborated our understanding of the regional cultural sequence and provided additional insight into the social processes of the Ahar-Banas. In five short seasons, the joint Deccan College/University of Pennsylvania team accomplished their initial goals, made some unexpected discoveries, and trained a new generation of archaeologists. It is hoped that the results of this project will contribute positively to the many debates and conversations on prehistory, protohistory, and archaeology in India and beyond.

Appendix 1

Radiocarbon Dates for Gilund

Radiocarbon analysis was performed by Beta Analytic Inc. in Miami, FL, USA.

Beta sample 140702, from Trench 5, Layer 4
Sample: charcoal found inside *chula* of structure 3
Analysis: Radiometric-standard delivery with extended counting
Measured radiocarbon age: 3450 +/- 80 BP
13C/12C ratio: -25.0 o/oo
Conventional Radiocarbon Age: 3450 +/- 80 BP
2 sigma calibration: 1954 to 1602 BC and 1590 to 1532 BC

Beta sample 215006 from Trench 4F, lot # 4F-4003, Stratum 29
Sample: charcoal
Analysis: AMS-standard delivery
Measured radiocarbon age: 3870 +/- 40 BP
13C/12C ratio: -25.9 o/oo
Conventional Radiocarbon Age: 3860 +/- 40 BP
2 sigma calibration: Cal BC 2460 to 2200 (Cal BP 4410 to 4150)

Beta sample 215007 from Trench 4F, lot # 4F-4004, Stratum 30
Sample: charcoal
Analysis: AMS-standard delivery
Measured radiocarbon age: 3800 +/- 40 BP
13C/12C ratio: -25.4 o/oo
Conventional Radiocarbon Age: 3700 +/- 40 BP
2 sigma calibration: Cal BC 2330 to 2130 (Cal BP 4280 to 4080) *and* Cal BC 2080 to 2060 (Cal BP 4030 to 4010)

Beta sample 215008 from Trench 4F, lot # 4F-4006, Stratum 32
Sample: charcoal
Analysis: AMS-standard delivery
Measured radiocarbon age: 3840 +/- 40 BP
13C/12C ratio: -25.0 o/oo
Conventional Radicarbon Age: 3840 +/- 40 BP
2 sigma calibration: Cal BC 2450 to 2190 (Cal BP 4400 to 4140) *and* Cal BC 2170 to 2150 (Cal BP 4120 to 4100)

Beta Sample 216401 from Trench 57, lot # 5570012, Stratum 2
Sample: Charred seeds found inside an in situ pot underneath a house floor
Analysis: Radiometric-standard delivery
Measured radiocarbon age: 3290 +/- 40 BP
13C/12C ratio: -23.2 o/oo
Conventional Radicarbon Age: 3320 +/- 40 BP
2 sigma calibration: Cal BC 1690 to 1510 (Cal BP 3640 to 3460)

Beta Sample 216402 from Trench 65, Lot # 5650027, Stratum 2
Sample: Charred seeds found inside an in situ pot underneath a house floor
Analysis: Radiometric-standard delivery
Measured radiocarbon age: 3220 +/- 40 BP
13C/12C ratio: -22.1 o/oo
Conventional Radiocarbon Age: 3270 +/- 40 BP
2 sigma calibration: Cal BC 1630 to 1440 (Cal BP 3580 to 3390)

Appendix 2

List of Supervisors and Student Participants in the Gilund Excavations

Co-Directors

Dr. Vasant Shinde, Deccan College
Dr. Gregory L. Possehl, University of Pennsylvania

Deccan College Team

Suvarnarekha Bhinde
Debashree Das Gupta
Shweta Sinha Deshpande
Gholamreza Karamian
Dr. M. Khajale
Shivaji Kshirsagar
Neha Kothari
Amul Kulkarni
Ashish Kulkarni
Shiva Kumar
Lopamudra Maitra
Swayam S. Panda
Nirmala Reddy
Reshma Sawant
Lajwanti Shahani
Salim Shaikh
Prabodh Shirvalkar
Gauri Thakar
David Tetso
Vaheesta L. Vankadia
Natha

American Team
(with other international participants)

Marta Ameri, New York University
Christopher Bayliss, Institute of Archaeology, UCL
Françoise Boudart (Belgium)
Alyce Dagorn, Queens College, CUNY
Dennys Franzia, University of Bologna
Lorena Giorgio, University of Bologna
Emanuel Grimaud, CNRS, Paris
Praveena Gullapalli, University of Pennsylvania
Neha Gupta, Institute of Archaeology, UCL
Neha Gupta, Toronto
Julie Hanlon, University of Pennsylvania
Suzanne Harris, University of Pennsylvania
Rita Jeney, Hungary
Peter Johansen, University of Chicago
Gwendolyn Kelly, Oberlin College
Mike Korvink, University of South Carolina
Matthew Landt, Washington State University
Lara Lang, University of Arizona
Megan McCormick, CUNY Graduate Center
Jon Meyer, Washington State University
Sarah Peterson, University of Pennsylvania
Alain Poljak, Belgium
Teresa Raczek, University of Pennsylvania
Gethin Rees, Institute of Archaeology, UCL
Uzma Rizvi, University of Pennsylvania
Robert Rollings, Florida
Camille Selleger, Switzerland
Erin Silverstein, University of Pennsylvania
Radhika Soundararajan, University of Pennsylvania

Japanese Team

Professor Yoshinori Yasuda, International Research Center for Japanese Studies, Kyoto
Azusa Yano, International Research Center for Japanese Studies, Kyoto
Junko Kitagawa, International Research Center for Japanese Studies, Kyoto

Fig. A2.1. Camp at Gilund, 2005.

Dr. Miroslaw Makohonenko, International Research Center for Japanese Studies, Kyoto

Dr. Takeshi Nakagawa, International Research Center for Japanese Studies, Kyoto

Kazuyoshi Yamada, Tokyo Metropolitan University

Tadashi Kudo

Yohei Tojima

Takeshi Takeda

Maharashtra Vidyapeth, Pune, Team

Prof. Shreemand Bapat

Jayant Aphale

Varsha Dhavade

Pikhil Jakle

Preeti Karambelkar

Gauri Mehendale

Arati Vaidya

Parag Vanarase

St. Xavier College, Mumbai, Team

Aniruddha Bose

Jayashree Coutinho

Jonathan Coutts-Zawadzki

Nishtha Dhoundiyal

Carmen D'Silva

Mario D'Penha

Yuki Ellias

Cletus Fereirra

Veer Krishna Gauba

Florence Lalmoikim

Fig. A2.2. Dr. Gregory L. Possehl at Gilund, 1999–2000.

Fig. A2.3. Dr. Vasant Shinde (top of ladder) and workers at Gilund, 2005.

Peitipushpa Mishra
Maria Mani
Prasad Menon
Amruta Nemivant
Zenaida (Zee) Pinto
Maryse Saldanha
Alicia Satrakot
Merrill Sequeira
Natasha Bridgette Shah
Pragya Vohra
Rohit Vishwanath

Bombay University Team

Dr. Kishore Gaikwad
Anjaivi Pandey
Ronette Gonsalvis
Radha
Anjali
Shweta
Smitha Kutty
Sajuta Panigrahi
Swapna
Savita
Urushali
Rajashree
Victor Demello
Pradeep Waghmare

Other Participants

Ashish Chadha, Stanford University
Neha Das Gupta, Calcutta
Sanjay Deshpande
Ambika Dhaka, Rajasthan University

Amitab Ghosh
Punkaj Gohel
Arunima Kashyap Chakrabarty, Michigan State
Dr. Manoj Kumar Kurmi, Indian Archaeological Society
B.M. Pande
Kishore Raghubans, M.S. University of Baroda
Praveen Singh, private
Talimenla, Pune University

Staff

Deccan College

Dighe Bharat Baburao, Drafstman, Camp Manager
Krishna Malap, Cook
I.V. Vishwasrao, Camp Manager

Gilund and Udaipur

Dilip Kumarwat, Sumo owner, Udaipur

Bibliography

Ali, R., A. Trivedi, and D. Solanki. 2004. *Chalcolithic Site of Ujjain Region: Mahidpur.* Delhi: Sharada Publishing House.

Ameri, M. 2010. Middle Asian Interconnections at the Turn of the Second Millennium BC: Locating the Foreign Elements in the Gilund Seals and Seal Impressions. In *The Gilund Project: Excavations in Regional Context. Proceedings of the 19th International Conference on South Asian Archaeology, July 2007, Ravenna, Italy,* ed. T.P. Raczek and V. Shinde, pp. 43–50. South Asian Archaeology 2007 Special Sessions 2. Oxford: British Archaeological Reports.

Anderson-Gerfaud, P., M.-L. Inizan, M. Lechevallier, J. Pelegrin, and M. Pernot. 1989. Des Lames de Silex dans un Atelier de Potier Harappéen: Interaction de Domaines Techniques. *Comptes Rendus de l'Académie des Sciences–Serie II* 308:443–49.

Andrefsky, W.J. 1994. Raw-material Availability and the Organization of Technology. *American Antiquity* 59.1: 21–35.

Andrews, P., and E.M. Nesbit Evans. 1983. Small Mammal Bone Accumulations Produced by Mammalian Carnivores. *Paleobiology* 9.3: 289–307.

Ansari, S. 2000. Clay Storage Bins in India: An Ethnoarchaeological Study. *Man and Environment* 25.2: 51–78.

Ansari, Z.D. 1969. Lithic Flake Tools. In *Excavations at Ahar (Tambavati),* ed. H.D. Sankalia, S.B. Deo, and Z.D. Ansari, pp. 15–17. Deccan College Building Centenary and Silver Jubilee Series, 45. Pune: Deccan College Postgraduate and Research Institute.

Ansari, Z.D., and M.K. Dhavalikar. 1975. *Excavations at Kayatha.* Pune: Deccan College.

Aruz, J., R. Wallenfels, and Metropolitan Museum of Art. 2003. *Art of the First Cities: The Third Millennium B.C. from the Mediterranean to the Indus.* New York: Metropolitan Museum of Art.

Banerjee, N.R. 1986. *Nagda: 1955–57.* Memoirs of the Archaeological Survey of India, no. 85. New Delhi: Archaeological Survey of India, Government of India.

Barker, G. 1972. The Conditions of Cultural and Economic Growth in the Bronze Age of Central Italy. *Proceedings of the Prehistoric Society* 38:170–208.

———. 1973. Cultural and Economic Change in the Prehistory of Central Italy. In *The Explanations of Culture Change: Models in Prehistory,* ed. C. Renfrew, pp. 359–70. Pittsburgh: University of Pittsburgh Press.

———. 1975a. Early Neolithic Land Use in Yugoslavia. *Proceedings of the Prehistoric Society* 41:85–104.

———. 1975b. Prehistoric Territories and Economies in Central Italy. In *Palaeoeconomy,* ed. E.S. Higgs, pp. 111–75. London: Cambridge University Press.

Barton, C.M., D.I. Olszewski, and N.R. Coinman. 1996. Beyond the Graver: Reconsidering Burin Function. *Journal of Field Archaeology* 23.1: 111–25.

Behrensmeyer, A.K. 1978. Taphonomic and Ecologic Information from Bone Weathering. *Paleobiology* 4.2: 150–62.

Bhan, K.K., M. Vidale, and J.M. Kenoyer. 2002. Some Important Aspects of the Harappan Technological Tradition. In *Protohistory: Archaeology of the Harappan Civilization,* ed. S. Settar and R. Korisettar, pp. 223–71. Indian Archaeology in Retrospect, Vol.2. Delhi: Indian Council of Historical Research and Manohar.

Bhandarkar, D.R. 1920. *The Archaeological Remains and Excavations at Nagari.* Memoirs of the Archaeological Survey of India, no. 4. New Delhi: Director General, Archaeological Survey of India. Reprinted 1998.

Bhattacharyya, R. 1991. Rangpur Seal—Probably Egyptian Connection. *Man and Environment* 16.1: 53–57.

Binford, L.R. 1981. *Bones, Ancient Men, and Modern Myths.* Studies in Archaeology. New York: Academic Press.

Blackman, M.J. 1999. Chemical Characterization of Local Anatolian and Uruk Style Sealing Clays from Hacinebi. *Paléorient* 25.1: 51–56.

Boivin, N. 2010. *Material Cultures, Material Minds: The Impact of Things on Human Thought, Society, and Evolution.* Cambridge: Cambridge University Press.

Brantingham, P.J., J.W. Olsen, J.A. Rech, and A.I. Krivoshapkin. 2000. Raw Material Quality and Prepared Core Technologies in Northeast Asia. *Journal of Archaeological Science* 27.3: 255–71.

Browman, D.L. 1976. Demographic Correlations of the Wari Conquest of Junin. *American Antiquity* 41.4: 465–77.

Brumfiel, E. 1976. Regional Growth in the Eastern Valley of Mexico: A Test of the "Population Pressure" Hypothesis. In *The Early Mesoamerican Village,* ed. K.V. Flannery, pp. 234–49. New York: Academic Press.

Chakrabarti, D.K. 1999. *India: An Archaeological History. Palaeolithic Beginnings to Early Historic Foundations.* Delhi: Oxford University Press.

Chazan, M. 2001. Bladelet Production in the Aurignacian of La Ferrassie (Dordogne, France). *Lithic Technology* 26.1: 16–28.

Chisholm, M. 1979. *Rural Settlement and Land Use: An Essay in Location.* London: Hutchinson.

Clark, J.E. 1991. Flintknapping and Debitage Disposal among the Lacandon Maya of Chiapas, Mexico. In *The Ethnoarchaeology of Refuse Disposal,* ed. E.L. Staski and L.D. Sutro, pp. 63–78. Anthropological Research Papers 42. Tempe: Arizona State University.

Clarke, D.L. 1972. A Provisional Model of an Iron Age Society and Its Settlement System. In *Models in Archaeology,* ed. D.L. Clarke, pp. 801–69. London: Methuen.

Cleland, J.H. 1977. Chalcolithic and Bronze Age Chipped Stone Industries of the Indus Region: An Analysis of Variability and Change. Ph.D. dissertation, University of Virginia.

———. 1986. Lithic Analysis and Culture Process in the Indus Region. In *Studies in the Archaeology of India and Pakistan,* ed. J. Jacobson, pp. 91–116. Delhi: Oxford & IBH and the American Institute of Indian Studies.

Crabtree, D. 1968. Mesoamerican Polyhedral Cores and Prismatic Blades. *American Antiquity* 33.4: 446–78.

Dasgupta, D. 2006a. A Study of Site Catchment Analysis of Gilund: A Chalcolithic Settlement in the Banas Ba-

sin, Rajasthan. *Man and Environment* 31.2: 70–74.

———. 2006b. Site Catchment Analysis of the Chalcolithic Settlement of Gilund in the Banas Basin. *Puratattva* 35:102–10.

Dennel, R.W., and D. Webley. 1975. Prehistoric Settlement and Land Use in Southern Bulgaria. In *Palaeoeconomy,* ed. E.S. Higgs, pp. 97–109. London: Cambridge University Press.

Deo, S.B. 1969a. Pottery Text. In *Excavations at Ahar (Tambavati),* ed. H.D. Sankalia, S.B. Deo, and Z.D. Ansari, pp. 28–162. Pune: Deccan College.

———. 1969b. Beads. In *Excavations at Ahar (Tambavati),* ed. H.D. Sankalia, S.B. Deo, and Z.D. Ansari, pp. 163–75. Pune: Deccan College.

———. 1969c. Terracotta Objects. In *Excavations at Ahar (Tambavati),* ed. H.D. Sankalia, S.B. Deo, and Z.D. Ansari, pp. 176–98. Pune: Deccan College.

Deshpande, S.S. 1999. Chalcolithic Social Organization in Central India: A Case Study of Balathal. *Puratattva* 29:50–59.

Deshpande, S.S., and V. Shinde. 2005. Gujarat between 2000 and 1400 BCE. *South Asian Studies* 21:121–35.

———. 2006. Development of Urbanization in the Mewar Region of Rajasthan, India, in the Middle of Third Millennium BC. *Ancient Asia* 1:103–22.

Dhavalikar, M.K. 1984. Chalcolithic Cultures: A Socio-Economic Perspective. In *Archaeological Perspective of India Since Independence,* ed. K.N. Dikshit. New Delhi: Indian Archaeological Society.

———. 2002. Early Farming Cultures of Central India. In *Prehistory: Archaeology of South Asia,* ed. S. Settar and R. Korisettar, pp. 253–62. Indian Archaeology in Retrospect, Vol. I, S. Settar and R. Korisettar, gen. eds. Delhi: Manohar and Indian Council of Historical Research.

Dhavalikar, M.K., H.D. Sankalia, and Z.D. Ansari. 1988. *Excavations at Inamgaon I,* Parts I and II. Pune: Deccan College Postgraduate and Research Institute.

Dhavalikar, M.K., V.S. Shinde, and S. Atre. 1990. Small Site Archaeology: Excavations at Walki. *Bulletin of the Deccan College Postgraduate and Research Institute* 50:197–228.

Dibyopama, A. 2006. Site Catchment Analysis of Balathal. Unpublished MA dissertation. Pune: Deccan College.

———. 2010. Site Catchment Analysis of Balathal. *Ancient Asia* 2:47–57.

Duistermaat, K. 2000. A View on Late Neolithic Sealing Practices in the Near East: The Case of Tell Sabi Abad, Syria. In *Administrative Documents in the Aegean and*

Their Near Eastern Counterparts, ed. M. Perna, pp. 13–31. Torino: Pubblicazióne degli Archivi di Stato.

Ellison, A., and J. Harris. 1972. Settlement and Land Use in the Prehistory and Early History of Southern England: A Study Based on Locational Models. In *Models in Archaeology,* ed. D.L. Clarke, pp. 911–62. London: Methuen.

Eriksen, B.V. 2010. *Lithic Technology in Metal-Using Societies.* Proceedings of the XVth UISPP Congress, Lisbon, September 7th, 2006. London: British Archaeological Reports.

Fagan, B.M. 1976. The Hunters of Gwisho: A Retrospect. In *Problems in Economic and Social Archaeology,* ed. G. de G. Sieveking, I.H. Longworth, and K.E. Wilson, pp. 15–24. Boulder: Westview Press.

Fiandra, E. 1981. The Connection between Clay Sealings and Tablets in Administration. In *South Asian Archaeology 1979,* ed. H. Härtel, pp. 29–43. Berlin: Dietrich Reimer Verlag.

Fiandra, E., and C. Pepe. 2000. Typology and Distribution of the Administrative Indicators in the Eastern Residential Area of Shahr-i Sokhta during Period II (2800–2600 B.C.). In *South Asian Archaeology 1997,* ed. M. Taddei and G. De Marco, pp. 467–83. Rome: Istituto Italiano per l'Africa e l'Oriente e Istituto Universitario Orientale.

Fisher, J.W., Jr. 1995. Bone Surface Modifications in Zooarchaeology. *Journal of Archaeological Method and Theory* 2.1: 7–68.

Flannery, K.V. 1976. The Village and Its Catchment Area. In *The Early Mesoamerican Village,* ed. K.V. Flannery, pp. 91–95. New York: Academic Press.

Frenez, D., and M. Tosi. 2005. The Lothal Sealings: Records from an Indus Civilization Town at the Eastern End of the Maritime Circuits across the Arabian Sea. In *Studi in Onóre di Enrica Fiandra: Contributi di Archeologia Egèa e Vicinorientale,* ed. M. Perna, pp. 65–103. Napoli: Diffusion de Boccard.

Ghosh, A., ed. 1990. *An Encyclopaedia of Indian Archaeology, Vol 1.* New York: E.J. Brill.

Ghosh, D.D. 2010. An Insight into the Economy of the Chalcolithic People of Gilund. In *The Gilund Project: Excavations in Regional Context. Proceedings of the 19th International Conference on South Asian Archaeology, July 2007, Ravenna, Italy,* ed. T.P. Raczek and V. Shinde, pp. 31–34. South Asian Archaeology 2007 Special Sessions 2. Oxford: British Archaeological Reports.

Gibson, M., and R.D. Biggs. 1977. *Seals and Sealing in the Ancient Near East.* Bibliotheca Mesopotamica, Vol. 6.

Malibu: Undena Publications.

Grayson, D.K. 1989. Bone Transport, Bone Destruction, and Reverse Utility Curves. *Journal of Archaeological Science* 16:643–52.

Hakemi, A. 1997. *Shahdad: Archaeological Excavations of a Bronze Age Center in Iran.* Rome: L'Istituto per il Medio ed Estremo Oriente.

Hamilton, N. 1996. Figurines, Clay Balls, Small Finds and Burials. In *On the Surface: Çatalhöyük 1993–1995,* ed. I. Hodder, pp. 215–63. BIAA Monograph 22. Cambridge: McDonald Institute for Archaeological Research.

Hanlon, J.A. 2006. The Gilund Terracottas: A New Look at the Ahar Culture in Rajasthan and Madhya Pradesh. Unpublished MPhil thesis, University of Cambridge, Cambridge.

———. 2010. An Overview of the Antiquities from the 1999–2005 Excavations at Gilund, A Chalcolithic Site in Southeast Rajasthan. In *The Gilund Project: Excavations in Regional Context. Proceedings of the 19th International Conference on South Asian Archaeology, July 2007, Ravenna, Italy,* ed. T.P. Raczek and V. Shinde, pp. 13–22. South Asian Archaeology 2007 Special Sessions 2. Oxford: British Archaeological Reports.

Hegmon, M. 1994. Boundary-Making Strategies in Early Pueblo Societies: Style and Architecture in the Kayenta and Mesa Verde Regions. In *The Ancient Southwestern Community: Models and Methods for the Study of Prehistoric Social Organization,* ed. W.H. Wills and R.D. Leonard, pp. 171–90. Albuquerque: University of New Mexico Press.

Hiebert, F.T. 1994. *Origins of the Bronze Age Oasis Civilization in Central Asia.* Cambridge, MA: Peabody Museum of Archaeology and Ethnography, Harvard University.

Higgs, E.S., ed. 1975. *Palaeoeconomy.* London: Cambridge University Press.

Higgs, E.S., C. Vita-Finzi, D.R. Harriss, and A.E. Fagg. 1967. The Climate, Environment and Industries of Stone Age Greece: Part 3. *Proceedings of the Prehistoric Society* 33:1–29.

Higgs, E.S., and D. Webley. 1971. Further Information Concerning the Environment of Palaeolithic Man in Epirus. *Proceedings of the Prehistoric Society* 37.2: 367–80.

Hodder, I., and C. Orton. 1976. *Spatial Analysis in Archaeology.* Cambridge: Cambridge University Press.

Hoffman, M.A., and J.H. Cleland. 1977. *Excavations at the Harappan Site of Allahdino: The Lithic Industry at Allahdino.* Papers of the Allahdino Expedition, No. 2. New York: American Museum of Natural History.

Hooja, R. 1988. *The Ahar Culture and Beyond: Settlements and Frontiers of "Mesolithic" and Early Agricultural Sites in South-Eastern Rajasthan, c. 3rd–2nd Millennia B.C.* British Archaeological Reports International Series 412. Oxford: British Archaeological Reports.

———. 1996. Expressing Ethnicity and Identity: Frontiers and Boundaries in Pre-History. *The Indian Journal of Social Work* 17.1: 91–114.

Indian Archaeology, a Review (IAR). 1954–55. Ahar, District Udaipur, pp. 14–15. Delhi: Archaeological Survey of India.

———. 1955–56. Excavation at Ahar, p. 11. Delhi: Archaeological Survey of India.

———. 1957–58. Exploration in Districts Bhilwara, Chitorgarh and Udaipur, pp. 43–45. Delhi: Archaeological Survey of India.

———. 1959–60. Excavations at Gilund, pp. 41–46. Delhi: Archaeological Survey of India.

———. 1964–65. Excavation at Kayatha, District Ujjain, pp. 18–19. New Delhi: Archaeological Survey of India.

———. 1967–68a. Excavation at Kayatha, District Ujjain, pp. 24–25. New Delhi: Archaeological Survey of India.

———. 1967–68b. Excavations at Bagor, pp. 41–42. New Delhi: Archaeological Survey of India.

———. 1968–69. Excavations at Bagor, pp. 26–28. New Delhi: Archaeological Survey of India.

———. 1969–70. Excavations at Bagor, pp. 32–34. New Delhi: Archaeological Survey of India.

———. 1998–99. Excavation at Chichali, District Khargone, pp. 92–107. New Delhi: Archaeological Survey of India.

———. 1999–2000. Excavation at Chichali, District Khargone, pp. 83–96. New Delhi: Archaeological Survey of India.

Inizan, M.-L., and M. Lechevallier. 1990. A Techno-economic Approach to Lithics: Some Examples of Blade Pressure Debitage in the Indo-Pakistani Subcontinent. In *South Asian Archaeology 1987,* ed. M. Taddei, pp. 43–59. Rome: Istituto Italiano per il Medio ed Estremo Oriente.

———. 1995. Pressure Debitage and Heat Treatment in the Microlithic Assemblage of Bagor, Northwest India. *Man and Environment* 20.2: 17–22.

Jarman, M.R. 1976. Prehistoric Economic Development in Sub-Alpine Italy. In *Problems in Economic and Social Archaeology,* ed. G. de G. Sieveking, I.H. Longworth, and K.E. Wilson, pp. 523–48. Boulder, CO:

Westview Press.

Jarman, M.R., and D. Webley. 1975. Settlement and Land Use in Capitanata, Italy. In *Palaeoeconomy,* ed. E.S. Higgs, pp. 177–221. London: Cambridge University Press.

Jarman, M.R., G.N. Bailey, and H.N. Jarman, eds. 1982. *Early European Agriculture: Its Foundation and Development.* Cambridge: Cambridge University Press.

Jarrige, J.-F. 1981. Economy and Society in the Early Chalcolithic/Bronze Age of Baluchistan: New Perspectives from Recent Excavations at Mehrgarh. In *South Asian Archaeology 1979,* ed. H. Härtel, pp. 93–114. Berlin: Dietrich Reimer Verlag.

Jayaswal, V. 1987. A New Look on the Clay Bull Figurines from Hastinapur in Rituals. In *Kusumāñjali: New Interpretation of Indian Art and Culture, Vol. I,* ed. M.S. Nagaraja Rao, pp. 111–14. Delhi: Agam Kala Prakashan.

———. 1989. Socio-ritual Significance of Ancient Terracottas in the Gangetic Plains: The Ethnoarchaeological and Literary Evidence. In *Old Problems and New Perspectives in the Archaeology of South Asia,* ed. J.M. Kenoyer, pp. 253–62. Madison: Dept. of Anthropology, University of Wisconsin.

Jayaswal, V., and K. Krishna. 1986. *An Ethnoarchaeological View of Indian Terracottas.* New Delhi: Agam Prakashan.

Joglekar, P.P., P.K. Thomas, and R.K. Mohanty. 2003. Faunal Remains from Purani Marmi: A Late Ahar Culture Settlement in the Mewar Plain Region of Rajasthan. *Man and Environment* 28.2: 99–109.

Joshi, J.P. 2003. Structures. In *Excavations at Kalibangan: The Early Harappans (1960–69),* ed. B.B. Lal, J.P. Joshi, B.K. Thapar, and M. Bala, pp. 51–94. Memoirs of the Archaeological Survey of India, No. 98. New Delhi: Archaeological Survey of India.

Joshi, J.P., and A. Parpola, eds. 1987. Collections in India. *Corpus of Indus Seals and Inscriptions.* Helsinki: Suomalainen Tiedeakatemia.

Kajale, M.D. 1996. Palaeobotanical Investigations at Balathal: Preliminary Results. *Man and Environment* 21.1: 98–102.

Kardulias, N. 2003. Stone in an Age of Bronze: Lithics from Bronze Age Contexts in Greece and Iran. In *Written in Stone. The Multiple Dimensions of Lithic Analysis,* ed. N. Kardulias and R.W. Yerkes, pp. 113–24. Lanham, MD: Lexington.

Kashyap, A. 2006. Use-Wear and Starch Grain Analysis: An Integrated Approach to Understanding the Transition from Hunting and Gathering to Food Production at Bagor, Rajasthan, India. Ph.D. dissertation, Michigan State University, Ann Arbor.

Kennedy, K.A.R. 1982. Biological Anthropology of Human Skeletal Remains from Bagor: Osteology. In *Bagor and Tilwara: Late Mesolithic Cultures of Northwest India.* Vol. I, *The Human Skeletal Remains,* ed. J.R. Lukacs, V.N. Misra, and K.A.R. Kennedy, pp. 27–51. Pune: Deccan College Postgraduate and Research Institute.

Kenoyer, J.M. 1998. *Ancient Cities of the Indus Valley Civilization.* Oxford: Oxford University Press.

Khanna, G.S. 1993. Patterns of Mobility in the Mesolithic of Rajasthan. *Man and Environment* 18.1: 49–55.

Khatri, J.S., and M. Acharya. 1997. Kunal—The Earliest Pre-Harappan Settlement. In *Facets of Indian Civilization: Recent Perspectives. Essays in Honour of Prof. B.B. Lal,* ed. J.P. Joshi and B.B. Lal, pp. 88–91. New Delhi: Aryan Books International.

Kramer, C. 1997. *Pottery in Rajasthan: Ethnoarchaeology in Two Indian Cities.* Washington, DC: Smithsonian Institution Press.

Kumar, V. 1970–73. Disposal of the Dead in Ancient Bagor. *The Researcher* 10.13: 53–58.

Landt, M. 2010. Cultural Developments at the Chalcolithic Site of Gilund, Rajasthan. In *The Gilund Project: Excavations in Regional Context. Proceedings of the 19th International Conference on South Asian Archaeology, July 2007, Ravenna, Italy,* ed. T.P. Raczek and V. Shinde, pp. 23–30. South Asian Archaeology 2007: Special Sessions 2. Oxford: British Archaeological Reports.

Lechevallier, M. 2003. *L'Industrie Lithique de Mehrgarh: Fouilles 1974–1985.* Éditions Recherche sur les Civilisations. Paris: Association pour la Diffusion de la Pensée Française.

Lee, R. 1969. !Kung Bushman Subsistence: An Input-Output Analysis. In *Environment and Cultural Behaviour,* ed. A.P. Vayda, pp. 47–79. Garden City, NJ: Natural History Press.

Lemonnier, P. 1986. The Study of Material Culture Today: Towards an Anthropology of Technical Systems. *Journal of Anthropological Archaeology* 5:147–86.

Lukacs, J.R. 1982. Biological Anthropology of Human Skeletal Remains from Bagor: Dentition. In *Bagor and Tilwara: Late Mesolithic Cultures of Northwest India.* Vol. I, *The Human Skeletal Remains,* ed. J.R. Lukacs, V.N. Misra, and K.A.R. Kennedy, pp. 61–85. Pune: Deccan College Postgraduate and Research Institute.

———. 2002. Hunting and Gathering Strategies in Prehistoric India: A Biocultural Perspective on Trade and Subsistence. In *Forager-Traders in South and Southeast Asia: Long Term Histories,* ed. K.D. Morrison and L.L. Junker, pp. 41–61. Cambridge: Cambridge University Press.

Lukacs, J.R., V.N. Misra, and K.A.R. Kennedy, eds. 1982. *Bagor and Tilwara: Late Mesolithic Cultures of Northwest India.* Vol. 1, *The Human Skeletal Remains.* Pune: Deccan College Postgraduate and Research Institute.

Lyon, P.J. 1970. Differential Bone Destruction: An Ethnographic Example. *American Antiquity* 35: 213–15.

Mackay, E.J.H. 1943. *Chanhu-Daro Excavations, 1935–36.* New Haven: American Oriental Society.

Meadow, R.H. 1978. Effects of Context on the Interpretation of Faunal Remains: A Case Study. In *Approaches to Faunal Analysis in the Middle East,* ed. R.H. Meadow and M.A. Zeder, pp. 15–21. Bulletin 2, Peabody Museum of Archaeology and Ethnology. Cambridge, MA: Peabody Museum.

Meadow, R.H., and A.K. Patel. 2002. From Mehrgarh to Harappa and Dholavira: Prehistoric Pastoralism in Northwestern South Asia through the Harappan Period. In *Protohistory: Archaeology of the Harappan Civilization,* ed. S. Settar and R. Korisettar, pp. 391–408. Indian Archaeology in Retrospect, vol. 2. New Delhi: Indian Council of Historical Research and Manohar.

———. 2003. Prehistoric Pastoralism in Northwestern South Asia from the Neolithic through the Harappan Period. In *Indus Ethnobiology: New Perspectives from the Field,* ed. S.A. Weber and W.R. Belcher, pp. 65–93. Lanham: Lexington Press.

Meena, B.R., and A. Tripathi. 2000a. *Recent Excavations in Rajasthan.* Jaipur: Archaeological Survey of India.

———. 2000b. Excavation at Ojiyana. *Puratattva* 30:67–73.

———. 2001. Further Excavation at Ojiyana. *Puratattva* 31:73–77.

———. 2001–02. Excavations at Ojiyana: An Unique Copper Age Site in Aravalli. *Pragdhara* 12:45–66.

Mehta, R.N., and A.J. Patel. 1967. *Excavation at Shamalaji.* Maharaja Sayajirao University Archaeology Series No. 9. Baroda: Dept. of Archaeology and Ancient History, Faculty of Arts, M.S. University of Baroda.

Mehta, R.N., and D.R. Shah. 1968. *Excavation at Nagara.* Maharaja Sayajirao University Archaeology Series No. 10. Baroda: Dept. of Archaeology and Ancient History, Faculty of Arts, M.S. University of Baroda.

Méry, S., P. Anderson, M.-L. Inizan, M. Lechevallier, and J.

Pelegrin. 2007. A Pottery Workshop with Flint Tools on Blades Knapped with Copper at Nausharo (Indus Civilization, ca. 2500 BC). *Journal of Archaeological Science* 34:1098–116.

Miller, H.M.-L. 2007. *Archaeological Approaches to Technology.* Burlington, MA: Academic Press.

Mishra, A.R. 2000. Chalcolithic Ceramics of Balathal, District Udaipur, Rajasthan. Ph.D. dissertation, Dept. of Archaeology, Deccan College, Pune.

Misra, V.N. 1967. *Pre- and Proto-History of the Berach Basin South Rajasthan.* Poona: Deccan College Postgraduate and Research Institute.

———. 1970. Cultural Significance of Three Copper Arrow-heads from Rajasthan India. *Journal of Near Eastern Studies* 29.4: 221–31.

———. 1971a. Two Late Mesolithic Settlements in Rajasthan—A Brief Review of Investigations. *Poona University Journal (Humanities)* 35:59–77.

———. 1971b. Two Microlithic Sites in Rajasthan—A Preliminary Investigation. *The Eastern Anthropologist* 24.3: 237–88.

———. 1972. Burials from Prehistoric Bagor, Rajasthan. In *Archaeological Congress and Seminar Papers,* ed. S.B. Deo, pp. 58–65. Nagpur: Nagpur University.

———. 1973. Bagor: A Late Mesolithic Settlement in North-west India. *World Archaeology* 5.1: 92–110.

———. 1982. Bagor: The Archaeological Setting. In *Bagor and Tilwara: Late Mesolithic Cultures of Northwest India.* Vol. I, *The Human Skeletal Remains,* ed. J.R. Lukacs, V.N. Misra, and K.A.R. Kennedy, pp. 9–20. Pune: Deccan College Postgraduate and Research Institute.

———. 1997. Balathal, a Chalcolithic Settlement in Mewar, Rajasthan, India: Results of the First Three Seasons' Excavation. *South Asian Studies* 13:251–73.

———. 2002. The Mesolithic Age in India. In *Indian Archaeology in Retrospect.* Vol. 1, *Prehistory: Archaeology of South Asia,* ed. S. Settar and R. Korisettar, pp. 111–26. New Delhi: Indian Council of Historical Research and Manohar.

———. 2005. Radiocarbon Chronology of Balathal, District Udaipur, Rajasthan. *Man and Environment* 30.1: 54–60.

Misra, V.N., V. Shinde, R.K. Mohanty, K. Dalal, A. Mishra, L. Pandey, and J. Kharakwal. 1995. The Excavations at Balathal: Their Contribution to the Chalcolithic and Iron Age Cultures of Mewar. *Man and Environment* 20.1: 57–80.

Misra, V.N., V. Shinde, R.K. Mohanty, and L. Pandey.

1993. Terracotta Bull Figurines from Marmi: A Chalcolithic Settlement in Chitorgarh District, Rajasthan. *Man and Environment* 18.2: 149–52.

Misra, V.N., V. Shinde, R.K. Mohanty, L. Pandey, and J. Kharakwal. 1997. Excavations at Balathal, Udaipur District, Rajasthan (1995–97), with Special Reference to Chalcolithic Architecture. *Man and Environment* 22.2: 35–60.

Mohanty, R.K., A. Mishra, P. Joglekar, P.K. Thomas, J. Kharakwal, and T. Panda. 2000. Purani Marmi: A Late Ahar Culture Settlement in Chittaurgarh District, Rajasthan. *Puratattva* 30:132–41.

Moore, A.M.T., G.C. Hillman, and A.J. Legge. 1975. The Excavation of Tell Abu Hureyra in Syria: A Preliminary Report. *Proceedings of the Prehistoric Society* 41:50–77.

Nagar, M. 1966. The Ahar-Banas Complex: An Archaeological and Ethnographic Study. Ph.D. dissertation, Deccan College and Poona University, Pune.

Neeley, M.P., and C.M. Barton. 1994. A New Approach to Interpreting Late Pleistocene Microlith Industries in Southwest Asia. *Antiquity* 68:275–88.

Nicholson, R.A. 1998. Bone Degradation in a Compost Heap. *Journal of Archaeological Science* 25:393–403.

Nielsen-Marsh, C.M., and R.E.M. Hedges. 2000. Patterns of Diagenesis in Bone I: The Effects of Site Environments. *Journal of Archaeological Science* 27:1139–50.

Noy, T., A.S. Legge, and E.S. Higgs. 1973. Recent Excavations at Nahal Oren, Israel. *Proceedings of the Prehistoric Society* 39:75–99.

Odell, G.H. 1998. Investigating Correlates of Sedentism and Domestication in Prehistoric North America. *American Antiquity* 63:553–71.

Oliver, J.S. 1993. Carcass Processing by the Hadza: Bone Breakage from Butchery to Consumption. In *From Bones to Behavior: Ethnoarchaeological and Experimental Contributions to the Interpretation of Faunal Remains,* ed. Jean Hudson, pp. 200–227. Center for Archaeological Investigations Occasional Paper No. 21. Carbondale, IL: Southern Illinois Univ.

Pandey, S.K. 1982. Chalcolithic Eran and Its Chronology. In *Indian Archaeology: New Perspectives,* ed. R.K. Sharma, pp. 249–56. Delhi: Agam Kala Prakashan.

Pappu, R.S. 1988. Site Catchment Analysis. In *Excavations at Inamgaon,* Vol. 1, Part i, ed. M.K. Dhavalikar, Z.D. Ansari, and H.D. Sankalia, pp. 107–20. Pune: Deccan College.

Pappu, R.S., and V.S. Shinde. 1990. Site Catchment Analysis of the Deccan Chalcolithic in the Central Tapi

Basin. *Bulletin of the Deccan College Postgraduate and Research Institute* 49:317–38.

Parry, W.J., and R.L. Kelly. 1987. Expedient Core Technology and Sedentism. In *The Organization of Core Technology,* ed. J.K. Johnson and C.A. Morrow, pp. 285–304. Boulder, CO: Westview Press.

Patel, A.K. 2009. Occupational Histories, Settlements, and Subsistence in Western India: What Bones and Genes Can Tell Us about the Origins and Spread of Pastoralism. *Anthropozoologica* 44.1: 173–88.

Peebles, C.S. 1978. Determinants of Settlement Size and Location in the Moundville Phase. In *Mississippian Settlement Patterns,* ed. B.D. Smith, pp. 369–416. New York: Academic Press.

Pelegrin, J. 1994. Lithic Technology in Harappan Times. In *South Asian Archaeology 1993,* ed. A. Parpola and P. Koskikallio, pp. 587–98. 2 vols. Annales Academiae Scientiarum Fennicae, Series B, Vol. 271. Helsinki: Suomalainen Tiedeakatemia.

Perna, M., ed. 2000. *Administrative Documents in the Aegean and Their Near Eastern Counterparts: Proceedings of the International Colloquium, Naples, February 29–March 2, 1996.* Pubblicazioni del Centro Internazionale di Ricerche Archeologiche Antropologiche e Storiche, 3. Turin: Ministero per i Beni e le Attivitá Culturali, Paravia Scriptorium.

Pfaffenberger, B. 1992. Social Anthropology of Technology. *Annual Review of Anthropology* 21:491–516.

Possehl, G.L. 2002. Harappans and Hunters: Economic Interaction and Specialization in Prehistoric India. In *Forager-Traders in South and Southeast Asia: Long Term Histories,* ed. K.D. Morrison and L. Junker, pp. 62–76. Cambridge: Cambridge University Press.

———. 2007. The Middle Asian Interaction Sphere: Trade and Contact in the 3rd Millennium BC. *Expedition* 49.1: 40–42.

Possehl, G.L., and K.A.R. Kennedy. 1979. Hunter-Gatherer/Agriculturalist Exchange in Prehistory: An Indian Example. *Current Anthropology* 20.3: 592–93.

Possehl, G.L., and P.C. Rissman. 1992. The Chronology of Prehistoric India: From Earliest Times to the Iron Age. In *Chronologies in Old World Archaeology,* 3rd ed., 2 vols., ed. R.W. Ehrich, pp. 465–90 and 447–74. Chicago: University of Chicago Press.

Possehl, G.L., V. Shinde, and M. Ameri. 2004. The Ahar-Banas Complex and the BMAC. *Man and Environment* 29.2: 18–29.

Raczek, T.P. 2007. Shared Histories: Technology and Community at Gilund and Bagor, Rajasthan, India (c.

3000–1700 BC). Ph.D. dissertation, Univ. of Pennsylvania, Philadelphia.

———. 2010a. Contextualizing Gilund: A Comparative Analysis of Technology. In *The Gilund Project: Excavations in Regional Context. Proceedings of the 19th International Conference on South Asian Archaeology, July 2007, Ravenna, Italy,* ed. T.P. Raczek and V. Shinde, pp. 35–42. South Asian Archaeology 2007 Special Sessions 2. Oxford: British Archaeological Reports.

———. 2010b. In the Context of Copper: Indian Lithics in the Third Millennium BC. In *Lithic Technology in Metal Using Societies,* ed. B.V. Eriksen, pp. 187–201. Proceedings of the XVth UISPP Congress, Lisbon, September 7th, 2006. London: British Archaeological Reports.

———. 2011. Mobility, Economic Strategies, and Social Networks: Investigating Movement in the Mewar Plain of Rajasthan. *Asian Perspectives* 50.1:24–52.

———. 2013. Technology and Everyday Crafts: Identifying Traces of Shared Histories in the Archaeological Record. In *Connections and Complexity: New Approaches to the Archaeology of South Asia,* ed. S. Abraham, P. Gullapalli, T.P. Raczek, and U. Rizvi, pp. 341–54. Walnut Creek: Left Coast Press.

Raczek, T.P., and V. Shinde, eds. 2010. *The Gilund Project: Excavations in Regional Context. Proceedings of the 19th International Conference on South Asian Archaeology, July 2007, Ravenna, Italy.* South Asian Archaeology Special Sessions 2. BAR International Series 2132. Oxford: British Archaeological Reports.

Raczek, T.P., N.S. Sugandhi, P. Shirvalkar, and L. Pandey. 2011. Researching a Living Site: Articulating the Intersection of Collaboration and Heritage in a Transnational Village. *Archaeological Review from Cambridge* 26.2: 119–35.

Rao, S.R. 1979. *Lothal, a Harappan Port Town (1955–62).* New Delhi: Archaeological Survey of India.

Rissman, P.C., and Y.M. Chitalwala. 1990. *Harappan Civilization and Oriyo Timbo.* Delhi: Oxford & IBH and the American Institute of Indian Studies.

Rizvi, U. 2010. Indices of Interaction: Comparisons between the Ahar-Banas and Ganeshwar Jodhpura Cultural Complex. In *The Gilund Project: Excavations in Regional Context. Proceedings of the 19th International Conference on South Asian Archaeology, July 2007, Ravenna, Italy,* ed. T.P. Raczek and V. Shinde, pp. 51–61. South Asian Archaeology 2007 Special Sessions 2. Oxford: British Archaeological Reports.

Robbins, G., V. Mushrif, V.N. Misra, R.K. Mohanty, and V.S. Shinde. 2006. Biographies of the Skeleton: Pathological Conditions at Balathal. *Man and Environment* 31.2: 150–65.

Robbins, G., V. Mushrif, V.N. Misra, R.K. Mohanty, and V.S. Shinde. 2007. Human Skeletal Remains from Balathal: A Full Report and Inventory. *Man and Environment* 32.2: 1–26.

Robbins, G., V.M. Tripathy, V.N. Misra, R.K. Mohanty, V.S. Shinde, K.M. Gray, and M.D. Schug. 2009. Ancient Skeletal Evidence for Leprosy in India (2000 B.C.). *PLoS ONE* 4.5: e5669. doi:10.1371/journal.pone.0005669.

Roper, D.C. 1974. *The Distribution of Middle Woodland Sites within the Environment of the Lower Sangamon River, Illinois.* Illinois State Museum Reports of Investigations No. 30. Springfield: Illinois State Museum.

———. 1979. The Method and Theory of Site Catchment Analysis: A Review. In *Advances in Archaeological Method and Theory,* Vol. 2, ed. M.B. Schiffer, pp. 110–40. New York: Academic Press.

Rosen, S.A. 1997. *Lithics after the Stone Age: A Handbook of Stone Tools from the Levant.* Walnut Creek, CA: Altamira.

Rossman, D.L. 1976. A Site Catchment Analysis of San Lorenzo, Veracruz. In *The Early Mesoamerican Village,* ed. K.V. Flannery, pp. 95–103. New York: Academic Press.

Sali, S.A. 1986. *Daimabad 1976–79.* Memoirs of the Archaeological Survey of India 83. New Delhi: Archaeological Survey of India.

Sankalia, H.D. 1969a. Preface. In *Excavations at Ahar (Tambavati),* ed. H.D. Sankalia, S.B. Deo, and Z.D. Ansari, pp. vii–ix. Pune: Deccan College.

———. 1969b. Pottery Introduction. In *Excavations at Ahar (Tambavati),* ed. H.D. Sankalia, S.B. Deo, and Z.D. Ansari, pp. 18–28. Pune: Deccan College.

———. 1969c. Strata and Structures. In *Excavations at Ahar (Tambavati),* ed. H.D. Sankalia, S.B. Deo, and Z.D. Ansari, pp. 7–12. Pune: Deccan College Postgraduate and Research Institute.

———. 1979. *Prehistory and Protohistory of India and Pakistan.* Pune: Deccan College.

Sankalia, H.D., S.B. Deo and Z.D. Ansari. 1969. *Excavations at Ahar (Tambavati).* Pune: Deccan College Postgraduate and Research Institute.

———. 1971. *Chalcolithic Navdatoli: The Excavations at Navdatoli 1957–59.* Deccan College Postgraduate

and Research Institute/Maharaja Sayajiro University Publication No. 2. Poona/Baroda.

Sankalia, H.D., B. Subbarao, and S.B. Deo. 1958. *The Excavations at Maheshwar and Navdatoli 1952–53.* Poona/Baroda: Deccan College Postgraduate and Research Institution.

Sarianidi, V. 1998. *Myths of Ancient Bactria and Margiana on Its Seals and Amulets.* Moscow: Pentgraphic.

Schmandt-Basserat, D. 1997. Animal Symbols at 'Ain Ghazal. *Expedition* 9.1: 48–58.

Shah, D.R. 1969. Animal Remains from Excavations at Ahar. In *Excavations at Ahar (Tambavati),* ed. H.D. Sankalia, S.B. Deo, and Z.D. Ansari, pp. 237–45. Pune: Deccan College Postgraduate and Research Institute.

Shah, H. 1992. Gujarat. In *Tribal India,* ed. S. Doshi, pp. 85–102. Bombay: Marg Publications.

Shinde, V. 1991. Craft Specialization and Social Organization in the Chalcolithic Deccan, India. *Antiquity* 65:796–807.

———. 2010a. Cultural Development from Mesolithic to Chalcolithic in the Mewar Region of Rajasthan, India. *Pragdhara* 18:201–13.

———. 2010b. Development from Mesolithic to Chalcolithic in the Mewar Region of Rajasthan: Contribution of Gilund Excavation. In *The Gilund Project: Excavations in Regional Context. Proceedings of the 19th International Conference on South Asian Archaeology, July 2007, Ravenna, Italy,* ed. T.P. Raczek and V. Shinde, pp. 7–12. South Asian Archaeology 2007 Special Sessions 2. Oxford: British Archaeological Reports.

Shinde, V., S.S. Deshpande, and Y. Yasuda. 2004. Human Response to Holocene Climate Changes—A Case Study of Western India between 5th and 3rd Millennia BC. In *Monsoon and Civilization,* ed. Y. Yasuda and V. Shinde, pp. 383–406. New Delhi: Lustre Press, Roli Books.

Shinde, V., and G.L. Possehl. 2005. A Report on the Excavations at Gilund, 1999–2001. In *South Asian Archaeology 2001,* ed. C. Jarrige and V. Lefèvre, pp. 293–302. Paris: Éditions Recherche sur les Civilisations.

Shinde, V., G.L. Possehl, and M. Ameri. 2005. Excavations at Gilund 2001–2003: The Seal Impressions and Other Finds. In *South Asian Archaeology 2003,* ed. U. Franke-Vogt and H.-J. Weisshar, pp. 159–69. Aachen: Linden Soft.

Shinde, V., G.L. Possehl, and S.S. Deshpande. 2002. The Ceramic Assemblage in Proto-historic Mewar (Rajasthan), with Special Reference to Gilund and Balathal.

Puratattva 32:5–24.

Shinde, V., and R. Pappu. 1990. Daimabad: The Chalcolithic Regional Centre in the Godavari Basin. *Bulletin of the Deccan College Post-Graduate Research Institute* 50:307–16.

Shinde, V., and T.P. Raczek. 2010. Introduction: A Review of the Gilund Excavations and Related Research. In *The Gilund Project: Excavations in Regional Context. Proceedings of the 19th International Conference on South Asian Archaeology, July 2007, Ravenna, Italy,* ed. T.P. Raczek and V. Shinde, pp. 1–6. South Asian Archaeology 2007 Special Sessions 2. Oxford: British Archaeological Reports.

Singh, G. 1971. The Indus Valley Culture, Seen in the Context of Post-glacial Climatic and Ecological Studies in Northwest India. *Archaeology and Physical Anthropology in Oceania* 6.2:177–89.

Singh, U.V. 1967a. Eran: A Chalcolithic Settlement. *Bulletin of the Department of Ancient Indian History and Archaeology* 1:29–30.

———. 1967b. Further Excavations at Eran. *Journal of the Madhya Pradesh Itihasa Parishad* 5:19–27.

Stein, J.R., and S.H. Lekson. 1992. Anasazi Ritual Landscapes. In *Anasazi Regional Organization and the Chaco System,* ed. D.E. Doyel, pp. 87–100. Maxwell Museum of Anthropology, Anthropological Papers vol. 5. Albuquerque, NM.

Subbarao, B. 1955. Chalcolithic Blade Industry of Maheshwar (Central India) and a Note on the History of the Technique. *Bulletin of the Deccan College Postgraduate and Research Institute* 17:126–49.

Sugandhi, N., T.P. Raczek, P. Shirvalkar, and L. Pandey. 2010. The Chatrikhera Research Project. *Antiquity* 84.325. http://antiquity.ac.uk/projgall/sugandhi325/.

Thomas, P.K. 1975. The Role of Animals in the Food Economy of the Mesolithic Culture of Western and Central India. In *Archaeozoological Studies,* ed. A.T. Clason, pp. 322–28. Amsterdam: North-Holland.

———. 1977. Archaeozoological Aspects of the Prehistoric Cultures of Western India. Ph.D. dissertation, Dept. of Archaeology, Deccan College, Poona.

———. 1984. The Faunal Background of the Chalcolithic Culture of Western India. In *Animals and Archaeology.* Vol. 3, *Early Herders and Their Flocks,* ed. J. Clutton-Brock and C. Grigson, pp. 355–62. International Series, 202. Oxford: British Archaeological Reports.

———. 2002. Investigations into the Archaeofauna of Harappan Sites in Western India. In *Indian Archaeology in Retrospect.* Vol. 2, *Protohistory: Archaeology of*

the Harappan Civilization, ed. S. Settar and R. Korisettar, pp. 409–20. New Delhi: Indian Council of Historic Research and Manohar Publishers.

Thomas, P.K., and P.P. Joglekar. 1996. Faunal Remains from Balathal: A Preliminary Report. *Man and Environment* 21.1: 91–97.

Tosi, M. 1968. Excavations at Shahr-i Sokhta, a Chalcolithic Settlement in the Iranian Sistan. Preliminary Report on the First Campaign, October–December 1967. *East and West* 18:1–66.

Vishnu-Mittre. 1969. Remains of Rice and Millet. In *Excavations at Ahar (Tambavati),* ed. H.D. Sankalia, S.B. Deo, and Z.D. Ansari, pp. 229–36. Pune: Deccan College Postgraduate and Research Institute.

Vita-Finzi, C., and E.S. Higgs. 1970. Prehistoric Economy in the Mount Carmel Area of Palestine: Site Catchment Analysis. *Proceedings of the Prehistoric Society* 36:1–37.

Voigt, M. 2000. Çatal Höyük in Context: Ritual at Early Neolithic Sites in Central and Eastern Turkey. In *Life in Neolithic Farming Communities,* ed. I. Kuijt, pp. 253–93. New York: Plenum Publishers.

Wakankar, V.S. 1967. Kayatha Excavation. *Journal of the Vikram University,* Special Issue on Ujjain.

Webley, D. 1972. Soils and Site Locations in Prehistoric Palestine. In *Papers in Economic Prehistory,* ed. E.S. Higgs, pp. 169–80. London: Cambridge University Press.

Wengrow, D. 2003. Interpreting Animal Art in the Prehistoric Near East. In *Culture through Objects: Ancient Near Eastern Studies in Honour of P.R.S. Moorey,* ed. T. Potts, M. Roaf, and D. Stein, pp. 139–60. Oxford: Griffith Institute.

White, E.M., and L.A. Hannus. 1983. Chemical Weathering of Bone in Archaeological Soils. *American Antiquity* 48:316–22.

Wright, R. 1991. Patterns of Technology and the Organization of Production at Harappa. In *Harappa Excavations 1986–1990: A Multidisciplinary Approach,* ed. R. Meadow, pp. 71–88. Monographs in World Archaeology no. 3. Madison: Prehistory Press.

———. 1993. Technological Styles: Transforming a Natural Material into a Cultural Object. In *History from Things: Essays on Material Culture,* ed. S. Lubar and W.D. Kingery, pp. 242–69. Washington, DC: Smithsonian Institution Press.

Zettler, R.L. 1987. Sealings as Artifacts in Institutional Administration in Ancient Mesopotamia. *Journal of Cuneiform Studies* 39:197–240.

Index